Frozen Shield

Alaska Cover-up

Nick Mangieri

Veracity Press, Inc.
Williamsburg, Virginia

Library of Congress Cataloging-in-Publication Data
Mangieri, Nick
Frozen Shield: Alaska Cover-up / by Nick Mangieri
p.400   cm
Included index.

ISBN 0-9665364-2-8

I. Title.
2000

99-097632 CIP

Printed in the United States of America

Published by
Veracity Press, Inc.
Williamsburg, Virginia

Book editing and design by Karen T. Morgan, Hampton, Va.
Printed by B&B Printing, Richmond, Va.
www.bbprintnet.com

Great is truth, and mighty above all things.

1 Esdras 4:41

What is against truth cannot be just.

St. Augustine

Nothing overshadows truth so completely as authority.

Alberti Del Principe III

This is a true story.
All of the events depicted in this book
are a matter of factual record,
and the people are real.

For my children:
Tammy, Mark, Dawn and Michelle

... Contents ...

Other books by Nick Mangieri

"**Broken Badge**, The Silencing of a Federal Agent," 1998

About the Author

Nick Mangieri, a native-born New Yorker and Navy veteran, has served as Chief of Police in Alaska, Deputy Sheriff in California and Private Detective in New York. He was a Federal Agent with the Department of Labor attached to the Inspector General's Fraud Division, assigned to South Florida and Washington, D.C. His background and interests are wide and varied and include work as an analyst for federal and state governments and as a free lance writer for men's adventure magazines. As such, his self-imposed junkets took him into the interiors of Central and South America, where he diamond prospected in the jungles, hunted jaguar and mountain climbed. He graduated from the University of the Pacific and got his graduate degree from Virginia Commonwealth University. He's also attended law school and done post graduate work, including doctoral studies. He's an avid outdoorsman, jogs regularly, works out at a gym daily and has even been a rodeo rider. Married and the father of four, he is a licensed Private Investigator.

... Chapter 1 ...

On November 4, 1975, an Alaskan town lost its Police Chief, a Police Department was thrown into turmoil and municipal corruption would soon make a mockery of justice.

Six months before, the acting City Manager had appointed me to that position. A former City Manager replaced him shortly thereafter. I learned — too late — about that former official's questionable reputation while in office the first time. In addition, a powerful, supposedly nonprofit corporation had operated with impunity for years in the area.

That day, however, no outward signs of what was to happen emanated from either the City Hall or from the town itself. The weather, while not atypical for early November in Alaska, portended an ominous foreboding of events to come. Increasingly dark heavy clouds rolled in over the frozen fields and tundra of the Matanuska Valley. Light northerly winds compounded the outside bleakness by intensifying the biting cold of the minus four-degree low of the previous night. Even the gray low-lying buildings of the small rural town of Palmer, seat of the Matanuska-Susitna Borough 40 miles from Anchorage, contributed to the somberness of the atmosphere. City Hall, too, normally a center of activity for that time of day, was still — too still.

The Palmer Police Department, situated beneath City Hall and below ground, however, was not quiet and had not been quiet since I was appointed its Chief in mid-spring. Since my takeover,

I had tried to run an efficient, effective and aggressive law enforcement unit in a politically controlled community. When I was first becoming familiar with the department and the town, I knew nothing of the extent of that control and the direct involvement in it by long-term political figures. Yet, in spite of the rigid hierarchy that ruled the town and surrounding area, there were honest citizens who came forward to voice their concerns about the corruption that long had festered in the City and Borough governments. At first, the complaints were sporadic. My own integrity was no doubt being tested. As time wore on and they learned I could be trusted, the complaints became more specific. Not only did the people cite instances of massive land fraud, but they also hinted about past violence and death in the valley that had not been resolved to the satisfaction of the citizenry.

On that particular morning, nothing seemed amiss. It was business as usual. The dispatcher on duty was routinely going about her duties. Bob Lemoine, the administrative corporal I recently had appointed was thoroughly immersed in shift changes and the updating of our operating manual. Gene Wilcox, my new patrol sergeant, was on the street checking on one of the new officers. My secretary, Chris Boyle, was busily typing up reports, and I was prioritizing my activities for the day.

Midmorning I received a call from Rose Ann Kohlberg, the City Manager's secretary.

"Mr. Curtis would like to see you," she announced without her usual pleasantries.

"Anything special?" I asked nonchalantly, thinking that he might want me to make my periodic report to him before my normal weekly visit.

"I don't know," she replied icily. She was usually aware of what was going on in the City Manager's office so her abrupt answer struck me as kind of odd.

"All right," I said. "I'll be up in a minute. I'm just working on something that I want to give to Chris."

"He wants you *right now*," was her blunt emphatic response before she hung up.

I looked quizzically at the receiver in my hand before replacing it, wondering what the hell was the problem. There had been no citizen complaints, no questions from the City Councilmen or the Mayor, and nothing pending with the City Manager to generate that type of phone call or abrasive attitude on her part. She always had been congenial in the past, and we always got along well.

"I gotta go upstairs, Chris ... to see Curtis. Be back in a little bit," I called out.

"Okay, Chief," she said and nodded her head. Her fingers never left the typewriter keyboard.

As I passed Kohlberg's desk outside Bill Curtis' office, she avoided my gaze. I walked through the open door.

"You wanted to see me?" I asked.

Curtis was seated stiffly at his desk with his arms outstretched before him. Behind him stood Public Works Director Chuck Shaver, dressed in his work coveralls. Shaver had hired me while he was still acting City Manager, just before Curtis' return. I briefly nodded to Shaver.

No one acknowledged my greeting. I turned to the City Manager, who remained motionless and quiet at his desk. He raised his head slightly and eyed me coldly for a moment before he spoke. His voice was low and flat, devoid of any inflection or emotion. This was a strange characteristic I had noticed in him before.

"I want your resignation," he said.

Unbelieving, I looked at him and then towards Shaver who was equally frozen.

"You want what?" I asked incredulously.

"I want your resignation," he said, his tone flat, his face revealing nothing.

I still couldn't believe what I was hearing but one look at their unwavering expressions, left no doubt as to the message.

"Do you mind telling me what this is all about?" I asked, trying to fathom what was going on.

"This isn't *about* anything," Curtis replied.

"I'm the City Manager, and you work for me ... and now I'm asking for your resignation," he answered stonily.

I looked back at him hard, and at Shaver who was beginning to fidget.

"I'm not resigning from anything," I said. "I've done a good job since I've been here, and everyone knows it."

"I'm not concerned with everyone. You're an employee on a probationary status and it's my decision to terminate your employment."

"*I* need a reason," I insisted.

"*I* don't need a reason," he replied. "You're still on probation."

"Everyone is entitled to a reason," I continued to insist.

He ignored my remark.

"If you won't resign, you're fired — effective immediately."

I heard the words, but I was still having difficulty associating it with reality. I responded the only way that I knew how.

"You can't fire me," I said. "I'm conducting an investigation into City Hall."

He raised his eyebrows and looked at me. For the first time his expression showed concern.

"What for?" he demanded.

"As the Chief of Police, that's my business," I said.

"We'll see about that," he said, and for the first time there was emotion in his voice.

He called to Kohlberg seated less than ten feet from us and well within hearing distance of the heated exchange.

"Rose Ann, get District Attorney Balfe on the line," he barked.

She complied and quickly advised him to pick up the phone.

In his usual low-key, even-toned voice Curtis asked Balfe whether I was conducting an investigation of Palmer City Hall. Curtis then thanked him and quickly hung up the receiver. There was no mention over the phone of why he had asked, nor was there any indication of the fact that he had just fired me. On the surface, it appeared to be a normal business call.

His look of concern disappeared as suddenly as it arose, and there was a smugness in his reply.

"Joe Balfe just informed me that as far as he knew, you had not initiated any investigation here."

I was holding off on telling Balfe about the investigation until I had uncovered more information and some hard evidence to back it all up. Only his investigator, Ernie Beaucamp, a resident of the valley, knew what I had in mind.

Beaucamp was a long-term area resident and knew — or suspected — that things had long been amiss at City Hall. He once advised me, "Before you start anything, make sure you've got your tracks covered."

It was good advice that I should have heeded. Now I was fired, and the abruptness of my termination had caught me off guard.

As I mulled over what course of action to take next, Sgt. Mike Kolivosky of the Alaska State Troopers walked into the small office. Either Kohlberg had called him or it was pre-arranged before I went upstairs. Kolivosky said nothing. He just stood by the entrance as if waiting for some sort of cue from Curtis or Shaver. I, in turn, expected some type of recognition from him. For the past six months we had a harmonious profes-sional working relationship. I had even worked side-by-side with his men as backup whenever there was a need. Their small detachment was billeted in Palmer but covered thousands of square miles. With their workload, there was always a need.

At about that time, both Lemoine and Wilcox walked into the office and upon the tail end of the confrontation. They looked bewildered, as if they didn't understand what was occurring.

Curtis picked up the phone and dialed City Attorney Burton Biss to undoubtedly get some advice concerning his next move. After he relayed my refusal to resign and his immediate termina-tion of me, he listened to the voice at the other end of the line and shook his head in affirmation.

"Okay. Okay," he answered quickly.

He replaced the phone confidently and looked up at me and over at Kolivosky as he spoke.

"You've got to leave the area," he said firmly. "Now!"

It was a defining moment. I was torn between complying or taking some form of action. Two of my men were there, com-pletely loyal to me I believed, while Kolivosky appeared to be on the side of City Hall. I considered arresting Curtis on charges of Obstruction of Justice, but I knew I had no concrete grounds for the charge. To order Kolivosky out of my City jurisdiction also momentarily crossed my mind. However, I could also envision a scuffle in the small office and knew that innocent bystanders might be injured. I dismissed the thought just as quickly as it arose.

It was a *Mexican standoff*, two parties facing each other — both armed — with the law on each side.

As I briefly sized-up the situation, it didn't take long to realize I held no trump card. I very reluctantly acquiesced. I knew I had to personally see Balfe and lay my cards on the table with him, tell him what I had and in what direction I was heading to firm up my charges of municipal corruption. I felt I could trust him and knew I had a good rapport with Beaucamp.

I headed for the doorway and the stairway back down to the Police Department.

"Where are you going?" Curtis demanded.

"Back down to get some of my stuff."

"No you're not!" His voice rose. "You're forbidden from entering your office again."

I spun around, trying to contain my rising anger.

"How the hell am I supposed to get my own personal things?" I asked angrily.

"We'll see that you get them," Curtis replied. "I want the keys to your police unit now."

He had a superior smug look on his face that I was tempted to change on the spot. Instead, I took a deep breath, reached into my pocket and threw the keys on his desk."

"I'll drive you home, Chief," Lemoine offered softly.

"Make sure you don't use a city car," Curtis warned him.

I clenched my fist and strode out of City Hall.

... Chapter 2 ...

On the short drive from the Palmer Police Department to my home in the valley near the smaller town of Wasilla, Lemoine was quiet most of the way sensing my disturbed mood.

"I'm sorry, Chief. I'm really sorry," he said. "Is there anything that I can do? Is there anything that any of us can do?"

I shook my head.

"It's politics, Bob," I said grimly. "There's nothing that you can do, or any of the other officers can do."

"We've gotta do something," he stressed. "It's not right. The department was really shaping up."

"Yeah, I know, but Curtis didn't want it to. It was too much of a threat to him."

Lemoine reached the Dairy Queen that sat back off the Parks Highway and then the dirt road to my property.

He made a left turn, and the tires moved loose gravel as the car rolled slowly down the long road toward my house.

"Thanks, Bob," I said, getting out of the car and ending the discussion.

My wife was at the back door.

"What's the matter?" she asked anxiously. "Where's your car?"

I held my hand up to calm her down and motioned Lemoine off.

"Let's go inside," I said. "I'll tell you all about it."

As I relayed the events of the morning, she interrupted, "Why that son-of-a-bitch. He can't do that."

I snorted in disagreement. "That son of a bitch, can do anything he wants. He thinks he's God."

"What're you going to do now?"

"I'm going to Anchorage to see the DA, and we'll see what happens then."

"Does Wayne know?" she asked.

The *Wayne* she spoke of was my former police officer, Wayne Higgins, who was fired by Curtis just a few weeks before for no apparent reason. Since both of our wives were Southern girls and we both had large families and the same basic interests, we had become more than just colleagues; we had become friends. I supported the efforts he was making to gain reinstatement and had talked with his Anchorage attorney Bill Artus. If that support was a problem for Curtis, he never mentioned it. When I was subpoenaed to give a deposition in Higgins' civil case I explained to Curtis that I merely told the truth under oath — nothing more. At the time he simply grunted acknowledgement.

Emerging from those thoughts, I remembered to answer my wife's question.

"I don't know," I said wearily. "It just happened. Give him a call after I leave and tell him to call me later. We've got a lot of work to do."

"Okay, I'll take care of it. Don't worry," she said, trying to reassure me.

"Worry? Not me," I countered. "Curtis is the one who better worry."

I jumped into my pickup truck and slammed the door shut.

"I gotta go."

I headed out to Anchorage, a 40-minute ride from my house. On the way my thoughts turned to the strange events of that morning, and I wondered what had precipitated Curtis' abrupt actions. He couldn't have known of my suspicions about the corruption because I had kept them to myself. Maybe some eager citizen had let something slip to him or to some of the other valley officials. I would never learn what had caused my firing, but it was inevitable because of the trail of my investigations. I was about to step on too many toes.

Over the next few months I would learn, however, that the events of that morning would be twisted beyond all recognition to suit City Hall. I didn't hear *all* of the spurious reports that were told — and retold — over the months, but in January and February, I learned about two of the completely fabricated tales. Two reliable witnesses told me that Kohlberg had relayed damaging information about me at their workplaces. Both later wondered about her truthfulness and then subsequently voluntarily gave me signed statements of her accounts to them.

One such party, Marta Hensel, a local employee, stated that:

"On January 18, 1979, in the a.m., Rose Ann Kohlberg came into the office and began talking about the Mangieri case and the City. She mentioned how frightened she was of him when Mr. Curtis told him he was fired and how he stared at her and became irrational and that she couldn't leave the office because Mangieri was blocking the doorway and he still had his gun on and how everyone was scared of him and Trooper Kolivosky had to be called to quiet things down before she felt safe. She also stated that he was not allowed to go back into his desk to get any of his personal belongings and that they did find some questionable things in his desk."

Hensel's statement about Kohlberg's description of that morning became even more incredible as it continued:

"She stated that she felt he was the Mafia type and wanted his own men who were of questionable backgrounds, most of whom would not be chosen as policemen otherwise. She did say this was her own personal feeling about it. She mentioned that this type of person was also teaching Business Law and that he just wanted personal revenge and would go to any lengths to attain it. That if he didn't want to abide by the rules and regulations set forth he should just leave and go somewhere else instead of making trouble."

Nick Mangieri

The other witness, Mary W. Steiner, a courthouse employee, gave an even more bizarre account in her statement, dated February 26, 1976:

"Rose Ann Kohlberg — Bill Curtis' secretary came into the Palmer Recording Office in the courthouse on Wednesday, February 18, 1976, in the morning. Someone asked her how things were over at City Hall. Rose Ann stated that they had begun to settle down since Mangieri was fired. She told us how completely irrational he was and how he stood in the doorway of Curtis' office and glared at her when she wanted to pass and wouldn't move. She stated that until he was relieved of the gun on his hip, she was terribly frightened for all those there, and until Trooper Kolivosky was called and he came into the office, no one could get across to Mangieri that he was through.

"She stated that he was really mad when he wasn't allowed to take anything from his desk and that he prob- ably had good reason for some of the papers found in his desk were incriminating, leading them to believe he was planning on setting up the Mafia here in Palmer — hir- ing men of questionable character like himself ..."

Evidently both had been well rehearsed because they were virtually carbon copies of each other. In the earlier Hensel state- ment, Kohlberg concluded her recital with, "Mr. Curtis said there was nothing to worry about and that he didn't have a case at all." In the later Steiner version, she further noted that:

"A week later Rose Ann came in on a Thursday and in the course of conversation, she did again mention that she really didn't know why Mangieri bothered with all his (civil) suits because he would only lose anyway."

Both absurd accounts stressed the element of fear that I had supposedly instilled in City Hall and their dramatic recounting was designed to engender sympathy with the listener, and of course, support for the administration.

The latter reference to "my gun" was the only vein of truth in the telling of her whole story. Naturally, on the day of my firing I was on duty and since I was in uniform I had my gun "on my hip." That's where the truth ended, however. I was never relieved of my gun before I left the office and wouldn't have surrendered it if asked. It was my personal weapon, and I left City Hall the same way that I entered — with my gun.

What was even more ludicrous in Kohlberg's highly fictionalized accounts was her unabashed use of the word "Mafia." It was unquestionably a term that was deemed to instill dread in the local citizenry. As illogical as that plan of attack would be to a disinterested onlooker, to them it was logical. Because my last name ended in a vowel, they must have found it to be effective proof that Italian skullduggery was in the making. However, after reading the two statements ascribed to Kohlberg, whatever dark humor I found in her revelations soon turned to anger. That anger quickly turned to disgust with the realization that Curtis and his supporters were lying with impunity, getting by with it, and would continue to do so, unless they were stopped.

Shortly thereafter, on February 29, I hastily drafted and submitted the following retort to the *Frontiersman*, Palmer's City Hall-oriented paper. I asked that it be placed in the "Letters to the Editor" section:

"Dear Editor:

"It looks like Curtis & Company are 'running scared' and in the process are leaving no stone unturned in a continuous program of trying to discredit me. Fortunately, there are others in town who don't buy their line and keep me posted accordingly.

"A few days ago, I heard that the reason I was fired is that I was attempting to form a Mafia organization in Palmer and that my hiring of police officers reflected that policy. The movie producers of "The Godfather" would be flattered to learn that the image they've created has reached into the depths of the Matanuska Valley. However, I fail to see how my last three hires — McKibben, Leichliter and Higgins — have contributed to that childish misconception.

Nick Mangieri

"More recently, I was advised that the Elks and the Moose Clubs have terminated certain 'social functions' because of fear of my personal vendetta to destroy the town and its inhabitants. It's probably only just coincidence that this cessation of activities occurred about thirty minutes after my wife and I walked into the Elks Club on Friday night at the invitation of a friend and member — and also mere coincidence that Bill Curtis was there.

"Undoubtedly there are those individuals in town who have valid reason for concern because they will 'reap what they sow.' However, the vast majority of citizens have no reason for concern as I'm doing a job that must be done and should have been done long ago. City Hall finds it necessary to perpetuate the myth that I am synonymous with Attila the Hun ready to sack a civilization. If there are those in town who find it comforting to rely on that image, then 'be my guest.' If, on the other hand, there are those people who have common sense and can think for themselves — ask me first before you believe what is said without question.

> Sincerely,
> Nick Mangieri
> Former Chief of Police"

When I mailed the letter, I had no delusions that they would actually honor my request since I knew full well where their loyalties lay. I did harbor a slight glimmer of hope, however, that they might actually place it in the paper to prevent future legal action on my part against them as well.

When it appeared in their next edition on February 4, more than forty percent of it had been decimated. The entire first paragraph was deleted as well as an identifying portion of the second paragraph. The entire third paragraph and one-third of the last paragraph were omitted from my original letter.

On reflection, I could see why my third paragraph had been cut. My tongue-in-cheek reference to "certain social functions" at the Elks and Moose Clubs in Palmer, specifically referred to the prevalent gambling activities at both clubs. Furthermore, the fact that Curtis had been there the night that the Elks had slot machines in operation meant that he tacitly approved illegal activities within the City limits.

It gave me no small satisfaction to know that even as an ex-Chief, I still retained a small amount of power when I unexpectedly walked into the club that night.

Although I managed to extract a minuscule amount of favorable press from the *Frontiersman*, my wife didn't fare as well when she submitted her letter on January 4, two months after my termination. Her 1,200-word barbed epistle was justifiably caustic. She covered every topic imaginable, from the town's officials to the town itself. She called Curtis, Shaver, and even the Mayor Jack Maze, corrupt individuals. She even profusely denigrated the town in general for supporting them. She minced no words either when she spoke of Mayor Maze. He had been convicted of a felony in that same town years earlier and she made a point of mentioning it. Although it was common knowledge among the old-timers in Palmer, I only learned about it near the end of my short stint in office.

When she showed me her final draft of the letter before she mailed it, I couldn't help but smile at its content.

"Do you like it?" she asked.

"I like it," I answered truthfully. "I don't think they'll ever run it, though."

"I thought newspapers would always put letters to the editors in," she said naively.

"Theoretically," I said. "If they have space."

It wasn't the length of her letter that kept it from being printed, though. They had printed letters favorable to the City administration that were as long or longer than my wife's. It was the content that kept hers out of print. Specifically, it was the subject matter that pertained to my police duties. In one of her opening paragraphs, she wrote:

> "When Nick took over as Chief of Police of Palmer, I knew what a damned good cop he was when I had my children come home and tell me, 'Boy dad's sure cleaning up drugs in this town. It's dry. Kids are mad at us because they can't even buy grass and speed is at a stand-

still, and they're blaming Dad for it.' And Nick's reply, 'isn't that too bad.'

"So for once I was seeing a town finally getting a good start at getting rid of drugs, which I as a mother and my concern for other kids was more than glad to see. Coming form California, this was a dream come true. I didn't mind so much that my kids were being harassed so that some of your children would not be able to buy any drugs in this town. That made it all worthwhile.

"I felt for the first time in any town I might just see it free from drugs, and that's a lot in its self. I wasn't even afraid of my children being on the streets of Palmer town after dark because Nick was Chief and was doing a good job. He's not perfect, he's human and being human he has faults like everyone else, but when he does a job — he's the best. And he was doing the best possible job at being Chief. He had a slightly dirty Peyton Place and was beginning to clean it up. I think the real reason behind his firing was not his hiring two policemen, one of which is still there, and not for his handling of the budget, he's handled bigger budgets than this town has ever seen. But, because he would not be a 'yes man' for Mr. Curtis."

(Curtis' initial explanation following my dismissal was my hiring methods and the Police Department budget.)

The balance of her retaliatory letter was accurate and expectable, as her kneejerk reaction was a direct result of the shock of my arbitrary dismissal. There had never been any indication from anyone within City Hall that it would happen.

The same dismay emanated from all my officers and dispatchers. However, their feelings were muted at the work place, because their own jobs were in jeopardy.

Although Lemoine and Wilcox voiced their immediate support and concern to Curtis, following the morning incident, they were quickly silenced. Any more vocal demonstrations, they were told, "would not be tolerated."

In fact, two members of my department would, at a later date, advise me of specific threats made to them by the City Manager.

During that drive to Anchorage on the morning of my firing, however, I was unaware of all that would transpire in the near future. I was only concerned with regaining my job as quickly as possible. I also was equally concerned with my own immediate plan of action once I reached Anchorage.

What would I tell Balfe? I wondered. I knew he would need more than hearsay and rumors about corruption in general or the Alaska Rural Rehabilitation Corporation in particular. (That was the alleged nonprofit corporation that had been operating in the Matanuska Valley since the 1930s.)

I knew he was going to want to know what I had. *I should've dug deeper. I should've gotten more facts. Who did I need to see next? Maybe I should see Artus, too, since I was going to be in Anchorage.*

My thoughts were all a jumble as I pulled up in front of the Fourth Avenue courthouse in Anchorage.

Balfe saw me right away.

"What was that call all about from Curtis this morning?" he asked curiously.

I told him.

"You've got a problem," was his casual response. "How're you going to handle it?"

"From here, I'm going to see Higgins' and soon-to-be-my attorney Bill Artus, and then after that, who knows," I said half in disgust and half mysteriously.

I liked Joe Balfe. I first met him when I was the Administrative Officer for the Public Defender's Office, my first job in Alaska. At that time, I worked on the ground floor of the courthouse. He was around 40, had straight brown hair, wore glasses and dressed like an attorney. He also was easygoing and likeable — but he struck me as not wanting to stick his neck out. I didn't come away from our meeting very enthused or too encouraged.

"Dig up some more evidence, and then come back to see me," were his parting words.

"Thanks, Joe," I said, and left.

The next stop was to see Artus a couple of blocks away on West Third Avenue. As soon as I walked through the firm doors he saw me and came forward.

"I just heard, Chief," he said, reaching out to shake my hand. "I'm sorry."

"Thanks, Bill."

Although he was young, he was sincere. "I hope it wasn't because you supported Wayne," he said apologetically.

"That was part of it, but just a small part," I said. "There's a lot more to it."

"Yeah, so I gathered from Wayne."

"What's my next step, Bill?"

"I was just on my way over to the courthouse, so we don't have much time now to talk. Call me tomorrow morning if you want me to represent you also, and we'll have to get together. After that, I'll see how soon we can set up a hearing before the City Council — that's the procedure."

I nodded in acknowledgement.

On my drive back to Palmer, I began to form a plan of action. While Artus was working on the upcoming hearing, I would gather as much information as I could about Curtis and City Hall and present it at the open session. I knew I'd have to personally contact the Mayor and all the City Council members. I still believed, however, that they would support me since they all seemed impressed with my performance while I was in office.

I just didn't realize the depth of corruption that existed at City Hall or the extent of collusion or involvement of its members.

I soon would find out.

The following morning, November 5, the day after my termination, the first article hit the front page of the *Anchorage Daily Times*, with the headline:

"OUSTED POLICE CHIEF TO SUE CITY MANAGER."

The article opened with the comment that I would sue the City Manager because he showed "no just cause" in dismissing me. It also mentioned that I said Curtis fired me because I hired two officers and changed a work schedule "without (his) approval." It listed the names of Wayne Higgins and a John

McKibben as the officers. The short article further noted that, "following several complaints by citizens of 'irregularities' in City Hall," that I was about to launch an investigation prior to my dismissal.

Although the City Manager was quoted as saying that "there was no specific action" by me that caused my discharge, he later found it necessary to amend that statement to justify his actions.

The following day, on November 6, the second newspaper that reported on the event was Palmer's only weekly paper, the *Frontiersman*. Its front-page coverage included a short article under the headline:

"PALMER POLICE CHIEF FIRED."

The story, although superficially similar to the *Anchorage Daily Times*, departed from my side of the story when it commented on the City Manager's policies:

"As far as the hiring of police officers being Mangieri's jurisdiction, Curtis said Mangieri's duties were 'whatever I tell him they are...' "

The article ended with a casual — but prophetic — remark I had made:

"There's a lot more to this than meets the eye. A lot will be coming out soon. Mr. Curtis' problems have just begun."

That type of caustic analytical remark was never again to appear in that local paper.

On November 11, another front-page article appeared in the *Anchorage Daily Times* bearing the headline:

"EX-CHIEF TO APPEAL IN PALMER."

It noted that on the following night I would appeal to the Palmer City Council to reinstate me as Police Chief. It also repeated the initial lame reasons put forth by City Hall since my dismissal: that I was fired because I had "hired two officers and changed a work schedule without the City Manager's approval."

However, Curtis' comments were different in this account. This time he said, "But these (reasons) are the lesser part of the thing. ... There are literally a thousand reasons."

City Councilman John Dolenc, who Higgins and I had visited a few days earlier, apparently was unaware that the City Manager was amending his answers to the press. Caught unaware by the *Anchorage Daily Times* reporter, he merely reiterated the initial City Hall position: "This boils down to poor communication and probably some misinterpretation. The chief feels he has the right to hire and fire. The manager feels he has the authority."

From that point forward, because of that naive unchecked interview, all future remarks were to be stock "party line" and would only be issued by designated officials — either the City Manager or the Mayor.

The week before my scheduled City Council hearing, I had time to reflect on Curtis' original professed reasons for my abrupt dismissal. Neither the objection to my change in work schedule hours, nor the objection to my rehire of two former police officers made any sense.

The work schedule "change" referred to was my decision to place my officers on a 10-hour, four-day schedule similar to the one implemented by the Anchorage Police Department. Not only were Anchorage Chief Charles Anderson and I on very amicable terms, but I had established strong ties with his officers at all levels. I voluntarily attended their 11-week police academy, and in doing so, had almost become "one of their own."

The City Manager's adamant refusal to honor my placement of Higgins or McKibben on the police payroll was never explained to me. Both were competent, professional police officers, yet both were denied reinstatement without reason. Although I never knew Curtis' real underlying objections to their rehire, it raised conjecture. During their previous tours of duty with the former Police Chief Gary Eilers had they obtained information that Curtis considered damaging or derogatory? Did he think they possessed confidential knowledge?

It wasn't long before the truth would surface.

... Chapter 3 ...

Wayne Higgins came over to my house late that afternoon after my return from Anchorage.

I stopped him before he could open his mouth to say he, too, was sorry. I knew he was blaming himself for my open support of him.

"It was just a matter of time, Wayne," I said. "He just got to me, before I got to him."

"I know," he said huskily, the intensity in his eyes showing his concern.

"We've gotta move fast," I interjected. "Artus is gonna shoot for a hearing as soon as he can get one."

"What's your plan, Chief?"

"Tomorrow morning we call all the Councilmen, including the Mayor, and see if we get any support."

"And then?"

"Then then we see people who want to talk. We dig into public records, and we learn as much as we can in a short time."

"The ARRC, too?"

"Whatever we can. Unfortunately, it's been around for 40 years — and it's still going strong. It's going to take a lot of digging, and I don't know how much time we're gonna have."

He nodded solemnly.

"Beer?"

"Yeah, Chief."

He drank it like it was going out of style.

"What do you think your chances are?" he said, referring to an upcoming regular council hearing.

"Good — I hope," and raised the can of Budweiser in his direction.

"I hope so," he said forlornly.

"If it's good for me, it'll be good for you," I reminded him.

"Yeah, we gotta expose that scumbag. He's gotten away with it too long."

"Maybe we can get more from the guys at the PD," he offered, "This shit's been going on a long time. We gotta put a stop to it, Chief."

"That's my job, Wayne," I said assuredly, trying to put his mind at ease.

"Besides, that sonofabitch has flunked *the attitude test*," I said, quoting an oft-used expression among California lawmen.

He smiled.

"Another beer?"

"No thanks, Chief, I gotta get home to Libby and the kids."

"How they holding out?"

"Okay, I guess," he said morosely. "It's tough making ends meet without steady income."

"Yeah, I know."

"How about your wife and kids?"

"It hasn't really hit home yet. Shirley is really pissed off at the City. My kids aren't taking it seriously yet. They know I'm going to do something. I always do. They're not concerned."

"Well, I better go," he said, standing to leave. "What time tomorrow?"

"Probably in town about 9. I'll give you a call early."

"Okay."

We met at the Frontier Restaurant on Evergreen near the Police Department and City Hall.

"Let's give them something to talk about — and worry about," I said, motioning for him to sit at the counter.

"I spoke to Lemoine last night," Wayne opened up. "He said he went in to see Curtis ... again ... to support you."

"And?"

"He told Bob to mind his own business."

We sat in silence and sipped our coffee.

I spoke next to break the quiet.

"I called the Councilmen this morning and the only one who said he would see us was Dolenc."

At 71, John Dolenc was the oldest of the City Councilmen. I didn't know if he would have any influence with the other Councilmen, but at least he was willing to listen. I got along well with him while I was in office. I got along well with all of them for that matter.

"What about Maze?" Higgins queried.

"I haven't been able to get hold of him, but I'll keep trying."

"What next then?"

"Since we're downtown, let's go over to the Mat-Su Borough and check some records."

"Yeah, that ought to worry the Borough Manager too. I heard that he was mixed up in all this shit, too," Higgins continued.

"Yeah, the first time I met Wes Howe at a breakfast last June, I didn't like or trust him then either."

The downtown area was devoid of any traffic, and we didn't see anyone from City Hall. I knew it was just a matter of time before someone would report back to the City that we were both roaming around town. When they heard that we were checking borough records, it would really get their attention.

"What can I do for you?"

The Borough clerk's query was cold and informal.

"Not what can I do for you, *Chief?*" or "Can I help you, *Chief?*"

There wasn't even a look of recognition of me or of Higgins, who had been around even longer than I had.

"I want to see what you have on the Industrial Park."

"The Industrial Park?"

"That's right," I said, "everything you've got."

I previously had heard there was hanky-panky in 1972 when the nearly 130 acres of land was purchased for the Industrial Park. It was not my intent to question neither the purpose nor the concept of industrial property but merely its purchase.

I knew Curtis was the City Manager at that time and was

instrumental in the land's purchase by the City. I also heard other names connected to the deal and wanted to see where they all fit together.

The records revealed that of the 129.825 acres that comprised tracts A-F, State Senator Jalmar "Jay" Kertula owned a total of 63.825 acres, approximately half of the future Industrial Park.

His name was one I often had heard, especially regarding land transactions — his name and that of the ARRC's. I also noted that the 15 acres in Tracts C and D that the Senator owned was appraised at $6,000 in 1971 and later re-appraised at $3,480 for a substantial reduction in both value, and of course, taxes.

By 1972, just prior to the purchase of the Industrial property, I saw that his 48.825 acres in Tracts E, G and H were appraised at $86,800.

Higgins' eyebrows shot up when he saw the extent of the property the Senator owned.

"That's where the Industrial Park went," he said as if he couldn't believe it.

"Yeah. I wonder how much of a kickback Curtis got for that transaction?"

He gave a low whistle.

"Unfortunately, Wayne we don't have time to find out — but a Grand Jury could find out if they wanted."

The records also indicated that the total appraisal of the industrial property came to approximately $1100 per acre. Yet, the City purchased the property for three times that amount at $3,000 per acre.

In later months, I raised those specific issues with the State Attorney General's Office, expecting some amount of interest — and action. However, when I was informed that "the striking of a poor business bargain does not constitute a criminal violation," I was taken aback. I never expected that type of remark from one of the senior law enforcement officials in the state.

In and of itself, that statement was undoubtedly true. However, neither the number of such "poor business bargains" nor the steps that led up to those "poor business bargains" were ever discussed. All of the ramifications that developed as a result of those "poor business bargains" were never considered. Analyzing all of those transactions could very well "constitute criminal violations." Yet, I had difficulty making the State authorities realize that distinct possibility.

Subsequent investigation revealed that City and Borough bonds purchased the Industrial Park property. In addition, of the two banks involved in the financial transaction — the Alaska Bank of Commerce and the Alaska Mutual Savings and Loan — that same State Senator was on the Board of Directors of the latter.

Alaska Statute Section 29.23.555. *Conflict of Interest* specified that, "an officer or employee shall disqualify himself from participating in any official action in which he has a substantial financial interest."

The same conflict of interest that existed for Senator Kertula as the owner of the industrial property itself also existed for those who owned property adjacent to the right-of-way to the proposed land purchase.

The more we uncovered on that particular trip — and the more we discovered in the days to come — made me realize my limitations. I did not have the authority or the power to unlock doors or unseal lips to learn who were specifically responsible for its purchase. Neither would those rightful inquiries come from official state sources to whom I pointed out that "where there's smoke, there's fire." Instead, I was continually informed that I offered "no proof of wrongdoing."

Higgins and I left the Borough office that morning without running into Howe, the Borough Manager. I looked forward to bumping into him while we were there to ask him some very pointed questions. But I knew I was pressed for time and didn't seek him out.

As we made ourselves conspicuous downtown while we pursued leads and initiated inquiries, I learned additional information concerning the Industrial Park property: that Senator Jalmar Kertula retained rights to hay sales after it was sold to the City of Palmer.

A sweet deal, I thought. I didn't know what connection he had with the City entity, and I couldn't understand how he, as an individual, was allowed to benefit from the private sale of public properties.

Nick Mangieri

Knowledgeable local citizens told me that while Cooper Construction Company obtained the bid for work done at the Industrial Park and was paid $200,000 by Palmer, City crews assisted them with the work.

I was unable to learn the extent of City involvement in a contract that was let out, but presumably it was substantial for the locals to notice and comment on it.

In the days that followed, our time was constantly occupied by those who deluged us with continual information. It was almost more than we could handle, or categorize, so we kept it for future reference.

Another source stated that in a 1973 bid for data processing with the Borough, Scientific Computer Systems was awarded the contract for $14,000. Although they had started work, that company was subsequently advised by Borough Chief Howe that the contract was to be awarded instead to Alaska Data Systems. The amount of that contract came to $50,000 — more than two-and-a-half times the original bid. In addition, there was an overrun of between $60,000 and $80,000.

Not surprisingly, the bookkeeper was reported to be Jack Maze — Palmer's Mayor. The overrun also was reputedly buried in the Parks and Recreation Department of the Mat-Su Borough.

The same source mentioned that in the construction of the Susitna Valley High School in the Mat valley, an $80,000 "error" was made on the cost of excavation and back fill. The Borough Manager authorized its payment — and again Maze was reportedly the bookkeeper.

The more we dug, the more we learned. Although my original intention was only to find out what Curtis' specific involvement was, or had been in the past, it became intertwined with others. Maze's name kept popping up, as did Howe's, and even Kertula's.

As enthusiastic as Wayne was in our continuing discovery of what appeared to be mushrooming corrupt practices, he had to admit to his frustration early in our investigation.

"This is getting too involved, Chief. We're gonna need a lot of help on this."

"Yeah, I know," I admitted, "but I'm trying to compile as much as I can for the state so they can get into the act."

"I don't trust 'em. This has been going on for years and nobody's done nuthin'."

The more we uncovered, the more I realized that what he said was true. However, I refused to believe that I was fighting a useless battle.

In going over the voluminous notes that we both compiled, I found a very interesting and pertinent complaint that was mailed to the Attorney General's Office in Juneau, six months prior, with copies sent to both the Assistant Attorney General and the Public Defender's Office in Anchorage. Coincidentally, I was the Administrative Officer of that latter agency before my appointment as Chief of the Palmer Police Department. Because it was not a Public Defender issue, we were only receiving an informational copy, so there was no action on our part.

That following irate letter from an Anchorage woman was that complaint. It was addressed to an Attorney General "Abrams," which probably referred to Attorney General Avrum Gross, the official who held that position in 1975:

"May 20, 1975
Attorney General's Office
Pouch Y
Juneau, Ak 99811
Atty Gen'l Abrams,
RE: Tax billing procedures of the Matanuska-Susitna Borough

"We purchased a lot in the Mat-Su Borough in June of 1974. The original owner had paid the taxes for the first half of the year. Sometime later we received from that Borough a verification of our purchase and a brief questionnaire, part of which I understood was to be used for purposes of assessment for taxation.

"Toward the end of March we received an assessment notice for the year of 1975. At no other time have we received any other communication from that Borough.

"Last Thursday, May 15, 1975, our names appeared on the foreclosure list published in the *Anchorage Times* for nonpayment of taxes for the last half of 1974. My sister called me on Friday to let me know that she had read this — it would never have occurred to me to even have looked.

"On Monday, May 19, 1975, I called the Mat-Su Borough. The woman to whom I spoke said we should have gotten a delinquent tax notice somewhere around the end of March or the first of April. When I asked why we hadn't received an original tax billing in 1974, she said there had been so many changes (due to sales, etc.) that no one who purchased property after June 1, 1974, would have been billed during 1974. The first billing would have been a delinquent notice in March or April of 1975.

"I was aghast. Since we had already received our assessment notice for 1975 with a computer printout sticker showing our correct (and only address in Alaska), then obviously someone or something had this address.

"I immediately sent the taxes and delinquent charges by certified letter as well as a letter protesting the handling of this situation.

"On a rough basis of names per inch on the published list, there are approximately 2000 names. The total delinquent charges on each piece of property is $13.40 as far as I could see. My figures work out to approximately $27,000.00

"My reason for writing is to question the legality of the tax billing procedure in which the first notice of taxes due would be that of a delinquent notice with attendant charges.

"If I attempted this procedure in my business, I am sure I would be viewing the sky through gray bars. I will repeat what I wrote them — the whole thing smells like a major ripoff.

"Sincerely,
Penelope G. Merrell
(and David L. Merrell)
(Two of a legion of slightly disgruntled and highly
irate taxpayers)
CC: Assistant Attorney General/Anchorage Public
Defender's Office/Anchorage"

That particular citizen's remarks about the "viewing of the sky through gray bars" and the whole thing smelling "like a major ripoff" really amused me.

When I showed Higgins the letter, it was even more entertaining to him.

"They even had their number before we did," he chuckled.

Nothing that I was to learn, either about the City of Palmer or of the Mat-Su Borough, would surprise me from that point on.

When I first heard that Curtis, during his prior tour, was head of the Site Selection Committee for Palmer High School, I expected to find more dirt. Sure enough, my expectations were realized when I was told that he tried to force the acceptance of the site at a City Council meeting without the public in attendance. Although his tactics failed on his first attempt, they were successful a few weeks later. He also lied about the availability of a particular prime piece of property because of "the expense." It was referred to as the "Johnnie Martin property," and I cited it in a subsequent letter to the Attorney General's Office. It was property that Martin said he would have gladly donated to the City if he had been approached. He vehemently denied in a future City Council meeting that the City Manager had ever broached the subject to him.

The same ploy utilized in the Industrial Park, as to low appraisal — but high purchase price — was applied to the acquisition of the new Palmer High School. In the latter case, of the new high school property, it was appraised at $1,250 per acre and then reportedly sold to the City for $2,500 and acre. Of course, the fact that Curtis' own property was in close proximity to the new school was nothing more than mere coincidence. That same coincidence extended to City Councilmen who also had property on the school right-of-way. Undoubtedly, conflict of interest could not possibly apply because as my direct contact in the A.G.'s Office, the Deputy Attorney General was again to subsequently advise me, "poor business deals do not constitute criminal violations." The fact that there were *continuous* "poor business deals," should have given rise to concern, if not investigation. If there were collusion and kickbacks, certainly a Grand Jury should have been convened to ascertain that possibility. Those allegations had been prevalent in the City and Borough for

.mber of years but nothing was ever done to either put those
.ims to rest — or prove they were true.

Other allegations arose in the community as to whether former City Councilman Bill Hermann ever sold gravel to the right-
of-way at the new school and to the Industrial Park. If he did, as
the citizens claimed, was the contract open for bid, as the dollar
amount required, or was it just awarded to him based upon his
past association with the City?

These and other unanswered questions easily could have
been resolved by an investigative body but the pat answer I
received from the Attorney General's Office was that noncom-
petitive bidding was permitted "so long as such contracts do not
involve the construction of public improvements and are for
more than two years."

The AG's Office did not look into the scope of the work done
by Herman or into contract work performed by Bomhoff and
Associates, another name that I gave to their office. Nor was the
duration of such contract work analyzed. Instead, I was informed
that I did not:

"Allege or offer incidents of particular acts of wrongdoing on
the part of City Officials into entering into such contracts that
would in any way constitute a violation of state criminal
statutes."

In spite of what I was subsequently told by state officials in
the upcoming months, Higgins and I had a productive week gath-
ering as much information as we could. It all appeared detrimen-
tal to those concerned.

Although I spoke to Bill Artus on at least two occasions during the week, he had gotten nothing definitive out of City Hall as
to when my hearing would be scheduled before the City Council.
Finally, by the end of the week, he called.

"Chief, I think I've got good news for you — and for Wayne
too."

"I could use a little good news."

"The Mayor has said that you and Wayne would probably be
scheduled for a hearing next week at the regular Council meeting."

"What does he mean, probably?"

"He said that he'd have to coordinate it with the rest of the

Councilmen and let me know."

"I don't trust that sonofabitch. He's been ducking me all week."

"I know, Chief," Artus said sympathetically, "but I'll keep after him."

"Do you want to talk to Wayne?"

"No, not at the moment. Just pass the information on, and as soon as I get definite word, I'll have you both in so we can discuss strategy."

"Thanks, Bill."

Higgins who listened to the conversation, asked, "What's the word, Chief?"

"Maze is giving Artus, the runaround. It's tentative for next week, but we're not gonna know for sure until the last minute."

"Them bastards are getting away with murder. They make the rules and then they bend 'em anytime they want. The Charter says we have to have a hearing."

I tried to pacify him, even though I could see the handwriting on the wall.

"Bill's doing his best. He'll let us know."

"Yeah, I know," he said, his voice dropping. "It's just all this damn waiting."

"Let's try to see Dolenc; he said he'd listen."

I placed the call to Councilman Dolenc and explained that we would like to talk to him. He was a little reluctant to see us, explaining that we would have our opportunity at the Council meeting to make ourselves heard, but I pressed him.

"We're not going to take up much of your time. It'll give you the time to get all of the facts, not just Curtis."

He agreed.

"I can't give you much time, but I'll listen," he promised.

"What do ya think, Chief, is he just talk, or will he really listen?"

I shrugged, "We got nothing to lose."

Dolenc invited us into his house and listened while I covered Curtis' announced reasons for my dismissal — the hiring of the two officers and the change in work schedule. Higgins filled in the gaps when he described a meeting he once had with Curtis, who could not give a logical reason for not allowing him to return to duty in the Police Department.

Dolenc shook his head as if not believing what he had heard.

"I really haven't had time to meet with the Mayor to see what's been happening. I know that you're both supposed to appear before the Council and give your side of this whole affair."

He seemed thoroughly sympathetic — but neither I nor Higgins really knew if he was as sincere as he tried to sound.

"There should really be a special session of the City Council to get this resolved and not a regular Council meeting," I mentioned as we stood up to leave.

"Well, I don't know," he hesitated. "I don't know who would call one."

"*Any* Council member could bring it up," I stated, hoping it would galvanize him into some kind of action.

"Let me talk to the Mayor first, and I'll see what I can do," was his weak response.

Higgins and I looked at each other. We knew the outcome of any discussion with Maze. He was obviously in Curtis' corner.

We thanked him for his time and left.

Over the weekend, we both continued seeing people and getting whatever information we considered important.

Pat Boyle, the mother of my secretary, Chris, gave us what I thought was a piece of astounding news.

Curtis, years earlier, arbitrarily abolished the City Clerk's position and increased his own salary when he absorbed her duties.

"How did he get by with it?" I asked her.

"The man thinks he's God," she replied in an accent that I couldn't readily put my finger on. It was an expression that was used often in reference to Curtis. Although her name was Irish, the accent sounded Germanic and gave it the emphasis it needed. "You've seen what he can do since you took over," she added.

I nodded my head, realizing that I was just beginning to see the tip of the iceberg.

"And dats not all," she continued. "He's a wery wiolent man when he drinks."

My ears perked up when she said it, and Higgins started to

break into a grin.

"Find his former secretary, Colleen, she'll tell you all about him."

This information was what I wanted to hear. It gave me a little leverage that I could use against him when it came to the hearing. Although, I preferred a special session of the City Council where background such as I just heard could be brought out in detail. I also recognized that it was dynamite if it could be brought to the public's attention at a regular hearing. Obviously, it was well hidden, as it was the first time that it was brought to light. Pat, fortunately, was not only a longtime City resident, but a longtime vociferous critic of the local government.

On Monday morning, November 10, Higgins and I went to a local radio and electronic shop downtown to call the Mayor. The owner, one of our supporters, had suggested that if we were going to call Maze, maybe it would be to our advantage if we taped the recording.

"It's a good idea," I said. "Maybe we'll catch him in something."

The equipment was set up, and he dialed.

It rang a few times, and a male voice answered.

"Jack?"

"Yes."

"This is Nick."

"What can I do for you?" was the cold business response.

I glanced over at the recording equipment. It was operating, and the storeowner gave me a thumbs up sign.

"I've been trying to get in touch with you for the past few days."

"What for?"

"To discuss this whole situation concerning Curtis."

"You and Higgins are both scheduled to appear before the City Council on Wednesday. There's nothing else to discuss before then."

"Don't you think there should be a special session to bring this all out in the open?"

I used the guise of the *special* session to open the conversation.

"No, I do not," and he was emphatic in his response.

"You and Higgins will have all the time you need," and he stressed "all the time."

I shouldn't have believed him, but I did.

The conversation then bounced back and forth for a few minutes, but it soon became obvious that nothing was going to be resolved so I terminated the call.

I looked at Higgins and the owner, and threw my hands in the air.

"The son of a bitch has already made up his mind."

"At least he did say that we'd have all the time we needed," Higgins replied weakly.

"We're going to need it," I responded.

... Chapter 4 ...

The locals in the valley told me that I didn't know what I was getting myself into when I first applied for the Chief's job.

After I had gotten the job, some said, "If you don't like it the way it is here, go back to where you came from."

The announced opening in the Police Department presented itself almost magically. It came out of the blue. There were no rumors, nor advance notification of its existence, nor for that matter, was it necessary for me to prepare for it beforehand. It just appeared in print, and when it did, I knew that I wanted it.

The classified ad in the *Anchorage Daily Times* read:

"Position open. Chief of Police, City of Palmer. Send resume to Acting City Manager Shaver, Box 1368, Palmer, AK 99645."

The brief ad immediately caught my attention. It not only was an opportunity I considered right up my alley, but equally important, it was in my own backyard. I had been living in Palmer, or rather near Palmer, for the past 13 months in a 40-year old *colonial* farmhouse about seven miles from town. It was referred to as colonial because it went back to Alaska's territorial days in the era before statehood. The homestead was off the new Glenn Highway, the main road between Anchorage and Palmer, and then a mile or so on up the Parks Highway toward

Fairbanks some 400 miles distant. The property sat back about a quarter mile down a hardened dirt road and consisted of an old stucco farmhouse and huge weatherbeaten barn. The structures were on 10 acres of land. I leased an adjoining 30 acres for the four horses and a pony I had shipped up from California. It wasn't the smartest move financially but it was for the family, and I did it without question. We came up from Nevada City, California — horse country. It was 40 miles from Sacramento, where everybody had a horse and either went on trail rides or rode in horse shows and rodeos. I chose that casual lifestyle and did it all. My wife and four of my five kids participated in all of the trail rides as well. The oldest, Robert, my 17-year-old stepson wasn't into horses, but the other four were Tammy, 15, Mark, 11, Dawn, 9 and Michelle, 5.

Every day for 13 months I drove the 40-mile distance from my old farmhouse in the Matanuska Valley to my job as first Administrative Officer for the Alaska Public Defender's Agency in downtown Anchorage. It was a position I more or less had talked myself into, first as the Public Defender's Administrative Assistant and then into the upgraded Administrative Officer slot.

I first met the Public Defender, Herb Soll, on a door-to-door job hunting campaign in April 1974. The initial purpose of my first solo Alaskan trip was to follow my old boss, Jim Arnold, who had been appointed as a Court Administrator for the Alaska Court System. Jim was the Court Administrator for the Sacramento County Superior Court when I was the Assistant Project Director for a federally funded *Court Reporting Study*. Jim had retained the title of Project Director, but because his duties in the Superior Court were full time and then some, I virtually ran the study and daily kept him apprised of its results. The yearlong project dealt with the feasibility of using electronic recordings in courtrooms in lieu of the traditional court stenographers. I hired fifteen law students from the nearby University of Pacific's McGeorge School of Law — my own alma mater — to determine whether the electronic AKAI recorders were more accurate, faster and less expensive than the traditional system. Court testimony in numerous trials was listened to over and over again and compared with the court stenographers' transcripts. Not only were there innumerable variances in what was actually said on the stand — and what was reported — but we found reversible error a number of times. Jim, because of his position, had court reporters working directly for him and accordingly faced a great deal of flak when we were successful. However, the project was a success and I was retained for an additional four months as a consultant to explain my 100-page final report to the Evaluation Committee.

Coincidentally, with Jim's selection for the Alaska position, my project — as well as my job — ended. He suggested I follow him to Anchorage to apply for a position he knew about in the Alaska Court System. I flew there in frigid weather, was interviewed for the job by the Administrative Director, Art Snowden, but didn't qualify because of the technical requirements. What I saw of Anchorage and learned of the opportunities that existed there, however, interested me. It did more than interest me, it intrigued me. It was a frozen, mountain-bedecked world that was virtually virgin territory for employment. I started door-knocking.

In those days, the Public Defender's Office resided on a second story walkup in an old building on Fourth Avenue, Anchorage's main street at the time. The floor was warped and the individual rooms were situated on either side of a long rectangular-shaped office. The Public Defender himself sat at the rear of this narrow jumbled mess in a small cluttered cubicle. He was a small man, with dark straight hair and a thick mustache that covered most of his upper lip. His skin was very smooth, and he wore dark-rimmed glasses that accentuated his almost rosy cheeks. A soft-spoken person, he listened intently as I gave him my sales pitch. It was, I soon learned, perfect timing. Herb Soll needed administrative help desperately, and I knew that I was that man. I was hired on the spot. Not only did he need me to immediately clear the mountain of disorganized work stacked on his desk and put them into meaningful piles, but he also wanted me to rearrange his filing system. Before long, I was assisting him in all personnel matters and had become the focal point for all grant applications and the monitoring of their progress.

In spite of his subdued, soft-spoken demeanor, he was very shrewd and capable in court and preferred that type of work and other mandatory public appearances to the endless paperwork that is always part and parcel of administrative work. In a very short time, I became indispensable to him. I also freed him up to travel throughout the state to outlying offices located at Juneau, Ketchikan, Kenai, Bethel, Fairbanks and a contract office in Nome. It was in Juneau, the capital, approximately 600 miles south of Anchorage that he was constantly required to visit the Governor's Office. The Public Defender's Office worked directly for that office so I constantly was in touch with its staff.

Within a few months, our small cramped office was relocated out of our glorified cubbyhole and moved down the block to new spacious offices on the ground floor of the Alaska Court Building. Herb's duties expanded with the increased budget — as did my own. The Administrative Assistant slot rapidly developed into a high-pressure Administrative Officer position. Not only did my personnel responsibilities, and problems, increase drastically with the additional clerical staff, but my interactions with the Assistant Public Defenders mushroomed because Herb was away from the office more and more.

The Assistant Public Defenders were a highly dedicated and cohesive group, thoroughly proficient in their duties with their clients, the accused felons and misdemeanants who needed their services. In such a close-knit office, however, I often became too aware of their dedication. To me they were becoming wild-eyed, bearded radicals who would stop at nothing to win a case in court. I am sure the majority of them weren't so disposed, but as a former police officer who lived life on the other side of the fence, that was my impression. I was more police and prosecution-oriented than I was defense-oriented.

When I saw the ad for the Chief's job in Palmer, I was ready to make a career move. The salary was less, $1,700 a month compared to the $1,912 a month I was earning in Anchorage. But I also was teaching part time at nights for the University of Alaska system at the Mat-Su Community College in Palmer. That gave me an additional $720 per month which was to increase to $870 within the next two years. I figured I could make it.

(I couldn't know then that in December 1976, at the behest of Palmer's City Hall, the local College Administrator would fail to renew my contract as part-time Instructor/Lecturer.)

Being blissfully unaware of what lay in store for me, in spite of what I had heard from rumormongers, I eagerly submitted a hastily typed 4½-page resume that detailed my 14-year span of jobs. By today's criteria, it was too long and too wordy. However, I felt that for Alaska, I'd be highly qualified for the position. I had an undergraduate degree, over two years of graduate school in the two disciplines of Criminal Justice and government, over two years of Law School, and had been an Instructor at the University of Alaska's Anchorage Community College campus and Mat-Su Community College campus, teaching not only Criminal Law and Criminal Procedure, but also Business Law I and II. As to my work experience, I was a Deputy Sheriff in Stockton, California, prior to working for the Sacramento County Superior Court. I had completed an internship in the Crime Prevention Division of the State Attorney General's Office in Sacramento and had done a short stint with the California Assembly Select Committee on Prison Reform and Rehabilitation at the State Capitol. In addition, I had held responsible administrative and analyst jobs with the federal government. Further, my resume referred to three years of investigative experience gained prior to 1960.

Although no details of my investigative duties were shown, or ever questioned, my experience in New York was as a Private Investigator for very reputable attorneys in Wall Street's financial district. The assignments ran the gamut of surveillance, to insurance fraud and locating people, to the service of literally thousands of processes — summonses and subpoenas alike. The geographical areas that I handled solo included Harlem, the Puerto Rican section of the Upper East Side, the docks on the West Side and the slums and tenements in Brooklyn.

When I subsequently moved to South Florida and opened my own agency in Ft. Lauderdale in the mid-'50's I knew my field and consequently was in high demand by local attorneys. The City Officials, however, didn't mince words when they told me they "didn't want me snooping around." (It was a response and a reaction that was to hold true 5,000 miles away in Alaska 20 years later.)

To discourage me from operating in their City limits, a special ordinance was passed. It obviously was for my benefit as no one else had sought to open an agency there. One of the provisions of that special ordinance was that all Private Investigators were required to take a Police Sergeant's exam to prove their proficiency in the law. I did so but was never given a grade despite my repeated queries to City Hall. The existing law provided that until such time as an individual who had applied for a Private Investigator's license had passed such Police Sergeant's examination, he was prohibited from practicing within City limits. Violations would bring a $500 fine and/or 60 days in jail. Although, I had gotten a county license and could, therefore, only operate within the confines of Broward County, I needed the City license for business.

Such was my first experience with politics and politicians. It was memorable, and unfortunately, would be repeated in the future.

With that background, I knew I not only was qualified to fill the Chief of Police position, but was more than qualified to fulfill those duties in a small Alaskan town.

Friends in the valley warned me but I waved their concerns aside because I knew I could handle myself and the job. The fact that I was a valley resident and had been for 13 months also was in my favor, I thought. Although I had no influence in Palmer at all and had made no political contacts during my time in the valley, I did have an Investigator from the Palmer Police Department in one or more of my Criminal Law classes at the local college. He was Gary Meier, a former California police officer who also had relocated from the *outside*, the Alaskan term for anyone out of the state or from the lower 48. He was a fast-talking heavyset type with thick sandy hair. He reminded me of the late TV detective, William Conrad, and he was just as incisive. He had no input to the selection of the new Chief, nor was he privy to the goings-on at City Hall or in the Police Department. However, we had a good relationship, and I'm sure that he mentioned my name as a worthy contender because of what he had learned and observed of me while a student in my classes. Unfortunately, before I was hired, he left the department to take a higher-paid security job with the Alaska pipeline. Shortly after leaving, he tried hard to get back on at the department. I received an almost pathetic letter from what he sarcastically described as coming from "beautiful downtown Glenn Allen Camp." In the letter, he wrote:

"This security guard stuff is okay for the money —
I guess — but they have really limited our ability to do
much. We aren't supposed to arrest people — just write
reports on them — I think it is particularly difficult for
those of us who have been policemen because we are
used to taking some sort of action against wrongdoers —
not just write them up in reports. A lot of these "pipelin-
ers" go get drunk at night and are hard to handle. But I
guess I can stick it out for awhile."

In his letter he stressed that he would even take a patrolman's
position — "anything. I think that with you there the PD is going
to prosper and grow, and I'd like to grow with it."

It was a comment that I would hear over and over again from
the officers and dispatchers at the department and from those who
had left and wanted to return. I was told that the morale and performance of the officers was poor under the prior administration.
I didn't learn specifics until after I assumed office.

My initial interview with Chuck Shaver, the Acting City
Manager was unmemorable and my selection by City Hall unmo-
mentous. I merely was informed that I was chosen for the position, and told where to pick up my uniform and a police unit to
start work on the upcoming Monday.

As nonchalant as my administrative hiring process was, the
reactions of my family were, as expected, far more enthusiastic.

My wife and kids all gave me the once-over before I stepped
inside my big unmarked white 4-door Custom 500 Ford.

"Pretty, Dad," my youngest one piped up.

"Me or the car, Michelle," I joked.

"You, Dad," she insisted with little girl seriousness.

"You look sharp, Dad," 9-year-old Dawn chimed in.

"Hand—some," my 16-year-old stretched the word out.

"Thanks, Tammy."

I couldn't help but smile at all the girls' preoccupation with
uniforms. It was not the khaki and greens of my former department at the San Joaquin Sheriff's Office in Stockton, California,
but was of various shades of blue. In fact, most of the surrounding communities, including the Anchorage Police Department

and the Alaska State Troopers, wore blue. The shirt was a light blue with dark blue flaps over the pockets and dark blue epaulets. The pants were a medium blue, with yellow stripes down the side, and the hat was slightly darker than the pants. The hat, however, was to be my bone of contention immediately upon assuming office. It was what I called a *Smoky Bear*-type hat, because that's what it looked like. Every time I saw it, that's what it reminded me of. To satisfy everyone, especially the girls, I put it on, made a face, and then threw it across the seat beside me.

They all giggled and laughed at my expression.

My boy was more fascinated with my on-duty weapon than he was with the color of my uniform.

"Can you reach your .357, Dad?" my concerned and interested son asked in typical young boy fashion.

"Sure can, Mark," I said, patting the hi-rise pancake holster that I wore on my left side for a cross-draw.

"Be careful," my wife felt compelled to say.

"Don't worry. Police Chiefs don't have to be careful," I said half convinced of the statement as I pulled down the long dirt road to Parks Highway.

I picked up the mike.

"Base, this is 9G-1," I gave my official designation.

"9G-1, this is base, go ahead."

"En route. Should be there in about ten."

"Right, Chief. Welcome aboard."

It was the very pleasant voice of Dispatcher Lucille Ashworth, and it sounded good.

On the drive in to Palmer, I glanced over at the hat again. It still struck me that it looked more like a Park Ranger's hat than a police officer's hat. It was not what I had seen in any of the *lower 48* police departments, and it was not what I wanted for my men. However, the Palmer Police had worn the hats because that's what the Alaska State Troopers wore, and I soon learned that they wanted to emulate that state agency because there had been no esprit-de-corps within their own department. I didn't think they looked like a City police department, and that's what I wanted them to look like — and be proud of.

Within a very short time of my assuming the office, I ordered the traditional police officer caps, with visors to set us apart from the troopers. We retained the *Smoky Bear*-type hats and wore them on special occasions.

One such occasion was the yearly *Frontier Days*, a celebration held during the summers to commemorate Alaska's frontier days. At that time, three of my officers, Higgins, Lemoine, and Hessler, owned horses, so the four of us rode in the parade down South Colony Way. That was the scope of our mounted detail, parade functions, which were few and far between.

The rest of the year, we all rode individually, whenever we could find the time, which wasn't very often. In the very brief summers, the horses grazed. In the very long winters, they were fed hay and grain — and grew long hair. Horses there all looked like wooly mammoths during the protracted winters.

My first winter there, the winter of 1974, I learned why and how nature protected animals in Alaska, especially horses.

The temperature had been dropping steadily from early October on and I noticed that the coats on the horses had grown longer and longer, something I had never seen before. I was used to seeing sleek shining animals that glistened when the sun hit their well-brushed coats. These Alaskan horses began to resemble South American yaks.

One evening in early November it felt like the thermometer had bottomed out. The weather report had broadcast a frigid night and my thermometer already registered 35 degrees below zero. At the time, I had no idea of what the wind chill factor could produce, but I did hear that the wind was blowing at about 10 miles per hour with gusts up to about 20 miles per hour. What I did know was that it was cold enough to freeze the balls off the proverbial brass monkey, and I was worried about the four horses and the pony still out in the frozen pasture. My pasture consisted of 10 frosted acres that surrounded my farmhouse and barn, plus another 30 frosted acres that I leased. The 40-acre tract gave the horses plenty of space to roam and me equally as much space to look for them.

The rapidly falling mercury prompted my immediate search for the horses so I could lead them all back into the relative warmth of the barn, if warmth is a term that can be used in an unheated structure with openings for windows. Before I left the house, I slipped on light mittens and put on a medium-weight coat, not expecting to be outside very long. After it got dark, the horses would mill around outside the barn about 70 feet from the house. The sun had set about 3:30, which was normal for that time of year. By the time I set out, around 4 or 4:30, it not only had grown dark, but ice fog had crystallized, making it even harder to open my eyes, much less see. The horses were not near the barn and I couldn't see them anywhere.

"Chato!" I yelled for my horse. No response.

"Shawnee!" I yelled again, this time for my wife's horse, as I edged further into the field. Still no response.

"Shilo ... Cheyenne," I yelled myself hoarse for both my eldest daughter's horse and my son's. Nothing.

"God damn animals," I muttered as I shuffled further into the long field searching for them — and listening. I heard nothing, only the wind howling over the frozen ground and blowing up the snow on my face where it stung like little ice needles.

"Son of a bitch. Where the hell are they?"

I was talking to myself, and each time I opened my mouth, I could feel the frigid gusts numbing the back of my throat.

"Apache, Apache," I screamed for my middle daughter's pony, trying to cover my mouth with my hands at the same time. He was the ringleader. He was always doing something he shouldn't. If it wasn't breaking through the electric fence that my son and I had strung across several hundred feet of pasture, it was leading the other horses out onto the highway.

"I'll bet he's led them off somewhere," I said to myself. It was too cold to open my mouth again. My hands had begun to get colder in my mittens, which were too thin to be wearing out for any extended period. It was certainly too cold for that weather. My legs were getting numb from the wind beating against them because I wore only jeans not expecting to be outside as long as I was. I soon learned learn that people had frozen to death in weather such as this, especially when they were as ill dressed for it as I was. It was, however, my first winter, and I had not yet learned to respect it.

I was halfway into the field at least a couple of hundred feet from the house and the barn and still could not see or hear the horses. I knew I should go back to the house to put something warmer on to continue my search for them. However, I felt they must be just as cold as I was. I hadn't even considered the likelihood that their newly grown hair would protect them from the frigid elements. So, I continued looking and probing further into the long field. Finally, at the end of that pasture, I saw the five huddled shapes at the base of some stunted trees.

"Chato," I tried to yell through chattering teeth.

No movement.

"God damn it. Come here," I yelled again.

Still nothing.

By now, I was almost on top of the motionless animals and grabbed Apache's halter. He tried to pull free of me, but finally gave in and reluctantly followed me back up the field. The other horses trailed slowly.

When I reached the large doors to the barn, I opened them. The horses needed no coaxing and bolted inside to get away from the icy gusts that had swirled up in front of the building. The inside of the old structure didn't feel much different than the outside. The wind blew in through the three large uncovered windows. There were no shutters over them, and if there ever had been, they were long since gone.

"Shit!" I muttered, as I looked around.

The horses started to huddle together for protection again, and though I knew I had to do something for them, my hands were too damned cold to move.

I left the barn and trudged back to the house. I wasn't looking forward to coming back out again, but I knew I had to.

My wife and kids all greeted me with a worried look on their faces.

"Are you okay?" they all wanted to know.

I explained what had happened and told them I had to go back out and nail some boards over the windows.

"Do you want someone to go out and help you?" my wife asked.

"No, it's too damned cold for anyone, and if I don't get back out there soon we're gonna have five dead horses. Just fix me some hot coffee, and I sat in front of the wood-burning stove in the kitchen trying to thaw out.

Before I set back out into the icy darkness, I slipped on a zippered snowmobile suit and put on a black wool Navy watch cap. I also slipped on heavier wool gloves and grabbed a hammer and some long nails.

"Are you sure you don't want me to help you, Dad?" my 11-year-old son volunteered.

"No, it's okay, Mark."

The all-too-brief warmth of the house seemed to evaporate in just a few short steps out the door.

The horses were waiting, still huddled together and motionless.

"It's okay," I said aloud to them, trying to convince myself as much as assure them.

I located some loose boards and started nailing them across the windows to cut down on the draft. It seemed to help. Although the horses began to mill around more, I still wasn't satisfied. I found some heavy plastic and sealed any openings I could find. After twenty minutes or so, I felt just as frozen as I had when I was in the field and slowly trekked back toward the lighted house. Once inside, I headed for the bathroom, filled the old-fashioned tub with hot water and lowered my almost-numb body into it. I noticed that the inside of my upper legs were pinkish in color, and colder to the touch, than the rest of my body.

Within the next day or so, I realized that I had frostbitten them in that brief —but frigid — exposure to the outside. For the next month or six weeks, I felt as if I had severe sunburn on them, and was uncomfortable wearing any kind of clothing that touched the legs. I learned the hard way about Alaskan winters.

As for my horses, they fared well that winter, and all subsequent winters.

My brief elation at being back in uniform and the pleasant send-off by my family was somewhat sobered with my arrival at City Hall. It was a low gray building located near the intersection of South Cobb Street and West Evergreen Avenue and was hardly an imposing structure. With the City Administrative Offices on the first floor and the Police Department situated in the basement, the only entrance to the department was by way of a narrow cement stairwell that dropped off steeply before the basement doorway. My first thought at seeing its cavernous location was, *my God, any kind of fire, or explosion, would seal the only exit from the department.*

Before I descended into what was to be my new workplace, I sought out Shaver, who also was the Public Works Director. I was told that he was somewhere in the building or was alternating between the shops where City equipment was being worked on. Someone tracked him down for me and he welcomed me, not in any formal manner, but more like I was reporting for duty as a mechanic in his Public Works Department. He was a large, craggy-featured, big-boned individual who was more at home working on City equipment than on City administrative matters. There was no swearing-in ceremony; there was no official stance of any kind. The brief introductions to his secretary, to the bookkeeper and to other clerks were perfunctory and brief:

"I suppose you'll want to be getting to your duties now," he said, leading the way to my new quarters.

... Chapter 5 ...

The Police Station was unlike any other station house that I had ever been in, especially in California. It was dark, spartan and cramped. Immediately inside the main door to the department was an undersized dispatch area to the right with a counter separating the dispatchers from the minuscule waiting area on the other side of the small room. Beyond another doorway was a somewhat larger space. To the left was the squad room with about six desks pushed back to back in a space not much larger than 9-by-12 feet. To the right was my new office, a windowless cement block cubicle that measured approximately 6-by-9 feet. Straight back, at the rear of this larger space were three holding cells. The entire area probably was no more than 800 to 1000 square feet and served as headquarters to eight sworn officers, five dispatchers and me.

The reception I received in the department was totally unlike what I had received topside from City Officials. The men and the dispatchers welcomed me warmly and openly. It was a greeting I had never experienced before nor ever would again. The dispatchers were a very friendly, outgoing group who were eager to see changes implemented in the Police Station and even more eager to pitch in and do whatever I requested of them as quickly as possible. They were impatient with internal changes, whereas the officers looked forward to external changes.

The first couple of days were busy as I proceeded to interview the dispatchers and officers, meet with the Mayor and the City

Councilmen, and become acclimated to the office and the town.

Lucille Ashworth, the oldest of the dispatchers, was a gray-haired grandmotherly type who had a tendency toward excitability if a call or complaint was an emergency. However, she got the job done.

Diana Long, a jovial pleasant female in her late 20s or early 30s, was on the large size but a bear for work. She took it on herself to tackle big projects and always accomplished them with relish.

Debby Stone, a petite dark-haired vivacious dispatcher was very young and animated in all her conversations. Although she appeared to be flighty, she was very bright and would do anything asked of her immediately. Unfortunately, within a few months of my arrival, tragedy struck her family when her younger sister was killed by a drunk driver.

Christine Boyle, also one of the dispatchers, was small of stature. She was brown-haired and very quiet, and while she looked to be in her early 20s, she acted much more mature. She also was very efficient and organized. I selected her as my secretary shortly after assuming the post.

The last dispatcher — I'll call her Belle Roth — was a CETA hire, a federally funded Comprehensive Employment and Training Act employee. Although she also was very pleasant and cooperative, she had a problem I wouldn't find out about until later. She also was the girlfriend of one of the single officers, and in the short time she was on duty, performed well when required.

The officers, the majority of whom were around age 30, were fairly new to the Palmer PD and all had come from the *outside*. I later learned that at least 20 officers in the department had resigned or were fired in an 18-month period. I also learned in rapid-fire fashion from the officers I interviewed that they all had one thing in common — frustration. They were professionals and were eager to ply their trade. But they never had the opportunity to do so. They were not given proper working equipment or the training to adequately perform their jobs. The former Chief allowed the men and the department to drift. It was a rudderless police force with little hope for any change.

Even though Gary Meier tried to act as my advance scout in painting a brighter picture to the men, they took a wait-and-see attitude. Even Meier, out of frustration and the pay — among the lowest in the state — couldn't wait for me. He quit. The high pay on the pipeline attracted many good men in state and out, and law enforcement was not immune to the lure. No matter how much they loved police work, when it came time to feed a family, security jobs on the pipeline would invariably win out over being an underpaid police officer. In time, though, they all wanted to come back. Meier and Higgins were prime examples ... and there would be others.

Bob Lemoine was one of the first officers with whom I had a closed-door session in order to get a comprehensive picture of what I faced. He also was the most vocal. A slender, dark-haired type with a premature receding hairline, Bob was a spit-and-polish officer.

"Chief," Lemoine said as he took a seat across the desk from me. "I want to welcome you." He offered his hand. It was a long firm handshake that belied his size.

"Tell me about the department," I began. "What are its problems? What does it need?"

I had opened a floodgate.

"There's been a lack of leadership here, for a long time," he answered. "... a lack of coordination ... lack of training. The radio in unit No. 3 needs work. We need nightsticks. The first-aid kits should be updated. We need type A, B, C fire extinguishers in all vehicles; we have none."

He stopped to catch his breath, eyeing me for a reaction.

"Anything else?" I tried to sound casual.

He forged ahead, knowing he had my attention.

"We need new scheduling."

"New scheduling?" I asked, wondering what he meant.

"A four-day workweek, Chief," he replied. "The Anchorage Police Department is doing it."

"You mean four 10 hour days?"

"Yes sir. It would compensate for the low salaries."

Without stopping to catch his breath again and in a matter-of-fact tone he continued, "the dispatch quality is poor; there's a lack of pride in the men and a lack of respect from the public."

When I questioned him as to what he would suggest to instill pride in them he had a ready answer.

"The place is messy and the cars are dirty. The officers should take care of their own areas and their own units."

He stopped, looked at me and leaned back in his seat to relax. He was honest and blunt. He held nothing back.

"Anything else?" I said firmly.

"No sir."

"Who else is out there waiting to see me?"

"Officer Wilcox."

"Okay, send him in."

Over the first few weeks I grew increasingly impressed by Lemoine's demeanor, his perception and his efficient manner both in the station house and in his preparations of court cases. I eventually made him my Administrative Assistant and promoted him to Corporal, a move that Curtis would squelch.

Gene Wilcox was the next officer to enter. He was of average size, young looking, almost baby-faced, with a full head of reddish-blonde hair. He was more of the fidgety type and shook hands quickly. I learned in the coming months that his quickness was a definite asset, and that he could be relied on in troublesome situations. The other men respected him.

"Chief," he said, nodding to me as he sat down.

"I'm going to ask you the same questions I asked Lemoine and will ask the others as well."

"What is it you'd like to know?"

His reply was slower than he normally spoke, more hesitant. When I repeated what I asked Lemoine, however, his face brightened with relief. A couple of his points were similar to Lemoine's ... the training and scheduling of the officers' time — but his other concerns were more patrol-oriented. He thought the units should have cameras and the patrol spotlights needed repair or upgrading. He thought there should be limited foot patrol in the downtown area and indicated that it would be good if the Alaska Criminal Statutes were made available to all the officers. He explained that they needed to be able to quickly refer to specific violations and be able to review and understand the elements in them before they could properly charge a suspect with a violation.

He was like a racehorse eager to get started. His appearance and his attitude toward the job equally impressed me.

I later learned how dedicated Wilcox and Lemoine were to

their uniform when I found out that they virtually *carried* the department before my arrival.

In response to a question that I later proposed to Lemoine during his September 29, 1976, court deposition concerning the condition of the Palmer Police Department before I took over, he answered:

"It was poor, very unorganized. Chief Gary Eilers, who had resigned along with Sergeant Gary Lewis, had more or less just left the department very unorganized ... and left it up to the senior officers to carry through until the administration, City Hall, hired a new chief to take their place ... and that was myself and Gene Wilcox."

The "carry through" that Lemoine referred to was further clarified in that same deposition when he testified that the prior chief, "wasn't in the office for the last two months that he was employed as Chief of Police. This is why I'm saying the senior officers, myself and Gene Wilcox, were left to keep things going and make sure that the shifts were covered and that the calls were completed and so forth."

I soon selected Wilcox as Patrol Supervisor over the men after Higgins resigned to take a higher-paid security officer position on the pipeline. It was also Wilcox that I intended to promote to Sergeant after Curtis pointedly told me that I could not bring Higgins back as a Sergeant — or for that matter — even as a patrolman. They both were equally qualified to wear the Sergeant's stripes. Higgins had edged out Wilcox only because of his prior police experience. Curtis was equally adamant, however, that I not be permitted to give Sergeant's stripes to Wilcox, either.

At the end of our interview session, I asked Wilcox who else was in the Squad Room.

"Officer Higgins, Chief," he said. "Should I send him in?"

I nodded and thanked him for talking with me.

David Wayne Higgins strode in next. He always answered to *Wayne*, and it was the name that we in the department always used. Besides, it fit him more than his first name did. He was a combination of John Wayne and Errol Flynn. He acted like the former and looked like the latter. Solidly, if not powerfully built,

Wayne was a six-footer with broad shoulders and a narrow waist. To him nothing was impossible. "We can do it, Chief," was his stock response. It didn't matter whether I asked him to monitor local drunk drivers or to ride herd on the outlaw biker group, the *Brothers*, when they came into town to stir up trouble at the infamous Pioneer Lounge or *49er* as it was sometimes called. He was sharp-featured with a thin pencil mustache and thick dark hair. His expression always was intense, as though he were studying every word put to him, and he always replied in a low soft voice tinged with a slight Southern accent.

"You wanted to see me, Chief?" he asked in a low husky voice.

I nodded again and directed him to the chair opposite me. He sat on the edge of the seat, almost at attention.

"Relax, Wayne." I said. "That's what you want me to call you, right?"

He smiled easily, and did relax, and then moved further back into his chair.

"Tell me about the Palmer PD," I said.

He launched into basically the same diatribe that both Lemoine and Wilcox had given. His primary concern was the low pay of the department. His priority differed from the other two officers because they were single while he had a family to support. Because he had more experience, he also cited the necessity of personnel protection, such as having Personnel Resolutions, a Civil Service Commission and a Police Review Board. He also stressed the need for accountability of evidence and property, a condition that under the prior administration was virtually non-existent.

"Is that it?"

"That's about it, Chief." he said assuredly in his low, almost hoarse voice. "If I think of something else, I'll let you know." He grasped my hand firmly.

"Glad you're here, Chief. We really need you," he added. "Anybody else you want to see?"

"Who's around?" I asked.

"I think Officer Hessler's still here. If he is, I'll send him right in."

"Thanks."

Nick Mangieri

Of all the officers, Higgins was probably the most person-
able. I also discovered that I had a little more in common with
him than I had with the others. We both had Southern wives and
kids near the same age. Our association would develop into a
friendship while I still lived in the valley. After my ouster and his
non-reinstatement, we teamed up to conduct in-depth investigations, not only into corruption at City Hall and the Borough, but
also into the mounting allegations of the longstanding massive
land fraud of the ARRC.

Charles Hessler knocked on my door next and entered. He
was probably the oldest of the officers, maybe 35 or so. He stood
about six feet tall and was slim with brown hair with a slightly
bushy mustache. He was of Czech extraction and had a very
slight accent.

After our brief mutual acknowledgements, he was eager to
discuss his observations of the department, having already been
alerted to the scope of my queries from the other officers.

Undoubtedly, his Teutonic background accounted for his precise responses.

"Car No. 3 has a steering problem ... car No. 2's shotgun
won't release ... we need sample copies of reports, forms and the
like."

When I told him that I would see that the mechanical problems would be resolved as soon as I talked to Shaver to have the
units scheduled in for work, he looked pleased.

"As to 'sample copies', I'll see that you and each one of the
officers are supplied with whatever you need."

"Thank you, Chief."

He covered some of the other items that the others had raised,
and then mentioned another one that I hadn't heard.

"There's been a policy of allowing bartenders at the local
bars to go to work before we can check into their backgrounds for
arrest records and before we give the official okay."

"Any bars in particular?" I asked, not being aware of the
local scene.

"The *49er*, Chief."

It was a name that I would come to hear often, especially in regard to narcotics, gambling and prostitution. I also later learned that the proprietor, Leroy Herren, was a personal friend of Bill Curtis, the City Manager.

I thanked him for his cooperation, and he left. Two other officers were not immediately available, Michael Temte and Dennis Hubbell. Temte was by far the largest member of the department in size and weight and was the most easygoing and quietest. However, nobody ever gave him any trouble. If they did, there was never a reoccurrence of the problem. At a subsequent interview he concurred with all the complaints and suggestions offered by the others. After I left the department, I heard that Temte was selected as a Chief of Police somewhere outside — Minnesota, I believe. He was a good man.

Officer Hubbell, "Denny" to all, was also a former North Carolina police officer, the same as Wayne Higgins. He was just as quiet as Temte, maybe even a little more restrained, but he was efficient. A slim dark-haired, six-footer, he had been a detective in his former department. I made him an Investigator on the Palmer PD before long. A cogent observation that he made during my interview with him was the need for a better reporting system. Although he primarily referred to local police reports, I also discovered that our Uniform Crime Reports to the U.S. Department of Justice were seriously delinquent. The 1974 year-end statistical reports should have been submitted to the FBI by January 22, 1975. They had not been done by the time I took over in June. Diana Long, the dispatcher, labored long and hard to get it out the following month.

The two remaining officers that I saw shortly after my arrival were the two new hires, Lt. Robert Bassett, my new Deputy Chief, and the new patrolman, Joe Norris. Both had been hired just before my arrival and without my concurrence or, indeed, any input from me. I also fired both within my first 90 days.

Bassett, a bombastic former Sheriff from the Midwest, was a typical back-stabber. In our first meeting, he assured me that he was there to help me. Unfortunately, I later learned that neither the department nor I were on his loyalty priority list.

Norris was a very effusive, glib individual who could find anything you wanted. He would have made a good Supply Sergeant in the military. But he was too glib and too helpful — a good con man. I found out that while on duty in one of the patrol cars he was banging a female in a rock pit near some observant elderly female citizens. When it was reported to me and I called him in about it, he emphatically denied that it ever happened. A polygraph by the neighboring Anchorage PD indicated that he had not told the truth. He was terminated immediately. I also heard, subsequent to his departure, that he had a criminal record, something the former chief had never checked before his hire. Because my knowledge of his record "was after the fact" and because his dismissal was not based on his alleged prior record, it was not used to fire him. His misconduct on the job was sufficient.

In Lemoine's later deposition he spoke unfavorably of both the hires:

> "**Q.** What was your impression of former Lieutenant Robert Bassett?
> **A.** Very poor.
> **Q.** What was your impression of former Police Officer Joe Norris?
> **A.** Very poor.
> **Q.** Who hired those Police Officers?
> **A.** I believe Chief Eilers did before he left.
> **Q.** How did the other Police Officers get along with Officer Norris and Lieutenant Bassett?
> **A.** Not well at all."

After both men were relieved of their duties, I made two final hires for the Palmer Police Department. The first was a former officer, John McKibben, who had left and wanted to return. Wilcox had been in contact with him and told him "to come back to the department, that the department was really squared away and that things were going real well." The second officer was Harold Leichliter, a 27-year-old former Vietnam veteran and Marine Reservist from Liberty, Texas, who was eager to enter the PD. Both turned out to be excellent replacements and complimented a small band of dedicated and loyal officers who served their department and their community with distinction.

I regretted that our relationship was not long-term.

... Chapter 6 ...

My first public meeting before influential town people was a memorable one.

On Wednesday, June 4, the Greater Palmer Chamber of Commerce sponsored a luncheon at a local restaurant, the Colony Room, and invited me to attend. During the informal session, I was asked to express my views on a variety of topics. One member of the group apparently testing my opinion of my former employer, the Alaska Public Defender's Office, asked if I always agreed with the positions taken by the agency.

"No, I did not," I replied, "however, I did learn that there are two sides to everything, and I try to remember that lesson."

I didn't want to give anyone the impression that I was in any way soft on violators so I continued. "In my capacity as the City's chief law enforcement officer, I will do what must be done."

I also added that, "I would rather have one good arrest than several that might not stand up in court for lack of evidence."

The *Frontiersman* reporter — or perhaps it was the editor — took what I said at the luncheon out-of-context and headlined an article about me with:

"NEW CHIEF: ENFORCEMENT, NOT BRUTALITY."

That caused me a slight problem at an upcoming Alaska Peace Officers Association meeting I later attended in Fairbanks.

At our attitude-adjustment session after the meeting, a grizzled gray-haired Captain from the Fairbanks Police Department challenged me on that twisted statement and implied that I was probably soft on crime. When I tried to straighten him out about what I actually had said, he interrupted me.

"I'll bet you don't even carry a weapon off duty, do you?" he asked sarcastically.

I couldn't help but smile as I nonchalantly pulled back the flap of my sport jacket to show him my 2-inch Smith and Wesson Chief Special in a pancake holster. He just grabbed his drink and went off muttering to himself.

What I had actually said at that luncheon, before the full group was, "I'm for strict law enforcement. I don't mean the brutality that police are usually accused of, I mean strict and equal law enforcement."

Just so there would be no question at that luncheon of what I stood for — *full enforcement* of the law — I even added, "I also believe in the death penalty."

When questioned by Mat-Su Borough Manager Wes Howe about my feelings concerning some sort of review board for police officers, I replied, "I'm in favor of some kind of civil service commission that would offer a method of appeal or redress in police discipline cases."

"Don't you feel that bringing in a third party not part of the administration would dilute your authority?" he asked.

"No, I do not," I replied firmly.

I knew that several officers had been fired arbitrarily from the department. What I didn't know at the time was many more had been terminated during the previous two years.

Howe continued his questioning:

"To what extent do you believe marijuana contributes to asocial behavior?"

I was beginning to get an uneasy feeling that I couldn't put my finger on about the Borough Manager — but would as the months passed. His name was one of those that came up with Curtis, our City Manager, in questionable land dealings. It was his public property transactions, as well as those of Curtis, that I was to request investigations by the Alaska State Troopers.

At the time of the luncheon, however, I knew nothing of him

or his background. I just didn't like the scope of his questions, especially his last one concerning "asocial behavior" of marijuana users. His tone was as if he questioned *any* asocial behavior ascribed to such users. It was as if he personally condoned it.

"The use of marijuana," I replied emphatically, "brings out certain adverse changes in individuals — although many people will try to refute this."

I stopped and looked at him, expecting other questions. There were none.

Bill Curtis, as the *Frontiersman* reported in its June 12 issue, would be "back at the reins of City government" on Monday, June 16.

It was just 12 days after I started. If he was surprised at my appearance, he didn't show it. In fact, our first meeting was visibly amicable as we shook hands.

"Chief, you've got your work cut out for you."

I smiled. "I can handle it, Mr. Curtis."

"I know you can," he said, flashing his typical quick tight smile. "If there's anything that you need, just let me know."

"I will," I responded comfortably.

"After I get organized, too, we'll talk some more," he said.

I nodded and started for the door.

Before I could turn the knob, he added, "We're family here, just call me Bill." He turned his attention back to his desk.

Curtis, according to the *Frontiersman*, was the choice of the City Council for the permanent position of City Manager "after a long executive session" on Tuesday, June 10, in which five applicants were considered.

However, Rose Ann Kohlberg, Curtis' new secretary at the time, confided to Bernie Boyle, another longtime resident of Palmer and a member of the Boyle family, that Bill Curtis had been on the City payroll three weeks before the deadline of applications for the position. Kohlberg also told Boyle that it was Jack Maze, the City Mayor, who hired him. The hiring of Curtis apparently had been predetermined and the farce of the public application process went forward to make it appear that all was above-board.

The personal "hiring" by Maze of Curtis for the City Manager's position also was contra to the provisions of the Palmer Municipal Charter. Section 5.3 (a) of the Charter, stated that "The City Manager ... shall be appointed by the Council." It did not state that the Mayor had the final word in hiring an appointed officer. What it did state under Section 3.4 (f) was that the Mayor, "Shall make all required appointments subject to prior approval of the Council." Being on the payroll three weeks before the announced selection process on June 10 would appear to unquestionably violate the provisions of the City Charter.

Section 1.9 of the Municipal Charter also stated that:

"Violations of this charter, the code, or any ordinance of the City may be punished by a fine which shall not exceed $300, or imprisonment for not more than 30 days, or by both such fine and imprisonment."

However, the term "violations" would appear to be a meaningless word if neither the City Attorney — nor any other state counsel — would enforce such violations. I pointed out this condition not only in a subsequent letter that I sent to the Grand Jury, but also in later interviews with the Alaska State Troopers. Dan Hickey, the Deputy Attorney General, with whom I dealt directly, merely deflected my concern by repeatedly stating that "no violations of state law are applicable." He *never* showed any concern over any of the issues that I raised, nor did he address any other courses of action. As it was, none of the violations of City law were to be enforced or investigated for *any* possible prosecution.

Maze, in commenting to the local paper on the Curtis selection, stated, "He left a year ago because of personal problems, and we were all sorry to see him go. But now that we have him back again, we are very glad. He was the best choice we could've made — we couldn't have found a better man."

As I subsequently learned, that "better man" that the Mayor spoke of was, in the words of Curtis' personal physician, a "textbook case" ... a man who not only had all the manifestations of mental illness, but also a drinking problem. I learned that in the fall of 1972, while he and his wife were visiting a friend's house during one of these episodes, he virtually destroyed the interior of the home in one of his frenzies. Although apparently no one was injured during the course of his bizarre violent behavior, it was symptomatic of what could occur when he was without his medication, medication that his wife tried to see that he took regularly. It was said that on at least one occasion she insisted that Public Works Director Chuck Shaver take Curtis' medication to him while he was out of the City. On still another occasion, as a future deposition would note, his concerned physician warned his former secretary, Colleen Ribelin, that she should never be in the same room alone with him.

As public records showed, his wife, Anne, in her petition for divorce before the Superior Court in Anchorage on July 11, 1974, stated that Curtis constantly verbally abused her and "would strike me lots of times when he had been drinking." Divorce was granted on August 13, 1974.

I also learned that shortly after leaving the City Manager's post in 1974, a position he had held for four years, Curtis went to work for the Matanuska Telephone Association as its plant superintendent. Why he left the City Manager's position for the MTA job was never fully known. All we had was Jack Maze's curt explanation to the newspaper that Curtis had "personal problems." What reportedly was said in City circles, and those privy to its internal goings-on, was that his one-year deadline to put his "problems" behind him was up, and he was scheduled to return. Although the announced reason for the out-going City Manager Jim Boyd was that he was forced to resign "due to ill health," Shaver decided to expand on that reason. He told Officer Bob Lemoine that Boyd "cost the City a lot of money and that was one of the reasons for his leaving." Shaver also made further derogatory remarks about Boyd and the former Police Chief Gary Eilers. The contents of those remarks were that both men were incompetent. However, he categorically denied those remarks in a future deposition taken of him in conjunction with my civil case for reinstatement. He also denied any prearrangement for Bill Curtis to return.

These questions and many others I gleaned from Palmer

insiders would "set the stage" for the majority of my future court depositions. To most of my deposition questions I already knew the answers. The purpose of the depositions was not so much for me to gain information as to catch them in perjured responses.

The responses from Shaver, Maze, Curtis, and even his secretary, Kohlberg, were all either outright lies or non-responsive.

The first few weeks on the job passed quickly. With each day, I either tried to resolve past problems within the office or to establish new policies as rapidly as possible. Lemoine was especially pleased because in his new administrative capacity, he not only kept the time cards and rotated the officers' shifts but supervised the dispatchers as well.

One morning he stopped in my office and asked if he could reorganize the filing system.

"What's the problem, Bob?"

"It stinks, Chief," he said. "We don't have a good check-out system. Anybody can go into the files and take out what they want anytime they want. Sometimes it's put back, and sometimes it's not."

He looked frustrated.

"Who's in charge of the files?" I asked.

"Nobody has been Chief, that's the problem," he responded wearily.

"Okay, Bob, that's your new responsibility. Make sure that area is secured and that no one checks a case out without your knowledge. If you need one of the dispatchers to help you set up a checkout procedure, select one. If you have any problems in that regard, let me know."

"Don't think I will, Chief," he answered happily. "Thanks."

Things moved smoothly within the office, but the problems with poor or broken equipment were not as easily resolved.

Shaver's stock answers to my continued queries about the officer's initial complaints and my own observations were either, "They're always complaining," or "We'll get to it, when we get time." The police units were not his number one priority, if in fact they were on his priority list at all. It was like pulling teeth to get anything done. Not only were the other two police units constantly in need of some type of maintenance or repair, but so was my own.

Late one afternoon, shortly after taking over, I responded to a call for assistance from one of my officers and put my portable red light on the roof of my unit. I jammed my foot to the accelerator and took off down the new Glenn Highway toward town. I hadn't gone more than fifty feet when the flashing light jumped off the roof of the unit and went bouncing down the road beside the car, still hooked to my lighter.

"God damn it! What the hell...!"

I couldn't imagine what had happened.

I jerked the still flashing red light back into the car and disgustedly threw it onto the seat beside me.

"What the hell's the matter with this thing?" I later asked Shaver as I handed him the light.

He took it unconcernedly, flipped it over and looked at it for a minute.

"Magnet's gone," he said curtly.

"Can you fix it?" I wanted to know.

"Nope."

"Can you get me a replacement?" I continued.

"Nope, you'll have to order it yourself."

"If I get one for the grille, can you install it?"

He walked to the front of the unit as I popped up the hood. He looked inside.

"I can probably do it," was his unenthusiastic reply.

"What about a shotgun mount?" I pressed him.

He walked back to the driver's side and peered in.

"Don't know 'bout that," he said as he opened the door, bent down and probed the floorboard with his fingers.

"When will you know?"

"Get your gun and bring it in and we'll see."

Chief Eilers never carried one, nor was there an extra shotgun in the office, so I shopped around. The pump shotguns were more than I wanted to expend out of my meager police budget of $170,000. Of that total budget only $500 was allotted to *Arms and Traffic Control*, so I opted for a less expensive model. I found one at Nordstrom's Department Store in Anchorage, in their sporting goods section. It was a Rossi double-barreled 12-gauge shotgun. The stubby-barreled model was called a "carriage gun." The apt name undoubtedly originated in the Old West because that's where they were probably effectively carried to ward off stagecoach robberies.

It was an awesome-looking weapon, especially up close. It wasn't quite the shortness of a sawed-off shotgun, but there wasn't a great deal of difference between the barrel lengths. I was so impressed with it that I carried it in the seat beside me because Shaver wasn't able to mount it. It was a reassuring backup weapon, especially on the remote Alaskan roads. It also was my weapon-of-choice after I was relieved of my position and started receiving threats on my life.

Shortly after getting my Rossi I thought I'd get a chance to use it — or at least make its presence known. It wasn't as psychologically intimidating as the regular police pump 12-guage shotguns were, especially when a shell was racked into its chamber. The mere sound of that being done would quickly get the bad guy's attention. One of the times that I noticed its immediate effectiveness was four years before while I was on the 4 to midnight shift with the San Joaquin Sheriff's Office, in California.

My partner and I were patrolling the outskirts of Stockton when we received the report of a burglar alarm at one of the many warehouses in the area. We were always getting similar reports and usually found them to be false. It was probably our second or third one of the night, and we weren't pushing to get there.

We rolled up on the gates and got out of the black-and-white unit. My partner, who had been driving, noticed the gate was slightly ajar and motioned for me to grab the shotgun. I did, and we both entered the darkened compound, headed toward the first warehouse adjacent to the gates. A side door was open. We crept inside and listened.

"You go right," he whispered, "and I'll go left."

Suddenly, we heard movement on the long metal racks above us that held rows of 50-gallon drums.

I racked a shell into the shotgun. It sounded with a sharp ringing metallic noise that seemed to reverberate throughout the building, bouncing off the high metal walls and back inward.

If any sound was intimidating it was the immediacy of the threat of that 12-gauge in action.

The soft shuffling movement above us quickly changed to,

"Don't shoot. Don't shoot. I give up." We shined our flashlights upward to pinpoint the voice. A solitary intruder, his hands held high, was trying to maneuver his way to the ground without falling off the slippery racks.

It was that thought that strangely popped into my head as I raced up the Parks Highway to assist Trooper Holman of the Alaska State Troopers. I broke open the double-barrels of the shotgun and shoved two "00" buckshot shells into its chambers and clicked it shut. The weapon rested on the seat beside me as I pressed the accelerator to the floor.

Minutes before, I heard the panicky voice of Lucille, my dispatcher, yelling into the mike, "Guns and things. They've got guns and things," she repeated.

It was a Sunday afternoon, and I wasn't on duty. I had just walked into my house after feeding my horses. My police scanner was on, as it always was, and all I could catch were those final-piercing words. I snatched up my own mike.

"Base, this is 9G-1."

"9G-1, 9G-1, where are you?" Her voice was still excited.

"What's going on, Lucille?" I demanded.

"Trooper Holman just called in to tell me he was stopping two car loads of blacks who were threatening each other with guns," she said breathlessly.

"Then," she continued, "I heard a noise that sounded like a gunshot. Her voice trailed off to a weak, "I don't know." It then picked up again, as she continued rapidly, "and then he broke off," she said helplessly.

"Did he give a location?" I wanted to know.

"Somewhere up the highway near you," was all she could say.

I strapped on my gun belt with my duty weapon, grabbed my shotgun and bolted out the door.

The Ford wasn't great on acceleration. It lacked a pursuit package that should have come with the unit, but it dug hard into the loose gravel of my driveway and sprayed small rocks as I rumbled out. I flicked on my siren and the flasher I recently had installed in the grille and spurted down Parks Highway toward Fairbanks.

"Move it, move it," I muttered to myself, trying to coax the big car into going faster.

I didn't know how far he was down the highway and searched the sparsely traveled road ahead of me. Finally, about 10 miles from my place, I spotted vehicles parked off the roadway on the opposite side of the highway. As I got closer, I saw the trooper's flashing red light behind two vehicles. I pulled my shotgun closer to me. A couple of hundred yards from the three cars, I noticed Holman outside one of the two autos talking to two men. Nothing looked amiss. As I pulled beside him, I yelled out, "Are you okay?"

He nodded his head. I pulled my unit over to the side of the road, and he walked over to me. I relaxed my grip on the weapon.

"Are you having a problem?" I asked him.

"Not really, Chief. Not now anyway."

"What happened?"

I didn't want to go into a full explanation, however brief, of what I heard on the radio and what prompted my Code 3 dash down the highway toward him. He looked like he was anxious to get back to the men he was talking to. He glanced over at the occupants of the second car, who appeared to be a family group.

"Appears to be some kind of misunderstanding," he said. "Think I've got it resolved now."

"Okay, I'll be standing by if you need me," I said, somewhat relieved.

"Thanks, Chief," he gave me a quick smile as he said it.

He walked back toward the men, said something and they got into their own car. He then walked over to the second automobile and spoke to its male driver, who also appeared to assent.

Apparently, either the situation was in the process of being resolved or the appearance of a second police car sped up the process. In any case, Holman again nodded in my direction and waved goodbye as I turned my vehicle around and headed back down Parks Highway toward home. The drive back was done at a more leisurely pace, and the episode reminded me of a similar situation while I was with the Sheriff's Office.

Another partner, I'll call Frank, and myself were parked in our black-and-white on a side road west of Stockton and about midway to the small town of Tracy, California.

Radio traffic crackled over the air, and Frank picked up the mike.

"Be advised," the voice said, " there's been a 187 of an Oakland Police Officer and the vehicle is reported moving east at a high rate of speed."

"We're the closest unit. We'll respond," Frank answered.

"Description?" he asked.

"A black Olds, 2 door, late model, license unknown, two black occupants."

Frank kicked it into gear, tires squealing, as we made a sharp right turn on the divided highway leading toward Tracy, some 10 miles distant.

"They could be headed this way," Frank said as he glanced over at me.

Oakland was about 60 miles west of us, and depending on their speed and the time of the shooting, that would put them in our area somewhere between 30 to 60 minutes at the time of our call.

A few miles east of the cut-off to the federal installation at Defense Depot Tracy, the radio crackled again, and I grasped the mike and identified ourselves.

"Be advised that suspect vehicle has been tracked by a copter and is reported to be definitely heading into San Joaquin County, and is now parallel to your present location."

I acknowledged and glanced over at Frank, who was tightly gripping the steering wheel.

"They're probably on the super highway now," he called out.

"Yeah, probably are," I answered tersely.

The stoplight at the intersection was coming up fast.

Lights flashing and siren screaming, we blew the red light and made a sharp left turn to thunder north. Luckily, it was an early Saturday morning, and there wasn't much traffic out yet. The depot was closed for the weekend so the steady stream of federal workers and supply vehicles that dominated the roadways during the week was missing. The narrow state road stretched straight ahead of us toward the super highway some 10 to 15 miles dead ahead.

Frank held the accelerator to the floor and telephone poles

and trees zipped by. I was as intent on watching traffic or obstacles down the road as Frank was focused on staying on the road. It seemed as if we were airborne. It felt as if any small gust of wind could've picked us up and blown us sideways with no effort at all. As fixed as my eyes were on the narrow road, I had to see our speed. I jerked a brief look. The needle pointed at 125 mph. Franks' knuckles were white from grasping the wheel. My own grip on the door rest was almost as tight.

"It's coming up," he said tensely. "Ask them which way we turn."

I contacted headquarters and gave them our location and ETA.

"They're presently east of your location," I was advised.

"Another unit is proceeding westward and should intercept with you."

"Get the shotgun," Frank barked hoarsely.

I unlocked the latch, swung it open and grasped the stock in sweaty hands.

At the broad intersection, we took a sharp fast left and headed eastward toward Stockton on an almost deserted broad highway.

"There it is straight ahead," we both said simultaneously, as we spotted it.

A black late-model Oldsmobile sped ahead of us with two visible occupants. They were doing 90 mph when we stopped them and bailed out, hearts pumping and blood racing, to approach the "cop killers." Both were black and fit the broadcast of the shooters. They were ordered out and did so immediately. Frank was crouched down with his service revolver out, and I had the shotgun trained on them and ready to fire at any sudden movement.

Our supervisor, who was already on the road when the call came in, zoomed in from the other direction at about the time we were making our felony stop.

The alleged suspects were a husband and wife who were only trying to get somewhere in a hurry. Their young daughter was asleep on the back seat.

A case of mistaken identity.

Somewhere along the line, the suspects' car was lost. It did not, however, lessen the anxiety and the tenseness that we had worked ourselves up to — nor to the complete letdown after a fruitless car stop. We both expected a shoot-out and had mentally prepared ourselves for it, and when it didn't happen, it took us the rest of the day to wind down. Our vehicle had to be towed back in for repairs after the sustained speed of the pursuit.

My next episode as backup to the State Troopers proved a little more fruitful.

Because our dispatch handled AST calls as well as Palmer PD calls, we were always aware of their traffic. One overcast afternoon in mid-summer, a report came in that two inmates of the Talkeetna Jail Facility had escaped from Spike Camp on the Talkeetna Spur. They had overpowered two correctional facility guards and had beaten one badly. One of the inmates was subsequently captured elsewhere but one was believed to be hiding in our area.

I contacted Corporal Grutzmacher at the local AST detachment.

"Do you guys need some help in tracking that escapee?" I wanted to know.

"Sure do, Chief," he responded effusively. "We can use all the help we can get."

"Whom can you send?" he asked.

"Well, if he's outside our City limits," I answered, "I can't use any of my people, but I can go."

It was a statement I made many times during my brief period in office. However, it was not only a statement that I enjoyed making, but one that I looked forward to carrying out. The action was unexpected and the rapport with a brother agency made it even more worthwhile.

"We sure appreciate it, Chief," he replied easily.

"Do you know where he is now?" I asked.

"The last I heard he was in the area of Kepler Lake."

I hadn't been to the section, but I knew about where it lay. It was approximately six or seven miles outside of town, near the new Glenn Highway, en route to Anchorage. I figured that he was probably heading for the big city to lose himself.

"Who's handling it at this end?" I queried Grutzmacher, again.

"Trooper Lewis," he replied.

"Where is he now?" I wanted to know.

"He's at the lake area now."

"Who's with him?"

"He's solo, Chief."

"I'm en route," I responded.

"Thanks," was his quick response.

I covered the distance in about five minutes and found Lewis' white unit parked beside the road, with him nowhere in sight. I expected him to be on the lake side of the road and searched there briefly, calling his name. When there was no response, I crossed the road and began searching for him near what appeared to be a giant rock pit. He had just started into the upper section of the excavation when I spotted him.

"Lewis!" I yelled.

"Yeah, Chief," he yelled back, as he stopped.

I hurried over to where he was standing, his eyes still searching the lower part of the pit.

"Four eyes are better than two," I said as I reached him.

He smiled.

"Any luck?"

He shook his head.

"He was seen in this vicinity, Chief, so he's probably hiding somewhere around here," he noted.

"This oughta be fun," I said as I looked down into the huge rocky crater with the tangled low-lying bushes and small boulders that lined the bottom.

"I'll take the pit and you can cover the top section," I said.

Lewis nodded.

I started my steep descent down the 50- to 60-foot drop-off.

"Watch yourself, Chief, he's tricky," he called after me.

I nodded back.

En route to the bottom, I quickly scanned the bushes and rocks in my immediate vicinity and saw nothing. I glanced back up at Lewis who was scouring the larger area at the top. He, too, didn't indicate that he saw anything. I continued my minute search of every bush and every rock behind which someone could hide. The bottom of the pit was at least 100 feet in diameter, and I exhausted the possibility of his crouching behind anything. I shouted back up to Lewis that I was starting back up the far side of the pit. He, too, threw up his hands, indicating no success, and was circling over to where I would emerge from the crater.

When I was about five feet from the top and Lewis was about 40 to 50 feet from me, he suddenly stopped. Less than 10 feet from him was the inmate crouching behind a thick bush.

"Here he is!" he yelled out.

I leapt up the few feet to the top and ran toward him, gun out.

Lewis had drawn his own weapon on the escapee, and he sheepishly raised his hands as he saw us both approaching from different directions. He was cuffed and led back to Lewis' vehicle. He thanked me before he elatedly called in the capture.

Because of that particular backup assistance, and others before that, Kolivosky commented, "You should be on our payroll, Chief."

That expression of appreciation and camaraderie among fellow officers, unfortunately, would be forgotten — or ignored.

... Chapter 7 ...

For the balance of the summer and into the fall I was into street work as much as possible and was unaware of the problems developing in City Hall behind my back. I was too intent on doing my job and doing it right to worry about stepping on any politician's toes in the process.

One such indication of rubbing somebody the wrong way occurred when I cracked down on the local *49er* Club. As a follow-up of Officer Hessler's complaint at our first meeting, that of new bartenders being allowed to start work before background checks were made for prior arrests, I instituted an immediate change.

No bartenders were allowed to tend bar until after arrest records had been reviewed.

The immediate response from the co-owner of the bar, Leroy Herren, was to go over to City Hall and complain to Curtis.

I subsequently learned that there had been a longstanding relationship, if not a friendship, between the two.

At the time of his complaint I knew nothing of their association, not that it would have made a difference. If anything, I would have delved even deeper into whatever dealings they might have had in the past and used it to a better future advantage.

Officer Lemoine, in his future deposition on my civil case for reinstatement, responded knowingly to my questions put to him during that process:

> "**Q.** Did he ever make the remark to you, "he," meaning Leroy Herren, that Bill Curtis was his buddy and that I was no good, meaning Chief Mangieri was no good, or words to that effect?
> **A.** Yes sir.
> **Q.** Do you recall what exact words?
> **A.** That you were out to hang him and that he'd been there longer than you and that he knew the City Fathers and that because of that no harm would come to him."

Herren's allusion to immunity did not impress me, however, and on one particular occasion I even had him arrested on a charge of disorderly conduct in his own bar.

In extracting additional pertinent information from Lemoine in his deposition, he admitted that the *49er* "was always a trouble spot." He continued further:

"I think that — I can't even begin to tell you how many calls as far as disturbance calls, but that's the reputation..."

Therefore it came as no surprise to me when one of my officers rushed into my office one late afternoon in mid-summer to tell me about unsettling call he had just received from the Anchorage PD.

"The *Brothers* are heading this way tonight, Chief."

The *Brothers* were an outlaw biker group that liked to raise hell wherever they went. They were headquartered in Anchorage and would take their bike forays into the countryside, especially in the short Alaskan summers. I had never heard of them before, but apparently they had a reputation as troublemakers.

Anchorage intelligence reported that they not only were riding into the valley, but into Palmer.

One of the older officers who had been with the department for over a year volunteered some additional info that I could've done without.

"They're probably going to the *49er*," he said. "It's their favorite hangout."

Officer Wilcox had just come in and overheard the conversation.

"Yeah, Chief," he confirmed. "They drink, gamble, do some drugs, and fight."

"Bullshit, not in this town," I said.

Lemoine asked, "What're we gonna do, Chief?"

I thought about it a moment, before I spoke.

"We're gonna ride herd on them. We're gonna be wherever they go; we'll be on their ass constantly. They're gonna be so tired of being hassled, they're gonna leave."

"I like it, Chief," Lemoine answered.

"Sounds good to me," another said.

"Who wants some overtime?" I asked.

Everybody on duty volunteered.

Hubbell, who was in plain clothes, asked, "Do you want me to get in uniform?"

"If you want to work tonight," I answered.

"Sure do, Chief," he responded enthusiastically.

"Okay, we'll ride two to three officers per car, depending on who we got, and somebody can ride with me if we're jammed up on space. That'll give us three units on the street."

They all nodded.

"Anybody seen Wayne?" I asked.

"He's off today," Lemoine answered, "but he called in before and said he'd stop by."

"When he comes in, Bob, send him in."

"Right, Chief."

As long as it took for him to drive from his house 10 minutes away, he was there.

He walked in to my office in civvies.

"I heard about it, Chief. You gonna need me."

It was more of a statement than a question. His voice was a little louder than usual and a little huskier.

He anticipated my question, because I was staring at him.

"Oh, just a couple of beers, Chief," and he didn't look me in the eye when he said it.

"A couple — and...?" I wanted to know.

"I'm okay," he insisted.

"No, I don't think so." I answered him. "Get some fresh air and then drink a pot of black coffee. Just hang around awhile and we'll see."

They didn't roll in until about 7 p.m., and then you could hear the throaty rumble of the Harleys a mile down the new Glenn Highway before they pulled up in front of the *49er* on Colony Way. There were about a dozen shiny black expensive bikes, choppers and ape hangars primarily. Some had different designs on them but were primarily black. All the riders were "wearing their colors" — logos on their cutoff jean jackets that they wore over their leather jackets.

I was seated solo in my unit as I watched them ride in like they owned the town. Right behind them was one of the police units, and coming around the corner was our third car. There were three officers in the one and two in the second.

Watching them stretched out in a mechanized column reminded me of the last time I saw a similar sight.

It was at the yearly festival at Angel's Camp in Calaveras County, California. It was a hot Saturday morning with the temperature to steadily climb. That was typical for the muggy agricultural San Joaquin Valley, made famous in some bygone TV series known as the "Big Valley."

I was working the first shift with my partner, and we got the word to head over toward the Calaveras County line. The SJSO was part of a mutual aid agreement in which we all assisted other adjoining counties in need. Calaveras County was definitely in need.

Every year, Mark Twain's famed Jumpin' Frog contest was held in the town. What started out as a quaint custom degenerated over the years into a wild free-for-all in which outlaw bikers from all over the state — and beyond — congregated for "a party." These *parties* consisted of drunken, drug-induced brawls in which people were injured — and killed.

Our solitary mission that day was to monitor the traffic leaving San Joaquin County to enter Calaveras County. We could've been assigned to police the town, as others before us had done, but we were lucky — or so we thought.

As we sat at the crossroads and watched the steady stream of vehicles, I asked, "Were you here last year?"

"Naw, you?"

"Nope, my first time," I responded.

"A couple of the guys I know," he continued, "worked the town last year — or maybe the year before," he said. "I forget."

"What happened?" I wanted to know.

"They said it was a zoo. Drunks, fights all over the place. Bikers riding up on the sidewalk. Gals puking their guts out. A real ball."

"Yeah," I agreed. "I heard, too, that some drunk passed out on the main street and some truck backed over his head."

"I'm glad we're not assigned there this weekend," he stressed. "This should be a breeze." He waved his hand over the now-still crossroads in front of us.

No sooner had he said those words than we heard what sounded like thunder in the distance.

"Sounds like bikers," I said, straining my eyes for a glimpse of them.

"Shit, sounds like an army of 'em," he added.

Within minutes, the low rumble had grown and their distant silhouettes seemed to fill the road.

"Look at the sonofabitches, there must be a hundred of them," he continued.

"Sure looks like it," I said slowly.

Interspersed with the motorcycles, were pickup trucks with their *mamas* riding in the back. These were hard-looking gals, tattooed, wearing chains, leathers and skimpy outfits to expose whatever they had for all to see. The guys on the motorcycles weaved back and forth, and when they passed us, they revved up their bikes.

"Hell's Angels," my partner noted.

"Yeah, I know," I answered.

"As long as they're moving, we're okay," he said, "but if one of them breaks down, we got a problem."

"Whataya mean?" I said, "we got a problem? What kind of problem?"

"When one stops," he added, "they all stop."

"We'll have a fuckin' tie-up for miles," I said, "if that happens."

"Well, partner," he added grimly, "just keep your fingers crossed that doesn't happen."

The column of Harleys and trucks were now moving slower because of the intersection and the sharp turn toward Angel's Camp. The guys on their low-riders really didn't pay too much attention to our black-and-white unit. It was their tough-looking babes who looked like they'd knife you if given the chance.

Halfway through the procession, one of the bikes pulled off the road and stopped. They all stopped.

"Shit. We got a problem now," my partner said.

"Maybe, he'll get it moving again," I said optimistically not really believing my statement.

My partner took a deep breath. "We'll give him a couple of minutes," he said.

The minutes passed. No movement back on the road. Other bikers had gotten off to see what was happening. Nothing.

"We gotta check this out and get this sonofabitch moving," my partner noted.

"Right," I added, knowing that we had little choice in the situation.

Traffic was stacking up with drivers leaning on their horns because of their impatience.

We called in our location, gave the dispatcher the problem, and advised we'd be out of the unit.

We both approached the jean-vested biker, who had broken down, and asked if he needed assistance.

"No, man. I'll have it fixed in a minute," he said, as he wiped the sweat on his forehead with a greasy hand and shook the long hair off his face.

Other nearby bikers were resting on their bikes and taking long drags on their cigarettes as they watched him — and us.

It was the gals in the beds of the two pickup trucks who couldn't resist opening their mouths.

"Don't let them pigs give you a hard time," a bleached blonde yelled out.

"There's only two of them," a stringy-haired brunette spat out.

"Shut up bitches," the driver of one of the trucks leaned out and called back to the two females who had started to climb out.

"Get back in the fuckin' truck."

An older blonde with short hair in the other truck started to yell out something.

"We told you to shut up," a burly biker with a spiked helmet pointed his beefy hand at her.

She quieted down.

My partner nudged me to move, and we walked slowly back to our car as we looked at the bikers closest to us. Nobody moved toward us, and we relaxed.

As soon as we got back to our car, the biker who had stopped straightened up and mounted his bike. He rose up and kick-started the monster with his black boots. It sprang to life and he roared off. The others followed.

Unlike that earlier time, these bikers were riding in toward us, not away from us.

As one biker after the other pulled up in front of the *49er* bar, they dismounted and glanced around at the white police cars. They shook their heads as they went inside.

My men were parked outside — just waiting.

After a few minutes, one of them stuck his head out and saw the motionless police cars facing the entrance. He went back in.

A few minutes passed and two leather-clad bikers came out, climbed on their bikes and rode up the street.

I motioned for the closest car to follow them. The one with the two officers took off after them, staying right on their tail. The bikers had only gone a few blocks when they turned and headed back in the same direction. The white police car did the same. The bikers parked again, scrambled off and hurriedly made for the entrance.

I motioned to the men to stay put.

Five minutes crawled by and a lone *Brother* came out, mounted his bike and took off in the opposite direction. This time I followed and indicated to the other cars not to move. He deliberately rode slowly up two blocks, made a right, went two more blocks and turned again. I was behind him all the way. When he finally pulled up in front, he disgustedly dismounted and strode through the entrance.

As long as it took for him to relay the information to the other *Brothers*, they began to file out.

"We don't need this chickenshit," one of them shouted as he jumped on his Harley. Another held up a middle finger as he boarded his own bike.

Others spit in the street or in our direction.

Still others cocked their right arms in an obscene gesture over their heads in a final act of defiance.

They all boarded their bikes and rumbled east out of town. I motioned to the other two cars to follow them out and headed back to the station to wait. Higgins was still there drinking coffee.

"How'd it go, Chief?" he asked in a low voice. "I *really* would have liked to have ridden with you," he stressed.

"Don't think I'll be needing you tonight," I smiled. "Thanks anyway, Wayne."

Shortly afterward, the men arrived.

"They're gone, Chief. We tailed them to the City limits, and then they took off like a bat outa hell."

"Good work, guys. We don't want that kind in town."

"I kinda enjoyed that," Wilcox also smiled as he said it.

"Who's got the duty tonight, Bob?" I asked Lemoine.

"I'll check, Chief," he answered.

"Have the others hang around a half hour, and if there's no other action from the *Brothers* tonight, the men are free to go home," I said.

Although they were to return again at the end of August, it was only to visit the State Fair held at the Alaska State Fairgrounds. Because the Fairgrounds were outside the City limits, it was outside of my technical jurisdiction and was up to the State Troopers to watch them. I couldn't resist the temptation to check them out, however, and to assist the Troopers if needed. They caused no problems that I was aware of that day, nor did I ever hear any other complaints about the *Brothers*.

What I did hear about was the kidnapping of a 12-year-old boy from the Fairgrounds on Monday, August 25.

I was attending a class at the Anchorage Police Academy when I received an urgent call from Investigator Hubble on Tuesday morning.

"We've got a major felony, Chief," he announced.

"What's up, Denny?" I wanted to know.

"A carnival pitchman named Rodney Adams abducted a Sherrod School sixth-grader, Lennie Haskins, from the State Fair yesterday."

"Why, the delay in reporting?" I asked.

"The parents said he was due home Monday evening and when he didn't return, they waited until Tuesday morning to call us."

"What else did they have to say?" I continued. "Did they think there was any foul play involved?"

"No, they think that he was just persuaded by Adams to leave with him," he said.

"What have you done so far?"

"I've just seen the parents, and they're both concerned for his safety."

"Okay, issue an all-points bulletin for Adams, charging him with kidnapping. I'm heading back to Palmer right now," I announced.

"Right, Chief. Will do."

When I arrived back at the PD, Hubbell gave me other detailed information on the incident.

Adams was "the boss" of a dime-toss booth at the fair. The boy, Lennie, worked the booth with his older brother, John, and appeared to be very impressed with the tales that the man told. So much so, the boy gave glowing accounts about him to his parents and told them of his reputed around-the-world travels.

The other workers on the midway, upon being interviewed, thought "he was just too friendly with those young boys."

Although he reportedly left Fairbanks with another young boy that he met while working as a pitchman at the Tanana Valley Fair, he arrived in Palmer with a slightly older boy named Carl.

Both boys, Carl and Lennie, were last seen with Adams in his dusty silver Hornet that bore Florida license plates at about 3 Monday afternoon. As a result of Hubbell's investigation, the information was passed on to the FBI, the Canadian authorities, the Alaska State Troopers and to the Florida authorities.

Two days later, on Thursday, August 28, the *Frontiersman* headline blazed across the front page:

"SEARCH STARTS FOR 'DEMON' KIDNAPPER."

Below it a subhead said,

**"HE WAS KNOWN AS THE 'WARLOCK OF THE
MIDWAY' BY THE BOYS."**

I read the article and shook my head in disgust.

When I called the paper to find out who the hell was writing that type of sensationalistic copy, a reporter came on the line.

"I'm just reporting the story, Chief," he responded. "Did you read it all?"

When I calmed down enough for him to explain his story, he continued,

"He used to tell all the young boys that he was a 'warlock', and to prove it he used to hypnotize several of them on a daily basis. He used to tell them they were 'coming under his power'..."

I still grunted my disapproval.

"It's all true, Chief," he insisted. "The way I write it just makes good reading."

"What did you say your name was?" I wanted to know.

"Slim," he answered. "Slim Randles."

In spite of our brief run-in, he turned out to be the same reporter who would give me favorable copy after my dismissal.

In early August I started my voluntary attendance at the 11-week Anchorage Police Academy. Curtis gave his approval, as did Maze, although his okay wasn't required. Just to touch all the bases, I casually mentioned it to the Mayor a few weeks before I actually was to start.

I explained to both Curtis and Maze that not only would Deputy Chief Lt. Bassett cover for me during the day, but that I'd work nights for the duration of the 11-week course.

"That's fine, Chief. We know we can rely on you," they responded.

After academy classes, I put in night work during the week, and would also work shifts on Saturdays and Sundays. I did so not only because I thoroughly enjoyed the duties and the challenge of straightening up an office that needed it, but because I wanted no adverse comments on not doing my job. I was always back in the office before the end of the first shift, and met with those that worked it, and I logged an additional 378 hours of overtime. Those hours did not include the time when I was actually on call — which was virtually the balance of the 24-hour day. Even while at home, my police scanner was on all during my waking hours. It was, I considered, my duty as Chief of the department.

Our small academy class consisted of 17 members. I can't call them "recruits" because the great majority of them had already been on the street a year or more. Of the total, 12 were APD officers, three were Elmendorf AFB military police, one was a Game Warden, and I, the Chief of Police of a small town. Nobody was impressed or surprised. Not that I expected or wanted them to be. In our close-knit, homogenous group, there also were three female officers. It was an exposure that I did not expect, having never worked with female officers in my last department. They were, however, very professional and dedicated. They had to be to prove they were as good, if not better, than the male officers. One of the female officers was severely injured enough in a car chase within the year that she was forced to take a disability retirement.

The course curriculum was very comprehensive, and the instructors very knowledgeable. The academy instruction was as good as I had experienced in California, which ranked high in the *"lower 48."*

In addition to the more mundane subjects of Criminal Law and Evidence, Laws of Arrest, Radio Code, Traffic Code, Auto Theft, Hit and Run Investigation, Crime Scene Investigation, Interviews and Interrogation and of course the ever-present Report Writing, there were more exotic subjects. Anti-Sniper Tactics, Explosive Ordance Disposal, Mental Disorders, Sex Crimes, and Drug Investigation, topped the list. The more hands-on instruction included Apprehension Techniques, Handcuff and Search Procedure and Traffic, Crowd and Riot Control.

The topics were varied; a total of 25 comprised the course.

As the class continued, we became a cohesive unit that worked, studied and drank together. My 40-mile distance precluded most of the drinking together, except infrequently when I was off duty and would come into Anchorage or whenever they might stop by my place in the valley.

One particular subject that we all looked forward to was the Pursuit Driving Course. As it turned out, however, it was more dramatic than even the course instructor anticipated.

During the pursuit phase, a simulated "fleeing felon" takes off at a high rate of speed with a chase car tracking it at an equally high rate of speed in order to keep up with the "felon," as he attempts to elude capture.

APD officer Hank Allers — who was some relation to Wayne Higgins — was the driving instructor for the day and took three of us in his car to show us what to do and what to expect. We were the chase car and the "felon" did his best to outrun us. Behind the wheel, Allers sped up and maneuvered beautifully to stay behind him. After a few minutes of high-speed turns we all smelled gas inside the car and could hear something sloshing behind us. Allers braked to a stop, yanked his door open and shouted.

"Everybody get out of the car, now!"

He ran to the back of the car and jerked open the trunk. Inside were two or three inches of raw gasoline still sloshing around. There was a leak in the tank that no one knew about. Some jokester in the group volunteered, "first whoosh and then whoom."

Although the age range of the officers taking the course varied slightly, most were under 30. I, of course, spotted the oldest one among them by 10 years. However, in our physical training class, I was up near the top, especially in the short sprints. I always was within the top two or three of reaching the finish line first, an accomplishment I used to rub in among the younger members.

There were a couple of young hot shots who looked like something out of the TV versions of the LAPD. They were slim, wiry, fast and good looking and usually sported black riding gloves.

One such police officer was Chuck Adams, a sharp officer who always had something to say. When he first saw the four minuscule stars that I wore on my collar as Chief, his spontaneous reaction was, "They're way too small, Chief."

There was no question about their miniature size. The four stars were on an inch-long bar. You couldn't distinguish what they were unless you were right in front of me.

"You're right, Chuck, but they came with the uniform," I responded. "First chance I get, I'll rectify that," I said smiling.

He smiled, too, but didn't realize that his comment had made an impact that would spur me to action.

He was wrong.

After graduation, I visited the local commissary at Elmendorf AFB and found regular-sized general's stars.

When I visited the Anchorage PD and found Adams, he noticed the large four stars that I had pinned to both shoulders.

"They look absolutely obscene, he cracked — but I love 'em."

I always intended to switch from the original four "stars" that I was initially issued to the eagles of a Colonel's rank. That was the insignia that Police Chiefs usually wore, especially those in smaller towns. I figured, what the hell, I was given four stars, and four stars it would be. Although they were obscene for the size of our town, the only comments I ever received were from Adams and a few other members of our class. Even Curtis, Maze and the City Councilmen never commented on the obvious change.

One afternoon, while en route from Anchorage, something happened. I was midway to Palmer and cruising nonchalantly across the Eklutna Flats in my white unmarked unit. The road ahead of me was fairly clear, and the traffic behind me was still sparse. Suddenly, out of nowhere, a white Japanese sports car was behind me and just as swiftly pulled out and zoomed past me as if I were standing still.

"Son of bitch," I blurted out.

The speed limit in that area was 60 mph. He had to be pushing 90 mph.

I flicked on my lights and siren and took chase.

I grabbed my mike.

"Base, this is 9G-1."

"9G-1, this is base, go ahead."

I could hardly hear the dispatcher over the screaming of the siren.

"Am in pursuit of a white 2-door Celica, late model, license unknown and proceeding toward Palmer on the new Glenn Highway," I almost yelled into the mike.

"What's your location, Chief."

"I just passed Eklutna Village."

It was a native village that skirted the highway, and it

whizzed past me as I tried to get more speed out of the big Ford.

I replaced the mike and grabbed the wheel with both hands.

The Celica gave no indication that it was slowing down and instead sped past two vehicles in front of it. They both gave way as I pulled around them. I looked ahead and saw that the fast-moving car rapidly was out-pacing me. I cursed the sluggishness of my own car and its inability to quickly accelerate.

Another long stretch of highway lay before me and the Celica, and I started to gain on him. Traffic was interspersed in both directions, and I saw vehicles erratically getting out of his path. I knew that a narrow bridge across the Knik River was coming up soon and hoped that I could intercept him before we both reached the bridge.

The bridge was only a couple of hundred feet long at the most, but it was so narrow that it could barely accommodate traffic in both directions and was unsafe at high speeds. To make the situation worse, the sides of the bridge were low and easily susceptible to a car going over the side and into the swiftly moving river.

The previous winter, a motorist was forced to stop in the middle of that icy bridge at night for some unknown reason. His wife and children were in the car with him and he decided to get out of the vehicle to check on something at the rear of his car. His wife saw him jump back to get out of the way of a fast-approaching vehicle that raced past their own stalled car.

It was the last time that his wife and children were to see of their father. When he jumped back to avoid being hit by the oncoming car, he had toppled over the short sides of the bridge into the fast-moving current of the frigid, ice-laden Knik River. His frozen body wasn't found until the spring.

A short distance before the Celica reached the bridge, the driver took the right fork of the Old Glenn Highway toward Palmer. It was a move I didn't expect. The old road was narrow, winding and pockmarked, and was very dangerous at any excessive speed.

I took a deep breath and yanked the wheel to the right as I rumbled into the old road. The Celica was out of sight, but I wasn't going to let him get away. I decreased my speed to stay on the road. The lane turned sharply one way and then another. Where the frost had buckled the roadway, my big car went up and slammed down hard on the broken surfaces of the road. Stunted trees growing right to the edge of the old highway caused me to slow down, and then accelerate again when there were slight clearings. Not having been on that stretch of road before and being totally unaware of what lay around the next bend made it a tense drive. I almost went off the road a half dozen times.

Finally, when I realized that I was fighting a losing battle, I grabbed the mike again.

"Base, this is 9G-1."

The siren still screamed into the car radio.

"9G-1, base," the dispatcher kicked in. "Are you okay, Chief?" she asked concernedly.

"I'm on the Old Glenn Highway, near the Eklutna Power Plant and coming up fast on Goat Creek," I replied. "Have one of the officers stop a white Celica at the old Matanuska Bridge."

"Right, Chief, will do," she responded rapidly.

I replaced the mike and eased up on the pedal. I didn't think that the car had reached the old rickety bridge yet.

Minutes later, as I rounded another bend, I saw the white Celica sitting in the middle of the narrow bridge, with Officer Temte's large frame just stepping out of his unit. He had effectively blocked the small sports car.

As I pulled up behind the vehicle, and switched off my lights and siren, I was in no mood for polite professionalism.

Inside were a young white male driver and a young female passenger.

"What was that all about?" I demanded.

"I didn't see or hear you," was his weak inappropriate response.

His female acquaintance raised her hands slightly with her eyes upward, in a futile gesture indicating that she had no part in the speeding incident.

I disgustedly looked back at him.

"That's the wrong answer, let's see your license."

His arrest was truly one of the high points of my day, and his subsequent stiff fine before a Magistrate, made it even higher.

That rough chase resulted in the shocks to my unit being completely broken to the extent that the shock mounting couplers were actually destroyed.

It also was an episode to which Curtis would refer in the upcoming City Council meeting that my attorney, Bill Artus had arranged.

In the final few weeks of my commuting back and forth to the Anchorage PD, my weekends were always busy and filled with the unexpected.

One Saturday afternoon, I received a call from Warrant Officer Jessie Lee of the trooper detachment that sounded like he needed assistance.

"What's up, Jess?" I asked.

"I got a problem, Chief," he said slowly.

"What is it?" I wanted to know.

"I gotta transport a prisoner from Sheep Mountain to the Anchorage jail facility, and I'm gonna need help." His voice was almost pleading.

"Aren't there any troopers around to assist?" I asked again.

"Not now," he answered.

"How come it's gonna take two officers?"

"They say this guys a boxer and he's fast, and I'll probably need somebody to watch him while I'm driving," he continued.

"Don't you have a cage or an enclosure for your back seat?" I queried him again.

"Nope," his reply was emphatic.

"How far is this place you gotta go to pick him up, Jess?"

"It's about an hour from here," he said.

"I can't send one of my men, Jess. It's too far out of town."

"I know, I thought maybe ..." and his voice trailed off.

I knew what he was getting at.

"Oh shit, Jessie, I'll go with you. I got a damn cold, or the flu, and I'm feeling lousy but if you need me, okay," I answered reluctantly.

"Thanks, Chief," was his quick response. "I'll pick you up in about an hour at your place."

I could've kicked myself for saying yes. As the hour wore on, I was feeling rockier and getting warmer by the minute.

"You should've told him no," my wife reminded me.

"I couldn't. A favor's a favor," I said.

By the time he pulled up in front of my house, I was in no mood to go down the road a mile, much less the 60 plus miles we had to travel. The October weather had suddenly turned colder, and the gray overcast sky didn't add much to the somber afternoon.

"I sure appreciate this, Chief," he said as I slid slowly into the front seat.

"Yeah, I know," I said weakly.

I wasn't talkative on the trip further into the mountains. I felt like lying down in the back seat instead sharing it with a prisoner.

As we approached our destination, another police unit from an adjoining jurisdiction rendezvoused with us. I didn't know their origin, nor did I particularly care at that point.

Two officers got out with a handcuffed prisoner between them.

"Watch this guy, he's fast, real fast," one of them said. "He's already put two people in the hospital."

That's great, I thought, *this sonafabitch's a tiger and I feel as weak as a kitten.*

"That's okay, I'll manacle him," I said, as I slipped a chain over his cuffs and through his belt. "That'll hold him."

"He's all yours," they said as they turned to go.

"Thanks," I said sarcastically.

We put him in the back, and I got in beside him.

"Sit there, and just sit quietly," I commanded him.

"Sure, just don't get hot," he said. "I didn't do nuthin."

"You okay, Chief?" Jess asked.

"Yeah," I said. But I wasn't. I felt like hell. My head was hot, my insides were hot, and it felt like someone had started to work me over with a board.

I looked at my watch; it had been over an hour since we had started. We still had over an hour back to Palmer and then another half hour to the jail facility.

The trip back felt like an eternity, and by the time we dumped him off and I was home I felt like I should've been the one helped out of the car. The flu had hit me and hit me fast, but I had nobody to blame but myself for being out.

A couple of weeks later while I was in the office I received a call.

"Chief, this Stu Godwin of the Anchorage FBI office," the voice announced. I remembered him. He taught a class at the police academy. He was a stocky agent in his 40s.

"Yeah, Stu. What can I do for you?" I asked.

"I need some information," he continued.

"What is it you need?"

"Did you see the flyer on that Indiana fugitive?" he asked.

"Yeah, I was just looking at it this morning," I admitted.

I recalled seeing the flyer that he spoke of. It was a wanted poster that the Indiana State Police had just sent out on a fugitive, I'll call Joe Barker, who had fled the state after a bank robbery. He was one of several involved in the heist. It was believed that he might be heading toward Alaska.

I recapped the information to Godwin.

"He's the one," he answered. "Information we have is that he could be in your area. He has a sister near there somewhere that he could be holed up at."

He mentioned a road that I was totally unfamiliar with.

"It's not in my immediate area, Stu. I'll call the Troopers and see what I can find out. I'll give you a call back as soon as I do."

"Appreciate that, Chief. We'd like to check it out today, if possible."

"I'll do my best," I said.

"By the way, Chief," he added, "We'd sure like some help if we can get it."

"Let me ask them."

I called the Trooper's office.

"Is Jess around?" I asked.

"Hang on a minute."

Warrant Officer Lee came to the phone and I explained the situation and also gave him the name of the road that the Bureau was looking for.

"It's way out in the country, Chief," he said, and he then briefly described how to get there.

"It's out of my jurisdiction, Jess," I reminded him. "I can't send one of my officers way out of City limits."

"I'm on my way to serve a warrant, Chief. I can't go now either," he said.

"Is there anybody else around?" I wanted to know.

"I don't know where Sgt. Kolivosky is. I'll ask Corp. Grutzmacher if he's available, because the others are all out on the road."

I waited while he checked on available personnel, and then he got back on the phone.

"Grutzmacher said he'd go with them, if he could, but he has to cover the office until Kolivosky gets back from Anchorage."

"Okay, Jess. Thanks anyway."

I called Agent Godwin back and relayed Lee's message about their lack of personnel to assist. I also repeated the same information to him that I had previously made to Lee, that it was way beyond City limits, so I would be unable to send my own officers there.

"We could sure use somebody's help, Chief."

His voice had the same pleading tone that Lee had used on me to get help with his prisoner transport.

"Oh, what the hell," I said finally. "I'll go with you."

"Great, Chief. Jim Hill and myself will pick you up at the station within the hour."

Upon their arrival, Godwin introduced me to Hill, another stocky agent.

"Glad to meet you, Chief," he said. "We sure appreciate you giving us a hand." On the ride out of town, the conversation centered on the fugitive and the likelihood of him hiding out where we were headed.

"He probably won't be there," one of them said, "because that'd be too obvious." The other added, "and besides all the authorities know that he has a sister living up here in the boonies."

The desolateness of the area, however, lent itself to individuals trying to lose themselves in that type of wilderness. We were miles from nowhere with sparse houses and farms farther and farther apart.

When we came to a section that Jess Lee had described, I started looking for road signs. The houses seemed more rundown than those nearer to Palmer did.

There were the typical Alaskan husky dogs roaming around the structures and around a type of general store that seemed to serve the very loose-knit rural community.

"There's the road, Stu," I pointed toward a narrow dusty gravel byway.

As he started to pull into it, he said, "You know we're not the only ones looking for him. Word has it that he double-crossed some of the gang and split with the money."

"You mean he's going to be real kinky about anybody coming near him," I offered.

"You got it," Hill replied.

There was a two-story gray wooden house down the road and to our left.

"That looks like it should be it," I noted.

They both nodded silently. We noticed that there wasn't another house close to it for a half mile.

As the car swung into the large yard there were three or four vehicles parked out front. Two or three of them looked like they were abandoned. It looked more like a junkyard than an old residence. There was nobody outside, and there didn't seem to be any movement from within.

"Let's check it out," Stu said, and they both stepped out of the vehicle.

They headed for the broken down front porch and the front door. I didn't like the looks of it. No activity, no lights, no movement of any kind. It almost looked deserted, but I knew it wasn't. At least one of the vehicles in the yard looked operable.

"I think I'll hang back here," I said, as I positioned myself between two of the wrecks. "I can check the upper windows and still see the back yard."

I thought back to what one of my former partners at the SJSO had said to me. We had answered a domestic disturbance call, and as we stepped up onto the front porch of the home and he proceeded to knock, he turned to me and said, "Don't get too close to me. If someone wants to blast away, he'll get both of us at the same time."

It was sound advice and a precaution that I always remembered — and always followed.

As Stu rapped on the door, a woman answered. After the agents both identified themselves, he questioned her about her brother. Although I couldn't hear the full conversation, I could see her shaking her head several times.

She closed the door and they turned to leave. I still saw no movement from within, although it was hard to tell through the light-colored curtains that covered all the windows.

"Doesn't look like he's there," they commented as they returned to where I stood.

"No search warrant?" I asked.

They shook their heads, "We didn't have time to get one, and besides it was a long shot that he'd be here. She said she hadn't seen him in over a year."

Months later, as I talked to one of the shadier characters that always frequented the *49er* bar, he gleefully volunteered the following information:

"Remember that time when you and the two FBI guys went to Barker's sister's house looking for him."

I nodded acknowledgment.

"Yeah, I remember."

"Well, he was upstairs with a shotgun watching you," he continued. "If you'd a been with those two guys at the front door, he'd a blown you all away."

He cackled as if he enjoyed the thought of it.

... Chapter 8 ...

At 7:58 p.m. on Wednesday, November 12, 1975, Mayor Jack E. Maze tried to gavel into order a growing boisterous audience at the regularly scheduled City Council meeting. The night was clear and cold, approaching single digit temperatures an hour before the meeting was to commence. For Alaskans used to frigid weather the weather was not unusual for that time of year. The forecast for that evening called for even lower temperatures, a low of zero to minus 10 degrees. Still, the people flocked to City Hall, that cement pill-box structure in the heart of downtown Palmer, to attend what was expected to be a very tumultuous session.

Continuous newspaper coverage and the constant rumors around town about my abrupt dismissal virtually guaranteed an overflow crowd. And yet Curtis and Maze, in future newspaper interviews and civil depositions, both would emphatically deny that the overwhelming public curiosity lay in my termination and my expected rebuttal that night. They would steadfastly assert that community concern that evening revolved about "other" City business. According to the agenda for that night, the only item of new business was an "Approval of Club License for Palmer Moose Lodge No. 793." That new announcement was hardly worth the intense public activity that was being generated in and around City Hall in spite of what the City Manager and the Mayor would maintain.

Even the items listed under old business:

   a. Review current water and sewer connection.
   b. Agreement RE: Tourist Center (Alaska State Fair,
       Inc.).
   c. Council Agenda Format.
   d. Alarm Monitor Agreement.
   e. Report on Bicentennial R.R. Museum Project.

had failed to inspire any great amount of attention in the past. In fact, even later there was no sustained or continuing interest, by the crowd in those topics.

The category that had whetted the appetite of the local community and had even stirred the imagination of the somewhat-distant Anchorage community was Item No. 8a. *Persons to be Heard*: "Nick Mangieri, Wayne Higgins and group of not more than three persons."

That rather flat, deliberately uninformative category belied the true purpose of those "to be heard." My Anchorage attorney, Bill Artus, in his letter of November 5 to the City Manager, advised him that not only did Section XI (3) of the Palmer Personnel Regulations require that I be given two weeks notice — which did not occur — but informed him of further provisions. Subsection 4 required a written notice, and Subsection 5 mandated that a hearing be held within five days of receipt of my Notice of Appeal. It was in this regard that the City Manager reluctantly agreed to hold his "formal" hearing in my case, although he downplayed that agreement to the public by burying it in mid-agenda for the evening and by phrasing it as innocuously as possible.

Curtis also reluctantly acquiesced to Artus' demands to also have Higgins heard that night and cagily lumped that request to be reinstated in with my own. He further stated to Artus that we were both permitted to have "not more than three persons" speak on our behalf. Those three witnesses were to be Bill Artus, who had represented us both; Kermit Kynel, a professor at the University of Alaska specializing in Constitutional Law; and Pat Boyle, a voracious outspoken critic of City Hall. Of course Boyle was the mother of Christine Boyle, my secretary and Chief

Dispatcher at the Palmer PD.

In the days immediately following my arbitrary discharge, my secretary was constantly intimidated by both Curtis and Chuck Shaver, who was subsequently appointed by Curtis to assume the position of Acting Chief of Police. She told me that in a prolonged one-hour and 45-minute third-degree session, she was threatened with the loss of her job not only if she attempted to support me in any manner, but also if she failed to keep her mother quiet. In the days following the City Council meeting Curtis also told her that he'd like "to punch her in the mouth." I never knew the reason behind that outburst, but it was indicative of his potential when aroused. It was also consistent with what I had already heard and what I later learned about his demeanor.

In a voluntary signed statement that she gave me on November 24, Christine Boyle stated, "It is not right to work in an atmosphere that is as oppressive as the present Police Department is and to work under an administration in City Hall that runs it employees by intimidation. The United States Constitution guarantees freedom of speech to all and that certainly is not the case in Palmer."

Bob Lemoine echoed her feelings. In another voluntarily signed statement, Lemoine related to me that when he attempted to question Curtis about my being fired immediately after the event, he was told in typical terms, that it was "none of your business." Then, Curtis had added, "My suggestion to you is that to keep yourself out of hot water, keep your mouth shut and continue to do your job."

Lemoine also was repeatedly told by both Curtis and Shaver to "keep your nose clean" as he could be easily replaced because he was "still a probationary employee." It was a statement that he could not understand since he had been in the department almost a year and regulations clearly defined the probationary period to be six months. That similar type of intimidation that was being experienced by Christine Boyle prompted Lemoine to state that he felt that their ominous warnings were "a direct threat to my freedom of speech as well as my job."

In a logical suggestion on the day prior to the City Council meeting, Artus wrote Mayor Maze and requested that the hearing be relocated to larger quarters because it was his belief that a large body of citizens was expected to attend the session. Artus, a bright capable young attorney, who had been used to dealing with basically ethical issues in the Anchorage area, was ill prepared for what he would face that night. Truth and fairness were not to be the name of the game in rural Palmer. Instead, he quickly learned that his opponents would employ innuendo, half-truths and outright lies to bolster their positions.

As the time rapidly approached to open the meeting, Maze's florid round face flushed with annoyance as he banged the gavel to commence the proceeding.

"Order, order," he shouted. "We're trying to conduct a City Council meeting here."

Irate people trying to force their way into the cramped room drowned out his efforts. Chairs were banged around, people pushed and shoved and were loud and abusive not only to each other but also to the two police officers trying to maintain some semblance of order inside and outside of the chambers. It was later estimated that 80 to 100 people were trying to squeeze into the 54 seats in the room. When it became obvious to the City Officials within the room that the Mayor's gaveling was ineffectual in silencing the commotion, both Curtis and City Attorney Burton Biss, demanded that the police officers shut the doors to the chambers and turn people away.

One of those denied entrance was Herb Shaindlin, Chief of News Operations at KIMO television, Channel 13 in Anchorage. The other was a newspaper reporter from the *Anchorage Daily Times*. Two members of the audience, however, relinquished their seats to those two media representatives so they could enter. Two other reporters that accompanied the renowned Anchorage TV commentator were denied admission. Shaindlin, in a future formal deposition, testified that in his 26 years of experience that he had never been denied admittance to any public body that was open to the public. In response to one of the questions put to him at that deposition, "Did that session have the content of a hearing?" Shaindlin stated, "...I came to the conclusion not too long after being admitted that the technique employed by I believe it was the Mayor and the Council would have to be relatively heavy handed ... so much so, incidentally that I later wrote an editorial commentary over and above the specific news coverage which followed with what, I hope and think, was direct relevance to the manner in which the entire proceedings were conducted."

In response to my query, "Did you see any people turned away from the meeting?" Shaindlin answered, "Numerous individuals, couples, et cetera."

The following exchange extracted from Shaindlin's deposition, is contra to what City Officials would offer in their attempt to downplay the public's primary interest in the council meeting — my dismissal:

Q. Did you hear any remarks made by those people?
A. Many.
Q. Can you tell me what the contents of those remarks were?
A. Utter and gross dissatisfaction with their inability to attend the meeting.

Shaindlin had previously testified that prior to the meeting he had received numerous phone calls informing him of the scope of the session and indicating that he might "find it of interest."

The Mayor and the City Attorney, in their attempt to defend their actions in barring citizens from attending the council meeting, later cited a violation of the fire ordinance with respect to overcrowding. However, it was a contingency that had already been considered. Fire Marshal Dan Contini, on the previous day, was made aware of the potentially large crowd and advised City Officials to move the session to larger quarters. He, too, was given the stock reply, "Mind your own business." Local concerned citizens also being perceptive to a need for additional space, pointed out to City Officials that there were indeed larger quarters available; The Matanuska Electric Association facilities, St. Michael's Catholic Church, and even the R.R. Depot, which was not only a community center for the City of Palmer but was operated by the City of Palmer. Both Artus and I also were told in advance by these knowledgeable citizens of those suggested locations. Their proposals, however, were totally ignored by the City Mayor and the City Attorney.

As the crowd continued to build outside the chambers, even after the session had officially started, Officer Michael G. Temte stepped through the swinging doors and uncharacteristically bellowed in frustration across the room to the Mayor and requested that he consider moving the meeting to a larger place. For Temte, it was highly unusual, as he was normally an unflappable individual. Maze, however, firmly denied the request. Moments later, Jimmy Carter, a Palmer resident and Matanuska Telephone Association employee, who was not allowed to enter, became violent and got into a pushing match with Temte and Officer Lemoine after he attempted to force his way into the room. He promptly was arrested by Lemoine, hauled off to the Police Department and booked for disorderly conduct. While at the police station, Lemoine contacted Eleanor Baxter, the Deputy Magistrate of the Matanuska-Susitna Borough and advised her of the turmoil at City Hall because of the overcrowded conditions. Her reply was that "definitely the meeting should be moved to larger quarters." Lemoine, on his return to the Council chambers approached City Attorney Biss and informed him of what Baxter had instructed. Biss' reply was that even though she was the Acting Magistrate, she had no authority to have the meeting moved. Baxter, on reflection, after talking with Officer Lemoine, was concerned with his graphic reports of the public's agitation at the Council meeting, and located Magistrate Dorothy Saxton, in Anchorage. She was attending a court seminar. Baxter apprised her of the ongoing situation at City Hall and Saxton, immediately called Lemoine for confirmation. She was given the same information that he had passed on to the Deputy Magistrate earlier as to the conditions that existed there.

Lemoine in subsequent recalling of the events of the evening was of the impression that Saxton then spoke to Biss. However, whatever direction or intercession the Magistrate gave — if any — was not heeded. The meeting did not move. Although the Magistrate was an effective political force in the valley and had been for a number of years, there were those in the local community in the days, weeks, and months that followed who believed she was part of "the system" and that any show of apparent concern on her part to alleviate wrongdoing was merely a "smoke screen." It was a disturbing thought, but one that I kept uppermost in my mind whenever I would have any future dealings with her.

When it became obvious to my attorney and me that the Mayor had no intention of relocating the meeting elsewhere, we both agreed to what had been obvious to all in attendance, that the Council had to move to accommodate the public. We rose to protest but were gaveled out by the Mayor. The session promptly commenced with the reading of the roll call of those City Officials in attendance: Mayor Maze, Councilmen Hanson, Ekstedt, Ingalls, Johnson, Dolenc and Pedersen. In addition, City Attorney Biss and City Manager Curtis were both noted as being present.

All sat on a slightly elevated platform at the front of the room, smug in their demeanor because of their apparent ability to not only maintain dominion over the location of the meeting, but to do so in spite of the vociferous objections of the citizens.

The entire scene had an unreal quality to it. It was as if the inmates of an asylum had taken control over their keepers.

Higgins, a dedicated professional police officer, was being denied his livelihood over the whim of the City Manager. I on another level had my career abruptly terminated and my future held in doubt because of the unbridled capriciousness of that same official. We both were to be accorded the farcical remedies of a kangaroo court.

I recently had learned that one of our primary adversaries, Mayor Jack E. Maze, had been a convicted bank embezzler in that same town, and had served federal time. City Manager Bill Curtis, I was yet to discover — was a wife-beater and reputed violent psychotic who had to be controlled by medication. The majority, if not all, of the other City Fathers, I later learned, had much to hide.

Immediately following the roll call, and before the usual Pledge of Allegiance that always opened their meetings, a self-satisfied Councilman Willard Johnson, made a motion that undoubtedly had been agreed upon by all members at a prior private session. The dapper, bespectacled, middle-aged Johnson was the Manager of the Matanuska Electric Association and was the prime individual on the City Council well aware of the larger available quarters at MEA facilities. He moved:

"That (the) Agenda be amended to provide for the reading of an affidavit by (the) City Manager immediately before 'Persons to be Heard' and that the "Persons to be Heard' is to be limited to those whose names appear on the agenda and further, that each be limited to 10 minutes in his presentation."

Dave Ingalls, a weaselly, slight-of-build fortyish Councilman, who sported a dark Van Dyke-type beard, quickly seconded it.

Artus and I quickly looked at each other in amazement.

"What the hell is going on?" I asked him.

He shrugged, as if not fully comprehending what was happening either.

Both of us had been assured by the Mayor on separate occasions during the past week that "we would have all the time that we needed" at the Council meeting. Higgins and I had taped a phone conversation with Maze during that same week when the same assurances were given. Higgins, recalling the conversation, leaned over to me and questioned the City Councilman's motion.

"What are they trying to pull, Chief?" he wanted to know.

"The sons of bitches are trying to screw us!" I answered unbelievingly.

We were not only to be held to "10 minutes," each, in our appeal before the Council, which was not what we were expressly told, but we were also to be denied our witnesses, which was contra to what we were informed and was specifically stipulated in the formal agenda for the evening.

Shaindlin, who in his many years in the media, was to respond to the following questions in his deposition:

"Have you ever attended any similar sessions where neither witnesses nor attorneys were allowed speak?"

"No. I don't know how — you can't have a session like that if you have no attorneys, no participants, nor accused are allowed to speak. If only accusers are allowed to speak that isn't a session."

When it came time for the City Officials to initiate their part in their pre-planned program, Curtis rose to his feet. He requested and was given acceptance by Maze to read an extensive Affidavit that was to be 13 pages in length and 45 minutes in duration.

The City Manager was a tall, gaunt-like individual whose ashen-hued appearance and close-cropped gray hair made him appear older than his 44 years. His expression always alternated between somberness and smugness, and it was the latter one with which he began to read:

"William Curtis, being first duly sworn. on oath deposes and says: I make this affidavit in connection with the above captioned suit and the threatened suit by Mr. Mangieri. I have not given any reasons or explanation before because I did not think (and still don't believe) it is required or necessary, and because rebutting the kind of charges made by Mr. Higgins and Mr. Mangieri is like adding fuel to the fire. I have been instructed to reply, however, and I do so, discussing the two individuals together because of the circumstances."

He then launched into a lengthy diatribe in which he attempted to justify his prior action of terminating me by citing Personnel Regulations regarding probationary employees, upon which he relied to support his recent precipitous conduct. He did not, however, bother to note that the Personnel Regulations also specified that, "City employees shall be protected from arbitrary discharge by Code provisions." It was a Personnel Reg stipulation that I was only hurriedly able to refer to in my brief "10 minute" response to his attack, which became increasingly virulent as the reading of his affidavit progressed. There were references to bills that I owed in the small community, confirmed, of course, by their reporting of those local businessmen who had always been part-and-parcel of a close-knit group that depended on City Hall for their livelihood and support. Notable among this group was Lee Hartley, owner of Hartley Motors, the Ford dealership in Palmer. He not only was the individual who was awarded the contract for the three police cruisers — which turned out to be below acceptable police standards — but was the same individual who posted bond for Maze after he had been arrested for embezzlement years earlier. It also was Hartley that employed Maze in his garage while he was out on bond.

There was even reference to a $5 check written by my wife for a bottle of wine purchased from a local market. She had written the check in haste and never recorded it in the checkbook or told me about it so that I could enter it. With a large family and lower pay, we were always living from payday to payday. Unfortunately, it was returned for insufficient funds. I quickly honored it with an apology to the market for the oversight as soon as I learned of the error. The newly hired Lieutenant from whom I borrowed the $5 to immediately repay the money to the store, however, had his own private agenda, and lost no time in siding with the City Administration after I had fired him during the summer. Not only did our small town have no need for a Deputy Chief, the position for which Lt. Robert Bassett was unnecessarily hired before my arrival, but also I learned that as a Sheriff in Tomahawk, Wisconsin, in 1974, he had been suspended for four counts of misconduct in office. Although he was tried and acquitted of those felony charges, he had to agree to resign and not seek re-election. In addition to what I discovered about his background, I also learned that he was politicking behind my back in an attempt to ingratiate himself among the local businessmen. Undoubtedly, he was trying to replace me at some future date. My firm handling of the Lt. Bassett situation was thoroughly condoned by Mayor Maze, at the time and even received Curtis' concurrence. Having dealt with employee problems in the past I was well aware of the need for thorough documentation and of the necessity to advise employees of sanctions that were to be forthcoming if their actions did not change. Bassett chose to ignore my warnings by constantly undermining me. I rectified that problem before it was too late.

It also was Bassett who subsequently charged in a City Council meeting in August 1975, that Public Works Director Chuck Shaver was involved in serious instances of cruelty to animals in the local pound. When Councilman John Dolenc asked Bassett why he hadn't intervened, he hesitated and stated that he reported it to his superior. However, the first time that I heard of the occurrence was when it appeared in the local paper during the summer.

In spite of City Officials' hostility towards Bassett, it was he that they used to expand their smear campaign against me.

Curtis, in typical condemnation by innuendo and half-truths, continued his personal poisonous barbs as he read his extensive affidavit:

"There is substantial evidence to indicate that Mr. Mangieri has a very unstable marital situation at this time as confirmed by family disturbance responses by the Alaska State Troopers."

The reference to "at this time" was totally false taken in the context of my marriage. The only obvious "instability" had to do with my stepson, Robert, who as an 18-year-old decided not only to challenge my authority but also to engage in the use of illicit drugs while living under my roof. Neither my officers nor I could catch him in the act of either using or supplying drugs. I did on one occasion, however, find my orange Ford pickup truck abandoned beside the Palmer Highway a few miles from town after he had taken without permission. When I opened the door to the vehicle, it reeked of marijuana.

Officer Lemoine, who subsequently resigned from the department in the summer of 1976, was openly supportive when he described the situation in a deposition that he gave to City Attorney Biss on his cross examination. Apparently, the City Attorney was still trying to justify Curtis' remarks:

Q. Do you know whether or not any of Mr. Mangieri's family was involved in narcotics or marijuana?

A. Yes sir.

Q. Do you want to tell us about that?

A. Myself and Officer Wilcox received a complaint from a school bus driver that an individual described as being hippie-looking, long red hair and driving an orange pickup with a white camper shell on the back was spending an awful lot of time in the school grounds, in the parking lot, and this individual — and he went on to say that several of the students would come out, get into the truck and be in the truck for a short time and then leave, and that it looked very suspicious to her. Myself and Officer Wilcox worked it just as we would any other case, with the exception that we made the Chief aware of it. The Chief, in turn, told us to work it just like we would any other case, and that even more so because it was his stepson, that if he was involved in any kind of dealing in narcotics that he wanted him punished to the fullest extent.

The response by Lemoine in that deposition did not prove to

be the City Attorney's shining hour.

In the two years that followed my dismissal, Biss went far beyond the normal role of City Attorney in defending City Officials. His actions and his legal briefs exhibited the same pattern of innuendo, half-truths, and outright lies that Curtis and Maze had done — and would continue to do. Although I retained counsel for as long as I could afford it on my reinstatement case, I eventually was to be *pro se*, my own attorney, in that case and in additional actions that I would file. Biss, too, was named as a defendant.

As Curtis continued reading his inflammatory affidavit, "the spectators in and out of the Council Chambers," as Shaindlin later noted, "were becoming increasingly volatile." Curtis however did not stop. In his obsessiveness, he zeroed in on every scrap of information that he had in order to justify his actions.

He then mentioned that an "extensive knowledge of the principles and practices of modern Police Administration and methods" were necessary "for the job specifications of Chief of Police under the City of Palmer job classification." I did not possess that knowledge, he said. What he failed to consider, or for that matter, to make known to the audience, was that when my application was initially submitted and approved by those same City Officials on that City Council, it was done before his rehire. They were aware that my background had included, not only a bachelor's degree and a completion of all requirements for a master's degree in government, but substantial completion of a second master's degree in Criminal Justice and two years of Law School. In addition, I was working as a part-time instructor at the University of Alaska, teaching Criminal Law and Criminal Procedure. I also had listed under "experience," three years as an "investigator," having acquired that in-depth skill both in New York and in Florida. Although he also cited that the job specs stated "five years of law enforcement experience with at least two years in a responsible supervisory position," it was not the criteria that was applied in the selection of the former Police Chief Gary Eilers. Eilers had less than the stated five years, and it did not disqualify him, nor was it considered as disqualifying when I applied for the job. My prior service as a Deputy Sheriff with the San Joaquin Sheriff's Office in Stockton, California, coupled with my other experience and education apparently surpassed the other 20 applicants. It was a decision that was made before his return as City Manager and undoubtedly rankled him because I was not his "type" of subordinate. In a future deposition he let slip his autocratic style in dealing with his supervisors or department heads:

"They don't wipe their noses without my approval."

As Curtis continued to read his affidavit, he referred to two incidents in which he stated that he was able to "observe my day-to-day capability to operate and manage (my) department. In those observations, he said, he "questioned" my actions as though the mere use of that term meant that he would have done otherwise. One incident involved a Police Dispatcher who occupied a federally funded CETA (Comprehensive Employment and Training Act) position. The second incident involved a high-speed pursuit in which I was engaged with my own unmarked unit.

In the former incident, the inebriated off-duty female dispatcher had broken a store window in the nearby town of Wasilla. In her drunken state, she entered the store and called the Palmer Police Department for reasons unknown. An off-duty patrolman responded to assist her. In the interim, another call came in and reported an intoxicated woman in the same town. Having no police department of their own, the complaint was directed to the Palmer PD, although there was still an unanswered question as to why the Alaska State Troopers did not handle it. When the second call was received by the dispatcher on duty, she sent a second police unit to respond. She was unaware that the off-duty officer had taken the only other remaining unit to look into the problem earlier. When I learned of the situation shortly afterward, I immediately fired the intoxicated dispatcher and docked both officers two days pay each, the off-duty officer for taking one of the units and the second officer for leaving the City without proper authorization. Personnel and payroll were subsequently advised to proceed with the pay cuts. Either they weren't prompt enough to activate the deductions, or hadn't initiated the paperwork. Whatever the reason, their negligence gave Curtis a contrived opportunity to raise the issue at the City Council meeting, implying that I was somehow remiss in not following up on my actions.

Nick Mangieri

In the latter incident, Curtis, in one breath, loudly questioned my judgment for the high-speed chase over a particularly bad stretch of road, and in the next breath feigned his phony concern by adding, "where he could easily have lost control and destroyed the car and lost his own life."

Either the full extent of police work, or the inherent dangers involved, were alien to someone who should have known — or he conveniently chose to ignore my duty. He was well aware that other police officers, and I possessed a statewide commission, meaning that we could arrest any offender within the confines of Alaska's borders. He also knew that I would be derelict in my duties if I didn't give chase to someone who had been endangering the lives of others on the highway for his erratic driving at an excessive rate of speed. The individual was rightly arrested, charged with reckless driving and subsequently appeared before Magistrate Saxton, who meted out a stiff fine.

Curtis resumed his harangue and expressed his continued displeasure because I attended the Anchorage Police Academy, an action that he had personally approved upon his return as City Manager. Although as Chief of Police, I was exempt, by statute, from undergoing any Police Standards training, I felt that it was well worth the additional effort. First, and foremost, I would be up-to-date on all Alaska statutes and procedures. Second, and this was almost as important as my first reason, I would establish an ongoing rapport with the Anchorage Police Department, Alaska's largest department and also our closest neighbor. It was a move that my officers and I considered to be a favorable step in order to professionalize our small department, a quality that had never existed before. Neither Curtis, nor Maze, nor any of the other City Council members objected to my attendance before or during that 11-week session. They all knew before that involvement that I would work full night shifts and weekends to compensate for the time out of the office during the day. Curtis also knew that any urgent problems or questions could and would be resolved by rapid communication to the Anchorage PD where I was instantly available. Moreover, I had a police scanner installed in my home to monitor all police traffic in the valley. Inasmuch as that traffic also involved Alaska State Trooper calls, I not only was fully abreast of their police complaints, but also frequently assisted them as personal back up. It was an additional self-imposed duty that I willingly absorbed in order to gain support and greater interest in our department from their small detachment quartered in Palmer. Such an interest, and even recognition, was minimal at best before my takeover. However, truthfully, I enjoyed any increased police action that I could get into. Sgt. Mike Kolivosky frequently commented about my being "everywhere."

Unfortunately, as time passed, whatever relationship that Kolivosky and I had seemed to disappear. He always appeared available when Curtis called or wanted to see him. Their friendship, it was reported, extended back into his first tour as City Manager in the early seventies. It also was Kolivosky who was called on the morning of the fourth when Curtis abruptly ousted me from office.

As Curtis completed his prolonged denunciation of me, he made feeble attempts to vindicate himself by first engaging in a disjointed discussion of why he rejected Officer Higgins and then jumped to his objection of my institution of a 10-hour, four-day workweek, both actions which were his initial stated reasons for my termination (The issue of denying Officer John McKibben's reinstatement, however, was not raised for some reason).

During Curtis' protracted monologue to the public, he stated that Higgins could not possibly be rehired as a Sergeant, because the position had not been funded in the budget. However, in prior discussions with the former Chief I knew that he had a Sergeant on his payroll — his brother-in-law — and I also knew that it was within my prerogative to hire a Sergeant in lieu of a Lieutenant. I did not need the higher-paid Lieutenant's slot because I wanted to save my department money. When I questioned the City Council about it shortly after I had assumed office, I was told, "We never understood why it was, why it came about."

Yet, in true robot-like rubber-stamp fashion, they approved a Lieutenant's position with the glorified title of Deputy Chief all for an eight man department.

When I first learned that Curtis was adamant about my not rehiring Higgins as a Sergeant I offered him the Patrolman slot. Although he accepted that offer, Curtis still refused to allow me to hire Higgins back, even though he told him in a private session that he had previously been a "good officer" and had done a "fine job." Higgins then retained Bill Artus in order to gain reinstatement. In turn, Artus subpoenaed me to verify our prior conversations. Those actions apparently did not sit well with City Attorney Biss as manifested in his abrasive cross examination of me when I appeared in Artus' office to give the deposition. Coincidentally, that deposition occurred three weeks before my dismissal.

Curtis' final volley of ammunition as to his stated reasons for my unsuitability for the Chief's position was because I my changed the hours of the 40-hour workweek for my officers without his permission. Although he cited the normal hours for the "standard work week," he contradicted himself during a deposition a year later as to the scope of my authority.

With his full ammo publicly expended, Curtis defiantly looked around at the openly hostile audience before he spoke again:

"Both Mr. Mangieri and Mr. Higgins (if he was actually an employee) were probationary employees. The purpose of the probation is to sort out those who are not satisfactory, and if in doubt, to terminate before both the City and the employee get too much invested in each other. Whether or not all of the information given me is verified, there was enough, coupled with my own observations to make it incumbent upon me to act in these two cases."

He then pushed himself back from the podium, at which he stood. He looked smugly over at the Mayor, thoroughly satisfied with his performance, and then took his seat back at the table.

Rose Ann Kohlberg, his secretary, who had taped the entire City Council meeting, was to understatedly — but correctly — note in her transcription:

"During the reading of the affidavit by Mr. Curtis, a recess was called by the Mayor at 9:15 p.m. and reconvened at 9:20 p.m. due to confusion in the audience."

Maze then magnanimously announced "Persons to be Heard" and looked in my direction, acting as self-satisfied as Curtis. I glanced quickly at Wayne Higgins and at Bill Artus, both were quiet. Higgins was tightly clenching his jaw; Artus was looking down at the floor, slowly shaking his head from side to side. I gripped the chair in front of me tightly as I rose, trying to contain my anger over Curtis' farcical allegations, and at the same time trying to focus on a *10-minute* response to his 45-minute tirade. I outlined my education, my background and my experience and stressed that all this was known to then Acting City Manager Chuck Shaver and to the City Council before my hire. I pointed out that my stint with the Anchorage Police Academy and with its department was to the benefit of the City and that it was with the approval of the City Manager. I reminded the assembled group that my tour of duty constantly had been given favorable comments by the public, my officers and dispatchers — who all had been thoroughly demoralized before I arrived — by other Chiefs of Police, by the Alaska Peace Officers Association, and even by the Mayor and the City Council members themselves. I called attention to the fact that there *never* were any derogatory remarks from the City Manager; there *never* were any memos citing my failure to act in a given situation and that there *never* was any adverse publicity to the City during my administration. In short, I reminded them again that there was no documentation at all to support Curtis' absurd allegations *before* he fired me.

Although it was obvious to me after the meeting adjourned that whatever Curtis had raised during that session had to have been obtained *after the fact*. I did not, and could not, zero in on that mode of attack because of my time constraints. I knew as I spoke that I had to cover all his points as rapidly as possible.

I then cited a similar capricious action taken by Curtis when he was City Manager during his first tour. I loudly informed the City Council and the public in the packed room, that Curtis, in conjunction with a prior City Council, had violated their own City Charter by illegally voting out of existence the former City Clerk, Emilie St. Pierre, in April 1971, and that the City Manager simply absorbed her position.

I informed the audience that the City Clerk's position had been established by City Charter, and that any amendments thereto, provided in Sections 14.1-14.4, had to be first be initiated by Council vote, and then submitted to the electorate at an election "not less than 60 days after its proposal by the Council, or at a special election called by the Council for the purpose of voting thereon". I further stated to those in that packed room that the Charter could also be amended by an "initiatory petition" signed by the required number of electors, then filed with the Mayor, and then submitted "to the electors of the City at the next regular City elections which is to be held after ninety days following the filing of the petition." *Then* and *only then* could there be an amendment to the City Charter, and in the case of the City Clerk, could her position be done away with?

I stressed the fact that neither of these stipulations was followed, nor were their procedures implemented, and consequently, Emilie St. Pierre's administrative position with the City of Palmer, and her attendant responsible "checks and balances" type of duties were summarily abolished. Among those duties were the, "custodian of the official records of the City" and equally important, when necessary, to advise officials of "the conditions or requirements of all bonds, franchises, contracts, or agreements" — duties that would have made difficult many of the illegal actions that I investigated in City Hall. I subsequently gleaned from an October 1971 agenda, that three of the six City Councilmen that sat on the dais in front of me, were on the City Council in 1971: Willard Johnson, James Ekstedt and Arlyn Hanson. Those three specifically played a role in illegally abolishing the City Clerk's position.

By the time I finished citing the prohibitory actions of the City Manager and the City Council, I was aware that the brief response time that was allotted to me was fleeting rapidly.

"How much time do I have?" I directed my question to the Mayor.

Mayor Maze replied, "You have three minutes."

I barely had time to answer the issues that Curtis had raised: my justified firing of both Lt. Bassett and the intoxicated dispatcher, my sanctions against the two officers, my contested hiring of Officer Higgins, or my valid reasons for changing the workweek when I abruptly stopped. I knew that I had to quickly bring out the real reasons for my sudden termination — my investigation into the rotten politics of City Hall:

"Now, as to my conducting investigations, there is an investigation being conducted. The investigator at the DA's office was aware of it, the DA himself is aware of it now, the U.S. Attorney's Office is aware of it. By your own standards here, by the Charter, you are conducting, you are allowing bids that are above and beyond what the Charter says. We won't go into them now, I can go into them if anybody wants to question me on them."

The following verbatim excerpts were extracted from the transcription of that tape as recorded by Curtis' secretary:

"**MANGIERI:** Now, as to a little dirt...

"**MAYOR MAZE:** You are already one minute over...

"**WAYNE HIGGINS:** I will give him five of mine...

"**MAYOR MAZE:** The Council, at the beginning of the meeting, made a motion and approved it, to limit each of you to 10 minutes, PERIOD!

"**MANGIERI:** Can I respond?

"**MAYOR MAZE:** Mr. Higgins, at this time...

"**MANGIERI:** Okay, I'll cancel it.

"**MAN FROM AUDIENCE:** That seems like a pretty rotten deal to me.

"**MAYOR MAZE:** Well, he said he's got his day in court, so...

"**MAN FROM AUDIENCE:** Well, I'd like to hear it man, I can't go to the court meeting. I gotta work.

"**MAYOR MAZE:** Do you live in the City?

"**MAN FROM AUDIENCE:** Yeah.

"**MAYOR MAZE:** Fine, thank you.

"**MAN FROM AUDIENCE:** I would like to hear what he has to say, it sounds pretty interesting up to now.

"**MAYOR MAZE:** I agree.

"**WOMAN FROM AUDIENCE:** If Mr. Curtis can rake him over the coals, why can't he have a chance to get back?

"**MAYOR MAZE:** Mr. Wayne Higgins..."

Higgins rose slowly from his seat, looking slightly bewildered at the obvious stacked-deck that he faced, and of his own limited response time. His jaw had relaxed but his flushed face exhibited the same sense of anger and frustration that I felt. He tried to open his statement by referencing our initial conversation concerning my offer of employment to him but was immediately cut down by Councilman Ekstedt's questioning his resignation before he sought temporary employment with the Trans-Alaska Pipeline at the city port of Valdez. Higgins tried to explain the circumstances that surrounded his departure but was constantly interrupted in his replies. When he was finally able to continue, he did so in his typical southern drawl but in a delivery that was pointedly emphatic:

> "I was hired by Mr. Mangieri and when I found out that Mr. Curtis had overruled his decision, I requested to see Mr. Curtis on Mr. Mangieri's advice. I went to see him and I explained the circumstances to Mr. Curtis who told me that he made a decision that no former Palmer employee, especially a police officer, can ever work for the City again. He also said that he thought I was a good officer and that I did a fine job but that it was his bull-headedness that wouldn't let me come back; once he makes a decision, it'll stand. He is bullheaded. It's obvious. He also confirmed what I asked him specifically, let me understand this, I was hired before I got to go to work sir, that's right, you were, it's my bullheadedness. I slept on it and I don't want you back under any circumstances.
>
> "Also, I have worked for Fayetteville Police Department from 1970 to 1974. I have attended Northwestern University. I have attended other various police schools which I won't go into, but I have served under three Chiefs of Police, all of whom ... excuse me ... four Chiefs of Police, all of whom I thought were very good, but one. Mr. Mangieri, I have more respect for than any Police Chief I have worked for because he is a man of his word. He stands behind his people and it's obvious to me that you don't want anybody here to stand behind their police officers. That's all I have."

Higgins disgustedly sat down, heavily, and Artus reassuringly patted him on the shoulder, indicating that he had done the best he could under the circumstances.

He had brought out Curtis' irrationality, but unfortunately, it wasn't enough. The transcript then states, that Mayor Maze thanked Higgins. The transcript wording then continued in a more generalized summary fashion:

> "Others from the audience wished to speak, at which time, Mayor Maze asked the Council if they wished to hear more speakers from the audience or hold to their original motion.
>
> "COUNCILMAN JOHNSON: 'I made the original motion and I wish to hold to that motion and I request that the testimony be terminated at this time and go on with the meeting.'
>
> "MAYOR MAZE ORDERED HEARING ADJOURNED."

At this time someone from the audience shouted, 'We have another person here who wishes to speak.' Mayor Maze hit the gavel and said, 'We will go on with the meeting.' At this time, a gentlemen from the University wished to speak and was denied based on the motion at the beginning of this meeting."

That "gentleman from the University" referred to in the taped transcript, was Professor Kynel. Although he was originally scheduled to speak on my behalf as one of my three witnesses, he was not allowed to give any testimony in spite of being approved by the City Council.

Kynel, a former Lieutenant with the Los Angeles County Police Department later supportively told the Anchorage Daily Times reporter, who was one of those who was allowed entry:

"I feel this man was denied due process. In my opinion he is one of the finest police officers I've ever seen. You just can't dismiss a person without a cause."

... Chapter 9 ...

On the following morning the *Anchorage Daily Times* ran a two-page article about the City Council fiasco titled:

"SCUFFLES MARK PALMER HEARING"

Below my photo on the front page they appropriately commented:

"REBUTTAL IS CUT OFF"

The story further noted that:
"The Council without giving a reason would not allow three persons to testify on behalf of Mangieri and Higgins.
The evening's agenda had provided for such testimony."
One of the people who were prohibited from speaking was of course my attorney Bill Artus.
It was an unheard of occurrence not to be allowed proper representation in any such hearing but was an indication of the uphill fight that was in store for me.
The balance of the lengthy article accurately reported all of the events of the prior night including the final remark by the Constitutional Law professor.
The *Frontiersman* also carried a large front page spread on that same day:

"BIG CROWD AT CITY HALL
Curtis tells why he fired Mangieri"

Although the article was surprisingly factual it also was just as surprisingly slanted in my favor. Whether by editorial design or by coincidence the reporter Slim Randles would leave the paper a short time later.

It was the opening sentence of that creative piece that really appealed to me. The reporter had Curtis and I "crossing verbal swords in a crowded Council chamber." I liked the word-picture that it conjured up. However I doubt that the City Hall crowd shared my word-appreciation. Even the closing sentence of the story was the Higgins comment that I'm sure that City Hall frowned on as well: "Mangieri is the man I have the greatest respect for because he stands behind his word."

Slim Randles also was a sled dog musher and breeder. As much as I relished his article I was not too enthralled when he appeared one cold night after his departure with two fully grown Samoyed dogs that my wife had impetuously purchased from him. Feeding a family of five plus five horses plus two other dogs was not a contingency that I had bargained for especially in light of my recently unemployed status. However, what happened to them a few months later was not the resolution I would have sought or expected.

The editorial of November 20 in the *Frontiersman* was to set the tone of that paper from that point forward and confirm their City-oriented pitch. Under the headline:

"THE MANGIERI AFFAIR,"

the editor and publisher Jerome F. Sheldon presented a more City-biased account of the night of the City Council meeting. In his editorial, he stated,

> "Some people there may genuinely have felt that ex-Police Chief Nick Mangieri should have been reinstated. Others may have believed that City Manager Bill Curtis is a 'dictator' as an Anchorage television commentator put it. A lot more may have been spoiling for a fight of

sorts — spectators drawn there by Mangieri's effective use of the Anchorage news media in the days following his firing."

He followed up his twisted assessment of the situation with:

"His use of the media? Maybe indeed it was he who was being manipulated by Herb Shaindlin of Channel 13 who came with his portable camera to put on videotape the scenes of minor disturbance as people tried to enter the Council Chamber."

He tried to downplay the situation at City Hall that night although all others who attended that volatile session or viewed it on TV knew otherwise:

"Furthermore, many of the public were in attendance not on Mangieri's account but to protest the construction of a fence around the Palmer Airport expansion project."

His comment turned out to be a lame observation inasmuch as the "construction of a fence" was *not* on the agenda for the meeting.

The editorial, still carrying the City banner, then noted in warped logic:

"In any case, the Council was right in cutting off any prolonged discussion of the Mangieri affair. Under the City Charter, the right to hire and fire the Police Chief or any other City employee rests solely with the manager. Mangieri could not have been re-hired over Curtis' objections without the Council in turn firing the City Manager."

In a feeble attempt at objective reporting the editor appeared to gently chide the Mayor "or a Council member," for not stepping into the lobby "to explain the circumstances to the crowd as to why they had to be kept out." He evidently blindly accepted the City's explanation that the fire code prohibited additional seating and was unaware that the Fire Chief had already made a request to move the session elsewhere. The summary of his simplified explanation — however inaccurate — justified his whole editorial:

"Apparently there was no other space available that night to accommodate a larger audience."

In that same issue there was yet another extensive article about Curtis. It reported that he received a vote of confidence from the Palmer City Council concerning my discharge. That action came at a special meeting held on November 14 when the Council went into executive session for almost an hour to discuss the Police Department.

The article also stated that Maze referred to a comment that I had raised during that Council meeting concerning Curtis' residence outside of the City limits. I had informed the City Council during the night of the hearing that Curtis was in violation of the Palmer City Charter on yet another code. Chapter V Section 5.4(a) stated that the City Manager "shall be a resident of the city during his tenure in office." Curtis had not been. Maze, however, grandiosely announced to the other City Council members in that executive session that Curtis "said he was very willing to move into the City but we informed him that he was practically inside."

Maze further gleefully noted to the City Council members in a blatant undisguised move to protect Curtis, "If we wanted to annex the area as soon as possible he was agreeable; the paperwork is all but done."

On November 14, Bill Artus, working for the firm of Houston & Lytle, filed a Civil Complaint (No. 75-8520) in the Third Judicial District Superior Court for the State of Alaska. The defendants were "William Curtis in his capacity as City Manager for Palmer, Alaska, and the City of Palmer, Alaska." The numerous causes of action included my termination without reason or justification which was contra to the Municipal Charter that provided that all City employees be protected from arbitrary dismissal; my denial to a hearing and my denial to two-weeks notice

— both of which were provided for in the Personnel Regulations. The demand stipulated in the action was for reinstatement back wages compensatory time for an additional 378 hours — that I had fully documented — plus costs and attorney's fees.

I previously had sent a formal demand letter to Curtis on November 5 requesting payment at that time and reminding him that "former Lt. Robert Bassett was paid his compensatory time at his termination, as was former Chief of Police Gary Eilers."

It was ignored.

The demand for compensatory time would also suffer the same fate during the course of my first civil suit.

In addition, a claim that I subsequently filed with the Wage and Hour Division of the Alaska Department of Labor was handled poorly. Their method of resolving my compensatory time issue was to totally disregard my proof and merely write the City of Palmer for an explanation. The Wage and Hour Investigator did not bother to check with the former Chief or with the former Lieutenant. The expected response was that the City Attorney summarily denied my compensatory payments without making any reference to the precedent-setting pay of either of those former officials. He also failed to submit any payroll or personnel documentation to back up any of his allegations, and the Alaska Department of Labor never solicited them.

I was beginning not to rely on my civil remedies so I also initiated a series of criminal complaints. The first complaint, filed on November 19, was a letter to the Foreman of the Grand Jury of the Alaska Court System in Anchorage in which I requested "an investigation into the rotten City politics in Palmer."

In that four-page letter I repeated to the Grand Jury the same charge that I had made at the City Council meeting, that the City Manager had illegally abolished the former City Clerk's job and had assumed the position at an annual salary increase of $2,500.

I also informed the Grand Jury that not only was the City Manager not a resident of the City as mandated by the Municipal Charter but that the location of his residence was well known to the City Mayor and Council members who had likewise concurred in his hire.

I also wrote:

"A citizen just recently informed me that about four or five months ago, she was advised 'confidentially' by the City Manager's secretary that he was on the payroll three weeks before applications terminated.

"If that were the case it would also mean he was on the payroll before his official appointment. This citizen is willing to so state before any investigating committee. I attempted to obtain this specific information but was denied access as 'payroll records' are not public records."

I continued:

"He has violated the Charter in several other manners:
1. He would not give me the oath of office stating that it was not necessary.
2. I was discharged arbitrarily (as was another police officer who knew the truth about City politics).
3. The public was denied access to the public hearing in which the police officer and I were supposed to be given the right to appear and reply.
4. The granting of bids is done preferentially and not in accordance with the provisions of the Charter.

"In addition to the City Manager, the City Mayor is just as guilty. He hired the City Manager and took part in all of the above.

"Furthermore, the Mayor should not even be allowed to hold public office.

"He is an ex-felon, having been arrested and convicted of embezzlement 20 years ago. He is a voter and has been for a number of years. (See attached Alaska Statute 15.05.030 — *Voter Disqualification for Felony Conviction*.)

"All of the above, and more as yet unproven, exist here in Palmer. The public has traditionally 'looked the other way' and those that have dared to challenge the system from within or posed a threat to it are eliminated.

"There have been hints and warnings of violence yet to come made to others and myself because we refuse to tolerate a crooked City Hall. We have done our duty and will continue to do so. But we do not have the power to unlock the many doors that need opening or unseal the lips of those who refuse or are to afraid to speak — the Grand Jury does.

"Your intervention is earnestly requested by myself and by my fellow police officer Wayne Higgins, who also was unjustly fired, and for the people of Palmer. It would be a warning to other communities that this type of behavior in City Hall will be scrutinized and dealt with promptly and firmly."

I did not cite the ARRC because I had yet to formulate a causal relationship between them and the City.

After reviewing my letter, I was thoroughly satisfied that my shotgun approach would generate sufficient interest for them to look into my allegations.

I was even more certain my closing sentence would galvanize them to action:

"Inasmuch as the City Attorney is culpable and is therefore unable to bring charges, this request for an investigation is of necessity directed to your body."

Within a week, I received an answer. It was the first of many responses that I would receive. It would also become the norm in all my attempts to launch any type of political investigation:

"Dear Mr. Mangieri:

"It is the consensus of the Grand Jury that there is insufficient evidence at this time to warrant an investigation as suggested in your letter of November 19, 1975.

"If you feel you have evidence, which indicates a violation of state law has occurred, it would be our suggestion that you immediately contact the Alaska State Troopers so that an independent investigation can be conducted.

"In the event a violation of a State statute or regulation is uncovered, we will, of course, consider the matter upon its presentation by the District Attorney.

"Very truly yours,

William G. Lofflin
Grand Jury Foreman"

As disappointed as I was, I learned, much to my continued dismay, that everyone would defer to someone else.

No individual or agency would initiate any preliminary action in spite of what I considered to be strong indications of *probable cause*.

Within a day of my Grand Jury appeal and before its rejection, I called Chuck Delinski of the Anchorage FBI office to get his advice on civil rights violations especially concerning the apparent pre-determined exclusion of citizens from a public meeting.

"That's a little beyond me at my level," he responded.

"What do you suggest?" I asked.

"The best way to handle this is for you to write me a letter and request that a formal ruling be issued from our Washington office concerning your allegations."

I was somewhat disappointed at his answer but knew that I had to follow procedures.

"All right, Chuck. Thanks. It'll be in the mail to you."

"I'll pass it on as soon as I receive it," he said. "Good luck."

"Thanks again," I said halfheartedly.

In my letter of November 21, 1975, to Delinski, I stated as suggested:

"I hereby request a formal ruling from your Washington office to determine whether my civil rights and those of the citizens of Palmer have been violated."

In that letter I briefly outlined the facts as they occurred on the night of November 12 in the Council Chambers and then added:

> "It is my contention and that of the 20 to 30 people who were denied entry to a public meeting that the denial was a violation of the Right to Assemble and the Right to Free Speech and also infringed upon the Freedom of the Press because at least one member of the press was not allowed initial admittance even though his presence was well known to all in the meeting room."

At the time that I contacted Delinski and then forwarded my letter to him I did not — nor could I — conceive that there would be any delay or any inaction by the Department of Justice once my letter reached Washington. I anticipated a prompt favorable reaction. I was, however, wrong in that expectation.

With the passing of the months, I would have to renew my request again. Fortunately for me, I was blissfully unaware of Washington's lack of interest or of any intended direction by them. What I did know was that I had to continue going forward with my criminal complaints. I felt that the most expeditious method at the state level was to go through the State Attorney General's Office. It was with this frame of reference that I placed a long-distance call to the Attorney General's Office in Juneau in early December. I asked to speak directly to Attorney General Avrum Gross, having met him personally on at least two separate occasions. One of those occasions had been the year before when I was still with the Alaska Public Defender's Agency. Public Defender Herb Soll, my former boss, was a personal friend of Gross and had introduced me. He seemed congenial enough, and I felt comfortable in contacting him about my specific assertions. However, he passed me on to Deputy Attorney General Daniel Hickey with the comment, "He'll take care of you."

In hindsight, a call to Herb Soll might have opened the door to Gross, who might have been more prone to listen to my full story, but again, at the time, I didn't know that.

In my conversation with Hickey I hit all the highlights of what had happened and what I had uncovered. He wasn't completely taken by surprise as he had already heard what had transpired having followed the Anchorage papers.

"Why don't you put it all in writing he requested "and I'll review it and then be in touch with you."

"I can fly down whenever you want to discuss it further," I offered.

I was encouraged by his apparent interest in my complaints and followed up that night with an 11-page handwritten memo on legal-sized paper detailing my general complaints of impropriety within City Hall and pointed out specific violations of City and State law by Palmer officials.

As suggested, I wrote the memo to the Attorney General and sent it to the attention of Dan Hickey as his deputy. It was lengthy and comprehensive.

That December 4 letter not only dealt with the same issues that I had raised at the City Council meeting and in my letter to the Grand Jury: the barring of the public into a public hearing (and the refusal to relocate elsewhere); the nonresidency of the City Manager (although mandated by City Charter); the illegal abolishment of the City Clerk's position; the refusal to give me the mandatory oath of office (which I later rectified and had notarized as required by law); and even the Mayor's felony conviction — but went even further.

I advised Hickey that the Mayor simultaneously held the position of Director of Parks and Recreation, which I believed was a conflict of interest. I also stated that reportedly the City Attorney, in an action that would be considered unethical for an official in his position, turned his microphone down in a Board of Equalization hearing before the Mat-Su Borough Assembly. The reason for the requested hearing was to have his house assessment lowered.

The lowering of the microphone precluded the ability of the public to fully ascertain what was being said. His request was successful, however, and his assessment was subsequently lowered. When those in attendance realized what had happened, they spread the news throughout the unhappy community.

When I referred to the City Manager's questionable actions during his first tour (1970-1974), I told Hickey that Curtis also was head of a Site Selection Committee for the Palmer High

School. I elaborated further:

> "He was solely instrumental in having it placed in that locale over the practical objections of others. In addition, at a Borough Assembly meeting he tried to force its acceptance without the public in attendance. Although he was ruled down on that occasion, a few weeks later he succeeded. The prime property (a Johnnie Martin piece of real estate) was not considered by the City Manager because 'it was too expensive.' However at a subsequent Borough meeting this Johnnie Martin stated aloud that he was never approached by the City Manager at all. If he was, he said, he probably would have donated it to the City and not charged them for it."

This school property I subsequently informed Hickey was not only adjacent to Curtis' own private property but also was adjacent to right-of-way property that was owned by some members of the City Council.

I continued in my letter and cited yet another questionable acquisition of property:

> "The Industrial Park property, owned primarily by an influential member of the community, was sold to the City. Again, this was not a desirable or practical site but was nevertheless purchased by the City with City bonds, Borough bonds and the help of two banks, Alaska Bank of Commerce and Alaska Mutual Savings and Loan. This same influential community member and owner of the above property was on the Board of Directors of one of the banks. It would appear to be a conflict of interest for this individual. More importantly, this tract of land — approximately 123 acres — was appraised for about $1100 per acre in 1972, just before the City's purchase. The City, however, paid three times that amount at $3,000 per acre."

Although not originally stated in that December 4 letter — but subsequently given to the State Troopers for their own investigation — was the name of that "influential member of the community."

It was the State Senator from the Matanuska-Susitna Borough, Jalmar (Jay) Kertula, a longtime resident of the valley and an influential politician.

I also wrote Hickey that I had recently filed criminal complaints with Anchorage Investigator John Lucking of the Alaska State Troopers "against all members of City Hall for felony counts in their conspiracy of violating civil rights." For his information I noted further: The Alaska State Statute 11.60.340 *Conspiracy Against Rights of Persons* specifically states:

> "A person who conspires with another to injure, oppress, threaten or intimidate a person because that person seeks to exercise or enjoy or has exercised or enjoyed a right privilege or immunity granted by the Constitution or the laws of this state, is guilty of a felony and upon conviction is punishable by imprisonment for not more than two years or by a fine of not more than $1,000 or by both."

I felt that all of the City Officials had conspired "to oppress" not only Higgins and me in our freedom of speech in the Council meeting but the public's as well. Further, the "threatening" and "intimidation" of both Officer Lemoine and my secretary Christine Boyle by the City Manager were well within the elements of the crime.

In addition, I informed Deputy Attorney General Hickey that I also had filed with Inv. Lucking a misdemeanor complaint against Public Works Director Chuck Shaver "for his beating to death dogs in the pound with an iron hook." I cited AS 11.40.480 *Cruelty to Animals*, which stated that:

> A person who cruelly beats or tortures or otherwise maltreats or neglects an animal, whether it belongs to himself or to another, upon conviction, is punishable by imprisonment in a jail for not less than 10 days nor more than 30 days or by a fine of not less than $5 nor more than $50.

For confirmation, I submitted a copy of an article that appeared in the August 28, 1975, edition of the *Frontiersman:*

"EX-COP CLAIMS DOGS BEATEN TO DEATH."

The "ex-cop" referred to was former Lt. Robert Bassett who allegedly watched while Shaver beat three puppies to death with an iron-cant hook "to save ammunition." Bassett reported the incident after-the-fact at the City Council meeting held in August.

The killing of those three puppies was a three-count violation of the statute. Although Bassett not only was a Police Lieutenant but the Deputy Chief, he did nothing. Instead, he merely termed the killings "inhuman and nauseating," at the meeting. When Councilman John Dolenc asked him why he didn't intervene if he knew it was illegal, Bassett hesitated and then said, "I reported it to the Chief because he was my superior."

When a reporter subsequently asked me about his remark I said, "Bassett's a damned liar."

Had he informed me of Shaver's illegal actions at the time that it happened, I would have asked him the same question that Councilman Dolenc did. Yet he said — and did — nothing at the time. He decided, for whatever personal reason, to raise that issue at a regularly scheduled meeting.

Mrs. Lillian Detling of the ASPCA, who previously had been alerted by someone and was present at the meeting, addressed the City Council. She replied heatedly to the description by Bassett. "We feel that this is an emergency and we want to know what action the Council plans to take?"

Councilman Willard Johnson, who was Acting Mayor in Maze's absence, answered her curtly, "You've just informed us. However, we have other things that are more pressing than this," and he terminated the discussion.

She was shocked at his reply and responded quickly, "This will be reported to the national organization. How any one of you can sit on this Council and allow this is barbaric."

Curtis, however, reportedly intervened and promised the seven members of the local Humane Society and the Anchorage SPCA that were in attendance, that he would promptly investigate the charges and report back to the City Council.

Curtis never instructed me to pursue an investigation and I heard no more about the incident from him.

In my detailed memo to Hickey, I zeroed in even more specifically on other in-depth charges when I stated:

> "A farm loan agency has restrictive and repressive lending procedures; keeps out those it does not want; does not permit or encourage new potato growers in the Matanuska Valley unless they are part of a select group; forecloses loans on opponents who challenge or criticize the system and does not account to any lending institution bylaws or procedures that are imposed upon other statewide lending institutions."

The "farm loan agency" that I referred to was of course the *Alaska Rural Rehabilitation Corporation,* that supposedly public, nonprofit corporation with assets *supposedly* held in trust for the State of Alaska for 50 years (that time expiring in 1985). The ARRC was initially set up at the time colonists migrated into the Matanuska Valley in the mid-1930s and ostensibly was established to promote agriculture in the area.

The ARRC was a recurring acronym that I heard over and over again throughout the valley, and I found it to be synonymous with corruption and reports of violence that had existed in the area for years. It was also briefly referred to in Hickey's subsequent extensive memo to Colonel James P. Wellington the Director of the Alaska State Troopers concerning my "Allegations of Criminal Law Violations":

> "We are presently trying to determine the precise legal status of the ARRC, the precise nature of the alleged criminal violations which Mr. Mangieri intimates surround its operations, and whether any of these allegations are susceptible of further investigation. I will keep you apprised of the course and results of this investigation and will request the assistance of your agency if that becomes appropriate and further investigation is necessary."

Nick Mangieri

If there ever were any "further investigation" into the ARRC I never heard about it and neither did anyone else I spoke to.

Immediately after those specific disclosures to the state I expected some form of swift feedback. It did not occur. I couldn't understand the apparent lack of official interest or concern about my allegations. Over the years there had been many who had raised a "hue and a cry" over the questionable antics of the ARRC. Chief among those was Wayne Hunter a valley resident and an unrelenting critic of the ARRC. He in particular was one who could not be intimidated, although it had been tried many times in many ways. Those that knew him lovingly called him "the old man." His opponents had other names for him. Although I personally met him briefly on only one or two occasions he deluged me with detailed information. However, because he was pushing 80 and was unable to get around much, he relied on his friends to carry the banner for him. One such contact was Harry Lechwold a fortyish farmer who lived on the outskirts of Palmer. It was these two names that I expressly raised in all my future interviews with the state authorities so they could obtain the necessary confirmation.

In my letter to the Deputy Attorney General, I also mentioned an upcoming course of action that I had planned for the City Officials of Palmer — a Recall Election. I further cited stonewalling incidents that I had encountered within the Mat-Su Borough Office because of my intent to do so:

> "A petition for recall is being filed of the City Mayor and the City Council and have the required number of signatures. However there appears to be an impropriety that has recently occurred in that area. Three individuals who registered at the Borough Clerk's office and then signed the petition never appeared on the Election Supervisor's list in Anchorage although a full two weeks had elapsed. When I questioned the Borough Clerk about it, she advised me that she mailed out the forms immediately and that they must have gotten lost in the mails. However, three separate mailings would seem to be beyond the laws of probability. It should also be noted that this Borough Clerk is also a girlfriend of the City Manager Bill Curtis."

Before I closed out my lengthy memo to Hickey I advised him that I had also "filed a complaint with the FBI alleging violations of federal civil rights against the public," and that it was forwarded to Washington, D.C., for a "formal ruling."

I hoped that as a result of that additional information concerning my notification to federal authorities that the State Attorney General's Office would become actively involved themselves.

The next morning, Higgins stopped by and I showed him the letter before I mailed it.

"That should do it Wayne," I said as I pounded a moistened stamp onto the envelope.

"I sure hope so, Chief," he said hoarsely. "It's been a month now."

"Unfortunately," I reminded him, "justice moves slowly." I tried to make light of the situation.

Wayne picked up on the mood of our conversation and cracked a smile.

"Slow is one thing, Chief. This is absolutely crawlin'," and the partial smile broadened into a wide grin.

"What about the troopers?" he continued in his serious tone. "Whatta they doin'?"

"You mean about the conspiracy complaint that I just filed with Investigator Lucking?" I said.

He nodded.

"I haven't heard yet, but I told Hickey about it. Maybe he'll push it."

"If he doesn't, there's somethin' the matter with him," Higgins added.

"Let's give him the benefit of the doubt," I said optimistically.

"When are you going to Juneau?" he asked.

"Probably within the next week or so after Hickey digests the letter."

However, I was getting impatient. Rather than wait until I was contacted, I decided to fly down to Juneau a week later to meet with Hickey.

... Chapter 10 ...

Daniel Hickey was short, stocky and younger than I expected. I wasn't as impressed as I should have been, and I was unsuccessful in convincing myself that *you can't judge a book by its
cover*. After all, he was the Deputy Attorney General of the
Criminal Division for the State of Alaska.

There was an exchange of pleasantries, and then he
announced, "I've arranged for Investigator Hoffbeck of the
Criminal Investigation Bureau to interview you and make a
report to me."

I hesitated a moment. I was being shuffled off to someone
else down the line.

He noticed the look of displeasure that immediately creased
my brow and quickly added, "We're going to need all the information we can get, and this is the best way to go about it."

He sounded sincere.

I reluctantly agreed, hoping that the picture he had presented
to me was, indeed, the "best way to go." I always had gotten best
results by going to the top. I didn't like — or trust — going
through second parties. I would have preferred dealing with an
attorney face-to-face rather than being interviewed by someone
who was not fluent with the various elements of the law that I
wanted to discuss.

That initial gut feeling eventually was proven right.

My introduction to Hoffbeck was without fanfare, and we

settled into a small cubicle for the interview.

I reiterated all that I had shared with Hickey while Hoffbeck took notes. He had a copy of my detailed memo to Hickey and referred to it from time to time, asking brief questions about areas that he felt needed clarification. There were no specific questions about names, places or dates, only generalized questions. These I answered as fully as I could. I was unaware at that time that our limited interview session would encompass the totality of the state's involvement — or investigation — or whatever term it would be referred to in the future. I believed they would take all the information I gave them and be able to delve further into the situation than I ever could. I was only an individual. They had the official power to gain specific evidence that could only be uncovered through subpoenas and Grand Juries.

At the end of my session, I wasn't as optimistic about its results as I was before my arrival in Juneau. I tried not to give off any negative vibes about my Juneau experience when I returned home.

To my family, to Wayne and to all others who were interested in my trip I would only say, "Looks good so far."

The truth is it wasn't looking as good as I would have liked it to look. I wasn't getting good vibes about my meeting in Juneau. Bill Artus was the only one in whom I confided that feeling. As my attorney, I thought he should know about the amount of state involvement that we might expect — or as it turned out the lack of state investigation that we would receive.

I never received a copy of my first interview with the state nor would I receive one of our shorter second session two weeks later. At the time I thought no more about it, still believing in — and trusting in — the criminal justice system. I had no reason to question Hoffbeck's work, as he seemed interested enough in the investigation. However, I still had nagging doubts about the *effectiveness* of the interviews. It seemed to me that he could have asked more pointed questions, especially when the second meeting was scheduled.

After my second trip to Juneau on Christmas Eve morning, my wife and kids were excited.

"They must really be interested for them to call you down again," my wife exclaimed, after I got home from the Anchorage flight and long drive back to the valley.

"I think so," I responded cautiously. I didn't want her or the children, who were standing nearby, to be overly concerned about my lack of enthusiasm, so I quickly added, "I've given them enough stuff to really get into it."

"What's taking them so long, Dad?" my oldest, Tammy, asked.

"These things always take time," I answered. I was wondering the same thing myself, however. I just didn't want to vocalize it in front of the family.

"Dad'll fix 'em," my son confidently responded.

"They'll be sorry," my number two daughter, Dawn, joined.

"Yeah," little Michelle felt compelled to jump into the family discussion.

To change the subject, I reminded them that it was Christmas Eve and that we still didn't have a tree.

"We could all go out and look for one," my wife answered.

"Yeah Dad let's go," they all agreed.

The weather was cold but not frigid. A light wind was kicking up the dry snow that had accumulated in the pasture, and it felt much colder than it actually was. It was almost dark, but there was still enough light to discern the scattered pine trees at the end of our 40 acres.

"There's some, Dad," announced one of the girls who had run ahead.

There were several small trees bunched together where the horses usually herded to escape the wind ripping across the field. The one we chose was sparse and a little on the scraggly side, but it was a tree.

"I'll cut it, Dad," Mark volunteered, and within minutes we were all headed back to the house to over-decorate it.

When the kids were through contributing their part to the overburdened branches, they stepped back to proudly display their handiwork and look to me for approval.

"Looks beautiful," I said. "You all did a great job."

They beamed at my congratulations.

It was our second Christmas in the valley, and we worked hard to make it as festive as we could in view of the circumstances. Unfortunately, there would be another cloud to mar our festivities.

Near the end of the holidays, the two youngest girls rode down our long dirt road to visit Tammy, who was working at the nearby Dairy Queen on the highway. Suddenly they came galloping back down the road toward the house with tears in their eyes.

"What's the matter?" I asked when they rushed into the house.

"Nikki's dead. Nikki's dead," my little one blurted out between her heavy sobs.

Nikki was the male Samoyed that my wife had bought from Slim Randles a few weeks earlier.

I looked at the older one who dabbed at her reddened eyes with her mittens.

"What happened, Dawn?" I asked her.

She sniffled as she tried to explain.

"He's just laying beside the road, and he's not moving," she said haltingly.

I raced out of the house with the girls and the female Samoyed behind me.

"Dawn, hold on to Nanook," I yelled back.

When we reached the spot, the girls pointed out the still carcass of the dog.

Nanook whimpered and strained to reach her dead mate.

"Stay there," I commanded the girls.

I checked Nikki. He was dead all right and had been for quite a while. He was rigid.

He must've been hit by a car I told them. He was beside our road, almost at the Parks Highway.

"He was probably just crossing the highway," I told the tearful girls, "and someone hit him."

It was little consolation to them but they knew that Samoyeds were wanderers. They knew it could happen because another pet had been hit by a car in California. Still, they were understandably upset.

My son and wife, who had just joined us at the entrance to the road, saw Nikki's lifeless form.

"We're going to have to bury him," my wife commented slowly.

I looked at the pitiful expressions of the girls and nodded acknowledgment.

"Mark, run back to the barn and see if you can find some burlap bags."

While we waited, Dawn went over to the Dairy Queen to tell her sister what happened. When she, too, came over to view the lifeless body of the dog, she asked if there was anything she could do to help.

"No. It's okay, Tammy," I said quietly. "You better get back to work."

She tried to comfort both of her sisters but was just as sad as they were over the loss of one of their pets.

When Mark returned with the bags, I lifted the thick matted body onto them.

I felt what appeared to be dried blood under him but I didn't want to examine him in the presence of everyone.

"Dawn and Michelle, go look for a place for us to bury him. Mark, you better take Nanook back to the house so she doesn't try to dig him up. I also need you to find a pickax and a shovel."

"Okay, Dad."

They all left, with the exception of my wife, who had noticed me checking the underside of the dog again.

"What are you looking for?" she asked concernedly.

I didn't want to comment on what I thought was blood on his side so I just replied, "nothing special."

As I carried him up to the field behind the house where he would be buried, however, I did examine him a little more closely.

There was definitely dried blood on his side but because he was so stiff and his coat so thick I couldn't tell the origin of the blood.

Probably the impact of being hit, I thought.

I wasn't really convinced that's what happened, but I was so occupied with my own plans I didn't dwell on it.

Three days after Christmas I wrote a two-page letter to Glen D. King the Executive Director of the International Chiefs of Police in Gaithersburg, Maryland.

I knew I couldn't afford to leave any stones unturned in my quest to see justice done.

I wrote:

"Dear Mr. King:

"As a follow-up of our phone conversation of two weeks ago I have taken the liberty of enclosing all of the newspaper articles that have accompanied my firing as Police Chief by a corrupt City Manager in Palmer, Alaska. In addition, in the six weeks that have followed that event, there have been countless news broadcasts and commentaries regarding it.

"My staunchest and most vocal ally is the news commentator and producer of KIMO-TV in Anchorage, Herb Shaindlin, an individual who would, I am sure, willingly confirm all that has transpired.

"Since the date of my firing, I have subsequently learned that not only are the City Mayor the City Councilmen and even the City Attorney all involved in illegal actions but widespread and deep-seated corruption extends into influential members of the local community who have infested and become part of the Borough government and of the State government.

"My allegations have been presented to a local Grand Jury, which has temporarily deferred prosecution pending investigation by the Alaska State Troopers, who are in the process of compiling my information, and to the Attorney General's Office, which has given them the green light to proceed.

"I have also advised the local FBI office concerning civil rights violations, but because they have not encountered similar violations in this area, have referred the matter to their civil rights office in Washington, D.C., who hopefully will respond quickly and affirmatively.

"My reason for directing this inquiry/complaint to your association is that, as an active member of the IACP, I feel that I not only have a right to request your assistance but feel moreover that the IACP should be actively involved in resisting the type of corruption that by illegal decree can immediately eliminate a Police Chief who has sworn to uphold the law.

"As a 'yes man' who 'looked the other way,' and condoned the illegal antics of a corrupt administration, I could still be the Chief of Police today — but I couldn't live with myself for such behavior. I know there are many in the field of law enforcement who would do exactly as I have done faced with the same sanctions.

"I can and will fight the City, the Borough and those State members alone if I must, but if there are those within my profession who will at least lend a certain measure of support if they cannot actively assist, not only would many in my category be eternally grateful but law enforcement would be immeasurably strengthened by such solidarity and unit of purpose.

"In speaking to you, I can understand the reluctance of the IACP to lend support to a Police Chief they know nothing about, but I am hopeful that the enclosed articles will at least give you 'probable cause' to investigate further.

"I will gladly keep you advised of further developments to substantiate my charges and the correctness of my stand. In addition, I can offer further reputable testimonials as to my honesty and capability by substantial members of the criminal justice field.

"This same type of letter is being drafted to all members of the Alaska Chiefs of Police, and any letter to their president, Charles Anderson, Chief of Police, Anchorage, Alaska, will confirm my allegations. However, because time is of the essence in rectifying this situation, I specifically request that the IACP investigate my firing and my charges of corruption into City Hall and into the community.

"If that should be an impractical request — although such a request for justice should not be deemed 'impractical' — then perhaps legal support/advice can be offered. As an adjunct to this letter request would be a follow-up by the IACP to the Department of Justice in Washington and a letter of support to the Attorney General, Juneau, Alaska.

"I realize that this letter may very well be an unusual and perhaps an impetuous request but our strength can only come through such unity and I am not reluctant to seek it.

"Sincerely,

Nick J. Mangieri
Former Chief of Police"

Although I was also a member of the Alaska Chiefs of Police and stated in my letter that I would be drafting a letter to that statewide association I was unable to do so. I didn't have the money to hire a public stenographer to type those additional letters. Instead, I relied on whatever support I could get from the IACP — and waited for that response.

A week or so passed after the death of Nikki. Nothing eventful occurred during that period, and I temporarily put it out of my mind. I briefly mentioned the episode about the dog to Higgins and his immediate reaction was, "You never know what they're going to pull Chief. I'd be watchful — just in case."

I thought about it and agreed.

Neither one of us had heard anything from City Hall. It had been quiet — too quiet, especially in light of what I had been stirring up.

Then it happened again — only closer this time.

The kids were on their way out to catch the school bus at the end of the road on the highway early one morning shortly after classes resumed. They were only gone a few minutes when unexpectedly Mark ran back into the house.

"What is it?" I asked. "What's the problem?"

"You gotta come, Dad," he said breathlessly as he stood by the rear entrance to the house.

"It's happened again," and his voice rose as he said it.

I knew what he meant before I even left the house. I didn't see Nanook in the area. She usually was right outside the house in the morning.

I followed him around the house and saw the girls less than 100 feet away on the dirt road. They all were bent over a white furry figure on the ground. It was Nanook.

"God damn. Son of a bitch," I muttered as I saw the animal stretched out beside the road. This time I could see the blood in the snow. There were no tire marks nearby, only the dead dog.

The kids all watched my expression as I bent down over her to examine her.

"Someone shot her, didn't they, Dad?" Mark was the first to say it.

I took a deep breath as I looked at their concerned faces. They weren't crying this time. Their faces contained looks of shock mixed with disbelief.

"Why, Dad? Why did somebody have to kill her?" Dawn asked. "She never hurt anybody."

I just shook my head slowly.

"I don't know kids."

However, I did know. It was just a warning.

My wife came out of the house and knew it had happened again.

She looked at me and the dog and the kids and shook her head, too, as if not fully grasping the situation.

"You kids better not miss the bus," I said, not knowing what else I could say to comfort them at the moment.

"Who's going to bury Nanook?" little Michelle asked.

"We will," I said. "We'll take care of it. We'll bury her right beside Nikki."

The younger girls' eyes were starting to well up as they looked at their second dead pet in a week.

"Tammy look after them," I added. "See that they get on the school bus."

She nodded that she would and escorted them down the road.

"Give her a hand, Mark."

"Are you sure you're not going to need some help, Dad?" he asked.

"It's okay. You better get to school."

He took one last lingering look at Nanook lying motionless on her side and then ran after his sisters.

"Why would they do this?" my wife asked tearfully.

"You know why," I answered.

"They're no good, every last one of them," she said. "The

dogs didn't deserve this, and the kids sure don't deserve this either."

"I'll find out who's responsible for this, and I'll get the bastards."

I stood up as I looked at the dog again.

"I've gotta get more burlap."

"Do you need help?"

"No, I'll do it," I said, and I trudged up toward the barn.

After I had finished burying Nanook I went back into the house. My wife was sitting quietly at the kitchen table with our German shepherd, Thunder, lying at her feet.

"We've got to keep our eye on him, too," I warned.

"Thunder doesn't wander off like the Samoyeds did," she said. "And besides, he stays in the house at night."

She was right. Shepherds were territorial and stayed in the immediate vicinity of the home protecting the family. Samoyeds on the other hand liked to range far and wide and were not really watchdogs.

"Did you hear a shot last night?" I asked.

"I'm not sure," she said slowly. "I thought I heard a noise early this morning, but I'm not sure."

"Did you?" she asked.

"No. You know I'm a sound sleeper. I didn't hear a thing."

"What're you going to do?" she wanted to know.

"There's nothing I *can* do yet. I can't pin the blame on anybody because I don't know who did it," I responded.

"Are you going to report it?" she continued.

"You mean to the troopers?" I scoffed. "If I can't get them to move on Palmer do you think they'd be interested in a dead dog?"

"No, I guess not," she said wearily.

Higgins called later in the morning.

"What's up, Chief? Anything happenin'?" he asked casually.

I told him about the recent incident with the second animal.

"Them sonsabitches. Them lowlifes," he roared. "Who would kill a dog for no reason?"

"Like I told my wife, Wayne, their reason is to warn me off. First Nikki was killed near the highway a quarter of a mile away and now Nanook 100 feet away.

He thought about it a minute.

"You're right, Chief. Whataya gonna do about it?"

"Well, I'm not gonna file a complaint with Kolivosky's detachment."

"I know what ya mean," he said. "He wouldn't look into it."

"Right."

"Well you better watch your ass, Chief," he said concernedly. "You never know what they're gonna pull. I'll nose around downtown and see if I hear anything."

Before he hung up he started to say something I didn't quite hear.

"What did you say, Wayne?" I asked. "I didn't catch it."

He hesitated a moment.

"I was jus' thinkin'," he continued slowly.

"Yeah."

"Maybe whenever you ride out alone I better be with you," he added quickly.

I laughed at the offer.

"I wouldn't put nuthin' past 'em," he said. "Better safe than sorry, Chief."

"I'll be fine. Thanks, Wayne," I said. "I always carry the Rossi with me. I can do a lot of damage with two barrels."

"Yeah, I know," he agreed. "But you don't have eyes in the back of your head."

I thanked him again, but his concern stuck with me afterward. I started carrying the shotgun with me whenever I was out on the road alone. I didn't really expect trouble because I didn't think anybody would be that stupid. However, even when I was out in the car with the family I had it.

"You're not a police officer anymore," my wife would remind me. "Why is the shotgun necessary?"

"Just a precaution," I'd say, trying to make light of it.

While I didn't know for sure that the first one was shot, the deaths of my two dogs had raised my awareness around the property. I had never before been concerned about strange cars or people I saw in my area. Now, I noticed. There was only one other farm at the end of our solitary dirt road and that was another quarter of a mile beyond us. A second dirt road looped near the front of our property and ran off at an oblique angle away from our home. Although there were but a few houses scattered in the distance, it was that traffic that I watched. *I must be getting paranoid,*I thought. *This isn't some Grade B movie in the deep South, this is Alaska.*

A week or more passed with nothing of note happening except our continuing interviews of people in the valley. Sometimes I'd go solo, and sometimes Higgins would go with me. The children seemed to have quieted down about the deaths of their two pets, and the two younger ones would exercise their small horses by riding far out into our fenced field.

One night when I had gotten home for dinner, they both approached me excitedly to tell me what they had seen.

"It was a bear, Dad," my middle daughter exclaimed.

"Naw, Dawn. Bears don't come in this close," I tried to explain to her.

Although we were really in the sticks with nothing behind us but the vast expanse of the Palmer Hay Flats and the Matanuska River and Knik River miles away I had never seen nor heard of any bears in our vicinity.

"Yeah, Dad, we really did we saw a bear at the end of our field," said little Michelle as she animatedly backed up her sister's story.

"No, Michelle," I said, trying to calm her down, "You both thought you saw one."

"We did, Dad. We did," they both chorused.

"Okay, Mark and I will check it out tomorrow," I reassured them.

"You'll see, Dad. He's there. He was big," the older one insisted.

"All right, the both of you stay at this end tomorrow after school and I'll get back early tomorrow and look."

They were content that I believed them, although I really didn't.

Mark, who was standing nearby listening to their animated description, started to add a big brother's sarcastic comment but didn't when he saw me wink at him.

"We'll go bear hunting tomorrow, Mark," I said loudly for the girls' benefit.

"Great," he answered, doing a good job of convincing the

girls with his own animated tone.

As promised, the next afternoon I arrived home early enough to "bear hunt."

I grabbed my shotgun as my son and I headed out the door.

"Aren't you going to need your pistol too?" my wife asked.

I didn't know whether she was serious or not.

"I don't think so," I replied lightly.

"Dad's a good shot. He won't need his .357," Mark replied.

We both headed in the direction that the girls pointed out to us.

"Way down there," my middle daughter said. "Where the hedges are and the man's barn are."

You could barely see the barn because of the short trees and the thick hedges but I nodded acknowledgment.

"Okay. You girls stay right here," I convincingly cautioned them.

"We'll watch right from here, Dad," Dawn answered sincerely.

We trekked deeper into the field, into the area that they last saw "the bear," with our larger horses watching us curiously.

"Do you really think they saw a bear, Dad?" my son asked.

"No. I think they mistook one of his horses for a bear. You know how wooly-looking they get with the cold weather," I assured him.

As we reached the far side of the 40 acres, we searched the snow-covered ground and the immediate vicinity for any signs of movement. Mark stopped a minute and looked down in the snow.

"What's this, Dad?" he asked, pointing to tracks in the snow that lead away from both our properties.

I stopped to check them out.

"I'll be a son of a —," and I stopped mid-sentence in amazement. "It looks like bear tracks Mark — big bear tracks."

"You mean they were right?" he asked, his eyes wide in awe.

"Looks like it," I had to admit.

"Well, we've got a gun. Let's hunt it down, Dad," he said excitedly.

"We've got a *short-barreled* shotgun Mark," I reminded him. "This is only good up close. Besides, his tracks are headed back toward the flats," I noted.

"We should've brought the pistol too," he continued. "Then we could've tracked him," he said confidently.

I smiled at the simplicity of his analysis.

"Well, next time we better believe them," I joked. "Let's head back."

We were mid-field, 100 yards or so from the house, when suddenly a shot rang out. The nearness of the report startled me, and I tried to quickly discern where it came from. Within seconds I knew. The horses that had been milling around the outside of our barn abruptly came racing in our direction away from the report of the gunfire. The sound of it came from the woods behind the barn. Although I didn't see any movement, I told Mark to remain where he was and stay down.

I crouched as I ran in the direction of the shot, my own weapon outstretched before me. My eyes quickly scanned the woods. I saw nothing. As I got nearer, I searched the area but came up empty. If there were discernible tracks, they were lost in the underbrush. Because of the wide expanse of heavy trees on that side of the field it was almost impossible to pinpoint the site of the rifle fire.

It sounded like the sharp crack of a 30/30. What were they aiming at, I wondered? The horses — or me? I never knew for sure.

What I did learn shortly thereafter, came from Higgins.

"I heard there's a 'contract' out on you, Chief," he announced in his low gruff voice.

"Where did you hear that?" I demanded.

"It's the word in town," he said. "It probably came from the *49er*."

"That figures," I said shaking my head slowly. "Any names Wayne?"

"No, Chief, I'm sorry. Anything I can do?"

"Well you can't follow me around 24 hours a day so I'm going to have to have eyes in the back of my head."

"I don't like it, Chief," he said seriously.

"Well, I'm not too crazy about it either but there's not much else I can do."

From that point on, my sleeping pattern changed. Whereas in the past I would sleep straight through the night, now I would wake at the slightest noise. If the sound persisted, I would reach under my mattress for my loaded revolver, roam the house and then peer into the darkness until I was satisfied that there was nothing there. Sometimes it would happen several times per night. Although the shepherd was a good watchdog, he wasn't reliable. He still hadn't completely grown out of his puppy stage. At 18 months he was gigantic and an awesome-looking animal, but in reality I didn't know how good he might be in protecting the family.

My driving habits also changed. I became doubly cautious whenever I was out on the highway or some lonely road. Instead of just watching cars that would pass me on an open stretch, I was aware of their presence behind me first and then as they overtook me to pass I'd glance at the driver — or passengers — to try to observe any unusual actions within their vehicle. All the while, I'd have my shotgun readily available on the seat beside me. In addition, I also made a point of carrying my .357 Magnum with me. It became a precautionary routine whenever I was out on the road. It changed slightly whenever I had the family with me. Because of the bulkiness of the Rossi in the front of the car and the obvious safety concern having passengers in the car with a loaded shotgun, I relied on my revolver only.

Although I really didn't expect trouble whenever my wife or kids were in the car with me — I really didn't know for sure.

That pattern of watchfulness was to last for many months, subside and then be reactivated again with renewed threats against my life.

... Chapter 11 ...

The months following the holidays were hectic for many reasons. Two of the more important actions dealt with Artus' appearance in Superior Court on separate occasions in order to gain the reinstatement of both Higgins and me. That also was when I decided to initiate a recall election against the City Councilmen for their actions the night of the hearing.

Artus' first action was to file a MOTION FOR SUMMARY JUDGMENT that would have returned Higgins to his former position as a patrolman. He went before Judge Ralph Moody and argued that the City's personnel rules specifically gave a Police Chief the right to hire and fire. City Attorney Biss, however, argued that the personnel rules were not part of the City Code "but merely policy in assisting the City Manager — and are not binding."

It was Biss' biased interpretation coupled with Artus' regrettable failure to file a timely opposing motion that caused Judge Moody to rule in favor of the City thereby effectively denying Higgins' reinstatement.

In that interim period there was no response to my own reinstatement suit because the City had 20 days to answer. My case also was initially assigned to Judge Moody. However, in light of Moody's unfavorable ruling against Higgins, Artus was successful in a move to disqualify him. My case was then reassigned to Superior Court Judge J. Justin Ripley.

Earlier, on December 4, Artus had filed a Notice of Hearing on a MOTION FOR PRELIMINARY INJUNCTION AND AN EXPARTE MOTION FOR A TEMPORARY RESTRAINING ORDER that would have provided for my immediate reinstatement. The basis of his MOTION was the "irreparable injury" to my professional reputation and the "substantial hardship" on my family.

On December 17, the hearing came before Judge Ripley. Ripley, a pleasant-looking fortyish judge, was fairly new to the bench. From the scope of his questions and the tone of his comments to the City Attorney, however, he appeared to be in my corner.

Artus rose to speak:

"Your honor, my client, as an employee, is protected by the City Charter from 'arbitrary dismissal'. Further," he continued, "the City's personnel rules guarantee employees due process when being fired, which includes a hearing, two-weeks notice and a formal letter of dismissal. My client was denied this process."

Biss attempted to interrupt him, but Artus had already finished his brief monologue to the court and sat down.

Biss looked like, and had always reminded me of, a hulking teddy bear whenever he stood up. Other than his body mass there was nothing else that was memorable about him. With his gray hair and glasses, his face was as unremarkable as his slow-moving manner.

"Mr. Mangieri, as a department head," he said impatiently, "is not protected by the charter." He continued "Administrative officers, unlike regular employees, serve at the pleasure of the City Manager." He then stressed, "Regardless of the charter and the personnel rules, Mr. Mangieri was a probationary employee and no just cause had to be demonstrated in firing him."

He then sat his hulk heavily in the chair beside Curtis. Both looked as smug as they did the night of the City Council meeting.

Ripley appeared to sigh. He then took a deep breath and looked in our direction.

"Before a temporary injunction can be issued, irreparable damage has to be proved," he said hesitantly.

Artus and I looked at each other knowing full well what

would come next.

"Unfortunately," he continued, "I see this balance swinging in favor of Palmer."

I was totally disheartened by his remark, and Artus obviously was completely disappointed. However, before dejection fully set in, Ripley made an unexpected unfavorable comment about Palmer's strong monolithic form of government and then pointed toward Curtis:

"That man out there with a crew cut makes this decision — what is in the best interest of the City. There seems to be an awesome amount of power in the City Manager."

He stopped and let the full force of his words sink in. We held our breath, not knowing what else to expect. Neither Artus nor I anticipated that type of remark, nor were we totally prepared for the judge's final follow-up comment.

"I tell you that it's — with a heavy heart that I rule in favor of the City."

In spite of his apparent sympathy to me, I took a deep breath and cursed inwardly. It was merely the first of many such rulings by the legal system.

Coincidentally, in mid-December there was a lengthy news item in the *Anchorage Daily Times* that should have given me cause for concern but didn't at the time. It wasn't until much much later that, upon re-reading the article, I saw "the handwriting on the wall." An appropriate philosophical expression would have been "when you're too close to the forest you can't see the trees." In my case, I was way too close and didn't see what the hell was going on around me.

The heading of that article,

"NO CHARGES TO BE MADE AGAINST FORMER OFFICIALS"

had nothing to do with my own investigations or with my own allegations but set the tone for what I could expect had I been more aware of Alaskan politics.

The article stated that a seven-month investigation by two Alaska State Trooper investigators "found no evidence of indictable criminal offenses" against former Alaska State Housing Authority officials and that "no presentation will be made to the Grand Jury."

The article further stated that "the troopers were frustrated in their investigation efforts by material reportedly missing from files and files which could not be found — and that witnesses also made contradictory statements."

The newspaper account said that although the troopers "may have found evidence of possible favoritism and mismanagement within the agency," an assistant district attorney announced that "things like that are not criminal under the Alaska Statutes."

It was the same announcement that I would hear concerning my own allegations of municipal corruption in Palmer.

The ASHA investigation, according to the article, was ordered after the Alaska Public Interest Research Group alleged questionable transactions by the former Assistant to the Executive Director. That Assistant later became the Deputy Director of the agency.

The research group's Director made an appropriate comment after the investigation had been closed, stating that it raised more questions than it answered.

He also noted that, "We think it was limited either by design or effort. It was either gross negligence or an overt cover-up attempt was made."

An additional barbed remark made by the accusing Director was that, "Efforts should have been made to locate the missing files." An even more cogent statement from him was "that destruction of public records is a crime."

Although the article went on the say that the public interest group would "present information to Attorney General Avrum Gross" — the same official that I had directed my allegations to via the Deputy Attorney General Daniel Hickey — I never heard any more about the ASHA investigation.

My decision on the recall election came about as a result of my reviewing Title 29 of the Alaska Statutes dealing with municipal government.

Section 29.28.130 stated that "an elected official of a home rule or general law municipality may be recalled by the voters

He served six months in office."

after he had served six months in office."

Palmer was a home rule municipality and fell within the purview specified in the applicable section.

Section 29.28.140 further pointed out the provisions in which I was interested:

> "Grounds for recall are misconduct in office, incompetence or failure to perform prescribed duties."

Their outrageous conduct subsequent to my dismissal, in my opinion, bordered on "incompetence" in office, and certainly their failure to act responsibly violated their "prescribed duties" to do so. Both elements being part of the recall grounds, I felt that I was on solid ground for the recall. Subsequent grudging acceptance by the City Attorney bore out my contention.

While I doubted an early resolution of my lawsuit for reinstatement would take place, I knew that whenever I would be reinstated I would face a hostile City Mayor and Council. Armed with that belief, and still bristling from the mock City Council "hearing," I instigated the recall.

Section 29.28.070 (b) (1) specified that the required number of signatures necessary on a petition were to be 25 percent of the total number of votes cast at the last general City election. Although there were 945 registered voters, it was first announced that 264 had voted at the last election. This figure meant that 66 voters had to sign the petition (although Evelyn Thompson the Borough Clerk issued a "To Whom it may concern" memo on November 18th that stated 258 persons had voted "in the City of Palmer Precinct in the Borough election on 10-7-75"). This last official tally further reduced slightly the mandatory signatures to 64 voters. It was a goal I knew I could accomplish, so I set out to do just that.

By now, Higgins and I had become a familiar team working in and around Palmer, investigating and interviewing citizens. I felt the recall procedure would be relatively easy to accomplish.

"Wayne, feel like knocking on doors?" I asked just before drafting the petitions for recall.

"Anything you say, Chief," he replied in his typical low husky voice.

"I can get all the help we need," he added.

"I think between you, me and my wife we'll only need three or four more."

"Just let me know when, Chief," he replied enthusiastically.

Less than a week after the City Council meeting, I prepared and had typed up separate petitions for both the Mayor and City Council. The heading on both petitions had the mandatory citings of the appropriate authorities under which the recall was sought: Section 2.12 of the Municipal Charter entitled "RECALL," and the similar section under Title 29 of the Alaska Statutes.

The Mayor's wording began with:

"The following registered City voters seek a recall of Jack E. Maze, the Mayor of the City of Palmer."

It then gave the necessary space for the voters to sign. Following their signatures was additional wording:

"This petition is prompted by:
1. His inept handling of the Police Chief's firing and his "rubber-stamp" concurrence of the City Manager's Actions in such firing — in violation of the City Charter and of said Title 29 of the Alaska Statutes dealing with municipal government.
2. His hiring of the City Manager a nonresident of the City of Palmer, which is an express qualification of the position and is therefore a blatant violation of the City Charter.
3. His denial to the public the use of larger quarters the night of the City Council meeting in which the Police Chief's firing was to be on the agenda and his specific orders to bar the door to those citizens who desired entrance and forced them to leave the building — all in violation of the City Charter and of Title 29 of the Alaska Statutes.
4. His failure to advise the City Council of many citizen complaints and his failure to follow up on other complaints.

5. His failure to honor promises put forward to the public who have had reason to put stock in his remarks and have acted or have not acted accordingly.

6. His failure as "presiding officer of the Council" to properly advise/direct the Council to hear all matters that are placed on its agenda or should be on the agenda — such acts being in contravention of his duty to represent the public who duly elected him to office."

The wording of the Council's recall was exactly the same as that of the Mayor's with the exception that it named them individually: "Willard Johnson, James Ekstedt, Dave Ingalls, Pete Pedersen, Arlyn Hanson and John Dolenc," and was also followed by:

"This petition is prompted by:
1. Their failure to exercise proper supervisory controls over the dictatorial actions of the City Manager in his firing of the Police Chief.

2. Their tolerance of the improper actions of the City Mayor in allowing the City Manager to act willfully and maliciously and in violation of the City Charter and of said Title 29 of the Alaska Statutes dealing with municipal government in such firing.

3. Not only denying the public larger quarters the night of the City Council meeting in which the Police Chief's firing was to be on the agenda, but openly turning away many of its citizens — all in violation of the Charter and of the Alaska Statutes.

4. Not advising the public of its many special meetings and their right to attend and be heard — all in violation of the Charter and of the Alaska Statutes.

5. Their ignoring of many citizen complaints and the failure to follow up on other complaints.

6. Their failure to honor promises of the City Manager and the City Mayor in their dealings with the public."

The final wording on both petitions concluded with the final identical sentence:

"These specific allegations and more best known to
the following signers are offered for this Recall Petition."

When it came time to gather the names, Wayne and I usually
went together because we had other motives in contacting supporters. We wanted to find out as much as we could about any
other allegations of corruption not only among City Officials but
also whatever we could learn about the Alaska Rural
Rehabilitation Corporation. The ARRC had become a buzz
acronym that we would follow wherever it took us.

My wife and three of our active sympathizers who also had
their own particular "axes to grind," canvassed Palmer for the
necessary signatures.

Within a few days we had gathered more than enough voters'
names — 73 signatures on each of the petitions.

Initially, the petitions were scheduled to be filed with the City
Manager's office on December 1, in his dual assumed capacity as
City Clerk, but were temporarily delayed while signatures were
checked for validity by the Borough.

Originally, I also had omitted placing Councilman Dolenc's
name on the recall petition, because as I reported to the
Anchorage Daily Times, "he was sympathetic and willing to listen to why things were being done."

However, I soon learned that his "sympathy" was feigned
and so his name was subsequently added to the list of other
Councilmen for recall.

It virtually took the entire month of December for the local
officials to validate the voter's signatures, but finally on
December 23, the petitions demanding the recall election were
filed at City Hall. Verna Euwer, a day-care operator, accompanied me when the petitions were handed to the City Manager. She
also had been a persistent critic of the City government because
of the manner in which they had dealt with her nursery. They
were insistent on her collecting and paying sales tax on her
Palmer child-care center, which she consistently had maintained,
was unfair. She contended that since the Children's House was
annexed to the City in 1972, her operation was a bona fide school

and therefore should be tax exempt. She cited the tax-exempt status of day-care centers in Kenai and Fairbanks as examples. The City, however, would not yield to her, and her willing signature to the petition and her part in its delivery gave her no small amount of satisfaction. It was a satisfaction that I gladly indulged.

Statutory provisions specified that the City had 10 days in which to accept or reject the recall petitions. If accepted, the council them would have 75 days in which to submit the questions to the voters.

The *Frontiersman* headlined the event on Christmas Eve:

"RECALL MOVE HITS PALMER MAYOR COUNCIL."

It also devoted a full column to the Mayor under the headline:

"MAZE SAYS RECALL 'JUST FINE'"

In the article, the Mayor gave me a left-handed compliment when he stated "I'm glad he's finally kept his word. I have more faith in the man."

His comment probably referred to the delay in filing the petitions that had been reported under way for a few weeks. It was a delay that he well knew was City- and Borough-oriented.

Curtis, on the other hand, was not as complacent as Maze. Although not personally involved in the recall because he was an appointed rather than elected official, he apparently was still very concerned. I knew it was because his job would be in jeopardy without his power base.

As he worriedly pointed out to the paper. "Should the Mayor and the entire Council be recalled, Palmer would be left without a City government. The Council then would have no power to order an election at which successors would be chosen."

He added, "I don't have the authority to set an election. We would probably have to turn to the courts."

This last statement concerning his non-authority to set an election was either a scare tactic to unduly distress an already confused public or a case of downright ignorance of the Alaska

Statutes dealing with municipal government. As to the former, Curtis was well aware that in his second role as City Clerk, he had that encompassing authority. As to the latter, it was highly doubtful that ignorance of the statutes could be claimed, as he should have been aware that all his actions would be carefully watched and analyzed and any such excuse would be unacceptable. It was the City Attorney's function to advise him accordingly even if he alleged such ignorance.

To refute his fallacious comment to the local paper the Alaska Statute was explicit on that point. Section 29.28.250. *Election of Successor,* clearly stated that:

"If the voters recall an officer, the clerk shall conduct an election for a successor to fill the unexpired term."

In that same newspaper edition under the "Letters to the Editor," whether by design or accident, was a lengthy informative piece by the former Palmer PD Investigator Gary Meier, with whom I had maintained contact and friendship since my hire as Police Chief. He referred to the court hearing before Judge Ripley on the 17th of the month and to the *Frontiersman* coverage of it immediately thereafter. Under his caption,

"DISTORTED NEWS"

it read:

"Dear Editor:

"After reading last week's news story in the *Frontiersman* titled: "Mangieri Loses," I thought maybe I had attended the wrong preliminary injunction hearing. I feel the news item may have distorted the true results of that hearing and am compelled to write this letter in retort.

"First of all, Mr. Mangieri did not and has not "lost" anything. The purpose of that hearing was to immediately reinstate him as Chief of Police if there was a showing of "immediate and irreparable harm." Unfortunately, the immediate and irreparable harm to the Palmer Police Department its officers and employees (and even the City of Palmer with its mushrooming crime rate) was not brought out at that session. If it were, however, the judge was willing to exercise his judicial prerogative and reinstate him as of that date. He did not, although he specifically requested additional reasons, but he left no doubt as to his sympathies in the matter.

"An *Anchorage Daily Times* article in the late afternoon edition reflected the judge's feeling when he stated that there is an "awesome amount of power" in that man (meaning Bill Curtis). The judge further stated during the hearing that he knew of Mangieri's background was impressed by it and his qualifications, as were others that he spoke to concerning Mangieri.

"Secondly, the *Frontiersman* article stated that trial would not come up for "two years." Either this was a misprint or erroneous information given to the paper. The truth is that a trial will be scheduled in about two months.

"There are many citizens very concerned about this situation in Palmer, and I wanted to set the record straight.

"Thank you.

"Sincerely,
GARY E. MEIER
Box 1172
Palmer"

Unfortunately, the "two-month" trial date did not materialize as expected. Undoubtedly the paper had greater input than I did.

At a special meeting on December 29, the Palmer City Council reluctantly accepted the certification of the recall petitions and ordered a special election to take place on Tuesday, January 20 1976.

By unanimous resolution, the Council then assailed me vehemently by asserting that the recall election was the result of my "personal vendetta" and described me in even more vivid terms as "a disgruntled ex-employee who wants to cause as much trouble as possible in any way he can because of personal spite against the City."

In the December 31 issue of the *Frontiersman*, Curtis, in his ever-present dual role of City Clerk, a role that he attempted to deny publicly a week earlier, placed a large ad in the paper with the heading NOTICE OF SPECIAL ELECTION in bold print emblazoned across the top of it. In the ad was the usual required information for voters as to time and place of the special recall election and qualifications of electors.

In it, also, was not only the necessary "grounds" as stated in the recall petition, but the inclusions of a 200-word rebuttal for both the Council and the Mayor. Although questionably permitted by statute, it nevertheless was done. It was this poisonous content that was to be the subject of a subsequent additional lawsuit for libel.

The Council's *rebuttal* statement followed the same basic wording that was adopted as their resolution against me at their special meeting of December 29.

In addition the statement said:

> "He threatened to 'tear this town wide open' if he were not rehired, and without regard for the damage to the community he has tried to spread discontent and dissatisfaction through misinformation and untrue charges all for his own personal benefit. He has used or been used by the Anchorage news media holding Palmer up to ridicule. The ill feeling and distrust irresponsibly created by him are an irrevocable loss to the community."

The Mayor, the most vocal of the group, was even more blatant in his denouncement of me by first claiming that I would never have been hired but for a "misleading job application." Of course, it was an application that was overwhelmingly approved by the Mayor himself and the full City Council before my hire. And it had come *before* the rehiring of Bill Curtis — and *before* my investigation into City Hall.

The Mayor's statement also stated:

> "Not qualified to be a Police Chief by experience,

he showed during his probationary period that he was not qualified by attitude or ability. In addition to problems created by his personal conduct, he refused to comply with the budget guidelines set by the Council and attempted to spend funds and hire his personal friends without authorization.

"A Chief of Police must bring dignity to the job and show an attitude of professional restraint, as well as be above personal reproach. Mr. Mangieri's hiring was a mistake that had to be corrected. The Mayor and Council unanimously supported the termination."

The openly supportive *Frontiersman*, in its January 15 edition, devoted full coverage to the upcoming recall election. The front page showed smiling inserts of the Mayor and the six Councilmen. The "Letters to the Editors" section, in virtually a full two-page spread, printed endless sympathetic letters with obviously biased captions:

"RECALL PERPLEXING"
"ADMIRES PALMER"
"LET'S KEEP COOL"
and
"BACK UP THE COUNCIL"

There was even a double 14-inch column that extolled the virtues of everybody in City Hall — almost back to their date of birth. However, the author of this elongated testimonial was to admit in her letter that she was a "relatively new resident of Palmer," citing September 1974 as her arrival. Even I, in my newcomer status, was to pre-date her by several months and couldn't possibly know everyone's good deeds — unless someone else prepared the script.

There was one particular letter, captioned "Citizens Alerted" that disturbed me even more than the other prejudicial epistles. In it, the author of the piece stated:

"If the Councilmen were listed separately, it would allow citizens to vote against individual Councilmen with which they have any grievance quite apart from the Mangieri issue."

It was a comment that I was completely in agreement with —
and it was a tactic, which I attempted to initiate. However, it was
Curtis, in his official capacity as City Clerk, who refused to permit me to do so. It was also to prove crucial to the recall.

Inasmuch as the entire *Frontiersman* issue appeared devoted
to full support of City Hall, it came as no surprise to me that no
favorable letters about me appeared in print. I don't think any
were allowed that were anti-Mayor or Council. It was a continuing complaint that I heard from those citizens that supported me
and tried unsuccessfully to have their views expressed in the
paper. Such is the awesome power of the press.

The day before the recall, the *Anchorage Times* — as it was
to be called in lieu of the former *Anchorage Daily Times* designation — put out its usual comprehensive and objective article
covering not only the "recall test," but also a detailed recap of all
events that had occurred prior to the recall.

In that issue, I decided to put in my own paid quarter ad,
alerting the people to the election that was to be held the following day:

"CITIZENS OF PALMER
WAKE UP!"

"Vote the City Mayor & the City Council out of
office in the **RECALL ELECTION** to be held
Tomorrow Jan. 20th in Palmer.
■ It was they who hired William E. Curtis as City
  Manager with the knowledge that he was not a resident of the City. This act was in direct violation of
  the City Charter, which specifically states that 'he
  shall be a resident of the City during his tenure in
  office.'
■ It is they who continue to violate that provision by
  continuing his employment while still a nonresident
  of the City.
■ It is this same group and the City Manager who constantly violates the provisions of the City Charter
  that deals with Special Meetings & those of the
  Alaska Statutes that deal with public meetings.

- It is this group who are not responsive or sympathetic to the needs of its citizens.
- **DO NOT ALLOW** them or any other elected official to dictate to the City or to place themselves above the law.
- **DO NOT BE MISLEAD** by William E. Curtis' words that he does 'not have the authority to set an election.' He does. The Alaska Statutes give him that authority in his dual role of City Clerk, a role he assumed in April 1971 when he initiated a drive to abolish the City Clerk's position, a move that was also contrary to the provisions of the City Charter.
- **DO NOT ALLOW** Curtis' statement before the City Council on the evening of Jan. 13th to become a reality: 'If my residency is a problem, all the City has to do is to pass an ordinance saying that I'm in the City, and I will be.'
- **DO YOUR CIVIC DUTY** and vote. Every vote counts. If there are those individual electors who are troubled by a recall "in mass" those Councilmen that you favor can be re-elected at the Special Election.

"Individual ballots could have been prepared by William E. Curtis but he declined to do so.

VOTE! VOTE! VOTE!

Paid by Concerned Citizens of Palmer & the Mat-Su Borough, Nick Mangieri, Chairman, S.R.A., Box 79 A, Palmer"

The phone rang off the hook that night.
"Good luck, Chief," one caller said.
"You can do it," another offered.
"We're all behind you," a voice encouraged.
"It's about time someone stood up to them," still another said.
I even got a couple of calls from guys I went through the Anchorage Police Academy with. "Hang the bastards Nick," one yelled.

"Give 'em hell, Paisan," another said.

The calls were endless — but all were supportive.

I was optimistic but not complacent. Higgins and I continued making the rounds in Palmer that night, contacting any and all who could give us any help or information as to what could be expected the following day.

The sun had not yet risen when the polling place at the Palmer City Library opened its doors at 8 a.m. on Tuesday, January 20. Outside, the weather was cooperative for both factions. It was in the low 20s with light winds and cloudy.

Councilman Willard Johnson was the first to cast his ballot with Mayor Jack Maze close behind. By sunrise at 8:48 a.m. almost 30 persons had voted. Councilman James Ekstedt, the 22nd person to vote, made a cautious but innocuous remark, "There's going to be a real strong turnout — the issue was debated very good."

It was true that the issue was debated very well. Unfortunately, the *Frontiersman* heavily influenced the Palmer "debate" — and it was the local community that relied on the local paper. The Anchorage community and many Mat-Su Borough residents were not swayed by the biased Palmer press. Regrettably, however, they could not vote.

By sunset that afternoon at 3:37 p.m., the somberness of the weather reflected the eventual outcome of the vote. Winds from the north picked up to 15 mph with heavier clouds and snow blowing in.

By the 8 p.m. closing time at the City library, the last of the voters had trickled in. I tried not to be concerned about the results during the day by keeping busy. Higgins and I had driven out further into the valley to follow up leads and question other people about mounting allegations against what came to be referred to as "Curtis and Company." Intertwined with this information came recurring references to the ARRC and even more sinister allusions to past political violence that was attributed to that long-term *nonprofit* corporation.

When the results of the recall election were finally tabulated, it was estimated that 38 percent of the 945 registered voters had cast their vote. Of the total votes cast, the Mayor received 127 votes to recall with 235 votes to keep him in office. The Council in mass tallied less to recall with 107 votes compared to the 255 votes to retain them.

"It was a good showing, Chief," said an obviously dejected supporter as he tried to bolster my feelings about the loss.

"Not bad," another said. "You've only been in the valley less than two years, and look what you did."

No matter what was said or how I tried to soften the defeat, it didn't lessen how I berated myself.

What else could I have done? What did I fail to do? I asked myself repeatedly.

It didn't dawn on me — nor would it as the months rolled by — that the old saying, "you can't fight City Hall," were more than just words. I still believed in all the age-old adages written and spoken about how *truth and justice* would triumph. That faith, however, would be tested over and over again.

The *Anchorage Times*, in its January 21 edition, objectively reported tally results with the heading:

"VOTE NIXES RECALLING IN PALMER"

The *Frontiersman*, however, in its weekly January 22 edition, headlined the issue:

"VOTERS DENY MAYOR CITY COUNCIL RECALL"

and then gleefully announced that the City Councilmen were "fresh from victory." They received "the community's vote of confidence — a substantial majority for their retaining office," the article further stated.

The difference in the reporting went further than the event itself in the Anchorage paper. The *Times* went on to say, "Meanwhile a radio report today states that Maze's eligibility to hold office is questionable because he is a convicted felon."

The paper, in interviewing Maze about his conviction, contained his indignant remarks, "I think it's a smear tactic. It's a matter of record. I think 90 percent of the people have known this thing for years. There's no reason to hide it."

The *Times* article then explained more in depth about his felony conviction.

"In the early 1950s, Maze was convicted of embezzling $125,000 from a Matanuska Valley bank where he had been employed, according to an early newspaper account. He served time in MacNeil Island Penitentiary in Washington State."

Maze's specific response to the Anchorage paper's coverage was that City Charter and State Law did not prohibit him from holding public office.

"I had the City Attorney look into this before I ever ran for City Council and Mayor."

My personal comment when asked by the *Times* reporter was, "I find it hard to believe that the public could re-elect incompetents back into office, and those accused of violations of the City Charter and Alaska statutes."

None of the references to the Anchorage radio broadcast concerning Maze's convicted felon status or any of my own remarks appeared in the *Frontiersman*'s coverage of the recall election. Instead, "victory" comments and actions dotted the article throughout.

During the City Council meeting the night of the 22nd, in which Maze triumphantly declared, "We are pleased with the outcome," he added a more cautious comment.

"We haven't heard the last of it."

At the time he said it, he was unaware of the full extent of that prophetic reference that would unfold in the coming months.

... Chapter 12 ...

With the recent defeat of the recall election and with criminal investigations hopefully being conducted by state authorities, I was temporarily at a loss as to my next move. Rather than sit around and wait for something to happen, however, I decided that probably the next most productive step would be to continue investigating not only "Curtis and Company" at the City but also Wes Howe, the Borough Manager. Recent delving into Borough records had indicated some sort of collusion between the City and the Borough. Interviews with knowledgeable disgusted citizens had revealed strong possibilities of kickbacks.

Late one afternoon, after Higgins and I had made the usual rounds of contacting people, I arrived home. My oldest daughter, Tammy, gave me an unusual message,

"Dad, somebody named Harry Lechwold called and told me to have you check into the ARRC sale of property to the American Legion in Palmer."

Lechwold, one of Wayne Hunter's protegees, was to become my main link with Hunter. Although still active at 79, he preferred to have the contacts come through Lechwold especially, when it dealt with the ARRC.

"What else did he say, Tammy?"

"He said that the land is south of Palmer and that the bus system is now leasing it and that they're paying the American Legion $1,200 a month."

"And?" I asked.

"But," she continued, "the American Legion has *no* accounting of the $1,200 a month."

"Did he say what that meant?" I wanted to know.

"All he said was that there were three people in the transaction. Somebody named Mullen, a George Hart and a Lee Hartley."

I didn't know the first two names, but I did know that Lee Hartley, owner of Lee Hartley Motors in Palmer, was part of the *inner circle* in town.

"Mr. Lechwold says," she continued "that Lee Hartley is the only one who has a key to the Legion Lodge. He also says that there are three freezers in the lodge with Hartley's name on all of them and that there's food in them. He said it looks like he's using the food supplies for his own personal use instead of for the American Legion."

"Thanks, Tammy. Anybody else involved?"

"Not that I know of Dad," she answered. "Maybe Mom and the others know. They're all out with the horses. Well, I gotta go to work," and she kissed me lightly on the cheek.

Although I didn't quite know what to make of this new information — or the torrent of other continuing information — I kept record of it as I would of all future input from Lechwold. What I did note, however, was still another reference to the ARRC. It seemed as though every time I turned around, I would hear that same acronym over and over again.

I called Lechwold later in the day to get clarification of the message and to find out more about the ARRC.

My questioning of it brought a flood of information from him.

"It was formed as a corporation in 1935 as a nonprofit organization to promote agriculture in Alaska," he began. "Then in 1953, the corporation was terminated and the federal government severed connections with it, but..." and he stressed the word, but "...the ARRC still continued operations."

I interrupted him "What operations?"

"Dispensing property, loaning money, etc.," he said.

"What about the assets of the Corporation?" I asked.

"In 1953," he continued, "the assets of the corporation should have inured to the territory — but it never happened."

"How can they still be functioning?" I asked incredulously.

He went on talking as if it were merely common knowledge and a matter-of-fact disclosure rather than an unbelievable explanation.

"The ARRC has been operating as a private group administering federal and state funds — even though it's illegal under state statute."

I couldn't believe what I was hearing.

"How can they get by with it?" I wanted to know.

"I don't know," was his direct reply. "They must have friends in the right places." He snickered as he said it.

"What does all this mean to the valley?" I asked trying to phrase some type of logical question.

"Well, if the ARRC didn't receive a title of assumption from the Territory or the State of Alaska, then no one has a right to have it — from the original colonists onward to this date. Furthermore, Alaska Title Guarantee, the title company, cannot guarantee a survey if in fact ARRC was not in a position to give clear title."

"That means," I added, "that Alaska Title could be sued for stating title was clear when it wasn't."

"That's right," he agreed.

I was still trying to sort the whole mess out in my mind when I asked him, "How does the City of Palmer figure into this whole thing?"

"Palmer," he answered, "was given rental buildings, sewer lines, land, etc. that was paid to the ARRC."

"Who was supposed to get that money?" I asked.

"Anything paid *before* 1953 should have gone to the federal government, and after that date, as I mentioned before, should have gone to the territory but it didn't because they are still functioning," he said disgustedly.

"Do you know what the City is doing now?"

He was unsure of their status when he answered.

"After 1953 the City of Palmer either still paid ARRC or they were given these assets without the approval of the territory."

It was just too big to take in his whole conversation and to try to understand it. I just couldn't imagine a corporation any corporation operating with such impunity on such a grand and prolonged scale and get by with it — especially as it related to the federal government. For that matter, I couldn't understand how the territory and then the State of Alaska could allow the ARRC to operate without any controls.

"Let me think about this, Harry. I'll see what sense I can make of this whole thing," I said slowly.

"Good luck, Chief. The 'old man' has been fighting them for 20 years — and they're still ahead."

"Who else has looked into this that you know of?" I asked, trying to put the puzzle into place.

"Try Bill Blessington," he answered.

"Where can I find him?"

"He does PR for the Municipality of Anchorage. He's one of the 'good guys'."

"Thanks. I'll be in touch," I responded. I was still mulling over all the information as I hung up.

I contacted Higgins.

"We've got our work cut out for ourselves," I said enthusiastically.

I briefly related my conversation with Lechwold to him.

He momentarily hesitated and then drew in a deep breath before he spoke.

"This is getting big, Chief. That's why Curtis and the City Council didn't want you in office. You ask too many questions."

"They're speeding the process up themselves," I said. "I wouldn't have even thought of these questions before. If they'd have just let me handle street crimes, I wouldn't have gotten involved in this white collar stuff."

"That reminds me, Chief. I ran across a farmer in my area who knows you and said for you to give him a call. He's got some info for you."

"What's his name?" I asked.

"Jim Vickaryous."

I knew Jim. He had a large dairy farm outside of town, and I periodically bought my hay for the horses from him. He seemed like a nice guy. He was young, mid-30s or so, and a hard worker.

"I'll give him a call," I said.

"Anything else you want me to do?" he asked concernedly.

"Yeah," I answered quickly. "Since we're into this ARRC thing, just nose around and ask questions."

"Sure thing, Chief."

I called Vickaryous.

"Chief, I hear you're interested in learning about the ARRC," he said without hesitation.

I acknowledged that I was.

"Well," he started, "you're aware that their purpose was to promote agriculture in Alaska for farmers through long-term financing."

"So I was told."

"Well, I'll bet that you're not aware then that between 1959 and 1972 the ARRC made loans to people who were not farmers," he said firmly.

The more I heard about the activities of the ARRC, the less I was surprised.

"Where did you pick that up?" I asked.

"It's common knowledge here in the valley," he answered. "Check on it."

"I will," I said, although I was unsure exactly where to start.

"Also, did you know that Alaska is the only state in the U.S. under the Farm Credit System that makes loans?" he continued.

"No," I answered, half-dazed with the constant flow of information that I was receiving.

"Do you want me to check that out too?" I asked, more in jest than in anything.

"The more you know, the better," he said. His reply was emphatic.

I agreed, but I realized that the scope of my investigation was quickly mushrooming.

"While you're at it," he continued, "you might as well look at Title 40 of the Alaska Statutes, *Public Buildings Property and Works*. I think you'll find Section 440 interesting and especially page 7468 — I think that's the page," he added.

"What does it cover?"

"You'll have to read it to fully understand what they've done," he answered. "Also, you should really examine Alaska Senate Report No. 403 re: 'Rural Rehabilitation Corporation Trust Liquidation Act' — especially page 2202."

I could surmise that it dealt with the termination of the ARRC the same as Lechwold had mentioned.

"Is that it Jim?" I asked wearily.

"That should keep you busy, Chief," he said quickly, apparently content that he had given me more than enough information to look into.

"Thanks," I said. "I'll be in touch." I hung up the receiver in amazement at the specifics of the conversation.

I was on a roll. Information was coming in quicker than I could check it out.

I was almost reluctant to call Bill Blessington as per Lechwold's suggestion because the incoming data was almost getting out of hand.

What the hell, I thought. *When you're hot, you're hot.*

I dialed him and introduced myself.

"I've heard of you," he quickly admitted. "You're really stirring things up," he added.

"It's not of my doing," I said half-defensively not wanting to alienate him.

"Don't get me wrong," he added just as quickly, "I'm on your side."

"Good," I said, relieved. "What can you tell me about the ARRC?"

"Had you heard that the ARRC provided money for unsecured loans?" he answered in response.

"Something on that order?" I replied cautiously.

"Well," he continued, "did you also hear that friends of the ARRC didn't pay off their loans and then had them written off?"

He hesitated briefly to let the remark sink in before he went on.

"Those loans amounted to several hundred thousand dollars."

That comment really had me going.

"No ... nothing like that," I had to admit.

He continued.

"There was a $100,000 loan to someone in 1968 or 1969, and allegedly there was a $25,000 kickback."

He named the individual. I had heard the name before.

"That's the way to do business," I said sarcastically.

"I'd also heard that the ARRC invested in dairy farms that

bellied up afterwards," he said.

"Do you know of any names involved or those who wound up with the property?" I wanted to know.

"Bank records would probably have that information," he answered. "As to who got the property afterward it was probably the ARRC. Who knows who owned it after the foreclosures."

I had already heard that the Matanuska Valley Bank had been involved in ARRC transactions and felt that their records would undoubtedly cast light on any corporate investments. All I had to do was to get the state directly involved in detailed financial investigations, something that was becoming increasingly unlikely. I thought at the time that it would be simple for the appropriate agencies to conduct their own in-depth investigations. However, I was to find out how naive I was if I expected that type of official investigation from the state.

When I mentioned my expectation of future state action, Blessington didn't seem as optimistic as I was.

"If I were you," he said, "I'd try to get copies of the ARRC tax records. That should tell you something."

I thanked him for his time and information and wondered where he had amassed that much background about the ARRC.

I later learned that he had been a broadcaster for KHAR-TV and as such had been involved in some investigative reporting for the station.

I made a mental note to get information on the ARRC tax returns. I believed that all nonprofit corporations were required to file yearly tax returns, and I was also fairly sure that they weren't required to pay any federal taxes because of their *nonprofit* status. What I didn't know was what actions would take them out of their nonprofit category since it was becoming clearer to me that there was profit involved in their transactions. Further, I knew that it wasn't only this amorphous corporation that had benefited over the years but also many individuals within the ARRC. I was sure that Wayne Hunter and Harry Lechwold could supply those names. They undoubtedly had been tracking them and their operations for years.

I spent the majority of the afternoon on the phone and sat back to relax a minute before I went outside to get the horses into the barn.

The phone rang again, and I picked it up for what seemed like the 10th time.

"Chief!"

"Yeah, Wayne. What's up?"

"You told me to nose around about the ARRC and I did," he said excitedly.

"What did you find out?" I quickly asked.

His tone had piqued my interest.

"I heard," he continued "that about five or six years ago the ARRC bought houses on the Eklutna Flats had them set up and then sold them to an individual who was supposed to have paid about $75,000 for them."

"Any other specifics on the deal?" I pressed him.

"Only that these houses have no tie-in with any soil bank or agricultural money."

"Doesn't surprise me, Wayne. Just make a note of the conversations and any other details that you can recall."

"These sonofabitch's are into everything, Chief. How do they get by with it?" he asked incredulously.

"That's what everyone wants to know," I said. "Did you learn anything else?"

"Only that Kertula owned Industrial Park property, and before that, it was ARRC property."

We had known that the state senator had owned a substantial amount of acreage in the newly developed Industrial Park property. What we didn't know was that it was ARRC property before he got it.

I was still musing over what Higgins had just told me when he interrupted my thoughts.

"Chief, you there?"

"Yeah," I said. "I was just wondering how we could get more background on that property."

"Me too," he confided. "The more we find out, the more there is," he said almost wearily. "What we need is for the state to step in and investigate. They've got more muscle than we've got."

He stopped a moment before he spoke again.

"Think we've got enough for them yet?" he asked.

I took a deep breath before I answered him.

"I don't think so, Wayne. They probably want it on a silver platter," I replied sarcastically.

"There's only two of us, Chief. We can't do everything."

His voice sounded tired and discouraged.

"Hang in there, Wayne. We just gotta do the best we can," I emphasized.

"Yeah I know," he answered. "I'll be all right. It's just that the more I hear about the damn City and the Borough crowd, the madder I get. Here we were both doing our jobs as sworn officers and we get canned. They've been screwing the state and the feds for years and they're still in power."

I knew Wayne had good reason to feel let down but I couldn't believe that I wouldn't get it all straightened out after I had gathered all the facts.

"Why don't you try to take it easy the rest of the night," I said, trying to console him. "We'll talk tomorrow."

"Right, Chief. You, too."

Tomorrow came and went as did the following days. The sporadic optimism that followed periodic splurges of information was being quickly replaced by the feeling that the state was dragging its feet in its investigation of all my allegations against the City, the Borough and the ARRC. To make matters worse, I had a growing realization that a reinstatement would take much longer than I had originally anticipated. I even started to doubt the effectiveness of the courts as I remembered the actions of Superior Court Judge Ralph Moody when he denied Higgins' reinstatement as a police officer. I mentioned the Moody episode when I spoke briefly to Harry Lechwold one afternoon.

"I have the old man's autobiography," he said. "I think you'll find it very interesting."

Higgins and I made a special stop that afternoon to pick up the material.

As I read the 60,000 word typewritten memoirs of Wayne Hunter's early years, which spanned a 23-year period from 1945-1968, I ran across Judge Moody's name. It was in connection with a civil action brought against the ARRC for abrogation of contract.

The plaintiff was George Engelmann, a highly decorated WWII veteran, who after serving in 12 major engagements in the

Pacific, including Wake Island and Guadalcanal, decided to try his hand at farming in the Matanuska Valley. Representing the ARRC at that time was George Crowther, the present manager of the corporation. Engelmann, according to the memoirs, had hired a Mrs. Helen Simpson as his lawyer.

The description of events as they occurred several years earlier are extracted from his account and are given in Hunter's unique words:

"The trial was held before Judge Moody, October 10, 1968. For those who think a fair trial can be obtained before Judge Moody, I will recount the day's happenings. Besides believing the decision was written before the opening of court that morning, I believe George's lawyer was paid by the ARRC to throw the trial. After you have read the happenings, you judge.

I arrived about three minutes late and walked quietly into the courtroom. The judge and clerk of court, George and his lawyer, and Crowther and his lawyer, were all present. No spectators and no witnesses except me. George's lawyer had a fine chance to have built a good case. I personally know of at least 10 witnesses who could have been and should have been called. I personally could have added much to George's case and could not at the time understand why I was not called. Why was quite obvious before the day was over.

Crowther's lawyers were Hahn and Jewell. I believe Mr. Jewell was the one in court that day. Mr. Jewell was talking when I came in. He had plenty of reason to not want me in that courtroom. He started to stutter and could not talk. Finally he got out 'Your Honor, I would like to request that Mr. Hunter be removed from the courtroom.' It being a public courtroom, this was clearly impossible. Once again he tried to speak. He could only stutter. Finally Judge Moody said, 'Let us call a 10-minute recess while Mr. Jewell composes himself.' One thing was certain, I did rather mess up their cut and dried deal. Of course I believe the decision was already written, but they would have to devise new strategy to meet

the emergency. Upon declaration of the recess, Mr.
Jewell again found his voice and said, 'Your Honor, I
would like to request that Mr. Hunter and Mr. Engelmann
be instructed not to confer during the recess.' How utterly stupid.

Too bad. He had hoped to wind up the thing that
morning, and from where I sit, I would say that
Crowther, Jewell, Simpson and the judge were all disappointed because I had appeared. Now they would have to
take longer to establish reason for that already written
decision. And now I will show you how innocent I was
of even believing that the court and Mrs. Simpson had
been corrupted. I thought that Mrs. Simpson was showing poor judgment in not calling the witnesses I knew
would have been at her disposal. But it wasn't until after
the trial that I began to suspect that she had acted to help
the ARRC and the court in this so-called legal thievery.
Must have taken quite a bit of the ARRC's nonprofits to
buy a court and two lawyers.

I walked over to George and Mrs. Simpson and
talked to them for a couple of minutes and so was a few
minutes late leaving the courtroom. However, I wanted
to go to the men's room, and as I stepped out the courtroom I saw Crowther and Jewell turn the corner towards
the men's room. I followed and turned the corner just in
time to see Crowther and Jewell go on past the men's
room. They proceeded on across the building and turned
down the corridor on the far side. I proceeded to the
men's room and then back to the courtroom. It was not
until later, after the trial, that I had occasion to go on
across the building and discovered that the corridor on
the far side of the building led only to the Judge's chambers.

It was then, after the trial, that I realized why Mr.
Jewell had been so composed when he came back into
the courtroom. He and Crowther had conferred with the
judge on the run of events brought about by my showing
up at the trial. It was also after the trial that I discovered
that Mrs. Simpson had apparently been bought and in

fact was probably in on the strategy to dispossess George in the first place. That happened in this manner.

When the trial was over and Judge Moody had announced his finding, George, Mrs. Simpson and I got together to work out plans for an appeal or so George and I thought. However when Mrs. Simpson discovered that we really meant business, she pled business in the Judge's chambers and went in promising to come out in a few minutes to discuss matters with us. Neither of us could figure why she had not called the witnesses available to her and had made no attempt to build a case. Nor could I understand a judge who did not seek the truth, the whole truth and nothing but the truth, but would deprive a man of many years of his life without seeking that truth. I personally have known of cases where judges have refused to finish hearing cases so poorly presented and insisted on the parties bringing the truth before him before he would allow the case to be heard. Having watched what went on, I am convinced that Judge Moody was privy to the theft that day of George's property.

In any case, we saw no more of Mrs. Simpson that day. Several days later, I dropped in to see her and urged that she appeal the decision but she refused and became very angry when I intimated that I thought the case was rigged. I retrieved the papers concerning the trial and now have them on file. Mrs. Simpson must have gotten the judge to let her out his private entrance. George and I stood by the door she went in at for over an hour and she did not come back out.

I know now how Mrs. Simpson must have lied about my case. But that is another story.

And now back to the courtroom. After the recess Jewell seemed well composed. He got George on the witness stand and proceeded to work him over. He apparently got his signals crossed though. He started calling the contracts George had submitted as evidence hearsay. Crowther signaled him frantically to shut up about that, and poor stupid me, I thought Crowther just had an irritated rectum the way he was squirming in his seat and waving his arms. Not knowing at that time about the visit to the Judge's chambers, I did not realize that this was old strategy and that new strategy had been cooked up. This just couldn't work with me there because I could testify differently. And of course I thought I was in a court of justice and did not know that no matter what George said, or Jewell said, or Crowther said, the decision would come out the same.

So now, Jewell browbeat George unmercifully, accusing him of typing the contracts himself (George wouldn't know how) and then forging the signatures and other crimes. I began to suspect something was wrong when George's lawyer, Mrs. Simpson, made no move to protect him in any way. George looked to her and to the judge for some protection from this insane attack staged by this so-called lawyer. Even when George denied any such things and was accused by Judge Moody of perjury — the tape was played back to prove he had not committed perjury — Jewell kept harping on the hearsay aspects of the contracts.

However, Judge Moody finally tired of that and asked Jewell on what he based the assumption of hearsay. Jewell again accused George of forgery, so the judge asked him, 'Why don't you ask Mr. Engelmann who typed the contracts?' This question was put and George, almost beat to a frazzle and certainly utterly confused, pointed to me and told the court I typed them.

This was true. I had even witnessed some of the signatures. This took the wind out of Jewell's sails, and Judge Moody called for lunch recess. Ah, yes, everything was going according to plan, and during lunch recess, Mrs. Simpson told us we had it made. Bound to win now.

I have been in courtrooms other places where true justice was being dispensed. Never have I seen such utter sadism as was allowed in that court. It is true that Judge Moody finally stopped it, but not until it had gone on for over an hour and a half.

After noon recess, Crowther was called to the stand.

He was not subjected to any indignity such as George had faced in any manner whatever. The main thing he emphasized to the court was that he did not impede Mr. Engelmann in his sale of the lots at all. All he did was to tell people their credit was no good and that they were foolish to buy property in the Wasilla area. The court however did not question his perjurous statements in any way, patted the criminal on the back and told him in effect, 'Go and steal some more.' He has."

As humorous and as down-to-earth as the memoirs were, a constant reference to the "theft" of agricultural property by the ARRC as well as to all those individuals associated with that *nonprofit* corporation became a recurring theme. It ran not only through Wayne Hunter's lengthy autobiography but also permeated his subsequent self-published periodicals, *The Alaska Farmer*. His periodicals continually called attention to what he considered injustice to individuals in the Mat-Su.

He billed himself as "the meanest s.o.b. in the valley," and as such he was a constant thorn in the side of the ARRC. Although he eventually lost his own property in the valley through foreclosure, he never stopped exposing them. When I eventually entered the picture, it must've been a huge relief to him.

... Chapter 13 ...

The retaliation against me was to take many forms. If I weren't looking over my shoulder literally, I was doing it figuratively. Creditors were getting very impatient and pushing for payment, especially those friends of City Hall. My bills and living expenses were a constant thing but my income no longer was.

The *Anchorage Times*, in a January 22, 1976, article called attention to the problem with the heading:

"FINANCES HAUNT EX-POLICE CHIEF"

Staff writer Ray Tyson, who had diligently followed and reported on my story for the past three months, noted that the Alaska Title Guarantee Company had recently foreclosed on my house. The article further stated that if the former owners of the house were not paid monies due them the property would be sold at public auction at 10 a.m. March 4 at the courthouse in Anchorage.

Although Tyson mentioned that I had a temporary state job, he zeroed in specifically on my former earnings. He stated that my salary had dwindled to "about $800 a month teaching business law and criminology part time at the Matanuska-Susitna Community College." Those earnings represented a *seventy per cent* decrease from my former wages as both Police Chief and college instructor, a drop that I could ill-afford. In time, even that part-time teaching position at the college would cease. Al

Okesan, the Director at the Mat-Su College, informed me short-ly thereafter that my services were no longer required at the end of that Spring semester. I had held the position for almost two years. When I ascribed that sudden termination to City Hall's direction he became flustered and attempted to deny it. I later learned from friendly City sources that he was, indeed, told to drop me from the teaching staff.

The reporter also correctly wrote that I had already incurred thousands of dollars in attorney's fees. But as Tyson commented "the ex-chief says he intends to fight on."

When Tyson questioned me further as to my reasons for doing so, I added, "You know by now that I'm not going to give up. When you're right you're right."

They were noble words at the time, but words were all I had then. Although the situation appeared particularly bleak for me, a series of events afforded me some glimmer of hope for my imme-diate future.

The first was my hire by Jim Arnold, my former boss from the Sacramento County Superior Court. In his new position as the Court Administrator for the Alaska Court System, he needed a Program Manager on a temporary basis to oversee a new project. The duties of that temporary job were to organize, hire and direct the activities of some 20 clerical personnel for a state-funded microfilming program that was scheduled to copy 5 million courthouse documents. My former boss had confidence in my ability to handle the project, and I jumped at the offer. The mere thought of being responsible for that awe-inspiring number was a challenge in itself. However, it was the duties themselves that kept me occupied and prevented me from dwelling too much on the Palmer aspects. My specific tasks entailed the training of new employees, the procurement of supplies and the maintenance of equipment that was being operated constantly. The time frame allotted for the completion of this assignment was eight weeks.

It was more than just a job to me at that time; it was a godsend. The pay was $1,441 per month, and while it was slightly less than my former Chief's salary of $1,700, it was enough to temporarily keep the wolf from my door. The job ended in mid-February with the successful completion of all documents microfilmed.

The termination of that state-funded position coincided with articles in both the *Anchorage Times* and the *Frontiersman* concerning possible state attorney general investigatory interest in my allegations. Their simultaneous interest was no coincidence but was the result of my own actions to see things done expeditiously.

My letter to the Attorney General's Office in early December, followed by two interview sessions with an investigator later that same month, produced no definitive action from that office in January. In early February 1976, I submitted copies of my letter to both the *Anchorage Times* and the *Frontiersman* to get them off dead center. The *Anchorage Times* ran a detailed two-page spread:

"VALLEY CHARGES BRING INQUIRY"

with the opening wording:

> "The State Attorney General's Office will advise the Alaska State Troopers to investigate land fraud allegations brought against City of Palmer officials by former Palmer Police Chief Nick Mangieri according to Dan Hickey Deputy Attorney General."

The *Frontiersman*, however, in an abbreviated two-page article titled:

"STATE ATTORNEY GENERAL REVIEWING MANGIERI CASE"

not surprisingly reported it differently. According to their lead-in:

> "The State Attorney General's Office is reviewing the results of interviews with ex-Police Chief Nick Mangieri but has not ordered an investigation into Mangieri's allegations of corruption among local officials according to Dan Hickey Deputy Attorney General."

Apparently Hickey was giving the widespread Anchorage public the perception that he was doing his job. Whereas the localized Palmer reader — and the politicians — were being told that the Attorney General had no intention of going forward. Hickey was to further amplify his stand when, in a telephone interview with the *Frontiersman,* he further stated:

> "Basically the situation is that the Attorney General's Office and the State Troopers are reviewing various memoranda rather than conducting an investigation."

His comment came as no surprise to me.

When Higgins saw the newspapers he called me in a highly irate state.

"What the hell are them sonsabitches trying to pull, Chief?"

"Your guess is as good as mine, Wayne," I answered him in a fed-up tone.

"They want it on a silver platter," he repeated what I had already said to him. "They don't want to do *any* of the work. They just want it all wrapped up nice and tidy. They just want you to do all the work *for them*," he said, spitting out each word.

"Yeah, I know," I said in a low voice.

I had to agree with him. I was getting sick and tired of trying to defend the state. It was becoming clearer to me that there would be little or no aggressive action on their part. However, I didn't want to discourage him completely.

"We just gotta do more, Wayne," I said assuredly, as if just that additional effort was all it would take to resolve state's inaction.

His mumbled grunt was indicative of what he thought of the suggestion. In a move to switch his discussion away from what he considered a disagreeable subject, he brought up the topic of the new lawsuit that I had considered and had been working on.

"How's it going?" he asked.

His tone was more animated because he had always liked the idea of not only suing Curtis, Maze and the City Council as individuals, but the City as well in a defamation action. That action was born as a result of the recall election.

"Good," I answered. "I think McShea is filing this week."

"That should get their damn attention," was his enthusiastic reply.

"I think so, too. Roger's a good man."

Although Bill Artus was still my attorney in my reinstatement suit against the City of Palmer, I recently retained the services of Roger McShea a middle-aged solo attorney-practitioner who was eager to take on City Hall. He had followed the stories ever since my dismissal, and when he saw and heard what those officials had done prior to, during and subsequent to the recall he was interested.

"I think you've got a good case here," was his low-key remark. "I'll handle it for you."

That comment and the subsequent actions that followed his representation were those welcomed spurts that offset the downers that I had experienced for months.

His quiet demeanor belied an incisive and methodical mind, and as a plus, he was a likeable guy. McShea was a former AAF navigator during World War II and was proud of his service background. He had a large picture of his flight crew hanging in his office. He didn't appear to have changed much from his Air Corps days. His dark thick hair was replaced by a graying mane, and a very slight paunch appeared where once a slim Captain fitted the chino uniform.

True to his word, he filed the suit on February 19 in Anchorage Superior Court. It was identified as Case No. 76-1271.

The *Anchorage Times* in its Sunday edition on February 22 headed the article:

"PAST PALMER POLICE CHIEF ASKS $7.5 MILLION IN SUIT"

Although the arithmetic was a little high as to total damages, the story was factual and comprehensive. I heard later that it also generated a lot of concern, not only in City Hall, but among Palmer residents as well.

The fairly lengthy article reported:

"A former Palmer police chief is asking $7.5 million in a defamation suit naming the Mayor, City Council and City Manager.

"The suit also asks that recall election results against

the government officials be set aside and a new election ordered. No one was recalled after the vote Jan 20.

"In a suit filed Thursday in Anchorage Superior Court, Nicholas Mangieri Jr., fired from his job in November, alleges malicious statements were made about him in a sample ballot for a recall election scheduled in January for City Manager William Curtis, Mayor Jack Maze, and Councilmen Dave Ingalls, Pete Pedersen, Willard Johnson, James Ekstedt, Arlyn Hanson and John Dolenc.

"Curtis said yesterday, 'I haven't thought about it but it seems ridiculous. I suppose we'll talk to the City Attorney next week.'

"Mangieri claims in his suit, filed by Roger McShea of Anchorage, that he was fired without cause and given inadequate opportunity to appeal his case before the City Council.

"Before and after the firing date Nov. 12, the Mayor, Manager and Council met to discuss the case in secret, the suit said, 'as a result of such meetings the Council voted to confirm plaintiff's discharge as Palmer Police Chief.

"The suit alleges the recall petition, 'contained malicious falsehoods concerning the plaintiff's integrity and truthfulness, his participation in the circulation of the recall petition and his qualifications to perform the duties of Police Chief for the City of Palmer.

"Said allegations were deliberately and calculatingly written and published by the individual defendants for the purpose of libeling and defaming the reputation of plaintiff,' the suit said.

"Mangieri maintains the libelous matter in the sample ballots include:

- That the recall election was a result of a personal vendetta by an ex-Police Chief.
- That he wanted to cause as much trouble as possible because of personal spite.
- That he threatened to 'tear the town wide open' if he were not rehired.
- That without regard for the community he tried to

spread discontent and dissatisfaction through misinformation and untrue charges all for his own personal benefit.

■ That he lied in his application for the job of Police Chief.

■ That he disregarded financial guidelines set out for him while police chief.

■ Innuendo that he tried to hire for his own personal gain while he was police chief and ...

■ Innuendo that he had incited public opinion against the City government in Palmer for self-gain.

"Mangieri asked $250,000 from the City of Palmer, $200,000 from Mayor Maze, a total of $2.1 million from the six Councilmen, $200,000 from Curtis and $500,000 in punitive damages and attorney's fees."

The *Frontiersman,* not to be out-reported by the *Anchorage Times,* wrote a substantially shorter article covering merely the filing of the lawsuit itself and the names of the City defendants and the amount of the damages. They did not cite nor comment on any of the grounds contained in the defamation action. City and Borough residents, however, were not to be denied the latest bit of news concerning my on-going battle with "Curtis and Company" simply because there was a lack of local newspaper coverage. The word coming out of Palmer was "What if he wins; where's the money coming from?"

Simultaneously, there was another plus action on my behalf. Jim Vickaryous, the local dairy farmer with whom I had spoken earlier about the activities of the ARRC, sent me a copy of a letter that he had mailed to Dan Hickey, the State Deputy Attorney General in Juneau. Perhaps the appearance of the recent articles in the newspapers concerning only lukewarm interest by the Attorney General's Office prompted that involvement.

The following cautious letter that Vickaryous forwarded to Hickey was dated February 23, 1976:

"Dear Mr. Hickey:

"I am a farm owner and life-time resident of the

Matanuska Valley that is interested in cleaning up graft.

"Mr. Mangieri's allegations of wrong-doing here have some sound basis in fact.

"I implore you to not consider these things lightly nor to allow 'pressure from the top' affect your decision in sending a charge to a Grand Jury.

"If such a Grand Jury were formed, I would be willing to bring forth what I deem valid documentation of corruption of the highest order and all the more vile because it has forced good people from our Valley at great financial loss, prevented new farmers from coming and allowed a few who control the farm lending agencies to profit in their side businesses of real estate appraisal and speculation.

"We were recently sued for foreclosure and the word put out that 'they will be pushed into bankruptcy and out of here.' We had the courage and resources to fight it. In getting a settlement agreement we were forced to sign a 'release from liability' to a loan manager whom we had discovered 'slandering our title' to property up for sale to solve our debt problems. He had got to our buyer, who got scared and forfeited $5,000 earnest money; but left us without a sale that we were depending upon to meet the needs of our complaining creditors.

"There is a lot more. But I will not bring these things forth except under the protection of the secrecy of a Grand Jury. We are still not out of the woods financially, and this little group can still wipe us out. I trust this letter will be held in confidence."

I fully expected some type of immediate follow-up as a result of Vickaryous' confirmatory letter.

It didn't happen.

Regrettably, he was *never* brought before the Grand Jury to testify as to what he knew. He was never given the opportunity to offer his "valid documentation of corruption" to anyone from Hickey's office.

Another unexpected bit of temporary uplifting news was a

slight reprieve in the foreclosure action on my house. The date that the foreclosure sale was to be held at the main door of the Boney Memorial Courthouse was changed from March 4 at 10 a.m. to April 6 at 10 a.m. It was the same courthouse that I had worked in both the Alaska Public Defender's Office and in the temporary state-funded position.

Although it was only a minor relief, any delay was welcomed. The trauma of being dispossessed from one's own house had not yet hit home. I could not I permit myself to dwell on neither it, nor on the anticipated emotional upheaval to my family afterward.

About this time, I also learned that my oldest daughter was making plans to move out immediately following graduation from high school in May. The news was met with mixed emotions. I was glad that she immediately found a job with the Criminal Affairs Division in the Warrants Section located in the courthouse, yet sad that I was also losing her so soon. All would miss her. The stress of the upcoming forced move on the other children was not readily apparent as yet. They all seemed to accept the fact that we were going to lose the house. However, what was to be even more upsetting to them was to be the loss of their horses. Initially, they managed to contain their disappointment. Perhaps because they knew of the underlying reasons for my abrupt dismissal and perhaps because of the cohesiveness of the family itself.

Events from that period onward moved rapidly — downward.

In April, the foreclosure sale was held on the steps of the courthouse, as customarily required.

In May, as a result of the sale, I received a *Notice to Quit* from the attorneys representing the owners of the property. It stated that I had to vacate the premises "on June 27, 1976, at midnight."

Also in that same month I was on another downhill slide. I received a copy of an extensive memo from the Attorney General's Office directed to the Director of the State Troopers Colonel James Wellington.

Anxiously I quickly scanned its content, and when I did, I couldn't believe what he had written.

The Anchorage Police Academy (1975). Participants are from several area police departments. The author, Nick Mangieri, is in the middle row, far left.

Mounted officers for the Pioneer Days Parade, from left, Bob Lemoine, Wayne Higgins, Chuck Hessler and the author, Nick Mangieri.

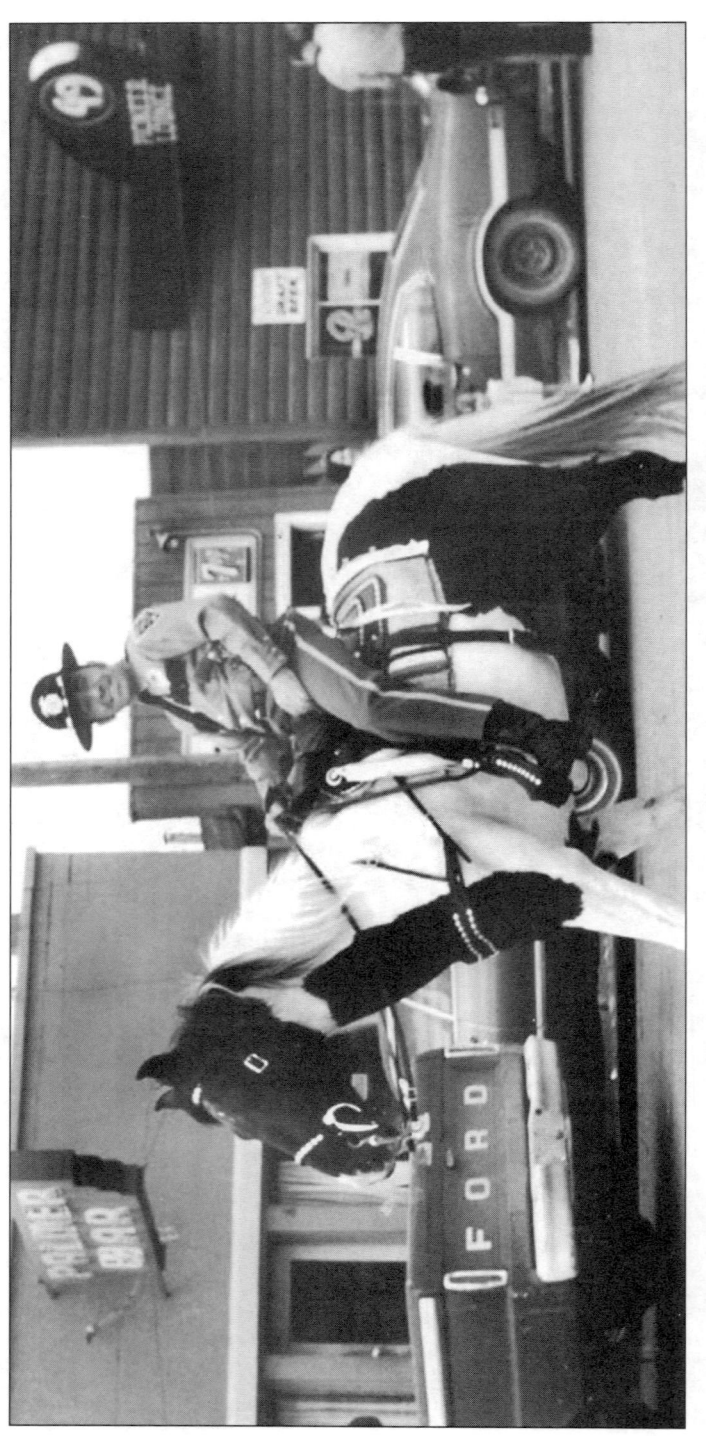

The author, Nick Mangieri, on his horse, Chato, during the Pioneer Days Parade.

The author, Nick Mangieri.

... Chapter 14 ...

The nine-page memorandum that the Deputy Attorney General forwarded to the head of the Alaska State Troopers in Anchorage was a whitewash.

Although he briefly mentioned the Alaska Rural Rehabilitation Corporation at the end of his letter, there appeared little interest in — or even knowledge of — my disclosures. He merely described it as a "farm loan agency" that I alleged had "engaged in restrictive and repressive lending procedures." He further claimed ignorance of its present existence, a corporation that had been in operation for 40 years. A full *five months* after my initial complaints to his office, he stated that "we are presently trying to determine the precise legal status of the ARRC." He further diluted his reference to them and to any possible criminality on their part by stating that he also was trying to determine the "precise nature of the alleged criminal violations that Mr. Mangieri intimates surround its operation and whether any of these allegations are susceptible to further investigation."

As taken aback as I was about his apparent lack of interest in the ARRC despite my own allegations and those of others over the years, the balance of his letter proved even more unbelievable. In that memo, he set forth what he termed as an "extensive review" of ten of my allegations that then were followed by his respective analyses of each one. He also stated in his memorandum that his decisions resulted from prior joint discussions with Anchorage

District Attorney Joseph D. Balfe. I never knew whether Balfe actually played a major role in the "review" process or whether the
information was just brought to his attention because he was in
charge. I never saw any individual memos from Balfe to anyone,
and I never received feedback from his Chief Investigator Ernie
Beaucamp. Although I wasn't a hundred percent sure they were
sympathetic to me, I didn't feel they had been underhanded with me
either. I felt I could trust them. That feeling was primarily based
upon my prior association with both of them before I took over as
Chief, while I was still in office and even after my dismissal.
However my perceptions could have been wrong.

Although the memo was from Attorney General Avrum M.
Gross to Colonel Wellington, Gross had not signed off or initialed
it to indicate that he had seen it and concurred in its content. I did-
n't know whether that oversight was intentional or accidental, but
I did not pursue it. Politics being as they were, the lack of Gross'
initials could very well indicate to all and sundry that he had
never seen nor authorized the memo should future questions
arise. The only flourished initials were "D.H.," above the writer's
name, the initials of Daniel W. Hickey.

Early in Hickey's protracted epistle he cited an "exhaustive
review" of the "following documents and supporting materials"
in his showcase attempt to acknowledge my issues. However,
once raised he then promptly disregarded them:

(a) the "minutes" of an October 11, 1971, meeting of the
City Council of the City of Palmer;

(b) a letter dated November 19, 1975, addressed to the
Foreman of the Grand Jury Alaska Court System
Anchorage, Alaska;

(c) a handwritten statement dated November 24, 1975, of
Christine L. Boyle Chief Dispatcher and Secretary to
Chief Mangieri:

(d) a handwritten, five-page statement dated November
25, 1975, of Nick J. Mangieri;

(e) a letter dated November 25, 1975, addressed to Mr.
Nick Mangieri from the Foreman of the Grand Jury;

(f) a handwritten, undated statement of David W.
Higgins;

(g) a handwritten, undated statement of Officer Robert J. Lemoine Palmer Police Department;

(h) a memorandum dated December 1, 1975, from Chief Investigator — Major Crime Unit — John H. Lucking to his immediate supervisor Lt. U. Dean Bivens Commander-Criminal Investigation Bureau Alaska State Troopers summarizing allegations related by Mr. Mangieri;

(i) a handwritten, 11-page letter dated December 4, 1975, addressed to Attorney General Avrum M. Gross, attention Deputy Attorney General Dan Hickey, from Mr. Mangieri setting forth the preponderance of the allegations that will be addressed below;

(j) a nine-page transcript of a statement given by Mr. Mangieri to Investigator Joseph D. Hoffbeck at my request on December 9, 1975;

(k) a three-page transcript of a further statement given by Mr. Mangieri to Investigator Hoffbeck on December 24, 1975;

(l) a 13-page copy of an Affidavit of William Curtis;

(m) a copy of Notice of Special Election dated December 24, 1975, described therein as a special recall election for the City of Palmer to be held on January 20, 1976;

(n) a copy of Sample Ballot — City of Palmer — Special Election Tuesday January 20, 1976; and

(o) a copy of the Municipal Charter of the City of Palmer Alaska.

The fifteen "documents and materials" referenced above by Hickey presumably "set the stage" for his ten selected allegations.

His methodology then included a comparative analysis of each one — followed by his reasons why they should be justifiably shot down.

Hickey's carefully prepared list of my complaints were followed by his own unique analyses that conveniently left out points I had raised.

It also failed to address any issues that would muddy the

water and confound his partial presentation of the facts:

Allegation No. 1: Violation of AS 11.60.340 —
Conspiracy Against the Rights of Individuals:
Mr. Mangieri alleges that he was unjustly terminated without cause as Chief of Police of Palmer by his immediate supervisor City Manager William Curtis.

He further alleges that he and others were denied an adequate opportunity to be heard at a City Council meeting, where the subject of his termination had been placed on the agenda, in that he and another former police officer were permitted to speak for only 10 minutes each, that others who were there to speak on his behalf were not permitted to do so, that an unspecified number of citizens who desired access to the meeting were denied entry because of fire code restrictions and that the City Council should have arranged to have the meeting held at a place that would accommodate more individuals because they were on notice that the meeting would require a larger than usual space.

Allegation No. 2: *Prior Felony conviction of Mayor:*
Mr. Mangieri alleges that the Mayor of Palmer was previously convicted of the offense of embezzlement approximately 20 years ago, that he is therefore disqualified to vote under AS 15.05.030 and therefore to hold public office, yet does both.

Allegation No. 3: *Residence of City Manager:*
Mr. Mangieri alleges that the City Manager of Palmer William Curtis is not a resident of the City of Palmer but rather resides one-fifth of a mile beyond the City limits in violation of Chapter V section 5.4 (a) of the Municipal Charter.

Allegation No. 4: *Abolishment of City Clerk Positions:*
Mr. Mangieri alleges that in April of 1971 the position of City Clerk was abolished and combined with that of City Manager by the actions of the City Manager, the

City Attorney and the City Council in violation of the Municipal Charter.

Allegation No. 5: *Special Meetings by City Council:*
Mr. Mangieri alleges that members of the City Council of Palmer, including the Mayor, routinely have breakfast together once a week at a local restaurant in Palmer where City business is discussed, that the City Manager and City Attorney also attend these meetings, that public notice of these meetings is not published in the newspaper although one or two members of the public attend these meetings "because they happen to know of it" and that he has been told that the City pays for the meals and will sometimes expend City monies for the meals of persons who are not Council Members.

Allegation No. 6: *Arbitrary Firing of City Employees:*
Mr. Mangieri alleges that numerous City employees have been arbitrarily fired or pressured into leaving City employment when they do not comply with the wishes of the City Manager and the City Council.
While he does not indicate any employees that have been terminated other than himself and Officer Higgins he has submitted handwritten statements from Officer Robert J. Lemoine and Police Dispatcher Christine L. Boyle which state that they have been informed by the City Manager "to mind their own business" in the matter of Mr. Mangieri's firing or they could jeopardize their own jobs.

Allegation No. 7: *Preferential Awarding of City Bids:*
Mr. Mangieri alleges that there have been preferential awarding of bids for work done in both the City of Palmer and "for the Borough as well."
As an example of this practice, he alleges that the City retained a private firm to perform street maintenance without first submitting such work for bid as required by the Municipal Charter and by City ordinances.

Frozen Shield

Allegation No. 8: *Conflict of Interest:*

Mr. Mangieri alleges that "the politicians in City Hall are corrupt" and that "this condition is one of long standing, and had of necessity, 'to come to a head' during his tenure as Police Chief." Specifically he alleges that the present City Manager was also the City Manager on a prior occasion from 1970 to 1973/74, and during that time he was head of the Site Selection Committee for the Palmer High School, in which capacity he was solely instrumental in having the school placed in its present location, which is in proximity to his own property, and which, according to Mr. Mangieri, was not the most desirable or economic site available.

Mr. Mangieri also alleges that collusion and one or more conflicts of interest were involved in the selection of property for the Industrial Park located in the Palmer area around 1972. He alleges that the site selected for the Industrial Park was not a desirable nor a practical site but was nevertheless purchased jointly by the City of Palmer through City bonds and through Borough bonds in conjunction with the Alaska Bank of Commerce and Alaska Mutual Savings and Loan, and that at least a portion of this property was purchased from an undisclosed influential member of the community who was on one of the Board of Directors of the two participating banks. He further alleges that prior to the purchase of this property it had been appraised at approximately $1,100 per acre but was subsequently sold for $3,000 per acre. He inquires "why the unnecessary profit?"

As a third specific allegation of conflict of interest, Mr. Mangieri alleges that the airport property in Palmer is of a size the City of Palmer does not need, is "a sore area among the residents of the City" and is "also an expensive boondoggle."

Allegation No. 9: Violation of AS 11.60.340 — *Cruelty to Animals:*

Mr. Mangieri alleges that the Acting Chief of Police and former head of the City of Palmer Public Works

Department beat dogs to death in the dog pound instead of shooting them or employing some more humane means in their destruction. Such incidents allegedly occurred a considerable period of time before they were first reported and were allegedly brought to Mr. Mangieri's attention by a former police officer in the summer of 1975 who was subsequently "fired for incompetence" by Mr. Mangieri when he was Chief of Police.

Allegation No. 10: *Criminal Libel:*
Mr. Mangieri believes that he has been criminally libeled by the Mayor, members of the Palmer City Council and by the City Manager through statements contained on both the Notice of Special Election and the Sample Ballot for the Special Election as well as through statements that have appeared in various newspaper articles commenting on his discharge as Chief of Police, on his efforts to recall the Mayor and City Council through a Special Election and on a number of the allegations set out above.

After I read Hickey's incomplete presentation of the facts I decided to do my own in depth analysis of his "extensive review." His presentation followed a similar pattern used by all who wished to avoid discussing the facts — just ignore them.

As I reviewed Hickey's first analysis of *Allegation No. 1*, I noted that he sidestepped the conspiracy issue completely by quickly brushing it aside and then stating a conclusion:

"Nor is there any requirement under Alaska law which addresses itself to the particular form or size of facilities that must be made available for participation in public hearings."

He totally ignored any legal issues of due process that had been agreed upon in advance with my attorney. He never considered nor pursued the assertion that other larger spaces were available nor that the Fire Chief himself raised the issue of moving elsewhere. He also failed to investigate the frustrated actions of the police officers themselves who not only also requested that the meeting be relocated but had contacted the local magistrate with their concerns. Furthermore, he never raised the legal issue that Palmer's Municipal Charter had a stated requirement that "the public shall have a reasonable opportunity to be heard."

The deliberate preclusion of thirty to forty percent of the public from being heard before a public meeting would appear to bear out my contention that a planned conspiracy had been formulated by all those officials as a result of prior meetings and agreements.

In addressing the limited speaking time that Higgins and I were allotted to respond, and in denying our witnesses (including our attorney) the opportunity to speak out in our behalf, Hickey's "analytical" statement was even more ludicrous:

"Furthermore, public comment was clearly allowed even if restricted by time limitations imposed by the Council."

The rigid censorship decreed by the City Council in advance would hardly indicate that "public comment was *clearly allowed.*"

In his analysis following *Allegation No. 2*, he noted that an Attorney General's opinion permitted a felon to run for public office. He did *not* however address the issue of the Mayor being able to vote as a convicted felon. That condition would only be permitted after his application to have his civil rights restored would be approved by the Governor.

In his respective analyses of *Allegation Numbers 3* and *4* of the City Manager's nonresidency and of the summary abolishment of the former City Clerk's position, Hickey's brief categorical statement of each allegation was that "no criminal statute of the State of Alaska is applicable."

As accurate as his pronouncement may have been, he totally ignored who or what entity would prosecute under the provisions of the Municipal Charter. He not only was aware — but was specifically informed — that the City Attorney was personally involved and would hardly bring charges against himself.

I found it hard to believe that with the inability of a municipality to investigate or prosecute City violations, that the state would not step to do so. To constantly raise the issue that "no criminal statute of the State of Alaska is applicable" seemed like a complete cop-out of the situation. I felt that other state jurisdictions in the *"lower 48"* would not back off when faced with the same complaints that I had offered.

That same hands-off policy as it related to possible state

prosecution of special meetings by the City Council that deliberately precluded the public was also cited in his next analysis.

As to the arbitrary firing of City employees and intimidation of other employees, Hickey again turned a blind eye when he disregarded the elements of AS 11.60.340 that dealt with conspiracy. He glossed over the statements of two of my former coerced employees and chose merely to discuss civil remedies in lieu of the criminal aspects.

In the analyses that followed *Allegations Numbered 7* and *8,* concerning preferential awarding of bids and conflict of interest, Hickey again took the easy way out by citing lack of specific evidence offered. He never once suggested that an in-depth investigation might be in order especially in light of the amount of violations that I had uncovered. Nor did he ever suggest that the presentation of any of that information to a Grand Jury would be done. It was their prerogative to consider a deeper probe into what appeared to be ongoing corruption.

However it was Hickey's off-the-wall defensive analysis of the dogs being beaten to death that convinced me that little or nothing would ever be done to investigate any allegations of misconduct in the City of Palmer — or for that matter in the Matanuska-Susitna Borough.

He opened his analytical statement by saying that "assuming" the dogs' beatings occurred, the event "took place quite some time before they were first reported" and could therefore "not be prosecuted because of the delay in bringing them to our attention."

In spite of Hickey's attempt to down play the situation, he was well aware that the event occurred at the end of August 1975, and that I was not advised of it until I read about in the local newspaper (a copy of which I initially forwarded to him with my December letter). Further, the article only identified the perpetrator as "a City official." I didn't learn his identity until *after* my ouster in November 1975. In addition, his comment that "due process requirements prohibit the initiation of any prosecution where there has been unreasonable purposeful and unnecessary delay between an alleged criminal act and the initiation of formal charges," was clearly inappropriate.

It wasn't so much the total inaccuracy of his statement as it was his next personal derogatory remark:

"One is, of course, forced to wonder why Mr. Mangieri waited until after he was terminated as Chief of Police to do anything about or bring to the attention of other law enforcement authorities incidents reported to him while he was Chief of Police, which he believed to constitute violations of state law."

Hickey was equally cognizant that the information was first disclosed at a public City Council meeting prior to its appearance in the City newspaper the following morning. Not only were ASPCA members in attendance, having been alerted by the former police lieutenant, but the City Manager was there also. He personally announced that he would look into the situation. Further, State Troopers operated out of the town as well and presumably read the local papers. They could have as easily initiated criminal charges against the individual who was subsequently identified as the Public Works Director inasmuch as the City terminated me eight weeks later. Therefore for Hickey to "wonder" about the incident would not appear to hold water.

His final comment dealt with a faulty and incomplete analysis of *Allegation No. 10* concerning the possibility of criminal libel charges. He again quickly sought to dispel the validity of that complaint by stating:

> "There are a line of United States Supreme Court cases commencing with *New York Times v. Sullivan* 376 U.S. 254 (1964) which make it absolutely clear that an individual who holds himself out as a public figure is properly subject to comments and opinions concerning his abilities and general reputation."

Hickey's explanation that because I was a public figure it was "absolutely clear" that I had no recourse to an attack of my reputation was apparently done to support his contentions. What he failed to cite however was an equally long line of cases in which the use of malice in a libel case would vitiate any alleged privileged defenses on the part of those who initiated an attack on a public figure.

In view of my constant reiteration of the maliciousness of the Palmer officials, Hickey was well apprised of their ongoing actions against me and in their unwavering propensity to malign any individual who crossed them. With a minimum of delving into their conduct, Hickey could have uncovered their *modus operandi* and easily could have pursued them for criminal libel — had he wanted to.

His closing remark, however, was chosen very carefully. "Beyond the possibility of additional investigation that might follow as a result of Mr. Beaucamp's present investigative efforts, we perceive no additional avenues of investigation at this time."

My response to the copy of that letter was immediate and unrestrained because of my total disillusionment with the Alaska criminal justice system. Although I tried to contain my anger, my frustration and sarcasm were not easy to hide, nor did I try to be diplomatic in my letter to him of June 2, 1976:

"Dear Mr. Hickey:
"I have thoroughly reviewed your extensive memo to Colonel Wellington of the Alaska State Troopers in your response to my allegations of both City and state criminal violations against Palmer City Officials. Needless to say, your reluctance to prosecute leaves me more than a little disappointed in the criminal justice system in Alaska, especially as it applies to small communities. I was of the belief that I offered you substantial probable cause to conduct your own in-depth investigation of the state violations; I was of the belief that if the City would not prosecute its own, then it was the duty of the state to step in and do so.

"Perhaps my expectations of aggressive law enforcement are inappropriate to a rural "frontier state" and are more applicable to other "outside" urban communities. Perhaps my condemnation of public officials is too harsh and unrealistic in our present society and I should learn to be more tolerant of their actions. Whatever the case, it is not my intention to be embroiled in controversy with your office as I have always been of the opinion that prosecutors and police have a common goal and should therefore work hand-in-hand toward that end. However I am compelled to "set the record straight,", as it appears that there are some elements missing from your memo and that there are other elements that are in need of clarification. Briefly:

1. In regard to my allegation of preferential awarding of bids I did not, as you stated in your memo, "allege or offer incidents of particular acts of wrongdoing on the part of City Officials ..." because I was of the belief that specifics would be requested of me at a future session.

2. There was no delay in my report that a "City Official beat dogs to death." I did not know, for certain, his identity until after my ouster as Police Chief in early November because of information given me by an ex-employee subsequent to my firing. That incident was reported at one of my interview sessions during mid-November, and it was also mentioned in a letter to your office dated December 4, 1975.

3. The names of individuals involved in land transactions between the City of Palmer and the Industrial Park and the airport were not solicited of me nor offered by me during my interviews because these preliminary sessions were merely intended to be highlights of general information and were not meant to be detailed charges. Again, it was my impression, and that of the interviewer, that specific information was to have been sought at future sessions after your review of the preliminary information. Please note, however, that in my December 4th letter I did name an individual, who could and would undoubtedly confirm improprieties in the selection of the new Palmer High School site.

4. Many of the "special meetings" held by the City Manager and the City Council did not conform to the criteria set forth for acceptable "executive sessions" outlined in A.S. 44.62.310 and would therefore appear to be in violation of Alaska Statues Section 29.23.580 *Meetings Public*. As you undoubtedly know, this section applies to home rule municipalities of which the City of Palmer is one.

5. A.S. 29.23.555 *Conflict of Interests* applies to the City of Palmer because it does not have its own conflict of interests ordinance. As you know, its provisions provide that "an officer or employee shall disqualify himself from participation in any official action in which he has a substantial interest." I believe minimal investigation by your staff could easily uncover possible conflicts of interest, especially since there has been such an extensive acquisition of certain properties by the City of Palmer over the past few years by the same group in City Hall. I have only very recently become aware of some members of the City Council who own property adjacent to the recently acquired right-of-way to the new Palmer High School. Names and locations of the property are naturally available upon request.

"It is certainly not my intention to cause your office any unnecessary embarrassment, but when there is skepticism attached to my allegations, and I know otherwise, I must respond accordingly. I am not in the habit of raising frivolous charges without having substantial bases upon which to rely. My experience and education, I believe, might be classified as fairly responsible, and it is from this background that I operated as Chief of Police, and it is from this background that even as a former Chief I attempted to uncover and expose wrongdoing. For your edification, enclosed find my resume together with past letters of recommendation from various sources. In summary, you will note that I have:

a. Six years of police and investigative experience;
b. 12 years administrative experience;
c. 11 years of college (nine years of study at the undergraduate graduate and law school levels and two years as an instructor at the University of Alaska in the fields of Criminal Law Business Law and Torts).

"I have offered my services to your office in the past as a Special Investigator to probe into my allegations of graft and corruption. I do so again. I believe that my background has indicated that it is entirely possible and probable that I could and would be objective in any investigation that I pursue. I also believe that "facts are facts" and will speak for themselves.

"In closing, my appreciation and the appreciation of many citizens of the valley, are extended to your office for any investigation of State violations that you are presently pursuing or will initiate as a result of this letter. However any violations of the Municipal Charter cannot go unnoticed and must not go unprosecuted. They are criminal in nature and should be treated accordingly. Section 1.9 of Palmer's Municipal Charter, *Penalties for Violations,* provides that: "violations of this charter the code or any ordinance of the City may be punished by a fine which shall not exceed Three Hundred Dollars or imprisonment for not more than thirty days or by both such fine and imprisonment."

"Therefore, if the City of Palmer will not prosecute itself and the State of Alaska cannot prosecute, then it is my opinion that a strong unbiased Special Prosecutor *must* be appointed to investigate. and where appropriate, prosecute those City Officials who have violated City ordinances. This approach is not unique, as this procedure is followed in other states and the results are most effective. City Officials cannot hold themselves above the law and must be held to the same standards as those they expect of the public.

"I am sure that you are aware of the deterrent effect that this law-oriented procedure would have on other public officials in the many communities throughout Alaska, a procedure that is long overdue in the interest of public welfare and one that would give your office the much needed control over law and order in a burgeoning state that it must have.

"Sincerely,
Nick J. Mangieri
Former Chief of Police
Palmer, Alaska"

I forwarded three copies to the same individuals that had received Hickey's original letter: Attorney General Avrum Gross, Department of Public Safety Commissioner Richard L. Burton and District Attorney Joseph D. Balfe.

I also gave the *Anchorage Times* a copy of my letter, and within the week they ran my rebuttal under the heading:

"MANGIERI OFFERS SERVICES."

In it, they called attention to the fact that I had offered my services to the State Attorney General's Office as a special investigator to probe land fraud allegations. The balance of the article was, as usual, comprehensive and accurate.

Unfortunately, however, it brought no sudden change of heart nor immediate results form the capital. I realized that I wasn't endearing myself to the Juneau politicians with my constant barrage of publicity, but I didn't particularly care at that point. In time I would hear from them again.

The rest of the month of June didn't get any better.

The Matanuska-Susitna Borough issued a *Notice of Foreclosure* against delinquent taxpayers that appeared in the June 10 issue of the *Frontiersman*. In that six-page edition, there were approximately 1,500 names that were delinquent for real estate property taxes for the year 1975. My name, of course, appeared on that list as well. However, by that time it didn't really matter. Two weeks later I was forced to vacate the house in accordance with the *Notice to Quit* that I had received the month before.

It was hard to leave what had been home for two years. As rustic as the old homestead had been, it was livable. Even harder to leave behind was the 40-acre property with its fairly secluded pasture and large barn — and of course — the horses. They were all sold to farmers in the area, but because horses in Alaska are not in great demand, they didn't fetch much on the open market.

The girls tearfully said goodbye to their equine friends, and even my son, who was not as prone to sentimentality as his sisters, found it hard to part with his as well. They had ridden them for the past four years, two years in Alaska and the two years before in the Sierra Madre Mountains in Northern California. Our former home outside of Nevada City was horse country, where feeding and taking care of their mounts was a way of life.

As I patted my own black and white pinto, Chato, before he was being led off I heard the kids yelling after their own animals.

"Bye, Shilo," my oldest called out.

"Bye, Cheyenne," my son said.

"Bye bye, Apache," the two younger girls cried in unison.

Red-eyed, they looked at the last horse to go, Shawnee. It had been my wife's for the past five years and had been with the family the longest. She patted him longingly before he, too, left the area.

"We gotta go," I said, trying to defuse the situation. However, before we got into the pickup truck packed with personal belongings that we had to store in a friend's barn, we all took one last look at the place.

Higgins, who was there to help, looked as crestfallen as the rest of the family.

"I'm sorry, Chief. I'm real sorry it had to end this way," he said slowly.

"It's not over, Wayne. I'll get the bastards yet."

He was silent as he nodded and climbed into the truck. I had rented it to take our furniture to a small house in Anchorage.

"I'll see you at McCarthy's," he said as he drove off.

John McCarthy, father of one of my former dispatchers, Debby Stone, had volunteered to store many of my personal effects that I couldn't take with me.

"I'll get them out as soon as I can, John," I said after I had unloaded them in one of his sheds.

"No rush. They're not in the way," he replied quietly.

McCarthy was one of the few who couldn't do enough to help. It was his younger daughter who was killed by a drunken driver a year earlier. Although the driver was located and apprehended within a short time, McCarthy doubly appreciated all the efforts in tracking that individual down. Regrettably, I was never able to retrieve any of those possessions that were left behind. Months later I had to give him reluctant permission to get rid of them so that he could use his own storage space.

As sad as the trek was from Palmer to Anchorage that day and as low a point as my own spirits had reached, events in the upcoming months would prove to be fruitful and encouraging.

Not only would my civil cases be a thorn in the side of the Palmer officials but also the discovery process was giving me even more information than I had possessed initially. In addition, I would learn greater details — some startling — of events in the valley that had preceded my takeover of the Police Department.

... Chapter 15 ...

In early June, just before my forced relocation to Anchorage, the *Anchorage Times* carried two articles. Their upbeat coverage was a welcomed respite from all that had recently happened.

The first article, a shorter one under the general headline:

"CANDIDATES"

showed a smiling picture of me as one of four hopefuls who had filed for the upcoming November elections. Above the optimistic photo was the heavily captioned:

"LAW FACES CHALLENGE"

Below it was the brief notation,

"RUNS FOR SENATE"

I had decided to announce my candidacy after supportive Palmer citizens encouraged me to do so. I did, however, face an impediment.

The article called attention to the fact that although I had not lived in Alaska long enough to be a state senator, I had filed as a Republican for the District D seat anyway. The paper also noted that the district took in the "Matanuska-Susitna Valley and the

Kenai area," which was a large area south of the valley. It also mentioned that I had been fired as Police Chief of Palmer and that I had led an unsuccessful recall election against the Mayor and the City Council. It added that I had "sued City Officials for $1.5 million, claiming libel and slander during the recall election early this year."

The reference to this lower amount was an accurate one compared to the last time that the amount for damages appeared in their February edition, that of $7.5 million. At that time, however, I liked to believe it was a Freudian slip instead of just an honest mistake. In any case, it was that initial figure that really alarmed Palmer residents, not that they were any happier with the reduced figure of $1.5 million.

The article explained my problem in my filing for the state senatorial seat:

"Mangieri has lived in Alaska two years and three months. State law requires a minimum residency of three years for legislative offices."

When questioned about how I would resolve that residency problem, I confidently answered, "I decided to challenge the three-year residency requirement, I believe it is unconstitutional."

The paper further noted that I would "campaign on law and order issues."

I also mentioned that "my primary concern is graft and corruption in local government."

In addition, the article cited the fact that "Mangieri said he was a Democrat but switched parties because of the upcoming election. Sen. Jay Kertula, who holds the office now, is a Democrat."

Although I had neither the time nor money to pursue the constitutional residency issues, it was a campaign I really could have sunk my teeth into and enjoyed.

Many of my former supporters in the valley and in Anchorage relished the idea of my running against State Senator Jay Kertula, the individual whose name continually popped up in my investigations. However, it was not meant to be. Neither fate nor politics dampened my ardor for a long time afterward, whenever I thought about it, because I knew that I would have been a formidable opponent.

Even the *Susitna Valley Chronicle*, a weekly newspaper published in Talkeetna by the former reporter to the *Frontiersman*, Slim Randles, and his wife, Pam, took note of my filing for the Senatorial seat. The paper colorfully identified me as "the feisty ex-Police Chief from Palmer."

The second article that appeared a few days later in the *Anchorage Times* was, of course, my offer to the State Attorney General's Office as a special investigator. It not only reported on their decision "not to investigate (my) charges" but noted further that, "Hickey was unavailable to comment on Mangieri's offer."

As unpleasant as it was to move to Anchorage, the City had certain definite advantages that didn't exist in Palmer. These advantages were especially pronounced in both of my pending lawsuits. Not only was I close to both of my attorneys, but at all hours, the Courthouse law library was available to me so that I could conduct my own legal research.

My first civil lawsuit, No. 75-8520, dealt with the reinstatement and was still being handled by Artus. However, before the summer was out, that representation would change. My second civil suit, No. 76-1271E, the libel action, was being handled by Roger McShea. For financial reasons, I decided to become directly involved in all the legal aspects of my former case.

As the days wore on, the benefits of the close proximity of the courthouse and of McShea's accessibility became immeasurable. Although I had general knowledge, from my law school days, on how to research particular topics or to locate pertinent law cases relevant to my reinstatement suit, it was the myriad details in the technical aspects of how and what to file that I needed help with. In particular, how and when were motions filed, memoranda, replies, oppositions, certificates of service, interrogatories, and the taking of depositions, to name but a few. McShea was always there for guidance or ready to answer a question about how I should proceed.

I immersed myself. The more I did, the more I realized I could do. It was true that the *content* of my court papers didn't contain the legal niceties that are prevalent in most — if not all — court documents, but the *format* was correct. I was not interested in polite legal bantering, but in results. My methods and terminology, although crude, were acceptable to the court. Even more important, it constantly grated not only on the defendants in the case but more specifically on their counsel, City Attorney Burton Biss.

I filed my first MEMORANDUM in late September.

That initial action was in direct response to City Attorney Biss' attempt to have my case dismissed when he filed a MOTION FOR SUMMARY JUDGMENT. Because I could no longer afford to retain the services of Bill Artus on my case, he withdrew on September 14. Although it might have been different had he been a sole practitioner, he was working for a large firm and was unable to carry me any longer.

That official reply I considered to be my first masterpiece acting as my own attorney — however amateurish it might have appeared at the time — and I was justifiably proud of its content.

My MEMORANDUM appears in its entirety:

IN THE SUPERIOR COURT
OF THE STATE OF ALASKA
THIRD JUDICIAL DISTRICT
NICK J. MANGIERI,
Plaintiff,
vs.
WILLIAM CURTIS in his capacity
as CITY MANAGER for PALMER,
ALASKA; THE CITY OF PALMER,
ALASKA,
Defendants.

No. 75-8520
MEMORANDUM OF PLAINTIFF IN SUPPORT OF
PLAINTIFF'S OPPOSITION TO DEFENDANTS'
MOTION FOR SUMMARY JUDGMENT

The main thrust of defendants' MOTION FOR A SUMMARY JUDGMENT is that because plaintiff was in his capacity as Chief of Police of the City of Palmer, a "department head," he was not entitled to any of the customary safeguards accorded any other City employees. He was not "protected from arbitrary discharge" as the Municipal Charter so magnanimously proclaims. He was not entitled to avail himself of the detailed conditions appearing under the sections entitled *Employee Appeal* and *Appeal Procedure*, so dutifully delineated under the Personnel Regulations governing City of Palmer employees. For that matter, neither could plaintiff place himself under the protective cloak of management. As defendants so aptly noted in their MOTION FOR SUMMARY JUDGMENT:

The Council may remove the City Manager, the City Attorney and members of boards, regardless of term of office. The person so removed from office shall have the *right to a public hearing before the Council concerning the cause for his removal.*" (Emphasis supplied.)

It is not equitable, nor is there any logical reason to exclude plaintiff from the traditional and constitutional safeguards of capriciousness.

Defendants, on the one hand, are seeking to exclude plaintiff from rights and benefits due "employees" because he is a department head. However, on the other hand, they are seeking to include him in the employee category. Defendants, in an extensive 13-page affidavit (Exhibit "A"), continually referred to plaintiff as an "employee" and held him to the same standards as all other City employees. Repeated references were made to his being a "probationary employee"; yet, he was not entitled to afford himself the hearing mandated by the Personnel Regulations nor come within the purview of the Municipal Charter prohibiting such arbitrary discharge.

It would appear that the doctrine of estoppel would prevent defendants from holding and actively pursuing diametrically opposed views.

An equally strong issue proffered and reiterated by defendants is that plaintiff, as Chief of Police, and all other administrative officers "shall serve at the pleasure" of the City Manager. Defendants, unfortunately, have misinterpreted and misapplied this directive. If these words were followed literally, it would:

(1) violate the due process clause of the U.S. Constitution;

(2) violate the due process clause of the Constitution of the State of Alaska; and

(3) be inconsistent with the method of appointment and mode of removal of the City Manager, the City Clerk and the City Attorney.

As to point (1), the United States Constitution, Article XIV, Section I, provides inter alia:

"...(N) or shall any state deprive any person of life, liberty, or property, without due process of law..."

As to point (2), the Constitution of the State of Alaska, Article I, Section 7, provides:

"No person shall be deprived of life, liberty or property, without due process of law. The right of all persons to fair and just treatment in the course of legislative and executive investigations shall not be infringed."

Point (3) refers to Section 5.3 of the Municipal Charter. This section, quoted by defendants' recent MOTION, states that the City Manager, City Clerk and City Attorney are appointed by the Council and that they too hold office "at the pleasure" of the Council. However, as stated above, they all have the "right to a public hearing" before removal.

Therefore, it would flow that all administrative officers, including plaintiff as Chief of Police, would be placed in the same constitutionally protected grouping as the City Manager, the City Clerk and the City Attorney.

It is not only plaintiff's contention of the necessity of due process safeguards, and of the due process provisions in the statutory authority quoted from the U.S. and the Alaska Constitutions, but case law is rife with similar decisions. Quoting from a 1974 Alaska case *Behn v. Sharp*:

"The major case on point in this state is *Nichols v. Eckert*. 504 P. 2d 1959 (Alaska 1973). That case concerned a mid-year dismissal of two non-tenured teachers for incompetence. The procedure under which they were terminated did not call for a hearing. However, because of the gravity of the charge and the serious reflection dismissal would have upon the teachers' future prospects for employment, reputation and livelihood, a fair hearing must be held. Specifically that hearing must include the right of the employees to present witnesses on their behalf. The court held that a hearing in which only one side — the School District — presents evidence is inherently unfair ... One further point. A majority of the Alaska Supreme Court held that a hearing must be held prior to the suspension or discharge of the employee. Id. at 1366. This holding requires that any new hearing in the case must be held prior to dismissal."

"Due process" requirements were also mandatory in *Mills v. City of Winchester*, 162 N.E. 2d 97, where firemen were not accorded procedural requirements in their dismissals.

In *Birnbaum v. Trussell*, 371 F. 2d 672, the Second Circuit Court analyzed other cases at 678-679 and stated:

"The principle to be extracted from these cases is that, whenever there is a substantial interest, other than employment by the state, involved in the discharge of a public employee, he can be removed neither on arbitrary grounds nor without a procedure calculated to determine whether legitimate grounds do exist."

In *Boulware v. Battaglia*, 327 F. Supp. 368 (1971), a case dealing with the "unconstitutional manner" of internal police procedure, the court in analyzing other cases said:

"The true issue in cases such as Wieman, Birnbaum and Attreau is not the job or profession in question. Rather, the fundamental similarity in the cases is the public employee's right to pursue his employment without arbitrary vilification and reckless injury to his reputation and employability by the state."

The list of cases is long and impressive dealing with the due process requirements.

In the case at bar, the plaintiff was never allowed a

formal hearing, although one was specifically requested. The request was made timely, and in writing, but was ignored. Instead, plaintiff was placed on the agenda at a regular Council meeting, under the standard classification *Persons To Be Heard*. (See Exhibit "B".)

Before the Council meeting was scheduled, the City Mayor advised plaintiff that he "would have all the time you need to speak." The City Manager instead vilified plaintiff in the 13-page slanderous affidavit (see Exhibit "A") that consumed 45 minutes. Plaintiff was advised he had exactly 10 minutes to respond, was not allowed to present his three witnesses and was gaveled-out by the City Mayor when he voiced his objections. The session was terminated in accordance with prearranged agreements among all members of the Council and defendant City Manager.

Inasmuch as the minimal elements of due process require a hearing and inasmuch as the actions of defendants and City Council precluded a fair and impartial hearing, the minimal requirements for due process were never met.

Defendants also raise the issue that Holiday Pay and compensatory time are not available to plaintiff because he is at the administrative level and because there was no prior approval by the City Manager. Again, defendants are estoppel from these assertions. First, prior supervisory personnel at plaintiff's level received such compensatory pay. Second, knowledge and approval by the City Manager for a recurring 10-week period would counteract defendant's allegation.

Further, defendant raises the issue that plaintiff was not employed for a fixed period of time. Plaintiff's contract for employment was for an indefinite term and *Williston on Contracts*, 3rd Edition (Jaeger), S 1012-1019 A, at page 36, states that:

"...where doubt exists as to whether there was reasonable ground for the dismissal of an employee, the question of justification must be left to the jury." *Schumaker v. Heinemann*, 99 Wis. 251, 74 N.W. 785.

Finally, Section 5.4 of the Municipal Charter of the

City of Palmer states that the City Manager "shall be a resident of the City during his tenure in office."

Defendant City Manager was not at the time of his hire a resident of the City, has never been during his present tenure, and is not now.

It is prayed that defendants' MOTION FOR SUMMARY JUDGMENT be denied and that plaintiff be permitted to continue his present cause of action.

DATED this 27 day of September, 1976.
NICK J. MANGIERI
Pro per

When McShea saw my completed memorandum, before I filed it with the court, he read it over carefully and gave me a half smile, "Good Luck," he said.

I didn't know what the smile meant then, but I knew that I had done a good job. When the judge's decision finally came out, McShea's smile was even broader.

Superior Court Judge Peter J. Kalamarides in his decision on November 8, 1976, denied the City's request for SUMMARY JUDGMENT when he held "that issues of fact and law exist concerning plaintiff's rights and job classification under Palmer Charter."

"Congratulations," was McShea's curt comment when I showed him the decision.

"Thanks," I beamed.

He continued, "You're the kind of opponent that drives the other party up the wall. They never know what you're going to say or do."

I smiled at the comment.

"I've got to admit that you're effective though," he added.

My *effectiveness* was to continue, but it was as much the City of Palmer's unwitting contribution as it was my own.

That first MEMORANDUM was to be the beginning of a long string of MOTIONS that continually had the City "on the ropes."

In a series of future Depositions that I conducted, the defendants, or their employees, constantly fed me ammunition that I could use against them.

Nick Mangieri

The first individual that I scheduled to appear before H&M Court Reporters, to give a Deposition, was Rose Ann Kohlberg, Curtis' private secretary. It was she who had mentioned that Curtis was on the payroll prematurely to Palmer resident, Bernie Boyle. It was also she who had spread the word that I was setting up a Mafia, and I had previously obtained signed statements from both Marta Hensel and Mary Steiner, attesting to it. She also was the one that was privy to all that occurred in City Hall. In short, she was my pigeon and she knew it.

She was very nervous when she appeared before me with City Attorney Burton Biss, counsel for the City. I had assiduously prepared a list of 55 questions that I was prepared to pepper her with.

The questioning started out innocuously enough, by my first dealing with personal and generalized data and then expanded to her knowledge of past City information, including prior officials and employees. I then zeroed in as to her specific knowledge about me, what she had heard and what she had said. Interspersed throughout my questions were pertinent questions that caused her to catch her breath. She was becoming more flustered as the general questioning took on the form of an interrogation.

Examples:
- Did you ever mention in confidence to anyone that Bill Curtis was "on the payroll 3 weeks before the deadline of applications" for the advertised vacancy, as City Manager of Palmer?
- Did you ever mention in confidence to anyone that the City Mayor, "Jack Maze, hired him?"
- Are you aware that it is criminal slander to "willfully speak defamatory or scandalous matter concerning another with intent to injure or defame him" and that punishment can be imprisonment in jail between 6 months to a year?
- Did you ever speak derogatorily or maliciously of former Chief Mangieri to another?
  (**a.** To Whom?)
  (**b.** What was the content of those remarks?)
- Did you ever tell another that Chief Mangieri was set-

216

ting up a Mafia organization in Palmer?
- Was the idea solely yours, or if someone else instigated that remark, who was that person?
- Did you ever tell another that questionable or incriminating documents were found in Chief Mangieri's desk?
 (**a.** To Whom?)
 (**b.** Describe those documents)
 (**c.** Did you personally search that desk?)
 (**d.** Who told you of their existence?)

Her negative answers were not forthright, but were all hesitant replies, especially those that concerned me.

When I exhausted that particular line of inquiry, I concentrated on the "special meetings" that were conducted at the Frontier Cafe, in which City business was discussed and the public were not allowed to attend — all in violation of the Alaska statutes that dealt with public meetings and their exceptions. Those specific statutes had already been pointed out to Hickey in prior memos.

The 10 questions that I put to her all involved her personal participation as recording secretary and I pointedly asked how they were handled and recorded. Her responses were either vague or unresponsive.

At the conclusion of that block of questions, I asked her one more:

"Are you aware that it is a misdemeanor to withhold information regarding public records, and if you are the custodian of such records it is your duty to safeguard those records?"

Another negative response, however, she was obviously disturbed at my line of questioning and was anxious to leave at the termination of her session.

I made a mental note to analyze her perjurious statements after her Deposition was transcribed and then charge her accordingly.

While awaiting that transcript, which proved to be a time-consuming process — as did all the other transcripts — I filed a subsequent MOTION FOR CONTEMPT against her when she failed to produce specific City records, requested at the

Nick Mangieri

Deposition, after she had been duly served with a SUBPOENA DUCES TECUM. The named records requested were the:

Personnel Records for & *Payroll Records* for:
Nick J. Mangieri, (6/75-11/75)
Gary Eilers, (1/75-6/75)
Robert Bassett, (5/75-9/75)
Joe Norris, (not applicable)
James Boyd, (1/75-6/75)
William Curtis, (5/75-7/75)

The purpose of the personnel records was to establish specific dates of hire, termination, experience and comments contained within.

Eilers was the former Police Chief; Bassett was the former Lieutenant who was hired by Eilers and then fired by me; Norris was the former officer hired by Eilers and then fired by me; Boyd was the former City Manager before Curtis.

The primary purpose of the payroll records was to prove that prior administrative heads (Eilers and Bassett) did receive compensatory time, whereas I was denied such pay. As to the payroll records of Boyd and Curtis, not only would any of their compensatory pay be examined, but an exact starting date for Curtis was sought, since it was reported that he was hired before it was formally announced in the newspapers.

When the requested records did not appear at her Deposition, she brazenly and falsely submitted an Affidavit alleging that she did not "have the care, custody, possession or control" of them.

I immediately responded to her Affidavit as to her reasons for the non-appearance of the records with a, REPLY TO AFFIDAVIT OF ROSE ANN KOHLBERG. In it I spelled out in no uncertain words why she should be held in contempt:

> "Contrary to Mrs. Kohlberg's allegations that she does not "have the care, custody, possession or control" of either personnel records or payroll records, the following is offered:
> **1.** The file cabinet containing such personnel records is physically located in her office, and is situated but a

few feet from her desk.

2. During plaintiff's tour as Chief of Police, defendant City Manager ordered the removal of all police personnel records from plaintiff's office to that of the affiant. Included in this group of records were those of Gary Eilers, Robert Bassett, Joe Norris and of the plaintiff.

3. Plaintiff was ordered to hand over these personnel records to the affiant, with which order he complied.

4. Affiant personally assumed custody and control of such records and associated them with other City personnel records located in her office in the same file cabinet that is situated but a few feet from her desk.

5. All personnel actions and paperwork dealing with former and present City employees were handled by the affiant and personally filed in their respective personnel folders.

6. At the time plaintiff relinquished possession of the aforementioned personnel records, the file cabinet was not locked and affiant held full sway over such records, and so acknowledged that fact to the plaintiff.

Therefore, it is held that the affiant actually does have the care, custody, possession and control of these records ..."

In a legal decision that I did not fully comprehend, in view of Kohlberg's deliberate thumbing her nose at the court, Judge Kalamarides denied my MOTION to hold her in contempt and to compel production of the records by her. He stated that the contempt motion was "inappropriate" and that the MOTION TO COMPEL PRODUCTION was "premature."

I learned as time went on in my cases, that the vagaries of the law were indeed wondrous things to behold and contemplate.

I did not take the judge's ruling personally, however, although I did scratch my head over what I considered to be an illogical decision. I liked the judge in spite of what I considered a cop-out at the time. He was a ruddy-faced, white-haired, affable individual who had a good reputation in the courthouse. His prior denial of the City's request for a SUMMARY JUDGMENT in my reinstatement case, however, confirmed my original opinion of him, that he was fair and impartial.

I was not to hold some of the other judges in the Superior Court in that same high regard, when their turn "came to bat" in my cases.

As well as my reinstatement case seemed to be going, especially by the end of the summer, I didn't want to rely on it solely. I still felt that the criminal violations that I had raised were primary, and I never stopped trying to get them across to the proper officials.

In late August, I approached Frank Flavin, the new State Ombudsman. He was selected for a newly advertised position that I had also applied for after my dismissal. It was one of many state openings for which I was qualified, and it was also one of the many for which I was never even considered. It should have come as no surprise to me that as controversial as I was, that nobody would touch me, but it did. I was still naive enough to believe that truth and integrity were in high demand in public office.

At our initial meeting, Flavin appeared interested in my complaints and said that he would pursue them. Knowing that he was new to the office, and that the office was new to the state system, I wasn't overly optimistic, but I had nothing to lose. Apparently, subsequent to our first meeting, he contacted the Department of Public Safety in Anchorage. He then confirmed it with a letter, on August 31, 1976, to the Director of the Alaska State Troopers, the same procedure that the Deputy Attorney General had followed months earlier.

"Re: Ombudsman Complaint 76-0952

"Dear Colonel Wellington:
    "This matter, as previously discussed with you, involves allegations of criminal law raised by Mr. Nick Mangieri, former Chief of Police for the City of Palmer. As you will recall Mr. Mangieri was interviewed by Chief Investigator J.H. Lucking and Lt. U. Dean Bivens who issued a report on December 1, 1975. This matter was turned over the District Attorney's Office and even-

tually reviewed by Daniel Hickey, Deputy Attorney General for Criminal Affairs Division. Mr. Hickey issued his memorandum on May 12, 1976, essentially dismissing most of the allegations raised by Mr. Mangieri. On June 2, 1976, Mr. Mangieri responded to the memorandum to you from Daniel Hickey.

"Succinctly stated, Mr. Mangieri's complaint is that he has not had an opportunity to fully explore the allegations of criminal misconduct which he raised at a session with the State Troopers in November and that the matter has not been actively pursued by the Criminal Affairs Division or the State Troopers. Additionally, Mr. Mangieri feels that he should be appointed Special Investigator for these matters.

"As there appears to be a different perception between Mr. Mangieri and the original State Trooper investigators involved in this case concerning the initial meetings I can make no determination concerning the conduct of the investigation at this time. Mr. Mangieri felt that the initial session was merely an overview and that more specific information would be required of him as a later date. My understanding is that the State Troopers felt that the initial session was to be complete. With this in mind I reviewed Deputy Attorney General Hickey's memorandum of May 12th and feel that numbered *Allegations 1,2,3,4,5,6, and 10* have been fairly resolved to the satisfaction of this office by that memorandum. I feel that Mr. Mangieri has additional information regarding *Allegations 7 and 8* which would shed more light on Mr. Mangieri's allegations in these areas. It is my suggestion that an additional meeting with Mr. Mangieri be established to explore these allegations.

"In regard to *Allegation 9* concerning the dog beating it would appear that substantial delay has resulted in prosecuting this matter. However, I am not sure as to where to fix responsibility for the delay. Mr. Mangieri indicates that the information was conveyed to the State Troopers in November but that no action was taken at that time. He feels that he was not aware of the violation until that time and that the violation had occurred in the Summer of 1975 which was not an unreasonable period of time to preclude prosecution. Did the State Troopers subsequent to the meeting with Mr. Mangieri and the information provided, conduct interviews with Chuck Shaver and ex-police lieutenant Robert Bassett to determine whether a violation may have occurred? If not, what were the reasons for not proceeding at that time?

"I feel that Mr. Mangieri's complaint that he was not appointed a Special Investigator is unsupported. Because of his involvement in civil litigation and a public dispute and recall election involving officials of the City of Palmer his appointment would, in appearance, if not in actuality, lack the independence and impartiality that the public would expect from law enforcement officials. While it is true that "facts are facts," it is also true that the degree of cooperation and the degree of credibility afforded those facts both in the public or potential jury's eyes would be substantially diminished if the investigator were not considered totally impartial and independent by the public or fact finders.

"Thank you very much for your patience and consideration in this matter

"Sincerely,
Frank Flavin
Ombudsman"

cc: Daniel Hickey, Deputy Attorney General for
Criminal Affairs
Joseph D. Balfe, District Attorney

After reviewing a copy of his letter, I was even more firmly convinced that his correspondence was kowtowing to the state officials. In spite of his proclaimed interest in my complaints, it was merely lip service to placate me. There was little, if any factual analysis on his part.

In his third paragraph, he stated that my impression of the initial interview session with the State Troopers was at odds with theirs. However, in light of that misunderstanding as to the conflicting dual intent of the interview sessions, Flavin failed to discuss any of the aspects from my viewpoint. Instead, he glossed over it by saying:

"With this in mind I reviewed Deputy Attorney General Hickey's memorandum of May 12 and feel that numbered *Allegations 1,2,3,4,5,6* and *10* have been fairly resolved to the satisfaction of this office by that memorandum."

His statement of "with this in mind" automatically took as gospel the State Trooper's belief that the "initial session was to be complete," and adopted their position without question. The distinct *possibility* that my belief was valid was not considered. Therefore, his review of Hickey's memo was biased from the beginning, and any subsequent analysis of it was not objective. He could have chosen to wonder what entity would have the power to enforce municipal violations, when they would not do so themselves — but he did not. He could have indicated that conspiracy against the rights of individuals, and intimidation of employees should be investigated — but he did not. Being made aware of the elements of criminal libel, and my own testimony regarding its strong likelihood, he could have suggested the possibility of Grand Jury review — but, again, he did not.

All he did was recommend that the remaining allegations concerning preferential awarding of City bids, conflict of interest and the cruelty to animals be reviewed again.

Even in his closing paragraph, Flavin cited specific reasons why I could not, under any circumstances, be appointed a Special Investigator. As compelling as those arguments were, not once did he intimate the possibility of appointing an impartial independent Special Investigator — a point he himself had stressed.

I waited days, and then weeks, for some type of response.

My patience was wearing thin when I heard nothing from Flavin, nor from Colonel Wellington's office in the period that followed Flavin's letter. It had been 10 months since my termination, and I was getting fed up with the slowness and the inaction of the state bureaucracy. I decided to pursue my complaints in the federal arena again.

... Chapter 16 ...

On September 26, I filed a Civil Rights complaint with Kent Edwards, the U.S. Attorney in Anchorage, listing the same facts that I had brought up in previous letters to state officials. This time, however, I specifically referred to pertinent sections of Title 42 of the U.S. Code that covered Civil Rights violations and to Title 18 of the U.S. Code that dealt with conspiracy.

"Dear Mr. Edwards:
"I hereby officially file Civil Rights complaints against the City Manager, the City Mayor and the City Councilmen of the City of Palmer. Specifically, William Curtis as City Manager; Jack E. Maze as City Mayor; and Councilmen — Willard Johnson, James Ekstedt, John Dolenc, Peter Pedersen and Dave Ingalls. (At this time, I do not wish to include City Councilman Arlyn Hanson.)
"Applicable sections are as follows:
(1) Title 18, Chapter 13, Section 241. *Conspiracy Against Rights of Citizens.*
(2) Title 42, Chapter 21, Section 1983. *Civil Action for Deprivation of Rights.*
(3) Title 42, Chapter 21, Section 1985. *Conspiracy to Interfere with Civil Rights.*
Sub-section (1). *Preventing Officer from Performing Duties.*

Sub-section (3). *Depriving Persons of Rights or Privileges.*

"Facts bearing on the above complaints:

"On November 12, 1975, I was ostensibly scheduled to appear before the City Council to appeal my ouster as Chief of Police of Palmer on November 4th by the City Manager. The City Mayor had advised me several days prior that I would "have all the time I needed" to speak in my own behalf.

"I had personally requested of the Mayor and of all the City Councilmen that a special session be called to listen to my appeal prior to the regularly scheduled session of the City Council. It was, however, denied, and I was advised to formally place my name on the agenda. I complied, and when the agenda was printed, my name with that of a former police officer and "group of not more than three persons" was placed under the standard category *Persons to be Heard.* There was no mention of any "appeal procedure" or "hearing" or anything other than a regular meeting.

"At the onset of the meeting, many members of the public were excluded under the guise that the fire ordinance precluded greater occupancy and that other space was not available. These were self-serving statements that were not only not substantiated by fact but could be proven otherwise. (This specific complaint was registered with the local FBI office on November 21, 1975.)

"At this Council meeting, the City Manager read a 13-page slanderous affidavit that consumed 45 minutes. When it was my turn to speak, I was advised that I had exactly ten minutes to reply — no more. The Mayor gaveled out my objections and those of the public. At the conclusion of my brief reply, at a prearranged signal from the Council table, all members concurred that the session would terminate and that I would not be allowed to present any of my witnesses — in direct contravention of the agenda agreement and of Personnel Regulations. My attorney also was refused permission to speak on my behalf. Again, when I voiced objections and other mem-

Nick Mangieri

bers of the audience concurred, the Mayor again gaveled
out our responses.

"All of the above is in violation of the U.S.
Constitution, Article XIV, Section 1, which provides
inter aila:

" '... (N) or shall any state deprive any person of life,
liberty, or property, without due process of law ...'

"Case law is also consonant with this "due process
of law" requirement. See *Boulware v. Battaglia*, 327 F.
Supp. 368 (1971) and *Birnbaum v. Trussell*, 371 F. 2d
672 and all appropriate and related cases cited therein.

"On December 4, 1975, I advised the State Attorney
General's Office that the City Manager, City Mayor and
City Councilmen had violated AS 11.60.340, *Conspiracy
of Violating Civil Rights*, "for threatening, intimidating
and oppressing several individuals, including myself, in
various constitutional rights." Nothing was done. I do not
wish at this time to register formal complaints against
that office but merely wish to place your office on record
to the fact that I did initiate complaints with the State and
that I was denied due process as a result of their nonfea-
sance.

"Inasmuch as a great deal of time has been wasted
because of the inaction of others, I hereby request that
immediate charges be filed against the individuals mentioned above. My allegations are supported by witnesses
(including the press) and tape recordings. Other allegations of a conspiracy beyond City Hall will not be presented at this time but suffice to say my firing prevented
me from performing my official duties as Police Chief.
Your prompt response is requested.

"Sincerely yours,
Nick J. Mangieri
Former Chief of Police"

My reliance, cited above, on the Civil Rights chapter of the
U.S. Criminal Code under Title 18, Section 241, *Conspiracy
Against Rights of Citizens*, was based on the applicable elements

226

and the punishment thereof:

"If two or more persons conspire to injure, oppress, threaten, or intimidate any citizen in the free exercise or enjoyment of any right or privilege secured to him by the Constitution or laws of the United States, or because of his having so exercised the same ..."

They shall be fined not more than $5,000 or imprisoned no more than ten years, or both."

It would certainly appear that the prearrangement of the City group to not only deny *me* my due process but to preclude the *public* from exercising their right to assemble and their right to free speech would fall within the gambit of the Civil Rights section on conspiracy.

It would further appear that my citing Title 42 of the U.S. Code that fell under the Public Health and Welfare statutes was equally appropriate. Under Chapter 21, Section 1983, *Civil Action For Deprivation of Rights*, the official actions of a municipal entity in denying me and the public our "rights and privileges," would certainly apply.

There appears to be no question that the above elements are contained in the following section:

"Every person who, under color of any statute, ordinance, regulation, custom, or usage, of any State or Territory, subjects, or causes to be subjected, any citizen of the United States of other person within the jurisdiction thereof to the deprivation of any rights, privileges, or immunities secured by the Constitution and laws, shall be liable to the party injured in an action at law, suit in equity, or other proper proceeding for redress."

As important as the first two sections were that I cited in my letter, i.e. the criminal prosecutability of the former section and the civil actionability of the latter, it was my next sub-citation that I considered to be even more important. I believed it to be of foremost concern, and I was of the firm belief that anyone in the law enforcement field would share my opinion.

Under Section 1985, *Conspiracy to Interfere With Civil Rights*, Sub-section (1), *Preventing Officer From Performing Duties*.

There would again appear to be little doubt that those in power in City Hall, from the City Manager to the Mayor and down to the City Councilmen, had in concert and by predesign prevented me from carrying out my official duties as the number one law enforcement official in the City and in surrounding area.

The full wording of the sub-section appears below:

"If two or more persons in any State or Territory conspire to prevent, by force, intimidation, or threat, any person from accepting or holding any office, trust, or place of confidence under the United States, or from discharging any duties thereof; or to induce by like means any officer of the United States to leave any state, district, or place, where his duties as an officer are required to be performed, or to injure him in his person or property on account of his lawful discharge of the duties of his office, or while engaged in the lawful discharge thereof, or to injure his property so as to molest, interrupt, hinder, or impede him in the discharge of his official duties;"

Sub-section (3) *Depriving Persons of Rights or Privileges*, of that same section also could have been employed against the City Officials. The appropriate elements contained therein are extracted from that lengthy sub-section:

"If two or more persons in any State or Territory conspire for the purpose of depriving, either directly or indirectly, any person or class of persons of the equal protection of the laws, or of equal privileges and immunities under the laws; in any case of conspiracy set forth in this section, if one or more persons engaged therein do, or cause to be done, any act in furtherance of the object of such conspiracy, whereby another is injured in his person or property, or deprived of having and exercising any right or privilege of a citizen of the United States, the party so injured or deprived may have an action for the recovery of damages, occasioned by such injury or deprivation against any one or more of the conspirators."

After I reviewed my letter to the U.S. Attorney and then reexamined the appropriate elements within each section of the violations that I cited, I believed that I was on solid ground in requesting federal prosecution of the Palmer officials. Because I still had not heard from the Department of Justice in Washington relative to the complaints that I had filed with the local FBI office in November 1975, I felt that I had nothing to lose in renewing my complaints — and of being very specific in my charges.

However, as I mulled over possible reasons for the long delay in Washington's determination, I could also envision their specific unsatisfactory responses — which could have been satisfactorily resolved.

If in spite of all the publicity that had attended my ouster, and *if* in spite of all the extensive testimony that I had given the state officials, and *if* in spite of all the allegations that had been raised by *other* witnesses, I still were not believed, then an independent investigation could have been ordered. The Bureau could have been called in. A federal Grand Jury could have been convened to hear all the evidence that would have been presented to them. Where there was smoke there was certainly the possibility of fire. In my case, there was unquestionably a great deal of smoke generated, not only by myself but also by others who had been aware of ongoing municipal and borough corruption for a long time. Unfortunately, it appeared that their past attempts to initiate any actions were unsuccessful.

I hoped that I would not be lumped in with those same individuals.

On the same date that I wrote the U.S. Attorney requesting those federal Civil Rights actions against the Palmer defendants, I also decided to write Anchorage District Attorney Joe Balfe the same type letter, modified to fit Alaska violations:

"I hereby officially file a criminal complaint against the City Manager, the City Mayor and the City Councilmen of the City of Palmer for conspiracy...

"The applicable section is AS 11.60.340, *Conspiracy Against Rights of Persons*, which states that 'A person who conspires with another to injure, oppress, threaten, or intimidate a person because that person seeks to exercise or enjoy, or has exercised or enjoyed a right, privilege or immunity granted by the Constitution or the laws of this State is guilty of a felony...

"The Constitution of the state of Alaska, Article I, Section 7, provides:

" 'No person shall be deprived of life, liberty or property, without due process of law. The rights of all persons to fair and just treatment in the course of legisla-

Nick Mangieri

tive and executive investigations shall not be infringed.'

"I was denied 'due process of law' when I was not given a fair and impartial hearing before and after my firing by the City Manager. Nor was I allowed to present any witnesses in my behalf at a 'kangaroo' session contrived at a regular City Council meeting, a full week after my ouster."

I also noted in the body of his letter that case law was "rife with the necessity for due process hearings," and cited half a dozen appropriate cases.

In addition, I mentioned:

"For more factual information regarding my allegations of conspiracy, see the attached copy of a letter addressed to the U.S. Attorney Kent Edwards, regarding violation of my Civil Rights."

I was unaware at that time that talking to the District Attorney's Office was the same as talking to the Attorney General's Office, since basically they were the same entity. In other states in which I had lived, District Attorneys were local in jurisdiction and were not part of the state jurisdiction. Therefore, unbeknownst to me, my letter to the Anchorage DA was a waste of time since the AG's office, through Hickey, had already decided to manifest a hands-off policy concerning my allegations.

The *Anchorage Times* in their continuing coverage ran an article about the contents of both my letters in their edition of October 3.

"PALMER EX-CHIEF FILES COMPLAINT, NAMES OFFICIALS"

In the article, the paper noted that I stated that I did not wish to include City Councilman, Arlyn Hanson, in either of my complaints. Although, I did not feel it was necessary to offer a reason in my complaints for his exclusion, the paper did their own checking. They mentioned that he was "at home recovering from a serious intestinal disorder."

I was aware of his illness before I filed my complaints and did not want to compound his problems at that juncture. Therefore, I left him out. It was unfortunate, however, that my compassion for him was not reciprocal. When I subsequently learned not only of his recovery, but also of his own apparent lack of any interest in my behalf, I also included him in all of my future actions.

A week after the article appeared in the *Anchorage Times*, I was contacted by the State Troopers again. Investigator Hoffbeck of the Anchorage office called me back on October 11 for another interview to cover "three distinct allegations" that Ombudsman Flavin had cited in his letter to Colonel Wellington in late August. I recalled Flavin stating in that memo to the Director of the State Troopers that he felt that I might have "additional information regarding *Allegations 7* and *8* which would shed more light on (his) allegations in these areas." Those allegations concerned City bids and conflict of interest by the Palmer officials. When I questioned Hoffbeck as to the specific purpose of the interview, he confirmed that *Allegations 7* and *8* were to be covered. He also stated that he was interested in *Allegation 9*, about the beating of the dogs. Flavin had also validly questioned the "dog beating" and properly wondered why the Troopers did not interview Chuck Shaver or former Lieutenant Bassett.

Whether Flavin's bland description of the beating to death of several puppies as merely "dog beating" was intentionally downplayed, or whether it was just a reference to the incident I never knew. However, in the interest of truth and objectivity he should have referred to it accurately instead of merely touching on it lightly.

The interview began at 1:10 p.m. on that same date by Investigator Hoffbeck with the verbatim text shown below exactly as it was transcribed and forwarded to me. Unfortunately, lack of editing compromises its clarity.

Q: Mr. Mangieri, I've asked you to come back in and —
to talk about three distinct allegations that you —
we've covered briefly last time we had spoken or last
I believe November and December. I think the last

time you and I spoke was about December the 9th or there — correction, December the 24th and since that time Deputy Attorney General — Attorney General Dan Hickey and also a Frank Slaven, the ombudsman have had opportunity to review and to go over everything that's been and so what they would like now is to talk about three separate allegations. The preferential awarding of City bids, the conflict of interest and the allegation of the violation of cruelty to animals that you had brought up previously. So why don't we just begin from there and — and any — in the order that you want to talk about them and as detailed and as specific as you possibly can make.

A: Okay. The first area that I claim there as a violation is in the conflict of interest Alaska Statute 29.23.555. This as is known as applicable to all home-municipalities of which Palmer is included, if they fail to adopt such conflict of interest ordinance, quote, within ninety days of September 6, 1972, unquote, the Alaska Statues would apply. The City of Palmer did not adopt their own conflict of interest and any violations along this line are violations of Alaska Statutes. On the present right of way to the new Palmer High School, I'll submit a copy with this allegation to Mr. Hoffbeck. There are City Councilmen present and former who own property on that right of way also the wife of the City Mayor or at least he's in the City — in the City Mayor's wife's name and the — also the City Manager has property in the vicinity of this new right of way property. The individuals I'm speaking of now are John Dolenc, spelling D-O-L-E-N-C, Peter Pedersen, spelling P-E-D-E-R-S-E-N, these are both present City Council members. Bill Hermann, spelling H-E-R-M-A-N-N, is a former City Councilman plus Bill Curtis is the City Manager and Jack Maze, spelling M-A-Z-E, is the City Mayor. My suggestion is that on the course of action number one, find out the date that the right of way was approved by the City Council. Number two find out if the above councilmen cast their votes in favor of it, number three same information for the mayor, number four also ascertain what the City managers affirmative part in the acquisition of this right of way property. Another point, in addition the industrial prop — property was purchased, as I mentioned I believe before, by City bonds which were purchased by the Mat-Su Borough, by the Alaska Bank of Commerce and by the Alaska Mutual Savings and Loan of which Senator Jalmar Kertula, C-E-R-T-U-L-A, is on the board of directors of this or was on the board of directors of the Alaska Mutual Savings and Loan. My suggested course of action this area is number one, find out what City Councilmen own property adjacent to the Industrial Park, two, find out...

Q: Can I interject?

A: Certainly.

Q: Which ones own now or which ones owned at the time of...

A: Which ones owned at the time.

Q: Okay..

A: Two, find out what date that the purchase was approved at the City Council meeting, three, find out if any of the press — present Councilmen or Bill Hermann as former Councilman, cast votes in favor of it. The same course of action for the Mayor, Jack Maze. The same course of action for the City Manager, Bill Curtis. In addition, ascertain what Bill Curtis' affirmative part in the administration or the details that went into this acquisition. Further point number seven, in as much as Senator Jalmar Kertula was in the board of directors, ascertain if he voted for the banks purchase of this property, if so what appropriate state violation that Senator Certula was involved with. Point number eight, find out if Bill Hermann, who's in the construction business in Palmer, sold gravel to the industrial park and to the right of way to the new Palmer High School. In addition, a question that would arise, was that contract open for bid. I heard that it wasn't, I haven't — I don't have the — the ability in the — the information that I can get some of this information from the City because they're very uptight when I ask them questions. Okay. Want to go off for a minute while I just... As to the allegation of preferential awarding of bids, Bomhoff and Associates, spelling B-O-M-H-O double F and Associates has been under contract of the City of Palmer for a number of years. They have gone beyond the two-year limit required. I've ascertained that — the last I checked last year they had been under contract at least three or four years to the City of Palmer. In addition, Bill Hermann, as I mentioned before also, in the gravel business has been awarded several contracts according to — what I've been told, the City Hall. Further, proof of construction, I was told this before at City Hall, there was approximately two hundred thousand dollars of work done at the industrial park, this figure could be off. However, I was told that City crews were over at the industrial park assisting with the work when Cooper Construction should have been doing the work. In addition, I was told, and I haven't been able to — to check into the validity of the statement, is that even though gravel was used on that particular property, was industrial park or the old park property I'm not sure, the gravel was paid for and the gravel was never put in or at least not to the depth and to the extent that was required.

Q: Who would've finally okayed this before it would've been paved?

A: Well...

Q: (Unintelligible)

A: In the City part it would have been of course with the City Manager. If the Borough was involved — on some phase it would have been the City, would have been the borough manager. But since it was industrial park properties Mr. Curtis would have been — would have given the final okay. Bill Curtis. If you want to go off a minute and I'll get the next topic up. As to the cruelty to animals as I mentioned before. Acting City Manager and who then became the — who's also the acting public wor — who is also the Public Works Director and then became the acting chief of police, Chuck Shaver, spelling S-H-A-V-E-R. Last summer some time took dogs out to — to get rid of them, he would — he literally beat these dogs to death with an iron claw. Former Lieutenant Robert Bassett was there by his own admission, he saw it happen, he didn't stop it, this was the subject — this was brought up a City Council meeting, this was also in the newspaper, Palmer at the time. So there's no question that Chuck Shaver did it. I was not aware of it until after I was fired. My former police officer, Wayne Higgins, told me about — told me that he had been at one of these session where Chuck Shaver was about to beat a dog to death and he told him to stop and then of course at the next session was Robert Bassett, lieutenant, who witnessed the beating of the dogs to death.

Q: Um, hum. Where did they take them to?

A: There's a dump outside the City.

Q: Just to the City dump?

A: Well, it was just in the — in the boondocks some-place. I'm not sure whether this is — if it's a — a City dump per say that they use, it was — or it's another area.

Q: What — what are the City requirements to disposing of animals?

A: We had been just shooting dogs but...

Q: Does it say specifically how to eliminate dogs or if you're (Unintelligible)

A: No. It doesn't say specifically how to eliminate dogs. However, this beating dogs to death doesn't not appear to be a humane way to do it. Lead is not that expensive and according to Robert Bassett that the

235

dogs were not dead when he threw them on a heap. Now this is testimony that came from Bassett. They were not dead, they were still crying, the Humane Society was called to that particular area, they were very incensed about the way the dogs were handled, the way the dogs were destroyed and I'm just repeating what was mentioned at this hearing.

Q: Why would Chuck Shaver be involved with the dogs anyway? Whose responsibility was it?

A: The public ... Well, he...

Q: (Unintelligible)

A: Took it on himself as Public Works Director to probably assist us and get rid of more dogs. I don't know. It had been the Police Department's responsibility before that and we used to shoot dogs. Gather them up and after a certain amount of time shoot them. And this had been the accepted procedure and this was — Humane Society had no — no qualms about that as being shot but not beaten to death.

Q: Does the City have a storage area for...

A: Yes. Um, hum. A small enclosure.

Q: And there's so many days before people pick...

A: They're kept there a week to two weeks and if they're not picked up then they're destroyed.

Q: And who takes care of them during this time?

A: The City. Police officers.

Q: City does?

A: Police officers feed them.

Q: Okay. Go ahead.

A: Okay. So I suggest number one that you contact or in addition, this fact was mentioned to Slim Randles when I was there. Oh, I asked him to — to check out what I heard. Slim Randles who was the newspaper reporter for the *Frontiersman*, he now has his own paper in Talkeetna, he didn't believe what I had told him about Chuck Shaver so Slim Randles was — asked Chuck Shaver himself and Chuck Shaver's did not deny it. He admitted that he had beaten the dogs to death. Slim in turn came back and told me — this was after I was fired — came back and told me...

Q: Um, hum.

A: That he heard, that's what happened, he believed me. So I suggest number one, you contact Slim Randles who is in Talkeetna, Wayne Higgins who lives in Palmer area, former officer and Lieutenant Robert Bassett, you can contact him as well and then of course...

Q: Where does Bassett reside in at?

A: He lives in town someplace.

Q: Anchorage or Palmer?

A: In Palmer. He still lives in Palmer. The last I heard he was living in Palmer but I know the first two or three parties I mentioned live in that area.

Q: Um, hum.

A: And of course, leave Shaver for last and with those four individuals you can find out what happened.

Q: How often would he do this?

A: To my knowledge, that was the only time he had done it. On that first or...

Q: One time?

A: Yea. Well, I think he attempted to do it with Wayne Higgins and Wayne Higgins, at least he told me that he stopped him at that particular incident and then he did it once more with Bassett and to my knowledge it never happened again.

Q: About how many dogs are we talking about and when was this?

A: This was last — last — late summer of 75 cause Bassett was there and I — I heard about it at the City Council meeting and I don't know how many dogs are involved but it seemed to me in the neighborhood of six to eight, something like that. Perhaps more. Some pups involved, this was older dogs.

Q: Strictly dogs, no cats?

A: Strictly dogs, yea.

Q: Okay. Does that cover the...

A: Yea.

Q: Three items...

Nick Mangieri

A: That...

Q: That I wanted specifically covered?

A: Okay. That covers — that covers the area that I believe we initially spoke, why don't you go off a minute and I'll just check through...

At that point I went off the record while I checked my notes. In doing so, I noticed that Hoffbeck was getting ready to terminate the session. I asked to go back on the record again before Hoffbeck cut off the interview.

Then I immediately opened up with:

"Now another area that I brought to the attention of the Attorney General's Office and the Governor's Office was ARRC."

I briefly described — again — what it was, why it was set up and when it would expire.

Hoffbeck was giving me monosyllabic responses, apparently hoping that I would end because my additional information was not part of the "three distinct allegations" that he was directed to obtain. However, I knew that I had to get across as much as possible as quickly as possible:

"The State of Alaska should be cognizant of this property, not only cognizant of the — of the property itself but of the assets that would accrue to the state and the date — in the not too distant future. They should be interested in checking the books of the ARRC to look into the many thousands of acres, perhaps millions of dollars that would accrue to the state at this date. On the other hand, if the corporations not acting in accordance with the way they should operate a nonprofit corporation then the state can terminate this corporation and then take advantage of all the assets of the ARRC for the states purpose. Okay. There has been an individual who is the manager of the ARRC, name is George Crowther, spelling C-R-O-W-T-H-E-R, it's been brought to my attention by several individuals and I'll go into their

238

names further on, that this George Crowther has used his position as director or manager of the ARRC for his own personal gain. I speak specifically now of Wayne Hunter, H-U-N-T-E-R, living in the Palmer area and he has had property confiscated from or foreclosed several years back. George Crowther wound up with the property, it went to other individuals, nobody received title to the property and was subsequently sold at an exorbitant rate further down. Harry Lechwold, L-E-C-H-W-O-L-D, is aware of not only, he's living in the Palmer area as well, is aware of the Wayne Hunter property as well as another piece of property, the name I believe is Gagnom, I think the spelling is G-A-G-N-O-M, who also had his property foreclosed by George Crowther and it said that he wound up with the property in his own personal possession. Harry Lechwold is familiar with the — with the property and the individuals name and can advise on that particular property as well as on other property in that area. He can also put you in touch with Wayne Hunter. So much so for the ARRC property at the moment."

I caught my breath in my run-on attempt to get as much info as I could about the ARRC across to my interviewer.

Hoffbeck's impatient solitary response of, "All right," had an unquestionable finality to our session. However, when he hesitated, slightly, as if unsure what would come next, I jumped right in with additional information about areas that I had raised previously, but were not solicited in his "three distinct allegations."

"Again I go into public meetings, Alaska Statute 29.23.580 which states that meetings of all public bodies — excuse me, meetings of all municipal bodies shall be public as provided in AS 44.62.310. The assembly and council shall provide reasonable opportunities for the public to be heard at regular and special sessions. Question has arisen before and I brought this to the Attorney General's attention, I believe that at these special sessions the public is not required to appear and so forth. However, in looking over AS 44.62.310, agency meetings public, all meetings of an administrative body, etc. and that includes council and so forth are open to the public except otherwise as provided by the section. Section "B" says, if excepted subjects are to be discussed at a meeting, the meeting must first be convened as a public meeting and the question of holding an executive session to discuss matters that come within the exceptions contained in C of this section shall be determined by a majority vote of the body. No subject may be considered at the executive session except those mentioned in the motion calling for the executive session unless auxiliary to the main question. No action may be taken at the executive session. The following excepted subjects may be discussed in an executive session, they go on to the section to discuss the areas that are allowed to be brought up in these executive sessions, one of which is — oh, well, excuse me. I'll relate these, number one, matters to the immediate knowledge of which would adversely affect the finance of the government unit, two, subjects that tend to prejudice a reputation and character of any person provided the person may request a public discussion, three, matters which by law, municipal chart or ordinance are required to be confidential, four, this section does not apply to (the) traditional clause on judicial bodies when holding a meeting solely to make a decision in an adjudicatory proceeding or to juries or to parole or pardon boards. Six, reasonable public notice shall be given for all meetings required to be open this section, and seven, action taken contrary to this section is void. Therefore all of these executive sessions, special sessions were not held in accordance with the — the procedure in AS 44.62.310. The week — or the several weeks that followed my termination on November 4, 1975, were held without the public's knowledge, were held in special locations, all contra to public meetings. The public was never notified, the public never had any input. In addition as I have mentioned before, in these breakfast sessions that were held weekly at The Frontiersman Cafe, business was discussed at these sessions also contra to public meeting AS 29.23.580. Individuals that should be contacted to determine what was said in the scope of these meetings and the number of these meetings are number one, Verna Euwer, spelling E-U-W-E-R, in Palmer, she runs a day care center. Also Jerome Sheldon, spelling S-H-E-L-D-O-N, he's the editor of the *Frontiersman*, it was he who told, after I was fired, of the several sessions that were held in which my name was brought up and it was their course of action, they meaning the City Council, City Mayor, City Manager, in which they determined to do what there going to do. The — so these individuals can be contacted, they were substantiated. In addition, last week I took a deposition of Roseanne Kohlberg, spelling K-O-H-L-B-E-R-G, in which one of the questions that I asked her was how many special meetings were held subsequent to my firing. She was very evasive in that deposition and all she would say is that there were at least two. Vernie Euwer, I'm sure and Jerome Sheldon will certify that there were many more meetings than those two that she evaded answering."

I stopped abruptly, satisfied that I added as much as I could under the circumstances. I looked up at Hoffbeck, who seemed relieved that I had finished my monologue.

My statement was subsequently transcribed and forwarded to me for my verification. As I reviewed it, I noted its poor editing but concluded that there was little that I could do to rectify that problem. I also noticed obvious typos as they referred to individuals. "Slaven" was, of course, "Flavin," and "Jelmer Certula" was, unquestionably, the State Senator, "Jalmar Kertula." However, I was sure that the state authorities could properly identify the parties, and did not request that it be amended.

As I read, and re-read even more slowly, all that I had given Hoffbeck, I couldn't imagine that any of the details offered would not be verified, investigated or checked in any manner. However, if it was ever done, it was done superficially. Further, if any of it was ever looked into, I was never officially notified by the

Attorney General's Office, nor in particular, by Daniel Hickey, the one that I would have expected to inform me of the scope of their continued *in-depth coverage* of my allegations. Instead, I received a brief unfavorable response from Flavin, months later, advising that no further action would be taken on my allegations.

Even before Higgins had heard of my final letter from Flavin, he was incensed when I called and told him of my upcoming third interview with Investigator Hoffbeck.

"They're not going to do anything, Chief," he said. "I've known it all along. The only reason they called you back is because Flavin threw them a bone to chew on. And another thing," he ranted, "what the hell kind of an Ombudsman is he?"

Before I had a chance to answer the obvious, Higgins continued, "He's a company man. That's what he is," and he spat the words out.

"Yeah, they're all company men," I agreed. "It's all show-case."

"Whattaya got left to do, Chief?" he asked.

"Only the civil cases, Wayne," I answered. "Mine is looking better all the time, and Roger's working on his, too. There's a lot of work involved in it though."

"Bet you're giving Biss fits," he gloated.

"You know it!"

"Keep me posted, Chief," he added.

"Right," I said, and hung up.

Higgins was taking it harder than I was, or rather, than I allowed myself to take it.

When I saw McShea after the Hoffbeck interview and reviewed the scope of that session with him, he gave me his half-smile again.

"You really didn't expect it to be much different, did you?" he noted.

"I was hoping, Roger," I said, trying to speak with assurance. Then I lowered my voice and added, "I had a feeling."

"Well," he responded. "You've got to put all your present energy into your case."

I nodded, "I know."

"How's it going?" he asked.

"I'm still working on my depositions and my subpoenas."

"Good," he said, shaking his head confidently. "I think you've gotten the format down."

I not only had gotten the format down, but I was cranking out the depositions and the subpoenas as fast as I could. I needed to keep the Palmer officials off balance, and I needed as much info as I could get as quickly as I could get it.

... Chapter 17 ...

By the end of October I had scheduled four more depositions to be taken before R&R Court Reporters at their offices. I changed from H&M Court Reporters to R&R because the owner of that agency was a personal friend of an attorney buddy with whom that I had worked while I was at the Public Defender's Office He spoke highly of her and the reasonableness of her fees, and since money — or, rather, lack of it — was a primary consideration, there was little doubt that I wouldn't switch.

The first deposition planned for a Saturday morning was William Curtis, followed by Colleen Ribelin, his former secretary, then Jerome Sheldon, the editor and publisher of the *Frontiersman*, and finally Dr. James Ivey, Curtis' personal physician. Curtis also was hit with a SUBPOENA DUCES TECUM, as was Ivey. Curtis was required to produce the City personnel and payroll records that his secretary, Kohlberg, had failed to produce earlier. Ivey was instructed to bring Curtis' medical records.

When Curtis was served at City Hall, he advised the process server that because of "short notice," he would not appear. The other parties so served arrived as requested. Although Ivey appeared, Curtis' medical records were not presented because Ivey had to first obtain permission from Curtis' original physician, Dr. Harry Owens, who unfortunately was out of the country at that time. Of the other two parties that showed up at the deposition session, it was Ribelin who was the most productive.

Following a series of forty-plus questions that dealt with Curtis' purported mental instability and his proneness to violence, I prepared a subsequent affidavit in a reinstatement case that I filed with the Superior Court:

AFFIDAVIT OF NICK J. MANGIERI
STATE OF ALASKA
ss.

THIRD JUDICIAL DISTRICT
    NICK J. MANGIERI, being first duly sworn, deposes and states as follows:
1) That I am the plaintiff and my own counsel in this action.
2) That at her deposition in this case on October 30, 1976, Colleen Ribelin, former secretary to WILLIAM CURTIS, Palmer City Manager, testified as follows:
    a) That she was secretary to CURTIS in 1970 and 1971.
    b) That Dr. Harry Owens (presently in South America) told her that CURTIS is psychotic and a "text-book case", that he was dangerous and sick, and that nobody should be in a room alone with him.
    c) That his actions disclosed such psychosis.
3) That the deposition will be available by November 10th, and Plaintiff will cause it to be published at such time and utilized in later stages of this Motion.

NICK J. MANGIERI
PLAINTIFF

In an attempt to justify his absence at the session and his failure to produce the requested City records in accordance with the SUBPOENA D.T., Curtis filed his own AFFIDAVIT with the court. In it, he alleged that not only was the production of those records "an invasion of the privacy of those about whom the records represent," but that I did not include the proper fees for him to attend because I underestimated the time involved in a round trip from Palmer to Anchorage.

I immediately filed a MOTION TO PRODUCE DOCU-MENTS, and then in exasperation of his blatant defiance of the court, I followed up with a MOTION TO HOLD DEFENDANT WILLIAM CURTIS IN CONTEMPT OF COURT, and also an unusual — if not an amusing — AFFIDAVIT to cover my contentions:

AFFIDAVIT
STATE OF ALASKA
ss.

THIRD JUDICIAL DISTRICT

NICK J. MANGIERI, being first duly sworn, deposes and says:

Of the 27 months that I lived in Palmer, Alaska, the vast majority of that time was spent commuting to and from Anchorage, on a daily basis. The many, many hundreds of trips made were driven in favorable and in adverse conditions, at various times of the day, week, and month of the year, and I can say, without qualification, that I can never recall a round trip that took two and a half to three hours — as Defendant WILLIAM CURTIS alleges in his AFFIDAVIT.

In an effort to disprove affiant's gross exaggeration, I conducted an experimental "run" under controlled conditions to ascertain the exact time that would be expended. A report of that experiment is as follows:

"On Saturday, November 20, 1976, at 9:45 a.m., from a dead stop — ignition off — I departed from the Municipal Parking Lot at Third Avenue and E Street, thence onto Third Avenue and down to Gambell Street, up to Sixth Avenue and then proceeded on the Glenn Highway toward Palmer. During this brief span I adhered strictly to posted speed limits within the City. Once beyond City limits, I maintained rigid observance of the 55-mph speed limit. At or near the Thunderbird Falls area, I encountered a virtual standstill of a long line of cars. For a distance of exactly three miles, and for a period of exactly ten minutes, I averaged between 15-20 mph. (The reason for the delay turned out to be road equipment performing minor road repairs.) Traffic then resumed a normal flow pattern and I proceeded toward Palmer, again closely monitoring my speed limit to conform to the posted 55 mph. On but two occasions did I accelerate briefly to pass two slow-moving vehicles that were below the posted limit. Only then did I accelerate to speeds not exceeding 59 mph and quickly dropped back and below the 55 mph to compensate for my brief spurts. At precisely 10:48 a.m., I reached defendant WILLIAM CURTIS' driveway — at a total time expended of 63 minutes.

At 11:10 a.m., I proceeded from the vicinity of defendant's driveway on my return trip to Anchorage. I again monitored my speed zealously and constantly so as not to exceed the posted 55 mph. Again, on two occasions across the Eklutna Flats did I have reason to briefly accelerate to 59 mph to pass two other slow-moving vehicles, but again briefly dropped below the 55 mph to compensate for the excess spurts. As I approached 40-mph curves, I conformed to their requirement and maintained that same adherence to other differently posted speeds until I reached Anchorage City limits. At that time, I observed the speed carefully and proceeded down the same route that I had departed from. Again, I entered the Municipal Parking Lot at Third Avenue and E Street, pulled into an adjoining empty space, turned the ignition off and looked at my watch; it was 12:08 p.m. — time expended on the return was 58 minutes. The grand total involved was 2 hours and 1 minute.

Defendant and defense counsel further allege that "demand was made in advance for the appropriate fees." Be it known that no demand was made for any additional fees. If demand were justified, I would have gladly expended any additional minor monies required, having already expended mileage and witness fees for four witnesses. However, I did not expect the time to exceed three hours, having noted how a prior adverse witness responded.

NICK J. MANGIERI
Plaintiff

In apparent shock to my filing a contempt motion against Curtis, City Attorney Biss, in a knee-jerk reaction, responded inappropriately, a tactic he was to utilize frequently in replying to my motions. It was also a measure that I could not tolerate, still of the naive belief that false or misleading statements to the court would not be acceptable. Accordingly, I fired back a new salvo to counteract Biss' flailing response:

PLAINTIFF'S RESPONSE TO DEFENDANTS' OPPOSITION
TO MOTION TO HOLD WILLIAM CURTIS IN CONTEMPT
Defendant continues to maintain a policy of deliberately mis-stating facts, of concealing pertinent facts and of exaggeration of others in an attempt to prejudice the Court.

In order of context, the plaintiff will again continue his policy of analyzing and reporting.

First, defense counsel spoke to plaintiff in the office of the Trial Court Administrator at, or about 9 a.m. on Friday, October 29, 1976, and advised plaintiff that he would not attend the depositions on the following morning. When plaintiff informed him that all of the witnesses were being served, including defendant WILLIAM CURTIS, he stated, "You do what your little heart desires," and hung up abruptly on plaintiff. No other words passed, nor were there any subsequent discussions with defense counsel or with defendant. There was no request for any additional monies, as defendant CURTIS had not yet been served.

At 11:15 a.m. on October 29, 1976, defendant CURTIS was served. He received $21 — a fact that was neither mentioned in his Affidavit nor in the OPPOSITION. Of the $21, $13.50 was for mileage (over-computed at $.15 per mile for 45 miles), plus $7.50 for witness fees. Defendant CURTIS' specific remark to the process server was to the effect that he would not be appearing because the notice was too short. (See Exhibit "A", *Return of Service.*) No mention was made of any additional fees. In fact, defendant commented to the process server that it was not even necessary for him to receive any fees, inasmuch as he was a defendant in the action.

Defendant relies on Rule 9 of the Administrative Rules, which states that if more than three consecutive hours are occupied an additional $7.50 witness fee will be paid. However, contrary to defendant's allegation that two and a half to three hours would be consumed in the entire return trip, it is believed that, as plaintiff demonstrates in his Affidavit, only two hours would be required at most. Specifically, 2 hours and 1 minute were expended by plaintiff under rigid conditions — including a ten-minute traffic delay. (Plaintiff is again willing to duplicate that experiment, should the Court desire, with representative of its choosing.)

Defendant further relies on a Subdivision (F) of Rule 9 which states that a witness may demand payment of the fee "in advance, and when so demanded shall not be compelled to attend until the allowances are paid."

As plaintiff emphatically stated in his AFFIDAVIT, neither explicit nor implied demand was ever made of the plaintiff, by either defense counsel or by defendant. If it were, as plaintiff indicated in his affidavit, he would have been foolish not to have complied. The information sought in the personnel and payroll records was vital and informative to disprove many of defendant's false allegations. As it was, plaintiff overpaid defendant CURTIS $.03 per mile. Accepting defendant's claim of the one-way distance of 46 miles, in lieu of 45 miles calculated by plaintiff, defendant was overpaid $2.46 (90 miles multiplied $.15/mile — 92 miles multiplied by $.12/mile). Plaintiff had subpoenaed four witnesses that day, plus the fees to the process server. Therefore, total fees incurred on that date exceeded $130 (one witness avoided service, or it would have been more). To intimate that plaintiff was unwilling to expend an additional $5.04 does not comport with common sense, assuming of course that an additional $7.50 was in fact necessary.

It has been plaintiff's experience that adverse witnesses in depositions are extremely reticent, and hence not disposed to prolong any session in which they have an aversion to attending and giving evidence.

As proof of plaintiff's contention, the following example is offered:

"Plaintiff is in the habit of preparing his questions in written form to be given at the deposition. When plaintiff called in ROSE ANN KOHLBERG, defendant CURTIS' secretary, for a deposition, he prepared a list of 54 questions to be answered. She was extremely evasive and close-mouthed and consequently consumed about 35 minutes of time."

Plaintiff again prepared a list of questions for defendant CURTIS. However, because the records requested would be left with plaintiff, only 42 questions were drawn up. Therefore, with fewer questions involved and with defendant being as adverse a witness as could be expected, it is foreseeable that the deposition would have been extremely unproductive and short in time. Therefore, although plaintiff set aside 1½ hours, the time was not expected to be utilized, as it was merely an approximation. The time was set prior to plaintiff's preparation of the questions to be presented at the deposition.

In summary, total driving time was 2 hours and 1 minute. The Municipal Parking Lot, at Third Avenue and E Street, was half a block distant from R&R Court Reporters at 509 W. Third Avenue, at best a distance of approximately 200 feet. The lot has several hundred spaces, of which there are over 75 percent vacancies at that hour of the morning on a Saturday. Therefore, an additional five minutes, to and from the building, would be involved. This time, plus an additional 35-40 minutes for defendant CURTIS' deposition would involve no more that 2 hours 41 minutes — 2 hours 26 minutes, both of which are well within the 3 hour time limit specified under Rule 9 of the Administrative Rules.

Defendant has not only continually thwarted plaintiff's attempt at discovery but now brazenly defies an order of the Court to appear at a deposition with records required. His defiance was manifested the day of his service when he stated that he would not appear. His justification was a contrived excuse subsequent to the date of the subpoena duces tecum. Therefore, it is respectfully requested that the MOTION TO HOLD WILLIAM CURTIS IN CONTEMPT be granted and the plaintiff be awarded costs in the amount of $350.

NICK J. MANGIERI
Plaintiff

The motions judge, however, failed to hold Curtis in Contempt of Court, and also denied damage costs that I had requested, in spite of my factual description of events that prompted my action.

The deposition session was then rescheduled for Curtis to appear before R&R Court Reporters on December 10.

When he finally appeared on that date to give his Deposition, I revised the number of my questions from the initial 42 to 50 questions. Had I received the City records that I had originally requested in my SUBPOENA DUCES TECUM, the lesser number would have sufficed. However, because of Curtis' continuing uncooperativeness, an attitude that would remain throughout the pendency of the law suits, I expanded my line of questioning toward him.

Unlike my restrained approach toward his secretary, Kohlberg, in her Deposition, I immediately hit Curtis hard with my questions. His responses were all in his typical low throaty monotone, devoid of any expressiveness or even agitation. I thoroughly expected some sort of reaction, especially after the incriminating queries that were put to him.

During the early stages of the deposition, he surprisingly answered "yes" to all of the three questions that concerned Leroy Herren, the proprietor of the *49er*, that local bar that was always the site of criminal activity. His initial answers were surprising in light of the alleged close-ties between him and Herren:

Q: Did you concur with Chief Mangieri's denial of allowing Leroy Herren to hire liquor handlers without police clearance first?

Q: Were you aware that Leroy Herren had an extensive police record?

Q: Did you authorize his issuance of a business license?"

As the questioning progressed, in spite of his strange lack of emotion to the accusatory queries, his persistent negative answers directly contradicted prior information that I possessed:

Q: Did you ever personally search Chief Mangieri's desk?

A: No.

Q: Did you ever tell your secretary, Rose Ann Kohlberg, that Chief Mangieri was planning on setting up a Mafia organization in Palmer?

A: No.

Q: Did you ever tell her that he had incriminating evidence in his desk?

A: No.

Q: Did you ever tell her to spread "the word"?

A: No.

Q: Did you ever imply anything at all in that connection?

A: No.

Q: Did you ever tell anyone else that he was going to set up a Mafia in Palmer?

A: No.

His blatant denial of the truth continued in his responses, to my inquiries, concerning his threats and intimidations to both my former secretary and to, at least, one of my former officers:

Q: Have you ever threatened to punch Christine Boyle in

the mouth?

A: No.

Q: Have you ever threatened, intimidated or oppressed
any police officers or dispatchers?

A: No, never.

Although he was unaware of the signed statements that I had
from both Boyle and Lemoine, he was definitely aware that their
Depositions were to the contrary. Biss, undoubtedly, informed
him of the content of both their Depositions, as he had also been
present throughout their testimony to me.

His brazen denial, with evidence that refuted him, continued,
however:

Q: Did you ever tell the manager of the Elks Club to
close the gaming room down because former Chief
Mangieri was going to do something about it?

A: No.

Q: ...the Moose Club?

A: No.

When it must of become readily apparent to Curtis from the
type of questions I asked that I must've possessed specific
knowledge about the subject matter he changed his mode of
response:

Q: Have you ever voted or taken any official action on
any property that you had a pecuniary interest in?

A: Not to my knowledge.

Q: Did you ever deny giving Chief Mangieri his Oath of
Office upon your assuming office?

A: I don't recall.

Q: Was it ever requested of you?

A: Not to my knowledge.

Q: Did your secretary, Rosie, ever specifically request it
of you at Chief Mangieri's request?

A: Not to my knowledge.

The majority of his Deposition was in the same mode, either

unresponsive, vague, or pointing the finger of blame at someone else.

His answers were no different than those that I had received from him in the libel case. Although McShea was the attorney-of-record in that case, I was allowed to assist him in the preparation of MOTIONS and supporting MEMORANDA because of my background knowledge and my receipt of ongoing information in the companion case, my reinstatement action.

At the time of my December deposition session with Curtis, I still had not had a satisfactory response to the INTERROGATORIES that I had submitted to him in early July. Although I had replied fully to those submitted to me, Curtis had refused to answer his questions completely.

During December, I also still awaited a response from the court concerning my MOTION TO PRODUCE DOCUMENTS that had been served on Curtis.

Biss, again, in an obdurant effort to defend Curtis' uncooperativeness in producing the City records, filed an objection to my MOTION to force production of those documents.

Upon receipt of the City Attorney's farcical OBJECTION, I couldn't contain my irritation with a system that permitted such duplicity in legal documents.

"How are they allowed to get by with this shit in official court documents, Roger?" I asked him in a visit to his office.

"The court doesn't know what you know," he said seriously. "You'll just have to point it out to them..." He hesitated before he added, "...again."

McShea was right of course, but I was getting fed up with doing the same thing over and over again. However, I quickly wrote up my answer to Biss' OBJECTION:

PLAINTIFF'S RESPONSE TO DEFENDANT'S
    OBJECTION TO
MOTION TO PRODUCE DOCUMENTS

Defendants in typical half-truth fashion are still attempting to convince the court that their actions were proper in not producing documents requested by the Plaintiff in a SUBPOENA DUCES TECUM because they were "not served with proper witness fees".

The "proper witness fees", referred to by defendants, were based upon a contrived estimate that the round trip to Palmer plus the deposition, would involve more than a three hour period, thereby entitling defendant William Curtis to a full day's witness fee amounting to an additional $7.50, (actually plaintiff overpaid Defendant on mileage and the "additional" witness fee amounted to $5.04). Plaintiff shortly thereafter filed a MOTION TO HOLD DEFENDANT CURTIS IN CONTEMPT OF COURT — which was opposed. Plaintiff then very methodically drove a rigidly controlled round trip to Palmer to prove that it would take no more than two hours. Plaintiff's contention was proved correct and Plaintiff further offered to demonstrate to the Court again, if requested. Plaintiff further contended that less than an additional hour would be expended in the deposition process itself — thereby totaling less than the three hours specified for a witness fee that would require the $7.50 that Plaintiff originally submitted to defendant. Plaintiff carefully delineated his reasons for his OPPOSITION and filed an AFFIDAVIT to Support his allegations. The court subsequently denied PLAINTIFF'S MOTION FOR CONTEMPT.

Plaintiff then tendered an additional $5.04 to defendant Curtis who appeared at a deposition on December 10, 1976. Time expended in the deposition was 20 minutes, even less that Plaintiff anticipated and far less that the three-hour limit that was challenged by defendants originally.

Defense counsel in an ostensibly cooperative vein offered to produce whatever records Plaintiff requested upon Plaintiff's securing an ORDER from the Court. Plaintiff prepared such ORDER. However, instead of cooperating, defendants continue to "buy time" by claiming irrelevance — and thus continue to defy the Court by denying discovery to Plaintiff.

Defendants are illogical in their OBJECTION. On the one hand, they are saying that even if some of the individuals, whose personnel records are requested, have less academic background and work experience that Plaintiff has, their hiring is not an issue. On the other hand, they are saying that there is confidential information "including job criticisms, etc.", thereby implying that they could be unfit for their jobs. It would flow that any indications of one who is unfit for a job might then be a candidate subject to firing also. It is in this regard that Plaintiff seeks to examine all of the personnel files requested. Plaintiff is not on a "witch hunt" to unnecessarily expose all of the individuals foibles or proclivities to the public — only to those which tend to show that the individual was unfit to hold his position. Plaintiff has been slandered and libeled. It therefore is right that Plaintiff be able to offer the truth in defense.

Plaintiff is in possession of information, which indicates that Eilers, the former Police Chief, was incompetent in the performance of his duties and his firing would have been justified. There is also similar information about Hanson, the former Chief. Bassett, the former Lieutenant fired by Plaintiff has a personnel file documenting why he was terminated and Norris the former officer fired by Plaintiff has an equally enlightening file. Both, as mentioned in Plaintiff's MOTION were hired by the former Police Chief, Eilers. Shaver, the Public Works Director, admittedly beat dogs to death — a misdemeanor in the eyes of the law and an act that the Defendant Curtis is aware of and has admitted in his deposition. In addition, depositions against Shaver have damaging information and his file may possess pertinent information relative to his relationship with Curtis and Boyd. Boyd, the former City Manager who departed under strange circumstances leaving Plaintiff and others, to believe that his hiring and resigning were done by pre-arrangement. In addition, discussions between Plaintiff and Shaver, early in Plaintiff's career with the City of Palmer, indicated that Boyd should have been fired during his tour with the City of Palmer. The release of Defendant Curtis' personnel file is mandatory to check against his interrogatory in companion case No. 76-1271E and his depositions in the instant case and in case No. 75-6501E involving a former police officer who also instituted suit against Defendant Curtis for improper firing.

Cries of irrelevancy are ill founded and are raised to thwart any discovery pertinent to Plaintiff's allegation that his firing was conceived in malice and perpetuated by conspiratorial overtones. Plaintiff possessed information damaging to the Defendants and because of his unique position as Chief of Police was privy to much more. As 29 Am Jur 2d 302 so aptly notes, "relevancy means the logical relation between the proposed evidence and a fact to be established."

As Plaintiff has intimated there is much to be established and can be accomplished by specific information that Plaintiff now possesses. Those known facts, in conjunction with existing personnel files, are the "relevancy" that Plaintiff suggests and that which Defendants deny.

NICK J. MANGIERI
Plaintiff

Before I hand-delivered my latest creative product to Biss' office, I showed it to McShea, who read it over.

He glanced up at me with the same serious expression that he wore most of the time.

"Have you ever thought of going back to Law School?" he asked.

Surprised at his remark, I shook my head slowly.

"At one time," I said seriously, "but not now."

Not only had I become frustrated with the Alaska Criminal Justice system, but I had become disillusioned with the whole legal system, as well. However, those feelings of disenchantment and dissatisfaction with our system of justice didn't stop me from doing what I knew I had to do. If anything, it made me work even harder to accomplish the desired results.

Nick Mangieri

With the flurry of MOTIONS going back and forth between the City Attorney and me, I failed to notice a new article in a paper that had hitherto not reported any of the events that occurred during the past year. McShea pointed it out to me one afternoon.

"Did you see the *Anchorage Daily News* on December 4?" he asked casually.

"No, I don't usually get the *News*," I replied. "I get the Times."

"Well," he added more enthusiastically, "the *Anchorage Daily News* is finally taking note too."

He showed me the short, but informative article:

"FIRED COP GETS TRIAL"

"Former Palmer Police Chief Nick Mangieri has moved one step closer to winning a day in court in his year-long battle for reinstatement and back pay against the City of Palmer, as MOTION challenging the merits of the case was denied by Superior Court Judge Peter J. Kalamarides. The judge set March 7 as the date for a jury trial in the case.

Kalamarides denied a request for a SUMMARY JUDGMENT by the City of Palmer, ruling there was sufficient cause to warrant bringing the case to trial.

Mangieri was fired by Palmer City Manager Bill Curtis in November 1975, for hiring two new policemen and changing a work schedule without receiving approval from Curtis. Mangieri claims he was denied a fair hearing on his dismissal before the City Council."

"It's about time," I noted as I read it and tossed it on his desk.

"Your work is just beginning," he commented dryly.

As much as I had done throughout the year, I knew that it was still just the tip of the iceberg. In spite of my growing confidence to handle myself in the courts, I still couldn't help but wonder what 1977 had in store for me.

... Chapter 18 ...

Although 1976 had drawn to a close, there were still important actions that had been filed during the year that were still pending. Chief among these was the extensive exhaustive list of questions that I had very methodically prepared for Curtis in my first MOTION in the libel case, on behalf of McShea:

NICHOLAS J. MANGIERI, JR.,
PLANTIFF
vs.
JACK E. MAZE, et al.,
DEFENDANTS

No.76-1271E
INTERROGATORIES PROPOUNDED TO DEFEN-
DANT, WILLIAM CURTIS

"COMES NOW the Plaintiff, by and through his attorney, ROGER A. McSHEA, and under the provisions of Rule 33, Rules of Civil Procedure, directs the following interrogatories to the Defendant, WILLIAM CURTIS, to be answered in writing, under oath, within thirty (30) days from the date on which these interrogatories are served upon him..."

In that very detailed list of questions in the libel case I sought to extract any information that I considered pertinent to his prior actions in the new case. In addition, I pursued every possible related avenue about his personal background that would explain his irrational behavior, i.e.:

- Have the police ever responded to any complaints that you assaulted your wife?
- Have any of your friends or acquaintances ever interceded in any case where you were assaulting your wife?
- Have you, in fact, ever assaulted your wife?
- Are you presently on any form of medication? If so, give the name of such medication and the purpose for which it is given.
- Are you prone to violent behavior?
- Have you ever engaged in any behavior that can be considered violent or destructive?
- Did you about three years ago, totally or partially destroy a friend's apartment with a knife?
- Have you ever been confined or voluntarily admitted to a hospital, institution or sanitarium for your mental or emotional state?
- Have you ever interfered with an official police investigation while under the influence of alcohol or while intoxicated?"

Although I knew the answers to the majority of the above questions through witness statements or other documentation, I wanted to have his sworn written replies so they could be used against him. I sought not only to show his behavior in his personal life, but also how it affected him while he was acting in an official capacity.

In the last question given above, that of interfering with "an official police investigation," it was reported to me that while in an intoxicated state during his first tour as City Manager, he had to be ordered away from a crime scene. In his inebriated condition, he was walking through a bomb scene investigation being conducted by the State Troopers and was negligently handling evidence crucial to the investigation.

In addition to the type of questions shown, there were a great many that asked about the acquisition of both the Industrial Park and the Palmer High School, and feasibility studies thereof, and property ownership on the right-of-ways.

The final question on the INTERROGATORY dealt with his relationship with the Alaska Rural Rehabilitation Corporation.

As was expected, his reply was not made in a timely fashion, and his written answers were neither responsive nor truthful.

Finally, in a MOTION TO COMPEL ANSWERS TO INTERROGATORIES that I filed with the Superior Court in December 1976 for the libel suit, I advised the court that:

"Although Defendant has responded to many of the interrogatories, the veracity of those answered is in doubt. Analysis is presently under way of those interrogatories comparing their responses with those of existing depositions and other facts known to Plaintiff."

In the accompanying MEMORANDUM IN SUPPORT OF PLAINTIFF'S MOTION TO COMPEL ANSWERS TO INTERROGATORIES, I was even more specific.

In part, I stated:

"This memorandum is submitted in support of PLAINTIFF'S MOTION TO COMPEL ANSWERS TO INTERROGATORIES. These interrogatories were submitted to defendant, William Curtis during July 1976. Defendant in turn, submitted partial or incomplete answers to plaintiff, dated August 12, 1976.

Of the 193 interrogatories submitted to defendant, 25 replies were unresponsive with not less than 10 responses being labeled as "irrelevant" by defendant and hence not worthy of any response by defendant Curtis. Defendant has a unique propensity to ignore information that is damaging to his case, sidestep issues, or as mentioned above, label a question "irrelevant." This tendency to thwart discovery that is due plaintiff is also inconsistent with Rule 26, *Depositions and Discovery*, of the Civil Rules of Court. This total disregard for cooperation has been called to the court's attention before in the instant case and has been brought before the court on numerous occasions in plaintiff's companion case (No.75-8520)..."

Also in December, City Attorney Biss subsequently filed a DEFENDANT'S MOTION FOR SUMMARY JUDGMENT in the libel case in another vain attempt to get my albatross off his neck.

Nick Mangieri

Following receipt of his MOTION, I immediately launched into intensive research for my own well-documented reply. It entailed many sweat-soaked hours in its preparation. When it was completed, I submitted a timely rebuttal with my own MOTION and accompanying MEMORANDUM:

MEMORANDUM IN SUPPORT OF PLAINTIFF'S OPPOSITION TO DEFENDANTS' MOTION FOR SUMMARY JUDGMENT

Defendants in their MOTION FOR SUMMARY JUDGMENT address themselves to two main issues:
1. The setting aside of the special recall election of the City Mayor and the City Councilmen held on January 20, 1976.
2. That their actions in preparing and issuing to the public the defamatory "Notice of Special Election" were absolutely privileged and accordingly they should be granted full immunity as a matter of law.

Defendants, in extensive quoting of Municipal Ordinances and of Alaska Statutes have attempted to show that the contesting of the election was not performed in the manner prescribed by law, either by plaintiff or by other qualified parties.

Defendants have also attempted to show that the statements appearing in said "Notice of Special Election" were done in accordance with statutory requirements and with other sources of the law including, but not limited to, case law.

Plaintiff will address each of these claims separately, beginning with the latter claim first. However, before plaintiff delves into all of defendants citations — particularly those challenging plaintiff's allegations of defamation — it should be called to the court's attention that defendants are prone to cite statutory authority and precedent cases that are either not "on point" or have conflicted with prior allegations of defendants. It is with this background that plaintiff finds it mandatory to analyze and dissect for the court's perusal and digestion

Frozen Shield

much of defendants' request of summary judgment.

In their MOTION, defendants have asserted that their responses are defensive statements to plaintiff's prior publication of defamatory material in the recall petition and as such are privileged replies. As authority, defendants give *50 Am Jur 2d*, Secs. 210 & 211 and *41 ALR 3d* 1083.

Section 210 of 50 *Am Jur 2d* entitled *"Defensive Declarations"* states:

"If they are made in good faith and without *malice*, statements made in an honest endeavor to vindicate one's character or to protect one's interests are usually regarded as *qualifiably privileged* even though they are false." (Emphasis supplied)

Defendants must know that in plaintiff's complaint for libel, he has already raised the issue of malice. Defendants must also know that plaintiff's allegations of malice are already supported in his companion case (No. 75-8520) in depositions recently taken in that case. Therefore, the qualified privilege referred to above must apply in the instant case and accordingly, defendants cannot hope for that privilege — if in fact, that is the privilege sought after.

It is defendants who have repeatedly hammered away that they seek the umbrella-like coverage of absolute privilege; yet, they cite this particular section — that of qualified privilege — to apply to their defense.

This section further states: "It is also settled that when one person assails another in the public press the latter is entitled to make reply therein *and so long as the reply does not exceed the occasion*, he cannot be held responsible for any resultant injury" (Emphasis supplied)

It is the defendants who seek the sanctity of this section; however, it is the plaintiff who is able to avail himself of its restrictive wording. The section further states: "It is undisputed that defensive communication will lose its privileged character if the person making it goes beyond the scope of the original attack or indulges in language that is unnecessarily defamatory. It is the duty of

263

the trial judge to determine in limine, as a matter of law, whether the content of an alleged libel made in reply to a prior attack is pertinent or relevant to matter contained in the initial attack."

Therefore, it is the province of the trial court — not the petitioning method of a MOTION FOR SUMMARY JUDGMENT, to determine if the Notice of Special Election" has gone beyond the scope of the original attack or has indulged in language that is unnecessarily defamatory.

Section 211 of *50 AM Jur 2d*, titled, "*Statements made in course of controversy*" is also relied upon by defendants apparently in defensive retort to plaintiff who provoked the accusations. However, again, a section is cited that does not offer defendants the blanket solace they seek. As indicated "*While some courts proceeding on the theory that one defamation cannot be set off against another, hold that no privilege attaches to a libel or a slander merely because it may have been provoked by a prior publication of objectionable character*, others take the view that a defamatory communication in the course of a mutual controversy is qualifiably privileged if it bears a reasonable relationship to the original aggression." (Emphasis supplied)

Note, that even those jurisdictions that permit defamatory retorts, the term "qualified" privilege rears its ugly head to thwart malicious transgressions.

As stated above, defendants offered *41 ALR 3d* 1083 for a "complete discussion". Presumably they refer to the privilege of responding to alleged defamatory material by the plaintiff, as these are the preceding sentences to the citing of the above annotation. However, "1083" is not explanatory as *41 ALR 3d* is at 1083-1105. And all sections are explanatory of the obliquely oft-quoted "*Qualified Privilege of Reply to Defamatory Publication*." (Emphasis supplied)

Plaintiff will refer back to this annotation as he analyzes cases cited by defendants in their steady pursuit of the ever-elusive absolute privilege. Further, it is noted by the plaintiff that although this "hue and cry" is maintained throughout the MOTION FOR SUMMARY JUDGMENT, it is but a slender thread that attempts to entwine all of the precedent cases cited by defendants. Of the ten cases cited by defendants only four deal with the defense of absolute privilege. However, for purposes of comparison and clarity, plaintiff will attempt to examine each of defendants' cases in their appearance in the MOTION.

In referring to *Animation Equipment Corporation vs. Portman*, (1959) 192 NY Sup 2d 268, defendants state that:

"Once the court determines the privilege to exist it is treated as a complete defense." (The privilege spoken of is the conditional or qualified privilege.) Apparently, the defendants are using the above case in an analogy to their own replies in the "Notice of Special Election". The defendants, however, are premature in their analogous conclusion as *41 ALR 3d* 1089 in referring to the *Animation* case states that:

"Ruling on the plaintiff's motion to strike certain defenses, including the defense of privilege because of provocation, the court said that while provocation may be a partial defense, the privilege of reply is a complete defense, and in the opinion of the court it was a *question of fact for the jury to determine* whether the privilege should be accorded the reply." (Emphasis supplied)

Defendants again use the broad brush of generalities that are unsubstantiated in law when on page 8 of their MOTION they state:

"*All* Courts appear to hold that any inference of malice that might otherwise be imputed to the Mayor and Councilmen is overcome by the *existence of the privilege*." (Emphasis supplied)

Defendants state that plaintiff "subjected his own motives to discussion when he made the attack on the defendants and cite *Mencher vs. Chesley*, (1948) 85 NY Sup 2d 431 as apparent authority to support an unclear contention. Again, in *41 ALR 3d* 1089 referring to the

Nick Mangieri

Mencher case it states:

"The plaintiff contended that in repelling the attack the defendant went beyond his privilege, and that consequently it afforded him no protection, but the court disagreed, saying that the reply seemed to be relevant to the issues made by the plaintiff, *and the question whether the defendant went beyond his privilege was one of fact for the jury and could not be disposed of as a matter of law.*" (Emphasis supplied)

Also see *Collier v. Postum Cereal Co. Limited*, 150 App. Div. 169, 134 N.Y.S. 847. There the court said, 150 App. Div at page 178, 134 N.Y.S. at page 853:

"The important question is whether the defendant had the right to impugn the motives of its assailant, if it did so honestly without malice and for the sole purpose of repelling the assault upon it, and not with the view of injuring the plaintiff..."

Again, the issue of malice that must be resolved and in the *Collier* case as in the *Mencher* case it is one of fact of the jury to determine.

Defendants cite *Phifer v. Foe* (Wyo 1968) 443 p.2d 870, 41 ALR 3d 1078 in the expectation that the awarding of summary judgement to defendants will induce the court in the instant case "to follow suit." However, not only is the factual situation totally dissimilar to the case at bar but more importantly, the reason that plaintiff Phifer failed in his case is at page 872:

"In any event, plaintiff Phifer has failed to demonstrate by affidavits, depositions or otherwise that evidence is available which would show either Foe or Kendig participated in publication of the alleged defamation with knowledge that it was false, or with reckless disregard of whether it was false or not."

The court earlier stated at page 871 that:

"When courts say statements made in reply to defamatory attacks enjoy a "qualified privilege", they mean the statements made in reply are privilege unless and until plaintiff proves they are false and made with actual malice. *Collier v. Postum Cereal Co.*, 149 App.

Div. 143, 133 N.Y.S. 852, 853; *Ashcroft v. Hammond*, 197 N.Y. 488, 90 N.E. 1117, 1120. See also *Bailey v. Charleston Mail Association*, 126 W. VA. 292, 27 S.E. 2d 837, 844, 150 A.L.R. 348."

Defendants cite three cases which "summarize the case law concerning the right of fair comment" in an attempt to justify defendants' statements in the afore-mentioned "Notice of Special Election." The first case *Pearson v. Fairbanks Publishing Co.* 413 P.2d 711 (AK 1966) embraced the holding of the landmark case of the *New York Times v. Sullivan* with regard to malice. At page 715 the court states:

"We adopt for this jurisdiction the meaning of actual malice as given by the United States Supreme Court in the case of *New York Times v. Sullivan.* Actual malice exists when it is proved that the defamatory statement was made with knowledge that it was false or with a reckless disregard of whether it was false or not. Under this meaning of the terms, the use of the knowingly false statements or the false statement made with reckless disregard of the truth will abuse — thus destroying — the privilege that otherwise would be enjoyed in discussion and debate on public questions and issues."

The court had earlier stated at page 713 that "freedom of debate and expression on public questions and issues" should be allowed "even if such comment criticism and judgement involves mis-statements of fact — so long as such mis-statements are relevant to the subject matter spoken or written about by the one claiming to be defamed *and are not shown by him to have been made with actual malice.*" (Emphasis supplied)

In *West v. Northern Publishing Co.*, 487 P.2d 1304 (AK 1971), the second case cited by defendants dealing with fair comment was again totally alien to the instant case. In the *West* case there was illegal distribution of intoxicating beverages by cab companies to minors. There was little doubt that legitimate public interest was involved but the libel suit, unlike the case at bar was brought about by a private individual and not a public

official, a status that plaintiff found himself in, in the
instant case. Summary judgment was granted Northern
Publishing Company because appellant West failed to
show that the libel was uttered with "knowledge that it
was false or with reckless disregard of whether it was
false or not." The court maintained the holding set forth
in the *New York Times* case.

The third case cited by defendants is the oft-quoted
case dealing with public officials and their defamation,
The *New York Times v. Sullivan*, 376 U.S. 254, 84 S. Ct.
710, 11 L. Ed. 2d 686 (1964).

Defendants at page 11 of their MOTION state:

"Publications dealing with political matter and public officers are privileged by reason of the public interest
involved. Debates on such public issues as here involved
must be uninhibited, robust and wide open and may well
include vehement, caustic and unpleasantly sharp comments, but are nevertheless protected by the First
Amendment."

It would appear that defendants have misled the
court in presenting a partially true statement in the belief
that it would be accepted at its full face value. As plaintiff has so laboriously dissected cases cited by defendants
and has so painstakingly quoted from his own citations,
the issue of malice is ever present and must be considered and either acknowledged or discarded by the court.
As to the first part of defendants statement that such publications are "privileged." It has been shown repeatedly
that similar publications are only privileged when there
is an absence of malice and that determination is for the
trial court. As to the second part, "Debates on such public issues...etc.", again, there is additional information
needed to clarify this statement. First of all, the quote
should be accurate. At page 711 of 84 S. Ct 710 (1964)
under Item 9 Constitutional Law is the wording:

"*There is a national commitment to the principle*
that debate on public issues...etc. U.S.C.A. Const.
Amend. 1. (Emphasis supplied)

The "national commitment" stated above does not

offer the mandatory overtones of the law as implied in defendants' MOTION. Further, since the wording of that paragraph as seen above is used in the same context as the *New York Times* case, it would again appear that this is the holding of the case. At page 726 the holding is as follows:

"The constitutional guarantees require, we think, a federal rule that prohibits a public official from recovering damages for a defamatory falsehood relating to his official conduct unless he proves that the statement was made with 'actual malice' — that is, with knowledge that it was false or with reckless disregard of whether it was false or not."

The defendants are attempting to justify their libelous statements by using the pretext that because plaintiff "voluntarily thrust himself into the public eye" and subsequently became a "public figure" that he was then "fair game." Defendants have failed to consider that it was they who were the original aggressors by firing plaintiff from his position as Chief of Police, by issuing slanderous statements with knowledge of their falsity, by conspiratorial arrangements among all defendants and their agents to deny plaintiff due process and by further preparing and issuing the above-mentioned libelous "Notice of Special Election," which intentionally affected the recall election — a violation of AS 15.55.180, *Improper influence of election by election officials* — in which capacity one of the defendants resides.

As to the four cases defendants cited relying on the condition of absolute privilege they will be handled in turn and in the context that they were presented. Defendants state that "plaintiff invited and instigated the defendants' statements and cannot now complain of alleged damage which he brought about" and then cite *Williams v. School District of Springfield.* (MO. 1969) 447 SW 2d 256 as the authority that is representative of that contention.

Defendants, again, are not "on point." Plaintiff Williams in the above case *specifically requested* at a

Board of Education session the reasons for her non re-employment the following school year. At page 268, it quotes from the Restatement of Torts, Chapter 25, Section 583, p. 22 et Seq. as follows:

"General Principle. Except as stated in Sec. 584, the publication of false and defamatory matter of another is *absolutely* privileged if the other *consents* thereto."

Defendants further state that in *Scott vs. McDonald Douglas Corp.*, 37 Cal Apls. 3d 277, 112 Cal Rptr 609, there is additional authority vindicating their issuance of the libelous "Notice" so as to render their actions absolutely privileged. However, the difference in the Scott case and the instant case is as follows:

1. City Councilmen in Santa Monica wrote and circulated allegedly defamatory letters about the City Manager *at a session of the regular City Council meeting*.

2. The "Notice of Special Election" was placed in the newspaper by the defendant City Manager, who also acts as the City Clerk.

The Court in the *Scott* case stated that:

"In California this freedom from liability for statements made before a legislative body is codified in section 47 of the Civil Code. The privilege provided by section 47 (subp.2) has been held to be absolute."

Because the libelous statements were not specifically intended for nor presented to a legislative body (of which there is considerable arguments against a municipal legislative body) the absolute privilege would not apply.

In the third case cited by defendants, that of *Noble v. Turnyik* (Ore) 539 p.2d 658, it is also apparent that they seek the veil of absolute privilege. However, again, allegedly defamatory statements were made at a *port commission meeting*. At page 660, it states:

"The Congress and state legislatures have always been privileged in their statements. Prosser, Supra, at 781-784; 1 Harper and James, Law of Torts, 427, Section 5.23. There has been a divergence of judicial opinion, however, on the question of whether the absolute privilege extends to lesser legislative bodies."

The Court further states that the latest version of tentative draft Sec. 598A of Tentative Draft No. 20 of the Restatement of Torts is:

An occasion is conditionally privileged when an inferior administrative officer of a state or of any of the subdivisions of the state, makes a defamatory communication which is required or permitted in the performance of his official duties."

The Court in reaching its decision admits that the tentative draft of Section 590 of the Restatement of Torts "may never be approved by the American Law Institute" but that they would follow it.

The final case relied upon by defendants is that of *Bigelow v. Brumley*, et al 37 N.E. 2d 584. Defendants state that "government officials engaged in the discharge of duties imposed upon them by law are immune from libel suits arising from official communications in respect of matters within their authority."

Again, defendants are not "on point." The *Bigelow* case deals with The Secretary of State of Ohio who in his executive capacity is absolutely privileged against actions for defamation. In addition, members of the State Legislature were involved and in their legislative capacity were absolutely privileged. Nowhere does it discuss inferior legislatures and their absolute privilege. Accordingly, the above case cannot be relied upon by defendants in their search for absolute immunity.

Defendants, at page 10 of their MOTION, again reach the improper conclusion that said Election notice was absolutely privileged and base that erroneous determination on Sections 220,222 and 224 of 50 Am Jr 2d. However, inspection of those sections not only does not support that contention but also cites authority favorable to the plaintiff.

Section 220 states:

"The occasion and the office afford the test whether an allegedly slanderous or libelous statement by a public officer will be absolutely privileged, conditionally or qualifiably privileged, or not at all privileged."

As authority, this section cites *Mills v. Denny*, 245 Iowa 584, 63 .W. 2d 222, 40 ALR 2d 933, which holding is supportive of plaintiff's stated position herein. At page 734 of *50 Am Jur 2d* the *Mills* case holds that:

"Statements by the mayor during a City Council meeting were not absolutely privileged, under the circumstances, indicated that, as a general proposition, statements or utterances by members of the governing bodies of political subdivisions in the course of official proceedings were qualifiably, and not absolutely, privileged."

Section 222 although noting "that some courts refuse to extend the protection of absolute privilege to the proceedings of municipal councils and other subordinate legislative bodies" does mention that "other courts hold or recognize that *under some circumstances.*" (Emphasis supplied)

This section goes on further to say that:

"A statement by a Councilman which was not made on the floor of the Council, but was first published through a political headquarters, has been held to enjoy, at most, only a qualified privilege."

Section 224, entitled Communication by or between governmental officials and also relied upon by defendants states:

"Under this rule, absolute privilege is extended to the statements and communications of *cabinet officers, governors of states, and to state officers occupying positions corresponding to cabinet offices.*" (Emphasis supplied)

Plaintiff fails to see how any of the defendants fit this category and why it was so liberally interpreted and then cited as one of its authorities.

Defendants, in their excursion into the libel and slander sections of *Am Jur* have neglected to touch upon section 221 *Legislative proceedings.* Although such "legislative proceedings" were not apparent in the instant case, defendants have attempted to raise that "straw-man" issue throughout their MOTION. It should be noted that this section states:

"Moreover, there are decisions which hold that where the privilege attaching to legislative proceedings is abused for malicious purposes, such misconduct is actionable."

It is apparent that defendants have unwisely selected authorities that are inconsistent and contradictory to their tenacious position in an effort to seize upon the rampart of absolute privilege. It is believed that plaintiff has undeniably shown that defendants' contentions are without substance or merit and accordingly their request for summary judgement in this area should be denied.

As to defendants' claim that the special recall election of January 20, 1976 should not be set aside, it should be noted that defendants violated several sections of the Alaska Statutes, specifically AS 15.55.180 — *Improper influence of election by election officials,* cited earlier in this opposition; AS 29.23.580 — *Meetings public,* which provide that the assemble and council "shall provide reasonable opportunity for the public to be heard at regular and special meetings and AS 44.62.310— *Agency Meetings public,* which further amplify the content and subject matter of special meetings or executive sessions.

Plaintiff has raised these allegations on several occasions of defendants' violations of each of the above statutes and stands ready to prove his contentions in the proper forum. Discovery has already commenced in companion case No. 75-8520 and witnesses are still available to corroborate plaintiff's allegations. Defendants should not be allowed to take advantage of the results of a recall election that was favorable to them when they have violated Alaska Statutes dealing with Municipal Governments. These statutes are not unrelated to the special election as plaintiff's firing, illegal City Council meetings, the recall election with its attendant libelous "Notice of Special Election" are all directly and proximately related and have produced a domino-effect that cannot be ignored merely because plaintiff does not have "standing" to challenge the election nor was it done in a timely matter. Plaintiff was not apprised of all pertinent actions and motives in the instant case until subsequent to the aforementioned recall election. As statutory authority supporting plaintiff's contention that the court may act affirmatively in his behalf is paragraph (f) of the above-mentioned AS 44.62.310 which states;

"Action taken contrary to this section is void."

As plaintiff stated above, secret special meetings were held by defendants and agreements reached prior to the special recall election — all in violation of the statutes concerning public meetings. Therefore, any actions emanating from these meetings are void — including the recall election.

It is requested that summary judgement in this area be denied as "one cannot profit from his own wrongdoing."

McShea and I both waited for the Motion Judge's decision as to the merits of my OPPOSITION against Palmer's request for SUMMARY JUDGMENT. I felt confident as to the results, knowing that I had done the best that I could possibly do. McShea, however, was a little more circumspect in his views on its success, having been in the practice of law for many years. Unlike my reinstatement case in which Judge Kalamarides issued his DECISION in my favor regarding a similar request for SUMMARY JUDGMENT, the libel case was assigned to another Superior Court judge, Judge Eben H. Lewis.

Finally, a month later, the long wait was justified when it produced a partial — if not a substantial — victory over Biss' MOTION FOR SUMMARY JUDGMENT. On February 4, 1977, Judge Lewis also issued a favorable ORDER. It stated in part:

"...with regard to the allegations concerning defamation, this court finds that genuine issues of material fact remain to be resolved by the tryer of fact. These would include, but are not necessarily limited to, whether the statements were published by the DEFENDANT with malice, and whether the published statements were true or not."

My lengthy MEMORANDA concerning Malice had paid off, and the DEFENDANT'S MOTION to have my libel case dismissed was denied. However, the judge also denied my request to have the RECALL ELECTION set aside.

When McShea first showed me the judge's ORDER, he was uncharacteristically beaming.

"You must be doing something right, Mangieri," he said in an animated tone.

He liked to call me by my last name. Perhaps he liked the sound of it. In any case, he usually — if not always — addressed me in that manner.

"I worked my tail off on that MEMORANDA, Roger, and I had a feeling that it would fly."

"Well, you were right," he said, smiling again.

"Yeah, but it should've been a *complete* success," I argued. "The judge should've held that a new RECALL ELECTION was in order based on their behavior."

"Look at the bright side, Mangieri," he said. "Do you realize how much you've shaken them up because of the judge's decision?"

I nodded my head in grudging agreement.

"This is the second MOTION FOR SUMMARY JUDG-MENT that they've failed at," he said. "The first was your reinstatement case, and now this one. Both judges recognized the need to go to court, and," he added, "Biss has thrown the book at you in both instances — and has lost both times."

I had to admit that he was right.

"Come on, Roger. I'll buy you a drink to celebrate."

... Chapter 19 ...

In the weeks before Judge Lewis' heartening decision to deny the City of Palmer's MOTION to dismiss my libel action, the reinstatement suit was going through a perpetual seesaw ride.

During prior discussions with McShea we agreed that perhaps it was feasible to combine the cases into a single suit. On January 3, I filed a MOTION TO CONSOLIDATE case No. 75-8520 with case No. 76-1271E. The Palmer City Attorney naturally filed an OPPOSITION, and I in turn, filed an immediate reply:

PLAINTIFF'S RESPONSE TO DEFENDANTS'
    OPPOSITION
TO MOTION TO CONSOLIDATE

Plaintiff has shown in his answers to interrogatories in companion case No. 76-1271E that Defendant Curtis, acting as City Manager irrationally and without prior notification or valid reason abruptly fired Plaintiff from his position as Chief of Police for the City of Palmer.

Plaintiff in numerous depositions in the instant case, from both cooperative and hostile witnesses, has ably demonstrated that:

(1) His supposed "hearing" at a public City Council meeting was a "kangaroo court."

(2) His officers and dispatchers were subsequently intimidated by Defendants.

(3) Defendants, those in their employ/control, slandered Plaintiff after his discharge and still continue to do so.

(4) Defendant Curtis was motivated by malice in his:

a) Discharge of Plaintiff

b) Publications of the libelous "Notice of Special Election."

Plaintiff will show in the courts that:

(1) Defendants in the libel case (No. 76.1271E) all agreed with Defendant Curtis to illegally discharge Plaintiff without valid cause case (No. 75-8520).

(2) Defendants continued that illegal agreement with Defendant Curtis to publish the libelous "Notice."

Plaintiff will also demonstrate that the reasons for his discharge and for events that culminated in the aforementioned "Notice of Special Election," which prompted his libel suit, are all steeped in time, past events and intertwined personalities in the City of Palmer. Both actions by Defendants were a continuum and will be shown by Plaintiff to be inseparable.

Plaintiff can further show that in his performance as Chief of Police he was a threat to individuals and activities in the City of Palmer and surroundings and could not be allowed to continue. His being fired summarily by Defendant Curtis was concurred in during "back-room sessions" by Defendants City Councilmen and the 'Notice'" that "fell on the heels " of those actions was also agreed to by all Defendants.

Defendants in mocking justification of having the MOTION TO CONSOLIDATE denied, refer to Plaintiff's "dislike of the City of Palmer", as the reason for his lawsuits.

Defendants, however, confuse Plaintiff's devotion to a cause and his steadfast adherence to the truth as being directed against "The City." It is not the "silent majority" within the City of Palmer that Plaintiff is at odds with. It is the corrupt handful that runs the City for

Nick Mangieri

their own greed and benefit, and it is those who trod on the rights of individuals that are the subjects of these actions.

It is respectfully requested that the MOTION TO CONSOLIDATE be granted for the above reasons and to save the Court from considerable duplication of effort that will result in unnecessary time and expense to the Court System.

This new MOTION wasn't the only legal response with which I had to contend. In yet another battle with Biss and his continual foot-dragging to produce the required City records, I was forced to file still *another* unnecessary detailed MEMO-RANDUM, on January 6, in an effort to see the records that were being deliberately kept from me:

PLAINTIFF'S RESPONSE TO
DEFENDANTS' MEMORANDUM

Defendants' continue to deliberately misinform the court of their actions in what appears to be an on-going effort to try to convince that authority that they are fully cooperating with plaintiff. However, the instant case and that of companion case No. 76-1271E abound with contradictions that have previously been pointed out by plaintiff to the court.

In their latest bit of "misinformation," defendants allege that plaintiff was "repeatedly" informed by defense counsel that he could inspect and copy his own payroll records at counsel's business office. This grandiose gesture of cooperation — even if true — would be but a hollow response to the initial request for the payroll records of five individuals. As it were, defense counsel merely advised plaintiff *once* — at the December 10, 1976 deposition of defendant William Curtis — that plaintiff's payroll record would be made available to plaintiff. However, at that deposition, the defense counsel also advised plaintiff that the other four payroll records would be made available, as would the records of repairs to all police units. As plaintiff indicated in his MEMORANDUM IN SUPPORT OF PLAINTIFF'S MOTION TO PRODUCE DOCUMENTS, dated December 17, 1976, defense counsel advised plaintiff that there must have been a "misunderstanding" as to their production on a voluntary basis. Plaintiff is again forced to draft unnecessary memoranda in an effort to secure an ORDER of the court to force defendants to cooperate.

Plaintiff has recently been required to call defense counsel's office three times over a period of several days to establish a time certain for new depositions before counsel returned his call. At that point in time, more than two weeks had elapsed and the documents relating to repairs of police units had not yet been made available to plaintiff in defense counsel's office. When plaintiff again inquired as to the availability of those documents, he was advised they would be transmitted to counsel's office. They apparently did arrive in his office on January 3, 1977 — a full three weeks later (or so plaintiff has been informed by defense counsel's secretary). Plaintiff, however, is guardedly restrained in deriving any helpful information from those documents as defendants in their OBJECTION TO MOTION TO PRODUCE DOCUMENTS, dated December 21, 1976, have already interjected a note of negativity when they state that they would produce the documents "insofar as the same exist."

Defendants state in their MEMORANDUM that because plaintiff has amended his complaint to delete references to compensatory time and has filed with the State Department of Labor, he should be precluded from obtaining payroll records of some of the individuals requested because it would be immaterial to his cause of action. However, perjury by defendants and those in their employ would certainly be material and relevant and could easily be ascertained by inspection of the payroll records, since plaintiff already possesses information obtained via depositions and is of that belief.

Nick Mangieri

As defendants so dutifully pointed out in their MEMORANDUM and in their above-mentioned OBJECTION, that even if defendants were careless in their "hiring" of employees, it would not be relevant to their "firing." However, in PLAINTIFF'S RESPONSE TO DEFENDANTS' OBJECTION TO MOTION TO PRODUCE DOCUMENTS, dated December 30, 1976, that point was specifically addressed.

Further, defendants continue to libel plaintiff in the sanctity of a legal motion by expressly stating that "at least on several occasions when plaintiff *claims* (Emphasis supplied) to have been working overtime he was actually moonlighting on another job."

Plaintiff, as defendants are well aware, was teaching a course at Mat-Su College for the University of Alaska and the time expended was truthfully and forthrightly listed on his time card and explained in great detail in companion case No. 76-1271E in his SUPPLEMENTAL ANSWERS TO INTERROGATORIES. (See pages 15-16 of those Answers in Attachment "A").

For the foregoing reasons it is respectfully requested that the MOTION FOR PRODUCTION OF PAY-ROLL RECORDS be granted.

Reference made in the above MEMORANDUM for the requested "records of repairs to all police units" was for the purpose of refuting defendant's prior allegations concerning my car. Those claims implied that the damage to my own police unit in a car chase was unnecessarily excessive. Inspection of repairs to all units would have proved otherwise, as I was already in possession of copies of some requests to do repairs on the other units.

Those records, however, were *never* produced for me.

Again, for whatever reason, the Motions Judge did not accede to my reasonable requests for the City records. Nor, was such refusal ever explained to me. In fact, the reasons for any other denials were never given.

During that same week that I filed both MOTIONS with the court, I had both the City Mayor Jack Maze and Chuck Shaver

served to appear before the court reporters so that I could take
their Depositions.

As was my usual custom, I prepared a list of 78 probing questions to deluge Maze with. Also, as was my custom, I intended
to hit him hard in the early stages in the same manner that I had
previously questioned Curtis. It was pre-planned in order to
upset his equilibrium.

He, however, did not have the slow-talking, low-voiced
mode of speaking that the City Manager manifested. He was
indignant and loud even before the session started.

At precisely 3:07 p.m. on Friday, January 7, I began with my
litany of questions. They ran the gamut from his conviction for
embezzlement to his political dealings and to his knowledge
about Curtis and any specifics dealing with or about me. His
round, florid face flushed with annoyance at the type of queries
put to him, especially those that dealt with his actions before and
after his federal conviction:

- How much money were you convicted of embezzling
  from the Matanuska Valley Bank?
- When and where did you serve your time?
- How much money was recovered?
- Was your home foreclosed upon?
- Before you went to prison, where was your home
  located — i.e. the address?
- Upon your return from prison, where was your home
  located?
- Before you went to prison was your car repossessed?
  (What year and make was it?)
- Upon your return from prison, what type of car did
  you have (year and make)?
- Did you own any property before you were convicted
  of embezzlement? (Where?)
- Do you own any property now? (Where?)
- Does your wife own any property in her name only?
  (Where?)

The minute questions that related to his financial worth were
purposeful. In addition to knowing that he had served 18 months

in a federal penitentiary at MacNeil Island in the state of Washington, I also had heard from local citizens that he wasn't alone in his embezzlement of the $125,000 from the bank.

I was advised by several people that he was being "taken care of" by others, who were also involved. From my line of questioning, I wanted to concentrate on the "before" and "after" aspects of his financial state.

He was naturally unresponsive or evasive.

I also wanted to tie him into an employment position that he reputedly held as a bookkeeper for a construction company and an $80,000 *error* that reportedly was made in billing for excavation and back-fill for the Susitna Valley High School site.

Again, he was uncooperative.

When my line of questioning zeroed in specifically on Curtis, he looked even more uncomfortable as he responded:

- What was your impression of Curtis his first time as City Manager?
- Were you aware of his physical, mental and emotional state?
- Were you aware that he is on continuing medication?
- Were you aware that he was prone to violent episodes?
- Did you ever comment to employees at that time of Curtis' excessive absences?

As to the last question, I, of course, knew that he had made such pointed comments, but as to the other questions, I had no concrete proof — nor did he volunteer it.

However, additional in-depth digging easily could have discovered it. As a solitary investigator trying to uncover a multitude of facts, I was considerably hamstrung in my efforts.

At 3:47 p.m., the intensive interrogation terminated, and the sweating City Mayor looked over at the imperturbable expression of the City Attorney.

In unison, the bear-like hulk of Biss and the shorter rotund figure of Maze rose from the table, and both left the room quickly.

Subsequent analysis of some of Maze's other specific responses to me all indicated that he had undoubtedly perjured himself in that Deposition:

Q: Do you own any property now?
A: No.
Q: Do you or your wife own any property on the right-of-way to the new Palmer High School?
A: No.
Q: Have you in the past four or five years had full use of a red car?
A: No.
Q: You never used or had possession of a red car emanating from Jenson and Bridges?
A: No!
Q: Did you work as a bookkeeper about four years ago for a construction company?
A: No.
Q: You *never* worked as a bookkeeper?
A: No!
Q: Were you aware of his (Curtis') physical, mental and emotional state?
A: No.
Q: Immediately subsequent to Chief Mangieri's firing by Curtis, did you advise Mangieri that he would 'have all the time he needed to speak at the Council meeting of November 12, 1975'?
A: No, I did not!

His last defiant answer was unabashedly flagrant. Yet, he accomplished that response without any hesitation or any flinching on his part. I couldn't believe his audacity. I not only *knew* that he was perjuring himself in a sworn Deposition, but I had *proof*.

On November 5, 1975, Wayne Higgins and I had made a tape recording of my conversation with the Mayor. In it he said:

"The regular meeting where you're on the agenda is going to be sufficient because you'll have *all* the time that you want."

After a very brief interlude outside the hearing room, Biss returned with Shaver. Still clad in his City work clothes, he sullenly eyed the court reporter, briefly nodded to me and then sat heavily in a chair that I had indicated.

Biss, who was sitting nearby, leaned over and whispered

something to him, and he morosely bobbed his head slowly up and down.

"Can we start now?" I showed my impatience as I said it.

"Of course," Biss answered curtly, as if they were not at fault in the delay.

At 3:50 p.m. I began my attack on Shaver in a series of 73 penetrating questions. They initially centered on the prior Police Chief and the former City Manager, moved on to the dog beatings and his questionable use of City equipment, and finally to his actions against me. Interspersed throughout the rapid-fire questions were constant subtle references to illegality.

Typical of the stream of queries that I peppered him with were:

- Did you think that it was a "set-up," that Jim Boyd (the former City Manager) had to leave because Bill Curtis was scheduled to be City Manager again?
- Did you ever make any comments to anyone stating that Chief Eilers was incompetent and that the Police Department needed a revamping because of his poor supervision?
- Are you aware that it is a violation of the Municipal Charter and of the Alaska State Statutes not to give a municipal officer an Oath of Office before he assumes office?
- During the summer of 1975 did you beat dogs to death with an iron hook?
- Are you aware that there is an Alaskan Statute covering 'cruelty to domestic' animals, which carries a penalty of up to 30 days in jail or a $100 fine, or both?
- Is it customary for City equipment and manpower to assist contractors that are working on City projects?
- While you were Public Works Director did you ever personally authorize City equipment to work with or for private contractors who were engaged in City projects?

Shaver started to shift in his chair over the last two questions, and he glanced at the City Attorney.

I also looked over at Biss, fully expecting him to give Shaver some kind of signal or motion, but he acted nonchalant and looked straight ahead.

I continued pounding him:

- Are you aware that under the Alaska Statutes it is a felony to destroy or falsify public records or to permit another person to do so while you were Acting City Manager or Acting Police Chief?
- Did you ever instigate remarks to the effect that Chief Mangieri was attempting to set up a Mafia organization in Palmer?
- Are you aware that it is criminal slander to 'willfully speak defamatory or scandalous matter concerning another with intent to injure or defame him', and that punishment can be imprisonment in jail between 6 months to a year?

The questioning went on in that same vein for the next half hour. With each new topic, Shaver would lower his chin to respond and then raise his eyes upward again. Frequently he mumbled or was inaudible, and the question had to be repeated. In virtually all of the incriminating queries he had some form of negative answer, although he did admit the dog beatings.

At precisely 4:20 p.m. the session ended and Shaver audibly breathed heavily, undoubtedly thankful that it was over.

For me, however, my work was just beginning. I had to check and analyze statements and Depositions of other witnesses to catch him in the typical lies that had come out of the Palmer people.

There were a series of particular answers by Shaver, in response to my own specific questions that constituted perjury on his part. Half of those that he denied. I had proof to the contrary. The remaining answers could have been easily verified by either a follow-up state investigation or by a Grand Jury.

The following exchange — not taken in order of context — was extracted from the court reporter's tape and indicated not only my intense interest in his responses at the time but also my disbelief at his adamant denials:

Q: Did you ever make any comments to anyone stating that Jim Boyd was incompetent and should be in jail?
A: No.
Q: You never made those statements to Chief Mangieri?
A: No.
Q: You never made those statements in front of Rose Ann Kohlberg?
A: No!
Q: After Chief Mangieri was fired, did you intimidate officers or dispatchers of the Palmer Police Department?
A: No.
Q: You did not intimidate them? You did not threaten them? You did not harass them?
A: No, Sir, I did not!
Q: Was Bill Curtis on the City payroll three weeks before the deadline of applications for the advertised vacancy as City Manager?
A: No, Sir.
Q: Did you ever take any medication out to him while he was out of the City at the insistence of his former wife, Anne?
A: No.
Q: Never?
A: Never!
Q: Were you aware that there was gambling at the Elks or Moose?
A: No, I wasn't.
Q: Did you ever comment to anyone that even if Chief Mangieri were rehired, things would be "done right" the next time and he wouldn't last long?
A: I don't recall that.
Q: (A repeat of the same question)
A: I don't recall making any statement like that to anybody.
Q: You're sure?
A: Yes...(indiscernible comment).
With all of those Depositions behind me, including some

lesser ones, and with the upcoming trial fast approaching, there was a concerted effort on both the City's part and my own to get all our MOTIONS in to the court for the judge to act upon.

The Palmer officials did not want to go to court.

In early February, their defense counsel submitted an ORAL REQUEST FOR CONTINUANCE OF TRIAL.

In response, I not only filed an OPPOSITION to it and an accusatory MEMORANDUM, but also filed a MOTION and a MEMORANDUM FOR RECONSIDERATION OF MOTION TO AMEND COMPLAINT.

In my MEMORANDUM IN SUPPORT OF OPPOSITION TO ORAL REQUEST FOR CONTINUANCE OF TRIAL, I continued my personal attack on Biss:

> "Defense counsel in a 'last-ditch' stand dilatory move has attempted to convince the Pre Trial Conference Judge to continue or set aside the trial scheduled in this matter on March 7, 1977.
>
> "Defense counsel has for the past year resisted all attempts to provide discovery to the Plaintiff. He has, as Plaintiff has continually pointed out to the Court, omitted pertinent facts, taken many other facts out of context and has blatantly misrepresented issues and facts to the court.
>
> "The Motions Judge, being fully cognizant of the facts and issues in the instant case has issued a DECISION denying Defendant's Summary Judgement. If Defendant believed he had merit in his contentions he should have filed a timely RECONSIDERATION. Obviously, he has not done so. He is aware that the time limit has expired many months ago and he cannot now by devious means try to subvert the Motions Judge's DECISION. As Defense Counsel knows, the matter "res adjudicata". His only resort is to the Supreme Court after the trial.
>
> "It is respectfully submitted that the Court in the form of the Pre Trial Judge schedule an immediate date for issues to be presented at the trial."

In my MOTION FOR RECONSIDERATION OF MOTION

TO AMEND COMPLAINT, I referred to a prior MOTION that I had filed on October 11.

It was a MOTION FOR LEAVE TO AMEND COM-PLAINT, that I had previously filed and it included a claim for "punitive damages" against the City of Palmer and its officials. Regrettably, however, the court handed down a decision, dated November 8, 1976, that denied my MOTION and relied on an Annotation at 19 ALR 903 as its authority.

When I read over the annotation in the *American Law Review*, that the judge cited, I did not agree with his interpretation because he did not take into consideration an exception to that citation — which also appeared in the *American Law Review*. It was the basis of that exception that I sought to amend my initial complaint to include the punitive damages. Accordingly, when I filed my MOTION FOR RECONSIDERA-TION, I included with it a detailed MEMORANDUM that should have satisfied the judge:

MEMORANDUM IN SUPPORT OF MOTION FOR RECONSIDERATION OF MOTION TO AMEND COMPLAINT

This MEMORANDUM is submitted in support of Plaintiff's MOTION FOR RECONSIDERATION OF MOTION TO AMEND COMPLAINT.

Plaintiff filed a MOTION FOR LEAVE TO AMEND COMPLAINT so as to include a prayer for punitive damages pursuant to Rule 15 of the Civil Rules of Court. This MOTION was denied by the Court citing the Annotation at 19 ALR 2d 903 and holding that puni-tive damages cannot be awarded against a municipal cor-poration. Although Plaintiff agrees that *generally* the courts do not favor the recovery of punitive or exempla-ry damages against a municipal corporation, there are exceptions to this rule.

Under Section 2 of the Summary at 19 ALR 2d 906 it states:

"An exception to or a modification of this rule is adhered to by some courts which have stated that where there is a concurrence in the wrongful acts of the agent by the citizens of the municipality, or where there is a ratification or subsequent approval by the latter of such acts, so as to show concurrence therein, exemplary damages are properly recoverable against the municipality itself."

As noted in the instant case and in companion case No. 76-1271E, other members of the corporation, i.e. the City Mayor and the City Councilmen concurred in Plaintiff's discharge as Chief of Police. In addition, the citizens of Palmer concurred with the body politic — the City Council — by choosing not to believe the allegations for a recall election and putting their representatives back into office.

Quoting the last sentence from a statement of the Mayor that appeared in a Notice of Special Election in the *Frontiersman* newspaper and on the Special Election ballot itself:

"The Mayor and Council unanimously supported the termination."

The voting public, in turn, voted two to one to retain the City Mayor and all the City Councilmen in the Special Election of January 20, 1976. The reason for the recall election was directly as a result of Plaintiff's discharge and is evident in Exhibit "A."

Plaintiff's allegations of malice are well founded and substantiated, therefore, Plaintiff urges the court to reconsider its denial. Plaintiff further notes that Rule 15 provides that leave to amend a complaint "shall be fully given when justice so requires" and it is Plaintiff's strong contention that justice so requires.

I felt just as strongly with my RECONSIDERATION MOTION, as I did with my initial MOTION TO AMEND, that I was on solid legal ground and had offered the judge sufficient ammo to back me up. However, again, it did not happen. The judge quickly denied my RECONSIDERATION.

Nick Mangieri

Unfortunately, being unaware of the strict filing deadlines — and of being perpetually tied up with legal motions — I failed to file my MOTION FOR RECONSIDERATION timely. However, it didn't prevent me from trying a new approach. I filed another MOTION as a follow-up to other legal responses that I initiated as a result of my unsuccessful attempt:

MOTION FOR ORDER SHORTENING TIME

In accordance with Rule 77 (j) of the Civil Rules of Court, plaintiff requests the above MOTION in order that his MOTION pursuant to Rule 60 may be heard on February 28th. Plaintiff has filed a RELIEF FROM ORDER, dated February 22, 1977, because his MOTION FOR RECONSIDERATION OF MOTION TO AMEND COMPLAINT, dated February 7, 1977, was denied by the Court in a DECISION issued on February 9, 1977. However, as plaintiff pointed out in his RECONSIDERATION MOTION, the Court was unaware that there is an exception under which a Municipality can be made liable for punitive damages. It was this exception that was pointed out to the Court, but it was done untimely.

As plaintiff indicated in his RELIEF FROM ORDER and in his AFFIDAVIT, dated February 22, 1977, he is not an attorney and is acting Pro Per and should not be held to the same standards of performance that an attorney is held. Therefore, an error in procedure should not close all doors to plaintiff to which he is entitled as a matter of law.

I felt that when I filed that MOTION and asked the judge to take into consideration my layman *Pro Per* status, that it was a long shot. However, I had nothing to lose.

With the return of my ORDER, unsigned by the judge, that would have granted me a RELIEF FROM ORDER that denied me the RECONSIDERATION, I knew that I was in trouble.

Whether any judge would have so acted, I don't know. Undoubtedly, there were those who wore the judicial robes who might have considered that justice was not being served by such refusal, especially in light of all the information and documentation that I had brought before the court.

Legal events then moved rapidly downward for me.

On March 2, the Palmer City Attorney filed an extensive TRIAL BRIEF with the court and still sought a summary judgment.

On March 3, the City Attorney in yet another eleventh-hour attempt to have the case dismissed before it went to trial, filed a JUDGMENT ON THE PLEADINGS.

Not to allow the defendants to continue their duplicity on the court, I filed my strongest and most vehement attack on the City Attorney on March 7:

OPPOSITION TO MOTION
FOR JUDGMENT ON THE PLEADINGS

    Plaintiff moves that Judgment be denied Defendants on the ground that Defendants' MOTION FOR JUDGMENT ON THE PLEADINGS with attached MEMORANDUM IN SUPPORT contain deliberate fallacious and misleading statements calculated to influence the Court adverse to Plaintiff's interest.

I then filed my own MEMORANDUM to backup my strong MOTION:

MEMORANDUM IN SUPPORT
OF OPPOSITION TO MOTION
FOR JUDGMENT ON THE PLEADINGS

    In contravention of Rule 12(G), *Affidavits Made in Bad Faith*, defense counsel, in his AFFIDAVIT dated March 3, 1977, has attempted not only to delay the Court in a trial that was scheduled on March 7, 1977, but has attempted to have the case dismissed by deliberately violating the Professional Canons of the Alaska Bar Association's Code of Ethics (DR-7-102, *Representing a Client within the Bounds of the Law*).

    On Page 2 of their MEMORANDUM, Defendants

allege that Plaintiff was provided with a "work contract" which stated that Plaintiff served at the "pleasure of the City Manager."

Plaintiff categorically denies any such self-serving allegations; nor can Defendants supply any evidence to that effect.

Defendants further allege that the personnel regulations state that "all City personnel may be terminated *with or without cause.*" (Emphasis supplied)

Plaintiff again categorically denies ever being advised of any such capricious termination before his employment or during his tenure. Again, defendants deliberately mislead the Court when they state that the personnel regulations advise probationary employees that they may be terminated "with or without cause."

Defendants continue to deliberately mislead the Court by advising the Court in its MEMORANDUM that because Plaintiff admitted in an interrogatory in companion case No. 76-1271E to being an "administrative officer" as per Section 2.1(c) of the City Charter, he also admitted to serving "at the pleasure of the City Manager."

Plaintiff has never so admitted; had never been apprised of the content of the City Charter or had never been given a copy of the City Charter before his employment or during his tenure in office.

In contradiction of the contents of Defendants' MEMORANDUM that:

"The allegations of the above-mentioned paragraph 3 of defendants' answer set forth the basis for a judgment on the pleadings in favor of these defendants."

Plaintiff contends that all of the aforementioned paragraph 3 deliberately has misled the Court in a malicious effort to delay the trial and dismiss the case and hence forms no valid basis for a JUDGMENT ON THE PLEADINGS.

Defendants are well aware that the law of the case has already been resolved by Judge Kalamarides DECISION, when he denied DEFENDANTS' MOTION FOR SUMMARY JUDGMENT and that Rule 56 encompasses Rule 12(c) upon which they so tenuously rely.

Defendants continue to misadvise the Court by stating that only a FIRST AMENDED COMPLAINT exists, which does not contain a claim for compensatory damages. Defendants are aware that a SECOND AMENDED COMPLAINT was filed which again incorporates Plaintiff's claim for compensatory damages. Further, defense counsel continues to malign Plaintiff, knowing the falsity of his allegations when he deliberately sent a letter to the Wage and Hour Division, Department of Labor, State of Alaska which contained outright falsehoods and other misleading statements.

In accordance with the provisions of Rule 56 (c) that penalizes for bad faith that "the court shall forthwith order the party employing them to pay to the other party the amount of the reasonable expenses which the filing of the Affidavits caused him to incur, including reasonable attorney's fees", it is so requested.

Meanwhile, the media that had followed my activities with intense interest and coverage reported on the events as they were happening. In a recap of all that had transpired since my dismissal 16 months prior, the *Anchorage Times* on March 7 carried the timely headline:

"EX-POLICE CHIEF SUES FOR HIS JOB"

Under it, they began:

"Former Palmer Police Chief Nick Mangieri went to Anchorage Superior Court today in his continuing battle against the City Fathers...

"The former Chief was scheduled to appear before Judge Seaborn Buckalew's court at 10 a.m. Jury selection was to begin at 2 p.m. ..."

Events that transpired that morning, after 10 a.m. were a blur of unprepared, frantic activity, on my part, because of the improper and totally unexpected actions by the judge in his chambers.

... Chapter 20 ...

Just prior to my appearance before Judge Buckalew at an in-chambers conference on March 1, I had previously requested that my reinstatement case not go before Superior Court Judge Ralph Moody. Moody was the judge who dismissed Higgins' lawsuit for reinstatement to the Palmer Police Department months earlier and dismissed an ARRC-tainted case many years earlier. As Wayne Hunter, the vociferous critic of the ARRC had noted in his voluminous memoirs:

> "The trial (concerning abrogation of contract against the ARRC) was held before Judge Moody on October 10, 1968. For those who think a fair trial can be obtained before Judge Moody, I will recount the day's happenings. Besides believing the decision was written before opening of court that morning, I believe George's lawyer was paid by the ARRC to throw the trial."

Based on my personal observation of Judge Moody in the Higgins case and on my reading of Hunter's vivid description of the George Engelmann case, there was no way I would have accepted Judge Moody to hear my own reinstatement case. A snowball in hell would have stood a better chance of survival than I would have had in his court. However, when I disqualified him, I was unaware of the future ramifications I would face as a result.

The in-chambers session before the Honorable Judge Seaborn Buckalew proved no better than it would have before the Honorable Judge Ralph Moody. It was an attempt at an immediate resolution of what had been long referred to as the "Mangieri problem" by the Palmer people.

During the brief course of that in-chambers hearing before Buckalew, he first indicated his bias when he suggested to the City Attorney that a MOTION FOR JUDGMENT ON THE PLEADINGS would be considered by the judge himself. I strenuously objected to the judge's suggestion by pointing out that the time for such a MOTION had long since past. I also knew without a doubt that the natural outcome of any such MOTION would result in the immediate dismissal of my case.

As incensed as I was at what I considered a highly improper judicial remark, it was the judge's next comment that goaded me into action.

"I've known Mr. Biss for 25 years and I consider him to be a very honorable man."

I couldn't believe what I was hearing, although nothing should have surprised me after what I had seen and heard in the past 16 months.

In the days that followed, up to the trial date itself, I sought legal ways to have him disqualified as well. My decision was based on his prejudicial statements made during that conference. I learned that the Alaska Supreme Court would have to officially consider my unusual request. My short trip on March 7 to the upper floors of that same building, to the Alaska Court System, resulted in my brief appearance before some of the members of the Supreme Court. At that time they decided that I had to schedule an appearance before another Superior Court Judge, who would then hear the facts and then determine the validity of my allegations. I felt like I was caught in a revolving door, but dutifully followed instructions and went back down to the offices of the Superior Court and then to the court of Judge Victor Carlson to set up a time to be heard. At that point, it had become a farce. I had not yet lost all faith in the judicial system, but that was quickly changing. After hearing my presentation, Judge Carlson's decision was no different than any I had experienced all

that day in the courthouse. The hours I had spent in that building
— with the interminable waiting — had drained the anger from
me and left only frustration.

On March 3, both the *Anchorage Times* and the *Anchorage
Daily News* related the happenings of the previous day.

The *Anchorage Times* noted that:

> "Former Palmer Police Chief Nick Mangieri's court
> fight against City Officials was struck a blow yesterday
> when a judge here dismissed the ex-chief's lawsuit seek-
> ing reinstatement to his former job. But Mangieri, fired
> from his job in November 1975, says he'll appeal the dis-
> missal to the Alaska Supreme Court. He also said he'll
> file suit in the U.S. District Court here saying his Civil
> Rights to due process were violated.
>
> "Moments after a hearing in which Mangieri
> attempted to have the judge disqualified, Superior Court
> Judge Seaborn J. Buckalew granted a motion by Palmer
> City Attorney Burton Biss asking that the case be dis-
> missed.
>
> " 'I took the time to examine the file carefully ... I'm
> granting the City's motion,' said Buckalew about the suit
> in which Mangieri claimed he had been wrongfully dis-
> charged. The dismissal came just before a civil jury trial
> was scheduled to begin.
>
> "Earlier in the day Mangieri, acting as his own attor-
> ney, asked the Supreme Court for a hearing to determine
> if Buckalew should be disqualified from the case. The
> former chief claimed Buckalew was prejudiced against
> him.
>
> "A hearing was held before Superior Court Judge
> Victor Carlson on Mangieri's motion. Citing statements
> he claimed Buckalew made in a pretrial conference,
> Mangieri told Carlson, 'I had the feeling Buckalew
> already had made his mind up.'
>
> "Biss disagreed and Carlson decided that there was
> no reason for Buckalew to be removed from the case. 'I
> don't see where the court abused its discretion,' Carlson
> told Mangieri ..."

The *Anchorage Daily News* in an equally colorful opening by staff writer, Bob Porterfield, also wrote a newsworthy article. Excerpts from that piece appear below:

"A simmering dispute between Palmer City Manager Bill Curtis and former Police Chief Nick Mangieri apparently won't reach a jury for some time — if at all.

"Following a day of whirlwind hearings — including intervention by the Alaska Supreme Court — Anchorage Superior Court Judge Seaborn J. Buckalew Monday dismissed Mangieri's lawsuit against his former employer charging wrongful discharge.

"But, Mangieri said he'll head for U.S. District Court this week with a complaint charging his Civil Rights to due process were violated.

"And, he's going to appeal Buckalew's decision to the state's highest tribunal as soon as he 'can prepare the necessary documents.'

"Buckalew's action came after another Superior Court Judge Victor Carlson, denied Mangieri's motion to disqualify Buckalew for cause.

"Carlson entered the case after the Supreme Court ordered a hearing to determine whether Buckalew has abused his discretion when he refused to remove himself from the case. Mangieri had charged Buckalew was prejudiced against him and had succumbed to coercion by Palmer City Attorney Burton Biss ...

"Mangieri told Carlson he requested Buckalew's disqualification on the basis of statements the judge allegedly made during an unrecorded pre-trial conference in chambers March 1."

The *Frontiersman* also carried an article in the paper's March 10 edition. Although its slant was still obviously pro-City, the article was more circumspect because the paper also was named as a defendant in my libel action:

"Shortly before the case was to go before a jury on

Monday, Superior Court Judge Seaborn J. Buckalew dismissed the suit by former Palmer Police Chief Nick Mangieri that was aimed at recovering his job.

"The action by Buckalew capped a day of legal maneuvering that City Attorney Burton Biss described in conference to Mayor Jack Maze, the City Council and City Manager Bill Curtis. All were defendants in Mangieri's civil action but only Curtis went to the courtroom.

"Biss's summary was given following Tuesday's regular council meeting.

"Mangieri attempted to remove Buckalew from the case but, according to Biss, "he fired his silver bullet when he got rid of Judge (Ralph) Moody" earlier. Mangieri had used the one peremptory challenge permitted under court rules.

"He claimed that he had not received a fair and impartial hearing from Buckalew before the trial, according to Biss. The Supreme Court ordered a hearing before Judge Victor Carlson to determine if Buckalew had abused his discretion, but Buckalew was upheld ..."

Biss was right, of course, when he informed the City Council that I had used up my peremptory challenge when I got "rid of Judge Moody earlier," a challenge that is *arbitrary* in use. What Biss failed to tell the City Council during that conference was that I did not need a peremptory challenge to disqualify Judge Buckalew, as I believed that I had *just cause* to relieve him. Regrettably, Superior Court Judge Carlson found otherwise.

Unfortunately, McShea was not available to advise me how to conduct myself during those courtroom procedures when I acted as my own attorney. As much as I had learned in the preparation of my MOTIONS and DEPOSITIONS, I remained an amateur in the courtroom, and it was to my disadvantage.

In its lengthy coverage of the events in the courthouse, the *Frontiersman* also reported that:

"Biss said he had requested a pre-trial conference in

order to define the issues and prepare instructions for the jury. Judge Buckalew came to the conclusion that our interpretation was correct. We can't instruct the jury if there are no issues to be tried, Biss explained."

Of course there was no mention by either Biss or the *Frontiersman* that Judge Kalamarides, the Motions Judge, had stated four months earlier that, "issues of fact and law exist concerning plaintiff's rights and job classification under the Palmer Charter."

If the City crowd thought they had "won the war," they were being over-confident in their battle victory. Bloodied, but still not beaten, I moved forward again.

This time my new battleground was in the federal courts.

On March 12, the *Anchorage Times* came out with a new story:

"MANGIERI FILES FEDERAL SUIT AGAINST OFFICIALS"

"Former Palmer Police Chief Nick Mangieri filed suit in federal court here yesterday demanding reinstatement to his former job, compensatory damages and $100,000 in punitive damages against Palmer officials.

"Anchorage Superior Court Judge Seaborn Buckalew dismissed on Monday a state court lawsuit Mangieri had filed in an attempt to gain reinstatement to the position.

"At the time of dismissal Mangieri said he was going to appeal the state court action to the Alaska Supreme Court, file the federal court suit and continue to press a separate suit in which he seeks $1.7 million from Palmer Mayor Jack Maze, the City Council and the *Frontiersman*, Palmer's weekly newspaper, for alleged libel and slander damages.

"Mangieri, fired from his job in November 1975, filed the federal court suit against Palmer City Manager Bill Curtis, Maze, City Attorney Burton Biss, the City Council and City Public Works director at the time of the incident.

"In the federal court complaint Mangieri charges he was dismissed arbitrarily and without due process of law and was denied his constitutional right to a fair hearing.

"He contends the actions of the defendants constituted a conspiracy to deprive him of his constitutional and Civil Rights.

"Curtis has said he discharged Mangieri because he "felt he wasn't capable or qualified."

"Mayor Maze and the city council consistently have upheld Curtis' firing of Mangieri."

Not to be outdone in the feeding frenzy on the news, the *Anchorage Daily News*, while late to the foray, carried the following article on March 14, under the headline:

"EX-POLICE CHIEF FILES NEW SUIT"

"Former Palmer Police Chief Nick Mangieri Friday filed a $350,000 suit in U.S. District Court against Palmer City Manager William Curtis, Mayor Jack Maze, City Attorney Burton Biss and seven others, charging conspiracy to deprive the plaintiff of his constitutional Civil Rights.

"Mangieri's action came three days after Anchorage Superior Court Judge Seaborn J. Buckalew dismissed a lawsuit filed by the former police officer charging the same individuals with arbitrarily discharging him from his office, and seeking reinstatement and back pay. That dismissal following an afternoon of hearings during which another superior court judge ruled Buckalew's actions during a pre-trial conference were not an abuse of his judicial discretion.

"In his federal suit, Mangieri charges, among other things, that Curtis, Maze, Biss and then Councilmen James Ekstedt, Willard Johnson, John Dolenc, David Ingalls, Everett "Pete" Pedersen, Arlyn Hanson and Charles Shaver discharged him improperly and did not allow sufficient time for him to present a defense at a reinstatement hearing on November 12, 1975.

"Mangieri seeks $350,000 in compensatory damages, $100,000 in punitive damages, reinstatement and back pay.

"For over a year Mangieri, who is acting as his own attorney, has contended that his discharge was prompted by his investigation into dealings between City Officials and the Alaska Rural Rehabilitation Corporation — a state — chartered agricultural loan agency formed during territorial days — as well as other aspects of what the ex-policeman calls "municipal corruption."

"In the lawsuit filed Friday, Mangieri also has a libel suit pending in state court against several Palmer officials."

The *Anchorage Daily News'* reference to what I considered the heart of my ouster, "the Alaska Rural Rehabilitation Corporation," was the first time that a newspaper — any newspaper — had cited that connection. Although I continually brought the issue up, it did not make print until it was mentioned in the March 12 story. At the time I didn't think much about its omission, but after reading Wayne Hunter's memoirs I began to put pieces of the puzzle together. Hunter had written that Robert Atwood, the publisher of the *Anchorage Times* had also been on the board of directors of the ARRC. Whether or not his membership played a significant part in the decision to play down the corporation's involvement in municipal corruption, I never learned. However, hindsight is always 20/20.

During the preparation of my new Civil Rights case, because I was unfamiliar with the federal format, McShea helped me with the specific wording needed, and I again acted *Pro Per*, or as my own attorney. I also thought that the use of my full name would look more formal in the federal jurisdiction, and used it in lieu of the "Nick J.," as plaintiff. In addition, as reported in both newspapers, I enjoined my nemesis, City Attorney Burton Biss as defendant as well.

After McShea reviewed my case preparation he gave me his quick half-smile as be handed it back to me.

"You were an English major, Mangieri. Do you remember

what Henry II said to the knights of Thomas Becket, the Archbishop of Canterbury?" he queried in a serious tone.

Before I had a chance to think about it or to answer him, he continued.

"Who will free me from this turbulent priest?"

He went on, without waiting for my response.

"You are that turbulent priest, Mangieri," and he hesitated before he spoke again, "good luck."

I liked the literary comparison, and his dry sense of humor.

On March 17, the U.S. Marshal's Office in Anchorage served all of the defendants in the case the following federal action:

IN THE UNITED STATES DISTRICT COURT FOR THE
DISTRICT OF ALASKA
NICHOLAS J. MANGIERI, JR.,
Plaintiff,
vs.
WILLIAM CURTIS, JACK E. MAZE,
BURTON BISS, JAMES EKSTEDT,
WILLARD JOHNSON, JOHN DOLENC,
DAVID INGALLS, EVERETT "PETE"
PEDERSEN, ARLYN HANSON and
CHARLES SHAVER,
Defendants.
No. A77-55 Civ.
COMPLAINT
(**1**) Plaintiff is a citizen of the State of Alaska.
(**2**) The Defendants are all citizens of the State of Alaska, and residents of this Judicial District.
(**3**) The matter in controversy exceeds Ten Thousand Dollars ($10,000).
(**4**) This action arises under Title 42 of the U.S. Code, Sections 1343, 1983 and 1985, and this Court has jurisdiction of this action under Title 28 of the U.S. Code, Sections 1331, 1332 and 1343.
(**5**) At all times pertinent to this complaint, the Defendant, NICHOLAS J. MANGIERI, JR., was Chief of Police of the City of Palmer, State of

Alaska, the Defendant CURTIS was City Manager of
the City of Palmer, State of Alaska, the Defendant
MAZE was Mayor of the City of Palmer, State of
Alaska, the Defendant BISS was City Attorney of
the City of Palmer, State of Alaska, the
Defendants, EKSTEDT, JOHNSON, DOLENC,
INGALLS, PEDERSEN and HANSON were mem-
bers of the City Council of the City of Palmer, State
of Alaska, and the Defendant SHAVER was the
Public Works Director of the City of Palmer, State of
Alaska.

(6) On or about June 1, 1975, Plaintiff was hired as Chief
of Police of Palmer, Alaska. There was a six (6)
month probationary period that would expire
December 1, 1975.

(7) In reliance thereupon, Plaintiff proceeded to enter
upon his employment and perform his duties as
Chief of Police.

(8) On November 4, 1975, without any prior notice or
any indication that he had not performed his
duties properly, Plaintiff was notified by the
Defendant CURTIS that his services were being terminated short of the expiration of the six (6) month
probationary period, subject to confirmation by the
Defendants Mayor and City Council.

(9) On November 12, 1975, Defendants held what purported to be a hearing at the City Council chambers
for the purpose of confirming Plaintiff's discharge.
During the course of this hearing, defendant CUR-
TIS delivered a forty-five minute defense of his
action in discharging Plaintiff, whereas Plaintiff was
allotted only ten minutes in response. The meeting
chambers were also very small and cramped, and
few of Plaintiff's supporters were permitted to be
seated, and no testimony was taken in opposition to
the Plaintiff's discharge.

(10) At the aforesaid "hearing", the Defendant BISS was
permitted to speak in support of the Plaintiff's discharge, but Plaintiff's attorney was forbidden to

speak.

(11) That Plaintiff was dismissed arbitrarily and without due process of law, that the Defendants were acting under color of State and Municipal law, and that such denial of due process was unlawful in violation of the U.S. Code, provisions herein set forth.

(12) That as a probationary public employee, Plaintiff had the constitutional right to a fair and impartial hearing, and denial thereof was a denial of his rights under the 14th Amendment to the Constitution of the United States.

(13) That the actions complained of also constituted a conspiracy under the statutory sections herein set forth, by all defendants, to deprive Plaintiff of his Constitutional and Civil Rights.

WHEREFORE, Plaintiff demands relief as follows:

(1) Compensatory damages against the defendants, jointly and severally, in the amount of Two Hundred Fifty Thousand Dollars ($250,000.00), including salary from November 4, 1975 to date, plus unpaid compensatory time.

(2) Punitive damages against the Defendants, jointly and severally, in the amount of One Hundred Thousand Dollars ($100,000.00).

(3) Reinstatement as Chief of Police of Palmer, State of Alaska.

(4) For such other and further relief as this Court may deem just and proper.

DATED this 11 day of March, 1977.
NICHOLAS J. MANGIERI, JR.
Plaintiff

That night, I received a call from Wayne Higgins at home.

"Chief," he began excitedly, "You're really shaking those bastards up in City Hall."

"That's my intention, Wayne," I replied firmly and calmly.

"Maybe you'll get a fair shake this time in the federal courts," he said earnestly. "You sure as hell didn't get one in the state courts."

"Don't remind me," I said bitterly.

"Speaking about 'remind,' Chief, Wayne Hunter just called me and said that he wanted you to give him a call as soon as possible."

"Did he say what it was about?"

"Not really, something about the death of some judge and that you would really find it interesting."

... Chapter 21 ...

"Hey, paisan. I'm glad you called me right back."

It was a term that Hunter liked to use whenever we spoke, much as McShea would like to call me by my last name.

"You knew I would, Wayne. I always do," I said quickly. "If it wasn't for you I wouldn't have half my information."

"Well, I've got some more for you. I didn't want to overload you before," he said, laughing softly, "but I think the time is ripe for you."

"You mean about some judge that died," I said repeating Higgins' message.

"More than just died," he said, "more like died under mysterious circumstances."

He had my attention.

"Who?" I asked.

"Have you ever heard of Justice Boney?"

"You mean the former Chief Justice that the state courthouse is named after?"

"That's the one, my friend. Chief Justice of the Alaska Supreme Court."

"What about him?" I inquired.

Before I go into any more details about his death, just check past issues of the local papers. When you've read them, give me a call back, and we'll talk some more."

What he said intrigued me. I wanted to press him for more

information, but I decided to wait until I had read about it further.

"When did it happen, Wayne?"

"About five years ago," he replied. "Probably before you came to Alaska."

He was right. I arrived in the state in the spring of 1974, and Justice Boney's death must've occurred sometime in 1972. I wondered why I had never heard about it before. Not only had I worked at the courthouse for over a year, but in all my subsequent investigations, no one had ever mentioned anything that was questionable about his death.

As we spoke, I pondered the possibilities of mysterious death. I knew I would have to delve into it.

"I'll be in touch, Wayne," I said before I concluded our conversation.

"If I know you, my friend, I think you'll be very interested," he answered just before hanging up.

I couldn't wait to check the local papers the next day. The *Anchorage Daily News* was my first stop. When I inquired, the clerk seemed to recall that he died in the summertime, but she wasn't sure of the year. Armed with that additional piece of information, I started with June 1, 1972, and worked my way chronologically through the front pages of the microfilming reels.

By the time I reached the end of the summer, I had found what I was looking for.

The headlines of the *Anchorage Daily News* of Thursday, August 31, 1972, covered the front page:

"CHIEF JUSTICE BONEY IS DEAD IN ACCIDENT"

Beneath the bold caption was one of many articles and columns that were to appear about him.

> The chief justice of the Alaska Supreme Court, George Frank Boney, died Wednesday after his sailboat capsized off the shores of Cheri Lake, about 45 miles north of Anchorage.
>
> Boney, 42, was alone in the small craft about 300 yards from shore when it tipped. He drowned going underwater several times while swimming.

Two men, Raymond F. Peterson and William E. McBride, who were working on a cabin on shore, spotted Boney struggling and jumped into a motorboat to attempt to rescue him.

Peterson said, "We jumped into a motorboat and went out to get him. He was about halfway between our boat and shore. Just about 10 yards before we got to him, he quit splashing. He was sinking when we got there. I reached down and got hold of his hair and pulled him up out of the water. He was about a foot underwater.

"I got hold of his hair, and he was so heavy we couldn't do much with him, so I just held him up as best I could and we pulled him up on beach. I gave him mouth to mouth resuscitation and tried to pump the water out of him," he said.

Two other men who were working on the cabin, William Wheeles and his son, Larry, immediately drove to a nearby store to phone troopers about the 11 a.m. accident, but help arrived too late to save Boney.

"He wasn't exactly swimming when we first saw him. We were a long ways away, and all we could see was just splashing, like floundering in the water. He wasn't swimming, he was just splashing." Peterson said.

The four men on shore, who were taking a respite from Anchorage to build a cabin for a friend, apparently had seen Boney sail his little plastic boat and swim often during the last week.

Peterson said, "The water was cold. He must have had cramps or something because he swims there all the time. He sailed quite a bit, but I can't understand why he was out there today. It was real windy, damned miserable to be working."

Boney was clad only in a pair of fairly long shorts and a T-shirt when he was pulled out. He has a house on Cheri Lake, near Big Lake, where he often relaxed and studied legal briefs.

His body was taken by Troopers to Green's Palmer Funeral Chapel, then brought into Anchorage. Funeral arrangements are not complete..."

The balance of the article spoke of his family, his appointment by Governor Walter J. Hickel as an Associate Justice on December 20, 1968, and his being named Chief Justice on May 8, 1970, by Governor Keith H. Miller.

Not being privy to the manner in which Supreme Court justices were selected and then promoted to the Chief Justice position, I was unaware of the time usually involved in upward mobility. It did seem, however, that two years as an Associate Justice before promotion to Chief Justice was rapid, but I didn't dwell on it.

What I did notice, was an additional interesting comment about him:

"During his four years on the bench, Boney was a sometimes controversial, always voluble justice who often put lawyers through intensive question-and-answer sessions during oral arguments before the five Supreme Court justices..."

The article further noted that he, "also was known as an able, aggressive administrator of the court system..."

I next visited the offices of the *Anchorage Times* to view their back issues of the episode.

The *Times'* headlines in the Wednesday evening edition on August 30 surpassed even the large headline of the *Anchorage Daily News'* front page. It read:

"JUSTICE BONEY DIES."

In a subhead, it stated:

"MISHAP OCCURS
IN CHERI LAKE OUTSIDE PALMER."

When I read that it had occurred near Palmer, I started to get a funny feeling. I didn't know if it was because Hunter had already planted a question in my mind concerning the events that surrounded Boney's death, or whether it had been my unsavory experience with anything that smacked of Palmer.

As I nonchalantly flipped through the various articles about the Chief Justice, I came across an even more interesting one on the Editorial page of the August 31 edition.

It described a highly controversial figure who was facing an uphill political battle in his seeking of a long-term seat on the bench. That was to be decided at the upcoming election.

The following editorial raised even more doubts:

George F. Boney

"IN LIFE yesterday morning, George F. Boney was sailing a small boat on turbulent waters — pondering, perhaps, a stormy period approaching in his career during which time his continued service on the Supreme Court of the State of Alaska would be on the election line.

In death today, the 42-year-old jurist is the object of praise and tribute from associates and friends, universally shocked and saddened by a sudden tragedy on the small lake north of Palmer where the Chief Justice maintained a cabin retreat.

His death by drowning, apparently as a result of the accidental capsizing of his small sailboat in rough waters on an overcast and windy day, stunned people in all walks of life in Alaska.

Once more the sudden death of a man in the prime of life was a startling reminder of how quickly anyone can be called from this life — in an instant, as it were, at a time when death and tragedy seem far removed from the scene.

For George F. Boney, a Georgian by birth and an Alaskan by choice and by spirit, the unexpected came at a time when he was away from the office: at a time when it was known that he was seeking solitude to ponder some of the decisions facing him as the youngest chief justice of all the states.

Only four weeks ago he had announced his intention to stand on the ballot in November for retention on the Supreme Court, under provisions of Alaska's Constitution that require judges to run on their record on a non-partisan ballot if they seek continuation in office to which they originally are selected by gubernatorial appointment.

Frozen Shield

George Boney's decision was to seek a 10-year elective term on the bench, despite the fact that a behind-the-scene political effort was being launched to defeat him.

As a Republican appointee to the high court, the Chief Justice was a political target of those who wanted his seat taken by a Democrat. The immediate cause of the move against him, however, was his leadership in the recent Supreme Court reapportionment of the Alaska Legislature.

That came after the high court unanimously declared unconstitutional the redistricting plan announced by Gov. William A. Egan. The Supreme Court, under Chief Justice Boney, affirmed a lower court's finding of unconstitutionality. The lower court had ordered the reapportionment matter returned to the governor's office for further review by the State Reapportionment Advisory Board — meanwhile leaving in place the existing legislative districts, at least through the 1973 lawmaking session.

Chief Justice Boney, speaking for the Supreme Court, would have none of that.

Reapportionment, under provisions of the one-man, one-vote concept, could not be delayed, the high court held. And the court promulgated its own redistricting plan — the one under which candidates were nominated in last week's primary election, and the one under which the nominees will stand in the November election.

But George Boney will not be on the ballot with them.

He will not face the test at the polls of which he had no fear, despite the opposition he recognized was being mounted against him."

A two-page article in the Thursday evening edition of the then-named *Anchorage Daily Times*, under the sub-heading,

"JUDGES CALL CONFERENCE TO FILL SLOT"

noted the high court's concern over his immediate replacement

Nick Mangieri

because of his important position:

> "The Alaska State Supreme Court, stunned by the drowning yesterday of Chief Justice George F. Boney, moved quickly today to name an acting Chief Justice, with Justice Jay Rabinowitz mentioned as a possible temporary successor because of his seniority.
>
> The special meeting was called for today, just 24 hours after Boney died in the waters of Cheri Lake, but inclement weather in Juneau delayed the departure of Justice Robert Boochever. Court administrator Robert Reeves said the meeting might not be held until tomorrow.
>
> While the four remaining justices, Rabinowitz, Boochever, Roger Connor and Robert Erwin will ponder the question, Reeves said they could elect a Chief Justice for a three-year term or could name an acting chief and wait for the appointment by Gov. William A. Egan of a fifth court member before selecting a permanent Chief Justice.
>
> The death of Boney has confronted the court with precedent setting decisions concerning succession to the Chief Justice position. It is a position as administrative head of the judicial branch of government and is one of the most powerful in the state..."

It further stated that an autopsy was held and that "Coroner Ronnie Bray said she would announce the results when the pathologist's report is completed."

That report, upon its release, stated that as a result of witness' testimony on the day of Justice Boney's death, that it was indeed just a case of "accidental drowning."

The reading of those newspaper accounts held my interest sufficiently enough to warrant my learning more of the man, who had become a legend in his own time in the judicial field.

I subsequently located a 45-page bound booklet *In Memoriam of the Honorable George Frank Boney* from the Supreme Court Clerk in Juneau, and read more about the jurist who had garnered admiration and respect from not only those within the state, but from around the nation. The consensus of opinion among all those who knew him or who had worked with or around him, was that he was a "brilliant lawyer" and that he possessed "one of the finest legal minds." In the various testimonials given at his Memorial Ceremony, held on September 13, 1972, he was consistently described, as well, as being "gregarious," "amiable," and even a true "humanitarian." However, there were other phrases by which he was portrayed. Governor Hickel said that he was an "activist," who "never ducked an argument." Justice Connor, who was selected as spokesman for the other Supreme Court justices, stated that he "always fought for those things he believed in" and that he had a "certain reformer's zeal," and was even more eloquent in his description of him, when he said:

> "Nothing was more abhorrent to George Boney than the notion that the law should ever be applied unequally to persons similarly situated, or that anyone should ever be the victim of either malice or official indifference."

A still more absorbing insight into Justice Boney's character, was a similar description offered by his former law partner of ten years, Donald Burr:

> "In private practice, George was — I think most lawyers who have worked with him would agree — was absolutely relentless and ingenious..."

The mental picture that I was developing of Justice Boney was that as brilliant as he was, he had a tendency to be overly aggressive to those individuals or situations in which he was at conflict. It would undoubtedly be a recipe to create enemies over the years.

What I found to be even more insightful was the following characterization of Boney that his former partner gave in his memoriam address before the assembled group honoring the late justice:

> "I remember very well the first case that he worked

on in private practice because it was a case I had tried and lost in Fairbanks; a jury trial in which Bob Parrish represented the plaintiffs, two coal miners seeking damages from our client, Suntrana Mining Company. It was a bitterly and hotly contested lawsuit and my client lost. Although I did not feel the chances on appeal were favorable, George was new in the office at that time and he thought there was some chance of success on appeal. So, he prosecuted and argued that case to the Supreme Court of Alaska, which was one of the first cases, incidentally, the court decided. After some delay and in due course, the Supreme Court affirmed the trial court's decision, and by that time Bob Parrish was becoming somewhat restless to collect the money for his clients on the judgement. On the other hand, George, being the type of individual that he was, was contemplating further appellate procedures. He wasn't really sure at the time but he was thinking in terms of further review. To my knowledge, it had not been previously done in the state, but George made a special trip to Washington, D.C., and he succeeded in finding Mr. Justice Black at home on a weekend on his time off. He prevailed on him to issue a stay of execution on the Supreme Court decision. To make a longer story much shorter, I might add that Bob Parrish ultimately collected the judgement with considerable interest and costs, but that is an example of the way George tried cases. He didn't know the meaning of the word quit. He practiced law that way and he practiced it consistently that way..."

At the time that I read it, I was not only impressed with his multi-faceted personality, but admired his steadfastness to duty and his persistent pursuit of what he considered truth and fairness — traits, however, that would grate on some.

As incisive and entertaining as that detailed story was of Boney in his private law practice, the name of Bob Parrish was merely anecdotal then. It wasn't until future delving, on my part, that I would run across that name again. It also raised a deeper question in my mind, at that time.

I debated calling Wayne Hunter back before I went any further. I knew there was still more information out there, but I decided to give him a quick call and to let him know that I was not yet finished — and that I was *very* interested in what I had learned so far.

"It's just the beginning, my friend," he said seriously.

As I delved further, I managed to unearth a full cassette tape of Justice Boney's inquest from the Alaska Court System, and listened to it intently. Six jurors, the number required, were impaneled to appear on the Coroner's jury: Kathryn J. Grimstone, Howard Paul, Patricia L. Larouche, Guy H. Green, Judy Bee, and Helen B. Auckerman.

After they were sworn in, the first witness called was Dr. Michael F. Beirne of Anchorage, who testified that he performed the autopsy a few hours after death had occurred.

In his testimony, he noted that there were no bruises or external injuries to the body; that "changes in the face and eyes" went along with drowning; that his lungs were consistent with drowning (i.e. small amounts of foreign matter, leaves, etc., in the lungs); that his stomach was empty (no food of any kind); that his blood alcohol was negative, and that there were no drugs in his system at all.

In further discussion of his internal examination, he also noted that the brain and heart were normal, that the blood vessels were normal, and that no natural disease was present. In summary, he concluded that, "this man died of drowning."

The next witness called was William Lawrence Wheeles, a carpenter, who was working at Cheri Lake, at the time of the mishap. He testified that although he didn't see Boney when he was first on the lake, he did hear someone screaming for help after he had shut off a portable generator he had been using. However, because the sound was "similar to the birds and animals in the area," he didn't readily notice it. When the sound continued, he and two other carpenters went to a lower level of a cabin that they had been working on. It was at this time that he saw the Chief Justice in the water, and noted that his small boat had already capsized. He calculated that he was about 60 yards from the boat, and that he was "going up and down."

The other two carpenters jumped into a motor boat to assist

him, but upon reaching him had difficulty getting him into their own small boat. When they finally managed to do it, they brought him ashore and laid him on the beach in front of his own cabin, which was nearby.

Wheeles also stated that he went to call the state troopers for help. Upon his return, the Chief Justice's secretary and two other young men had just arrived. Shortly afterward, the troopers and an ambulance also arrived.

The second witness that was called to the stand was Raymond Frank Peterson, also a carpenter, who commented that the time "was around 11 o'clock." He said he saw a boat tipped over and someone in the water. He "could see him splashing" and also "could see his hands coming up — and like he would go down, and then up." He further mentioned that as their boat approached the Chief Justice, that when they were "10 to 15 yards from him, he quit splashing and started to sink." By the time they got to him, his head was just under the water. Peterson stated that he had to grab him by the hair to pull him up beside the boat and also reached down to grasp one of his arms.

The other carpenter, who was in the rear steering the boat, came forward to assist. He grabbed the other arm and both kept his head above the water until they managed precariously to get him into their own small boat. With the weight of the Chief Justice and with their craft tilting, they were afraid of capsizing also.

Peterson further testified that when they finally made shore, they got Justice Boney on the beach and tried to get the water out of him. They then gave him mouth-to-mouth resuscitation.

In reply to a question from the presiding Magistrate at the inquest, as to what the Chief Justice wore, Peterson said that he had on "a type of tennis shorts, a T-shirt, and no shoes."

In response to a question about the weather, he noted that it was "real windy" and that there was "rough water."

One of the jurors asked him about how far the Chief Justice was from his capsized boat, "about 65-75 yards," and from shore, "about 300 yards."

He was excused, and the next witness called was William John McBride, the third carpenter working at the same cabin. He was more specific as to the type of generator that they were using:

"It was a 1500-watt generator, and it was making a lot of noise," he said. Because of that noise, they couldn't hear Boney's cries for help. It wasn't until it was shut off that they heard something, but as had been testified previously, "because it was similar to the animals and wildlife, it was hard to hear."

McBride also testified that he saw the Chief Justice "splashing around in the water," before they started out to help him. He also noted that the wind was brisk and that it was "blowing harder than he had seen it in the past four or five days." In addition, in reply to a question about the time of day, he commented that he thought it was "between eleven fifteen and a quarter to twelve." A final question about the kind of boat that it was brought the response, "it was about a 12 foot styrofoam boat."

The next witness was Kermit A. Barker, Jr., a law clerk with the Alaska Supreme Court. He testified that he was "summoned by the Chief Justice to discuss certain cases that were pending before the Supreme Court, and that there were certain questions of law that he was concerned with." He also testified that he was accompanied by the Chief Justice's secretary, Charlene Hitchings, and another law clerk, Douglas J. Servely. He noted that when they all arrived in a state car "something on the order of noon," someone came up to them and advised them "that George had drowned." His immediate reaction was one of disbelief, but when he jumped out of the car and ran down to the shore, he saw Boney's body. He further testified that when he inquired of the two men there if they had administered "artificial respiration," the younger man stated that he had. After the younger carpenter had made the remark, because as Barker testified "he was distraught," he also said, "If you don't believe me, do it yourself." Whereupon, the law clerk also administered mouth-to-mouth resuscitation to the Chief Justice's body. However, he had done it only a short time when he "listened for a heart beat and couldn't hear one." He further noted, that "shortly thereafter the state troopers arrived."

The troopers that responded to the scene were those from the Palmer Detachment, Michael Kolivosky and Lyle E. Nygren. Because Kolivosky had not yet arrived at the inquest, Trooper Nygren was called to come forward as the next witness.

He testified that after he had arrived at the lake and inquired of those present as to what had been done for the Chief Justice, he also tried to revive him. He stated that he "administered 15 minutes of oxygen but there was no response at all." The ambulance then arrived at the scene, and both he and the attendant "tried recuperating him." Trooper Kolivosky, according to Nygren, also appeared about five minutes after Nygren's arrival.

Nygren also testified to queries from the Magistrate that he interviewed all people at the vicinity, checked the Chief Justice's boat out that had been retrieved and was now at the shore and that he took photographs of the boat and the scene.

There being no other questions of the witness, and because Kolivosky had not yet arrived, the Magistrate inquired of Nygren if Kolivosky's testimony "would be basically the same." Nygren admitted that it would, although he stated that Kolivosky had interviewed some other people. He also commented that Kolivosky had the photographs with him, although in a repeat question from the Magistrate, Nygren again stated that it was he that took the photos.

At that point, the Magistrate told the jurors that Trooper Nygren had informed her of the content of the photographs taken of the body and of the area and the "there would be no other evidence that we could offer the jury at this time." She also repeated that, "Trooper Kolivosky will probably testify very similar to what Trooper Nygren has told you," and also added that, "it may be a while before Trooper Kolivosky does arrive."

Her last statement was contra to what Nygren had said while on the stand, that Kolivosky should be there "in a few moments."

The Magistrate then instructed the bailiff to take the jurors to another room to deliberate.

Before they left, she charged them to find a verdict that would include three points: "the name of the person, the date on or about which he came to his death, and the cause of death as a result of your deliberations on the evidence that you heard here in court."

Upon the return of the six jurors, their verdict was handed to the bailiff who then gave it to the Magistrate to read.

It began with, "We the jury being duly impaneled and sworn in the above entitled manner and having heard the testimony of witnesses subpoenaed by the court."

It then identified the decedent, the date of his death and the place where it occurred, and then ended with:

"The cause of his death is accidental drowning, and that no person may be guilty of the crime thereof."

When I called Wayne Hunter that night, and not only told him about the contents of the inquest tape but of all else that I had read, he scoffed; "Justice isn't only blind," he said, "but it's dumb as well."

"What do you mean, Wayne?"

"Well," he began, "first of all, there were *other* witnesses to Boney's death."

"Other witnesses?" I asked incredulously. "Why didn't they come forward? Why weren't they at the inquest?"

I hit him with all the questions that popped into my head without giving him a chance to respond individually to them.

"I don't know all the reasons as to the whys," he said. "Maybe they were afraid. Maybe they thought no one would believe them. Maybe they just didn't want to get involved. Who knows?"

"Any specifics?" I pressed him.

"Are you ready for this?" he answered.

"Sure!"

"Well, a witness who had been at the lake that day came to me afterward and told me that he had seen two skin divers that had been in and out of the water before and after Boney's drowning."

Hunter's story caught me by surprise and I hesitated momentarily, trying to piece together what he had just told me.

"Who was the witness, Wayne?"

He didn't hesitate when he replied.

"It was Leon Schwartz."

I had never heard the name before, and although he didn't know the exact spelling, I wrote it down phonetically.

"Did you say witnesses, or was it one witness?" I asked him again.

"Schwartz was the one that came to me," he answered, "but I heard later form another source that one of those skin divers drowned a year later."

I took a deep breath, after he had finished giving me the information.

"God damn, Wayne, you're in the wrong business. You should've been a cop."

"And that not all," he continued, "I think there was something about it in *Diver's World*, afterward."

"*Diver's World*?" I asked.

"Yes," he said, "I think it's a skin divers magazine."

"Do you know when it came out or where I can get it?" I queried him.

"No, I don't know, but call Howard Weaver, he should know."

Another name I hadn't heard of. Hunter didn't have a number to contact him, but I wrote down the name.

"What do you think now, my friend?" he asked almost proudly.

"Yeah," I admitted, "it sounds like you're right about justice."

"Did you ever mention any of this to anyone?" I asked.

"Do you really think that they would have believed me?" he replied wearily.

"No, I guess not Wayne. I'm having trouble getting attention from the authorities as well."

"Well, paisan, it's in your hands now. Good luck," he said almost cheerfully.

"Thanks, Wayne. I wish I were here five years ago."

"I wish you were too," and his tone was serious again.

After I hung up on what was an almost unbelievable scenario of the Chief Justice's death, I planned my next move to obtain additional information. I decided I wanted to learn as much as I could about Boney, and especially about his last hours. I figured that if anybody would know anything about him, it would be his secretary, Charlene Hitchings.

On April 11, 1977, I contacted his former secretary, whose name was now Brown. I identified myself and told her I'd like to ask her some additional questions about her former boss. She was more than cooperative and stated that she would be glad to help since she "and others" had questioned his death "by accidental drowning."

Frozen Shield

She began by saying that "George" had called her the morning of his death and had asked her to come to Cheri Lake and to bring the two law clerks with her. When they all arrived at the lake, they discovered that he had drowned a half-hour earlier.

When I questioned her if she thought it was unusual for him to have drowned in that manner, she admitted that she did. She commented that "he went jumping in cold water all the time," and would usually do it after a sauna. She also stressed that he was "a good swimmer."

When I questioned her further about anything noteworthy that she might have seen after she had arrived, she replied that there was "nothing unusual at the cabin." She also commented that he "was disturbed that his wife had left with his children on the day of his death."

I didn't press her as to what she meant, whether it was just a normal trip "outside to the *lower 48*," or whether there were other reasons, as I didn't consider it important at the time. It was she who offered the information, not me who solicited it. What she did get across to me was that he had "never been depressed in the five years" that she had worked for him. She also was quick to point out that he "never wanted to endanger himself," and that he was "very analytical." In addition, she stated that he was a "very methodical man." When I questioned what she meant, she replied that he "*always* had breakfast."

As she said it, I remembered that the results of the autopsy stated "that his stomach was empty (no food of any kind)."

When I probed further, she said "he was having financial trouble because of his cattle business." She also added a questionable element when she stated that there was "a problem about his safety," and that she thought that he "was threatened."

I asked what she meant by that remark, and she said to ask Clarence Erickson at the Alaska Court System, as he would have more information about it.

Erickson had been an administrator in the courts, and although I didn't know or recall at what level, I had heard his name before.

However, what Hitchings did know about threats to Boney, when I asked her to be specific, was that he had some sort of protection. When I asked what she referred to, she said that an

Nick Mangieri

Administrative Assistant in the court system, a *"Sam,"* she believed was his name, "fashioned himself as a bodyguard, and that George didn't discourage it." When I pressed her as to where I could find this *"Sam,"* she replied that after he left Alaska, she heard that he had worked for the Florida Legislature. Other than that, she said, she thought that *"Sam"* was associated with Boney in the bodyguard capacity for about a year. "Clarence can give you more details," she added.

When I thanked her for her information, I asked if I could contact her again. She answered that she didn't mind.

That same day, I located and contacted Clarence Erickson. Although he was cooperative, he didn't have a great deal of comprehensive information to offer. What he did have was to fill in more pieces of the puzzle concerning the whereabouts of *"Sam."* He told me that a George Morrison, the Chief Accountant at the Alaska State Bank in Anchorage was formerly the Chief Accountant at the Alaska Court System when Boney was the Chief Justice. He also said that it was Morrison who knew where to find a Bob Reeves, who had been the former Administrative Director of the court system under Boney. It was Reeves, he said, who hired *"Sam"* and that he might know where he was.

It was Erickson's belief that *"Sam"* dealt with the Alaska Legislature for the Chief Justice, and that he worked "more or less as a gofer for Boney." Erickson also believed that *"Sam"* left about three or four months after Boney's death. He also added that he "didn't have much dealings with him."

As I thanked him for his information, I asked him if there was anything else that he could think of in connection with the Boney matter that would be of any assistance to me.

"The only additional information that I can think of," he said, "was that it was Dorothy Saxton who handled the inquest."

It was a name that I knew, and it was also one that I — and others — had come to question before, during and after my stint as Chief of Police in Palmer.

It was shortly after my conversation with Erickson that I learned about *"Sam's"* full name. It was W. Samuel Griffis, and the Alaska court records indicated that he terminated with the court system on September 29, 1972, less than one month after Boney's death.

Armed with this additional information, I called Boney's former secretary back the following day.

"I just have a few more questions if you don't mind."

"Not at all," she said.

"At what time did Justice Boney call you the morning of his death?"

"It was at approximately 9 o'clock."

"Did he say that he was going out in the boat?"

"No he didn't."

"Did he mention anything about Sam," and I gave her the last name, "Griffis?"

"No."

When I queried her about Bob Reeves, the former Administrative Director, who had hired Sam Griffis, she responded, "He was one of the good guys," she noted. "I think he's an attorney in Washington, D.C., now." She then added, "He didn't think very highly of Sam."

I asked her the same question about George Morrison, the former Chief Accountant.

"He was an honest man who just happened to have a bad job."

Because I seemed to be getting off the track, I didn't pursue that line of questioning.

"What was Boney's relationship with the other justices?" I then asked.

"As a whole, okay," she answered.

What about his relationship with Justice Connor and Justice Rabinowitz?

Again she responded, "Okay, although Rabinowitz thought him flamboyant."

She then volunteered some additional information.

"Boney and Nesbett had locked horns."

Nesbett, I recently learned from the *Anchorage Daily Times* coverage, was the former justice at the Supreme Court that Boney had succeeded on the bench. The paper noted that he had retired because of ill health.

I did not ask her when their "locking horns" had occurred, whether before or after he took office. At the time, it was not an important issue to me.

What were important were her next two comments to me. The first one was that Sam had been with Boney at his cabin the night before and on the morning of his death. However, according to Sam's remarks later, Boney had "told him to leave" and he did so. I never learned *why or when* he left.

Her next comment dealt with that of another party at the cabin.

She stated that Bob Parrish was also at the cabin with Boney and Sam Griffis the night before his death.

Bob Parrish, I recalled was the individual mentioned by Boney's former partner, Donald Burr. It was in his speech extolling Boney's virtues that he casually mentioned that Parrish and Boney had been prior adversaries in a bitterly fought civil suit. Burr merely raised his name in his memorial speech to give an example of the bulldog tenacity that Boney exhibited in his practice of law.

Although I had no way of knowing the context in which Parrish had been with Boney the night before, in light of what I had heard, I still considered it a little strange.

As I hung up the phone after that enlightening conversation with her, I couldn't help but recall the words from a narrative poem, by Sir Walter Scott, that I had read long ago: "Oh, what a tangled web we weave, when we first practice to deceive."

Those words seemed to fit all that had transpired in the Boney death.

I had to sit and analyze all that I had read and heard to either come to the same conclusion that Chief Justice Boney's death was "by accidental drowning" — or to disprove it.

First of all, I wondered why Boney would call his secretary at 9 a.m. to tell her to come out to the lake with his two law clerks if he was going sailing in his boat. He never mentioned to her that he might be out on the lake and to wait for him should he not be there. Then again, if as his law clerk Kermit Barker testified the justice wanted *both* law clerks to come out with his secretary because "there were certain questions for law that he was concerned with," in cases that were then pending before the Supreme Court, then *why* would he even be out on the lake at all. In that same regard, if for some reason he wanted to take a short sail on the lake because it was such a nice day, that was not the case at all. As both of the carpenters who attempted to rescue him testified, the weather was "real windy," and there was "rough water." The last carpenter on the stand, witness McBride, was even more explicit about the weather when he said that it had been, "blowing harder than he had seen it in the past four or five days."

If the weather were as nasty as it was described by both men, why would the Chief Justice be clad only in "a type of tennis shorts and a T-shirt," and of course, "no shoes." Someone could undoubtedly say that because the Chief Justice was used to *cold water*, his spartan dress was appropriate *for him*. Yet, his secretary, Hitchings, told me that he was an "analytical man" and would not "endanger himself." Being out on the lake in a 12-foot styrofoam boat in high wind and rough water would appear to be lacking common sense and totally out of character for him.

There, of course, was another disturbing fact. If Boney was a "very methodical man" and always had breakfast as Hitchings said, why was "his stomach empty."

In my attempt to analyze Justice Boney's prior actions before he got into the boat, these questions were merely *preliminary* questions. The harder questions were yet to be mulled over.

For example, why did the witnesses uniformly state that Boney was "going up and down." Witness Peterson, who was one of the rescuers approaching him in the motorboat, was even more graphic. He "could see his hands coming up — and like he would go down and then up again."

From various descriptions that I have heard over the years concerning drowning victims, the comment that they were "splashing" — as was Justice Boney — would be consistent with a panicky drowner. What would not be consistent, however, would be an account of a person "going up and down", and especially the portrayal of a person's hands "coming up — and down — and up again."

That particular depiction of a drowning person would appear to be more consistent with someone being *pulled down*. However, the possibility of such a bizarre incident would not occur to someone viewing a drowning person from a distance — nor, for that matter, even to someone approaching a drowning person. But, in light of witness Schwartz' statement to Wayne Hunter that he saw "two skin divers in and out of the water, before and after Boney's death," that bizarre report was an extremely likely causation of what actually happened.

Undoubtedly, there would be those who would say that the Chief Justice's antics of "going up and down" in the water were no more than his reaction to a cramp that he experienced. However, that explanation would not appear to be satisfactory. As noted by Hitchings, Boney was a "strong swimmer." The lack of food in the stomach, or drugs or alcohol in the system, as determined in the autopsy, would seem to preclude that type of cramp. Further, muscle spasms in the legs would not provoke the type of movements that Boney exhibited in the water.

While analyzing the pros and cons of the "accidental drowning" it also appeared clear that there was nothing in Dr. Beirne's testimony that denied that the Chief Justice died by other than accidental means. His statement that there were "no bruises or external injuries to the body" would not — and probably could not — cover the fact, that he was being pulled down by his feet, or by his ankles.

As unbelievable as was the scenario that I envisioned, the more I dwelt on it and the more convinced I became of its reality. This belief was especially fostered in view of Hitchings' comment that she believed that Boney "was threatened." That remark by his secretary was not just idle speculation. It was supported by the fact that Boney had a bodyguard in the form of Sam Griffis.

My final questions concerning Boney's speculative death "under mysterious circumstances," as reported by Wayne Hunter, then centered on his "bodyguard" Sam Griffis.

If he had been, as Hitchings stated, the last one to see Boney alive, why wasn't he questioned? If he were questioned, why didn't he appear at the inquest?

The same question applied to Parrish, although to a lesser extent. If he also was with Boney and Griffis the night before, why wasn't he questioned. And if he were, why didn't he appear at the inquest, as well? It would appear that his testimony might have some significance to the jurors.

My final question then centered on the magistrate, who I was told presided over the inquest, Dorothy Saxton. Why did she not wait for Trooper Kolivosky to appear? Although Trooper Nygren had said that Kolivosky's testimony "would be basically the same," he had also mentioned that Kolivosky "had interviewed some other people." Waiting the extra "few moments" for Kolivosky to appear, as Nygren said he would, would hardly have seemed unreasonable in light of the death of a Chief Justice of the Alaska Supreme Court, who by all accounts was one of the most important people in the state. Yet. the Magistrate elected not to do so. I was still not satisfied with the response that was given at the inquest.

Incredible as the thought was — much less the actuality — that Chief Justice Boney met death not by accidental means but by *person or persons unknown*, became more than an investigative obsession, it became a pursuit of justice that I knew *had* to be done.

Sadly, however, upcoming events in my personal life, would soon overshadow my time, my ability — and even my interest — in pursuing the Boney affair, or even my own pending law suits.

... Chapter 22 ...

The month of April didn't start out well. I should have realized at the time that it was to be a foreboding of what was to come, but I didn't want to dwell on it. I was too involved in other areas.

On April 4, I finally received an official response from the Ombudsman with whom I had initially filed a complaint in August 1976. That complaint resulted in my re-interview with Investigator Hoffbeck a couple of months later in October 1976. In the intervening six months I had heard absolutely nothing from the Ombudsman or the state troopers. So, when I received a very brief notification of the results, I was not surprised.

> Re: Ombudsman Complaint 76-0952
> Dear Mr. Mangieri:
> In reviewing your complaint before our agency, I feel that the District Attorney's office and State Troopers have given the matter sufficient attention and considera-tion, especially in light of the fact that there is pending civil litigation.
> Thank you very much for your patience in this matter.
> Sincerely,
> Frank Flavin
> OMBUDSMAN
> cc: Col. Wellington
> Joe Balfe

When I read it, I just shook my head and cursed under my breath.

What sufficient attention and consideration had I gotten, I wondered? *Besides, what the hell did my pending civil litigation have to do with valid criminal complaints against them?*

When I told Wayne Higgins about the response, he just took an audible deep breath on the phone.

"I *knew* they'd all cop out," he said disgustedly.

"I'm sorry to hear that," was McShea's curt comment.

My wife who had been living with the perpetual roller coaster ride and with its continuing disappointments, appeared to be sympathetic to the latest bit of news. However, because I was so deeply involved in my Boney investigation, I didn't notice whether she felt as strongly about that phase of my actions as she once would have.

I prepared a list of things that I knew I had to do in the Boney case in order to tie up all the loose ends. To name but a few, I had noted that: I should contact Boney's relatives to get their views on his death; contact his former partner and friend, Donald Burr; try to locate Schwartz, who allegedly had seen the skin divers; check on Hunter's reference to *Diver's World*; and even look into whatever the Chief Justice might have had under advisement.

I learned that there were numerous "action grants" that were in existence at the time of his death. Although none sounded as though they would elicit any *threats*, I made a note to look into them briefly, time permitting. They were: A District Court Video Project, a Bail Bond Project, a First Bush Justice Conference, a New Magistrate Orientation Program, and a Sentencing Conference.

Someone mentioned that perhaps the Bail Bond Project might prove interesting to look at. However, what sounded even more promising was new information to the effect that Boney had "co-signed a land deal with an Anchorage attorney, who was later disbarred." Although I later learned that Boney had gotten out of the co-signing, I wanted to know who that attorney was so that I could see him.

At about that same time, there was an article in the *Alaska Advocate*, a weekly newspaper I believe, that also referred to the ARRC. Although I hadn't noticed it, McShea called my attention to the "Letters to the Editor" section that appeared in the April 8 edition of the *Anchorage Daily News*.

"I think you'll find this interesting," he said, jokingly adding, "maybe it'll make you feel better."

Under a small headline,

"PROBE ARRC"

was the following letter:

Dear Editor:

Recent articles in some of our local newspapers (The *Anchorage Daily News*, *Times* and *Alaska Advocate*) have referred to Mr. Mangieri and his running battle with the "industrial giant of the Matanuska Valley," Palmer.

One of the issues mentioned was his attempt to investigate the ARRC (Alaska Rural Rehabilitation Corporation) which he says led to his dismissal. This letter is not a plea for Mr. Mangieri. From what I have seen, he can take care of himself. What I call for is an immediate in-depth audit of the records of the ARRC.

If the article published recently in the *Alaska Advocate* is accurate this "non-profit" corporation has not filed a financial report since 1959.

Now, you can say what you will, nobody should be allowed to do millions of dollars worth of business every year and not give an accounting of its finances to the people. What would we say if NBA or IBM refused to file reports for 18 years? Maybe Wayne Hunter's charge that they stole our land has more substance to it than the high and mighty ARRC wants to let on?

What do you say? How about some investigative reporting of ARRC to match your investigation of the Teamsters? The people have a right to know, and if you really want two newspapers in Anchorage, you need to tell us some of the facts about the dirt powerful people are trying to hide.

William P. Slabaugh

I did get a kick out of it as McShea had known I would, and I told him so in person.

"I really needed that," I remarked.

He smiled.

"I thought you would," he said.

I called Wayne Hunter to let him know that his name was still in print, and maybe something good would come of it.

"I've been in print a long time," he said, "and nothing's really happened yet, but," he added optimistically, "you just never know."

I also told him that I'd be doing some more delving into the ARRC, as soon as I could find more time.

He thanked me briefly and then abruptly changed the subject.

"While you're looking into the Boney thing," he continued, "you might just look into the Schmidtke incident."

"Schmidtke?" I asked, puzzled by the reference.

"You know, the former publisher of The *Frontiersman*," he responded as if I should have known the name.

"I knew he was the former Mayor of Palmer, before Maze," I answered, "but I didn't know that he published the paper."

"I forget you didn't arrive in the state until '74," and he paused, "that's what happens when you get old," and he laughed in a low voice. "The man died in '73." Then he added, "and now ask me how he died."

I hesitated briefly before I answered again, "Don't tell me he drowned too?"

"Give that man a silver dollar," he roared.

"C'mon, Wayne," I said. "Are you trying to tell me that there's something fishy about his death, too?"

"Your choice of words is appropriate for the circumstance," he chuckled to himself briefly, but went on, "that's exactly what I'm saying."

"Do you want to tell me some more about it?" I asked, "or do you want me to read up on it first?"

"I'll give you a little more detail than I did on Boney," he continued, "but you can still check the records on it, as well."

"Okay," I said in a low voice not wanting to interrupt him.

"Well, apparently the man did drink a little," he conceded,

"and when he was found, they thought there had been a robbery because he had no money on him."

"Was that unusual?" I asked.

"I would think so," he continued, "since he had been out drinking and *gambling* all night. I would expect that if he won, he would have a lot of money on him. Even if he lost, he would have *something* left. I don't think that he would be cleaned out completely."

"Makes sense." I said.

"Further," he continued, "even if he drank as much as they say he did, he would know the way home — he always did before," he stressed.

"Meaning what?" I queried.

"Meaning that he wasn't found on his way home, they found him in Wasilla Lake."

"Where did he live?"

"Well, the paper at the time said he lived at Rocky Lake, and that's in the opposite direction."

"Maybe he took the wrong road," I countered, trying to play devil's advocate.

"They're more than ten miles apart," he stressed again. "Wasilla Lake is just east of Wasilla, on the outskirts. Rocky Lake is due west of Wasilla, near Big Lake."

He stopped to catch his breath.

"Nobody," he said, "but nobody could make that kind of mistake. I don't care how much they've been drinking, especially if they can hold their liquor."

I thought it over a minute.

"I've got to agree with you, Wayne. It just doesn't add up."

"To use your expression," he quipped, "it just sounds fishy."

He continued, "People at the time thought something had happened to him then too, but nothing ever came of it."

"Was there an inquest afterward?" I asked.

"I don't know," he responded, "but I don't think so. I'm pretty sure there was an autopsy though."

"That's easy enough to check on," I replied.

"Sorry to load you down my friend," he said, "but I thought you should know."

"You mean so I should avoid large bodies of water," I countered lightly.

"That's a good start," he said in the same vein.

"Thanks, Wayne. The more info I have, the better," my tone was more serious. "Right now," I continued slowly, "it's just a question of the number of available hours in a day that I can get it all squeezed in with my job at Fort Rich now, too."

If he heard my last comment, he didn't respond as his mind was still on the Schmidtke incident.

"I don't know what it all means, if anything," he droned on before he hung up, "but it would seem to me that there are a lot of unanswered questions."

I had to agree with him.

At my next opportunity, I began checking into the Schmidtke affair, as well. Six months earlier, I had gotten a full-time federal job as a management analyst at Fort Richardson near Anchorage, so my spare time was limited. Nevertheless, I requested and received, not only a back copy of The *Frontiersman* reporting Schmidtke's drowning, but all the official documentation about his death, as well.

That documentation included: a synopsis of the investigating Trooper's report, a two-and-a-half-page autopsy report, a Certificate of Death, and an ORDER DISPENSING WITH INQUEST. That ORDER was signed five days after his death by the Palmer Magistrate, the same official who presided over Chief Justice Boney's inquest. However, in the case of Schmidtke, there was no inquest requested.

The official wording on that ORDER was:

"It having come to the attention of the coroner that Theodore O. Schmidtke died at or near Wasilla Lake, Alaska, on or about October 17, 1973, and it appearing from the findings of Michael F. Beirne, M.D., (a physician) and an investigation of the facts and circumstances surrounding this death, that no inquest is warranted in this matter;

IT IS HEREBY ORDERED that no inquest be held in this matter."

DATED October 22, 1973.

Dorothy B. Saxton

JUDGE/MAGISTRATE/CORONER

In its coverage of his death on October 18, 1973, The *Frontiersman* reported in part:

> "Theodore O. (Ted) Schmidtke, publisher of The *Frontiersman*, was found dead today in Lake Wasilla, apparently a drowning victim.
>
> His car went into the lake near a picnic area behind Green Acres. It was discovered late this morning by two hikers..."

The lengthy editorial about their publisher characterized him as "a mover," inasmuch as he had done "a lot for this town." It also cited his specific accomplishments, as well as calling attention to the fact that he had been publisher of the paper for 13 years, and Mayor of Palmer for seven years.

I also had previously noted from inspection of the minutes of a Special Meeting of the Palmer City Council on October 11, 1971, that he was the outgoing mayor and that Jack E. Maze, succeeded him as the new mayor of the town.

The autopsy was performed by Dr. Michael F. Beirne, the same individual who was to conduct an autopsy, a year later, on the Chief Justice.

In his opening *History* of the deceased Schmidtke, Dr. Beirne wrote:

> "According to information available at this time this middle aged white male was found dead in Wasilla Lake. Apparently his car was in the lake also, the door was open and this man was floating on the water alongside of the car. It is not certain when he was last seen. State Troopers are now investigating the case. Apparently the body was found on the morning of October 18 and brought to Anchorage to the Green Funeral Chapel. The autopsy was ordered by the coroner to determine the cause of death."

Dr. Beirne, in his report under the *Autopsy* section, also stated that:

> "The autopsy was conducted at the Green Funeral

Chapel in Anchorage on October 18, 1973, at 3 p.m.

"The body was that of a white male, fully clothed, well developed, well nourished, appearing to be about middle age with moderately thinning hair which appears tan to light gray, thinning in the front. All the clothing was removed and there was no sign of any papers or identification or any other material in the pockets. Everything had been removed from the pockets prior to examination. The clothing were removed."

Whether, all the material, including his papers and identification had first been removed by the investigating trooper was unknown to me, but it was strange for the medical examiner to specifically comment on the absence of *anything* in his pockets. However, I knew the investigating officer, Trooper Boatright, and made a note to ask him about it.

During the course of the autopsy, Dr. Beirne also noted that "there was no evidence of any external trauma to the body."

Laboratory studies of blood, urine, and gastric alcohols indicated a blood alcohol of .208 percent and Dr. Beirne also reflected the above information on his summary below:

"This middle aged white male was found dead (in) Wasilla Lake. Autopsy indicates that the cause of death was on the basis of drowning. No traumatic injuries identified. The man was very intoxicated with alcohol at the time of his death."

Presumably on the basis of those facts, it was decided that it was an open-and-shut case of drowning, and that a formal inquest was unnecessary. However, on reading the following synopsis by the investigating trooper, and then reading the newspaper article again, I had a few questions of my own:

"Synopsis:
"11 a.m., 10/18/73 Palmer AST advised of vehicle and body on Southwest shore of Wasilla Lake. Investigation revealed (victim) had been, between the hours of 11 p.m. 10/17/73 and 6 a.m. 10/18/73, drinking

quite heavily and gambling in the Palmer area. Robbery/homicide was initially suspected. Subsequent investigation indicating accidental death by drowning."

The *Frontiersman* had stated in its coverage that the car "went into the lake near a picnic area behind Green Acres."

After checking a Mat-Su Valley map, I learned that the Palmer-Wasilla Highway ran by Wasilla Lake. I also knew from the investigative synopsis that the vehicle was found on the "Southwest shore" of the lake, which would have been in the *general* vicinity of Schmidtke's drive back to his home, about ten miles west of Wasilla. What I did *not* know, however, was how far in was the "picnic area behind Green Acres." If it was *immediately* adjacent to the Palmer-Wasilla Highway, I could understand how an individual in an intoxicated state might have veered off the road and gone into the lake. If, on the other hand, the "picnic area behind Green Acres" was not on his direct route home, what would his car be doing in the lake at that point? If it were determined that the vehicle did actually drive into the picnic area first, why did it do so and what was Schmidtke doing there that time of morning? He had already driven the ten miles from Palmer — according to the investigative synopsis — and was almost halfway home to Rocky Lake. Why would he stop off there if he had another 10-15 minutes before he would be home?

If, as the synopsis indicated, he had gambled in the Palmer area until "6 a.m.," there would have been little likelihood that he would have *lost his way in the dark*, or for that matter, that he would have been *unable to see the road clearly*. In the first place, although the sun had not yet risen — sunrise being at 7:50 a.m. on October 18 — the sky was beginning to lighten. Further, the lake and the picnic area were off the main highway, with little question of obscure road conditions because of the darkness. However, had this incident happened later in the year, undoubtedly the question of darkness might have arisen. Still, another fact should have been considered, if it was ever seriously considered at all. *Why* had he pulled off the highway when he was so near to his own home?

Another important question arose concerning the wording of the medical examiner's *History*. If as the autopsy report stated, "apparently his car was in the lake also, the door was open and this man was floating on the water along side of the car," there were then problems of logic.

First, if his car was in the lake, with the door *open*, and Schmidtke *alongside* the car, it is safe to assume that the car was in fairly shallow water and Schmidtke managed to exit it. If he exited it, and the evidence indicated that he did because he was found floating alongside the car, then he must've drowned in that same shallow water. The next logical question would be *how* he had drowned in shallow water. The autopsy report stated that an "examination of the head, scalp, eyes, ears, nose, lips and teeth and neck areas fails to show any evidence of injury." Therefore, there is no indication of any external trauma to warrant his being knocked unconscious and then subsequently drowning in shallow water. Although there may be detractors who will say that in his degree of intoxication, that he just passed out and then drowned, it would appear to be highly unlikely. The water temperature in Alaska, even at that time of year, is still extremely cold, and would undoubtedly shock someone back into a conscious state.

The final question that loomed above the others was: Why were his pockets completely empty?

There were many questions that I would have liked answered to my satisfaction. If these same questions were pondered after Schmidtke's death, then an inquest certainly would have been in order. My next question was *why* did the Magistrate dispense with an inquest?

In an attempt to resolve some of these questions, I made a note to interview those who might have some answers or might have questioned his death themselves

The trooper was high on my list, as was the Magistrate, and, of course, the pathologist. Next on my list were those he worked with who might have their own opinions as to his tragic demise:

Karen Lee, the editor of The *Frontiersman*; Doug Haugom, the manager of the paper; Marilyn Ryder, a reporter; Don Shaginoff, close friend; Richard Jones, the Executor of his Estate; Siegfried Schmidtke, his brother; Billie Schmidtke, his wife, who I noted also was — or had recently become — the Publisher of The *Frontiersman*. Also, I wanted to get the views of his three adult children.

Before I could implement any inquiries into the Schmidtke drowning, however, a series of personal events in my own life arose so quickly and so unexpectedly that any investigative efforts by me was delayed for a prolonged period.

First, my wife walked out on me in mid-April. After 19 years it was somewhat of a shock since I had no advanced warning of her intention to do so. But even at that, it wasn't her leaving so much as her taking our three younger children to stay with her at a girlfriend's house that bothered me the most. I considered it an act that was irresponsible and harmful to their welfare. Not only was their home life totally disrupted, but also their schoolwork suffered. To make it even worse, the children had to live in what proved to be unwholesome circumstances.

From that point on, my entire summer was consumed with first getting my three children back, (my oldest daughter having married a day prior to the walk-out), then going through the pre-liminaries before the divorce, and then the ultimate attempt to reestablish normalcy after the divorce — for them — and for myself.

I make it sound simple, but that is a far cry from reality. At first, I hired an attorney, more as an attorney of record than to handle all the Motions and Affidavits that I knew from prior experience in the courts were necessary. I eventually went *Pro Per* again, to save on expenses. Even in the early stages, I saved considerable money by doing most of my own work. I knew from the onset that it would be time-consuming to do the necessary custodial investigation, but I also knew that I was very thorough in all my work. I didn't want to leave to chance the possibility of any slip-ups and then be unable to regain my children. Daily investigative efforts on my part placed all my other efforts on a back burner. In addition, there were continuing frustrations to constantly bring to the court's attention that their daily lives were in an abnormal state.

In the process of going through the divorce proceedings I was able to obtain temporary custody of the kids. Six months later when the divorce was granted, I was finally able to get permanent custody. In the interim, however, to describe the situation as *unpleasant* would be the understatement of the year. At first, I voluntarily relinquished my rented house so the children could return with their mother while the divorce litigation was under way. In doing so, I was forced initially to live out of my car because I had no extra money at all. Then, when that became intolerable, I lived in various cheap motels. Because of my temporary living conditions, which alternated between cramped and crowded to spartan and meager, I was unable to have with me my legal papers concerning my Palmer actions and various investigations. I was too preoccupied with my family situation to worry much about it at the time. I was too concerned with having my children returned to some semblance of normal routine and regularity, which they had lost in their lives. In addition to my full-time hours with my civilian job at Fort Rich, all my extra time was devoted toward my kids and the court papers that I was constantly working on and filing.

Although my legal endeavors to get custody of my children were successful they were not without a price. Their lives — and my own — had been unalterably changed. My other lawsuits became secondary to me. My children's welfare now became primary. Because I had initiated actions against the Palmer officials and still had to see justice done, however, I continued as best I could. To make matters worse, while divorce proceedings were still under way my estranged spouse informed me that she had turned over some of my confidential investigative papers to the Palmer officials. Gloating, she noted that there was another "contract" out on me and then added, "This time they'll get you..."

I understood that she felt justified in her retaliation against me for fighting her for custody of the children, but that didn't lessen its impact on me. I still had to go through the same precautionary measures I had undertaken eighteen months earlier. And I had to be concerned for the children, as well. If anything, the likelihood of something happening was even more pronounced because the Palmer people *knew* what I had. Earlier, they were somewhat in the dark and didn't know what to expect.

At the time I was told about the second "contract," I had long since given my Rossi shotgun back to the City. My reliance was then solely on my .357 Magnum, a thoroughly dependable revolver, but not as effective as I would have liked. In addition, I was forced to check my private vehicle over daily for any hidden explosive devices. This precaution was necessary after the car bombing of an Anchorage real estate woman, who was killed as a result of the blast. I happened to be a few blocks away when it occurred. It was around noontime, and I was having lunch with a friend at the lounge beneath the Captain Cook Hotel on Fourth Avenue, across the street from the Anchorage Court House.

"What the hell was that?" we simultaneously asked each other when we heard the explosion reverberate through the downtown. When we rushed outside to see what had happened, an Anchorage Police Officer told us what happened. The Anchorage papers carried the account of the murder the following day, but I was so involved in my own problems and my own attempts at thwarting violence that I was callously uninterested in the articles that followed. What stuck in my mind, however, was *another* method that could be used against me. With the announcement of the first "contract" supposedly out on me many months earlier, the constant media barrage — both newspapers and TV — had undoubtedly discouraged any implementation.

What the bad guys didn't need at that time was any more adverse publicity. Whether an attempt was successful or unsuccessful, there would have been more attention focused on my ongoing allegations of corruption.

Because of my time limitations and my continuing concern about my children's welfare I had no inclination to aggressively pursue my actions against Palmer during the summer of 1977. Then, City Attorney Biss decided to take further action and I had little choice but to jump back into the fray.

The Palmer defendants filed a MOTION FOR SUMMARY JUDGMENT in the case in early July. They knew I was vulnerable and were anxious to rid themselves of my federal action for Civil Rights violations against them. Their main issue was that of "res judicata," meaning that an issue had already been decided, that a second lawsuit was inappropriate and that, as a consequence, their issue of "collateral estoppel" would preclude my being able to initiate that lawsuit, i.e. my federal action.

Shaken out of my complacency and goaded into action because of their MOTION to dismiss my federal case, I immediately filed an OPPOSITION TO MOTION FOR SUMMARY JUDGMENT, on July 11, for Case No. A77-55 Civil, in the United States District Court again.

In it, I briefly stated that:

Plaintiff moves for Summary Judgment on the basis that Defendants' allegations of collateral estoppel and res judicata do not apply in the instant case. Further, Plaintiff, by Defendants' own admission, never gave Plaintiff the "hearing" to which all citizens are entitled and accordingly violated the "due process" clause of the Constitution.

This Motion is supported by Plaintiff's Memorandum filed herewith.

On that date I also filed another detailed, and well-researched MEMORANDUM IN SUPPORT OF (my) OPPOSITION with that MOTION:

Defendants cite Judge Buckalew's Judgment in his granting Defendants' Judgment on the Pleadings in Plaintiff's State action as though it were the final answer to what has proved to be complex issues between Plaintiff and Defendants in what Plaintiff has alleged to be wrongful discharge by corrupt officials. However, what the Defendants do not mention is that Judge Buckalew dismissed Plaintiff's action because in his opinion the discharge of Plaintiff was merely a "contractual matter" and nothing more. This issue was raised by Defendants' counsel in an in-chambers conference and conceded to by Judge Buckalew — much to Plaintiff's dismay — and contrary to the State Motions Judge in the case who found that "issues of fact and law exist concerning Plaintiff's rights and job classification under the Palmer Charter" (Exhibit A). Further, other issues raised by Plaintiff in his State complaint, No. 75-8520 (Exhibit B) were never considered by Judge Buckalew who, as trial judge, had never seen Plaintiff's file before the in-chambers conference. Therefore, for Defendants to advise this federal court that "after considering all the files in the State action..." is grossly misleading as the files were never considered — merely the issue of con-

341

Nick Mangieri

tracts. Further, the Defendants' reliance on the principles of res judicata and collateral estoppel are inappropriate because of the reasons cited above. If the court will note that in Plaintiff's MEMORANDUM IN SUPPORT OF MOTION FOR ISSUANCE OF TEMPORARY RESTRAINING ORDER and Writ of Mandamus, dated April 5, 1977, he cited other irregularities against Judge Buckalew. Unfortunately, Plaintiff, acting as *Pro Per*, neglected to name Judge Buckalew as a Defendant. This situation will be corrected in the near future.

The court will also note that under item 13 of the instant Complaint Plaintiff complains of a "conspiracy" by all Defendants. This conspiracy was never mentioned in Plaintiff's State action and therefore principles of res judicata and collateral estoppel would hardly apply.

Plaintiff raised the issue of a lack of a hearing in his State action and as Plaintiff has already mentioned above, Judge Buckalew did not take it into consideration. However, as *Davis v. Davis*, 247 A.2d 139, 143, 103 N.J. Super, 284 states:

There is no "hearing" within contemplation of due process when the affected party has not the means of knowing what evidence is offered or considered and is not afforded an opportunity to test, explain or refute it.

Further, *WUJ, the Goodwill Station v. F.C.C.*, 174 F.2d 226, 239, 84 U.S. App. D.C.1 holds that:

A hearing required by due process refers not only to a hearing on truth of allegations made by complainant, but also to hearing on questions of law as to sufficiency of allegations made by complainant.

In addition, In *Re Tate, D.C.D.C.*, 63 F. Supp. 961, 962 states that:

A person entitled to a "hearing" was entitled to be represented by counsel, present evidence and adduce witnesses.

Plaintiff was never given the hearing to which he was entitled and to which Defendants have never denied his right. See Page 8, Conclusion, of DEFENDANTS' RESPONSE TO PLAINTIFF'S OPPOSITION TO

MOTION FOR SUMMARY JUDGMENT (Exhibit C).

Plaintiff, as Chief of Police, was not a second class citizen and was entitled to all of the constitutional safeguards that all other citizens are entitled to receive. Case law is rife with similar holdings that all citizens are entitled to due process.

As *National Sur. Corp. v. Sharpe*, 59 S.E.2d 593, 597, 232, N.C. 98 emphatically states:

In its procedural aspects the constitutional guaranty of "due process of law" assures to *every* person his day in court and means that there can be no proceeding against life, liberty, or property without observance of those general rules established in the American system of jurisprudence for the security of private rights. (Emphasis supplied.)

Shioutakon v. District of Columbia, D.C. Mun. App., 114 A.2d 896, 899 holds that:

The indispensable elements of "due process" are a tribunal with jurisdiction, notice of hearing to proper party, and opportunity for fair hearing according to applicable procedures.

In addition, it was strongly noted in *Rudder v. U.S.*, 226 F.2d 51, 53, 96 U.S. App. D.C. 329 that:

Arbitrary action is not "due process of law."

Further, *Juster Bros. v. Christgau*, 7 N.W. 2d 501, 507, 214 Minn. 108 states that:

The "due process of law" clauses of State and Federal Constitutions are standing guarantees of substantial justice and prevent such capricious or arbitrary action as would prevent a litigant from having a substantially fair trial.

Ex Parte Lackey, Okl. Car. 279 P.2d 380, 382 also holds that:

"Due process of law" as used in constitutional provision that no person shall be deprived of life, liberty or property without due process of law is intended to protect the citizen against arbitrary action and to secure *all* persons equal and impartial justice. (Emphasis supplied.)

The list of cases is endless and all agree with the

same holding — that all citizens are entitled to "due process of law." Without such procedural safeguards, abuses can be heaped upon any individual and corruption can be the order of the day.

As Plaintiff indicated in his MEMORANDUM OF PLAINTIFF IN SUPPORT OF PLAINTIFF'S OPPOSI- TION TO DEFENDANTS' MOTION FOR SUMMARY JUDGMENT (Defendant's Exhibit "B"), the hearing of November 12, 1975, was a farce and Defendants have been able to act with impunity. Such reckless action on their behalf does not fall within the intent of the "due process of law" of the U.S. Constitution, nor did it set well with Judge Kalamarides, the Motions Judge in Plaintiff's State action mentioned in Exhibit "A" above.

Further, as to the allegations of conspiracy cited in Item 13 of Plaintiff's present Complaint under Sections 1983 and 1985 of Title 42, all of the Defendants fall within its purview for their actions.

Plaintiff should be entitled to Summary Judgment.

At the time of my immediate response to the Palmer defen- dants for their MOTION FOR SUMMARY JUDGMENT, I was unaware that Biss had given the case to Paul Waggoner, a staff attorney in his office, undoubtedly because Biss himself was also a defendant in the case.

On August 8, the Federal Motions Judge, United States District Judge James A. von der Heydt, responded as I hoped he would. He acceded to my OPPOSITION to the defendant's MOTION to dismiss my case. He issued a fairly lengthy ruling and also cited my present appeal to the Alaska Supreme Court as the basis for his decision:

MEMORANDUM AND ORDER

THIS CAUSE comes before the court on defen- dants' motion for summary judgment. The sole basis for this motion is that this claim is barred by the doctrine of res judicata.

The present case involves a claim for relief under various Civil Rights statutes for incidents allegedly

occurring during plaintiff's discharge from local government employment. Plaintiff brought an action in the State
court alleging various theories of relief but not including
those alleged herein. On March 14, 1977, defendants in
that case were granted a judgment on the pleadings.
Plaintiff has appealed that decision.

The doctrine of res judicata is intended to promote
judicial economy by preventing parties from splitting
causes of action in two separate lawsuits. The doctrine
essentially requires that when there has been a final
judgement on the merits in another action on the same
cause of action that further actions asserting different
bases for relief may not be maintained. *See* generally 1B
Moore's Federal Practice, 10.405(1). When claims that
could have been maintained in the former suit are asserted in a later suit the doctrine precludes the second action.

A review of the file in this case and in the prior State
action shows that the present claim arose from the same
general operative facts. Under Alaska Rule 18, which is
nearly the same as Federal Rule 18, this claim could have
been joined with the prior claim. *See* 6 *Wright & Miller,
Federal Practice & Procedure*, 1583, p.795. State courts
have concurrent jurisdiction over Civil Rights claims,
Long v. District of Columbia, 469 F.2d 927 (D.C. Cir.
1972), and res judicata applies to Civil Rights claims. 12
Wright & Miller, Federal Practice & Procedure, 3573, p.
499. The State court judgement appears to be a final
judgment and on the merits.

Although many of the requisites for the doctrine of
res judicata are present in the instant case the court cannot grant summary judgment at this time. The State court
judgment is presently on appeal to the Alaska Supreme
Court. The precise effect of an appeal on the doctrine of
res judicata is open to general uncertainty. *See* cases at 9
A.L.R. 2d 984, 994-1008. *See* also 1B, *Moore's Federal
Practice*, 0.416(3), p. 2254. The court's research has
revealed no Alaska decision or statue which would indicate the effect of an appeal upon res judicata and it is
Alaska law that controls this issue. 1B, *Moore's Federal*

Practice, 0.416(3), p. 2256. Given the countervailing considerations on this issue, see A.L.R. 2d 984, 987-88, the court concludes that the pendency of an appeal should prevent the application of res judicata. Hence, summary judgment cannot be granted at this time.

Should this judgment be affirmed the defendant should address the additional issue presented in this case of the effect of additional parties in the present suit on the doctrine. *See* 1B *Moore's Federal Practice*, 0.411(1); Restatement of Judgments 94, comment (b).

As a final matter the court notes that during the pendency of the State proceedings abstention may be appropriate. Wright, Federal Courts, p. 218-20.

Accordingly IT IS ORDERED:

THAT defendants' motion for summary judgement is denied.

When McShea saw U.S. District Judge von der Heydt's MEMORANDUM AND ORDER that denied the City's request for Summary Judgment, he was animated in his reaction.

"Not bad, Mangieri. That's three out of three," he acknowledged. "You're batting 1000."

As satisfied as I was with my latest victory against the City of Palmer, it wasn't the same feeling of elation that I had experienced before.

I was still very concerned about my kids, and it was draining my interest and my energy.

... Chapter 23 ...

Less than two weeks after my favorable decision by Judge von der Heydt I decided to put a little heat on the situation in an effort to speed things up in my federal case.

I called Waggoner, the new defense attorney in the case. He was surprised to hear from me since we had never directly communicated about the new federal action and all recent MOTIONS between us had been adversarial. He was even more surprised when I suggested that I *might* consider dropping the federal case in exchange for certain considerations. Since he obviously was in no position to unilaterally decide for the other defendants in the case — including Biss of course — he suggested I put my offer in writing. I agreed wholeheartedly and composed the following letter on August 19:

"Dear Mr. Waggoner:
"As per our telephone conversation of today's date, I am willing to withdraw my complaint in federal court against all of the ten defendants for conspiracy and Civil Rights violations and $350,000 in damages, in exchange for the following conditions:
1. Immediate reinstatement with full back pay, including compensatory time.
2. $25,000 in cash.
3. $25,000 in real property (appraisal value).

As to amplification of condition No. 1:

a. It is not my intention to resume office upon such reinstatement.

b. It is my desire to be on paid leave for the leave accrued during the past 21 months and to make my resignation effective the date that such leave terminates.

As to my reason for the above offer and as to the desirability of your clients considering and accepting this offer, the following is tendered for your enlightenment:

1. Four of your clients perjured themselves in depositions taken in *Case No. 75-8520* — specifically:
   - William Curtis
   - Jack Maze
   - Charles Shaver
   - Roseann Kohlberg

2. Depositions will be scheduled in the instant case, with the same questions proposed to them again. If perjurious statements are again put forth, appropriate proceedings, as discussed in our conversation, will be initiated in the federal system immediately.

3. In addition to depositions taken of the four stated above, depositions will be taken of all defendants, with similar questions proposed to all of them. If results are perjurious, the same proceedings as stated above will be initiated.

Your immediate action is requested and a response communicated to me no later than 4:30 p.m. on Monday, August 22, 1977."

I felt confident that much as defendants didn't want to capitulate in the lawsuit, by accepting my conditions for dropping the federal case, they would be less amenable to having charges for perjury instituted against them in federal court.

I waited for a response — but none came.

Their refusal to contact me — much less negotiate for a settlement — triggered an instantaneous reaction within me.

If that's what the sonsabitches want, I thought, *I'll be only too glad to oblige!*

I started to make preparations to draft the same depositions for Curtis, Maze, Shaver and Kohlberg as I had done in the state case. In addition, I compared other statements that I had with information obtained from other sources to make the content of their federal depositions even meatier. I began to get a new rush of adrenaline to accomplish rapidly what had lain fallow for too long.

I also felt that with their arrogance and with their false sense of invincibility that they would lie again under oath — and I was ready for them.

There was always the slim possibility that one or more of those four witnesses would tell the truth in the federal depositions to escape the very real specter of perjury, charges that I readily would have made a reality for them. Should the truth emerge in any of those depositions, it would have proven very effective. Not only was my reinstatement suit up on Appeal to the Alaska Supreme Court but my libel suit was due to come up for trial in the near future.

Meanwhile, McShea and I had been conferring frequently on the libel case, researching various aspects of defamation and compiling as much documentation that was appropriate to the case. Months earlier I had agreed to retain a high-powered Anchorage attorney named Edward Reasor to co-represent me with McShea. He was interested in handling the case and was well-versed in defamation suits.

The August 30 edition of The *Anchorage Times* carried an article noting that:

> "A $1.7 million libel suit brought by former Palmer Police Chief Nick Mangieri against City Officials has been scheduled for Sept. 12 in Superior Court here."

I was ready, more than ready, to resolve this whole issue. It had been almost two years. In addition, my divorce was almost finalized, and I was preparing to close that chapter, as well.

I had no immediate plans for when the libel case was over or the judge had signed the final decree. I had moved with my son and two daughters to a fairly decent new apartment complex during the summer but it wasn't easy. My ex constantly incited them, causing disrespect and disobedience in them, traits they had never exhibited before the marriage break-up. All the while, I tried to resume as normal a life as possible with them.

Both of those issues should have been resolved in September but that didn't happen. Although the judge signed the divorce decree on September 7, the relief was short-lived. Volatile episodes with my ex-wife increased in frequency and intensity making living conditions for the kids and me untenable.

A few days later, the libel case that was scheduled for trial on Monday, September 7, did not materialize. We were advised that the attorneys for the *Frontiersman* newspaper said they had not received official notice of the trial date. A new trial date was set for February 7, 1978, months away, and more than two years since the suit originally was filed.

When I heard the news, I couldn't believe it. I blew my top.

"Goddamn it! What the hell is going on? What are they trying to pull now?"

When I finally had quieted my ranting, McShea stepped in.

"This might be a blessing in disguise," he said quietly. "Reasor's going to be able to devote a lot more time to it."

"In the meantime, Roger," I continued, "I've got to get away for awhile. I'm fed up with the whole goddamn system. I need a change."

"That's a good idea," he said. "You *do* need a change. Any ideas?"

"Yeah, I've been thinking of visiting family on the East Coast."

"That's a wonderful idea," he was sincere as he said it. "For how long?" he queried.

"I don't know," I said. "A few weeks — maybe longer. I'm thinking of taking the kids to stay with family there. It's becoming too much of a hassle here. They need some stabilizing influence."

He looked at me for a moment.

"Then what?" he asked.

"You mean about the February trial," I answered. "Oh, I'll be back by then, or before then if I'm needed."

"I'm sure we can work it out," he said. "We still have five months to go. Have you set a departing date, yet?"

Frozen Shield

"No, but I've petitioned the court, to take the kids out of state."

"I don't think you'll have any trouble in that area," he said. I had kept him abreast of my own personal situation as well.

"I doubt it too, Roger," I said bitterly.

On October 3, Judge Justin Ripley concurred with my request and signed the ORDER that permitted me to leave the state with the children. He was the same judge who had spoken favorably after ruling for the preliminary injunction that Bill Artus had filed in my reinstatement action two years earlier. "It's with a heavy heart that I rule in favor of the City," he had said.

While I was busily making plans to return to the East Coast, I also had to continue my legal filings in my Appeal to the Alaska Supreme Court on the reinstatement case. Because I literally had used up all my money and couldn't afford to appeal, I filed a MOTION TO APPEAL AT PUBLIC EXPENSE with the court. An ORDER came down from the Supreme Court on October 7 that the matter was being remanded to the Superior Court for a hearing and that I had to file a MOTION with that court, "within 10 days following the date of this order."

A week later, in the midst of packing and continued dissension at home, I filed a MOTION and the following MEMORANDUM:

IN THE SUPERIOR COURT FOR THE STATE OF ALASKA
THIRD JUDICIAL DISTRICT
NICK J. MANGIERI,
Plaintiff,
vs.
WILLIAM CURTIS in his capacity
as City Manager for Palmer,
Alaska; THE CITY OF PALMER,
ALASKA,
Defendants.
No. 75-8520
MEMORANDUM IN SUPPORT OF POINTS ON APPEAL

It is the intention of Plaintiff to reply on the following points in the appeal:

(1) The Honorable Seaborn J. Buckalew was a biased
trial judge, swayed by prejudices toward the defense
attorney.

(2) Summary Judgement had already been denied defendants by Judge Kalamarides, the Motions Judge.

(3) Motion for Reconsideration was improperly denied.

(4) Motion Pursuant to Rule 60 was improperly denied.

(5) Plaintiff's employment "contract" was predicated
upon fraud.

(6) Plaintiff's employment was "permanent" and not
"indefinite".

(7) Plaintiff was an "employee" and not an "official".

(8) Plaintiff was wrongfully discharged.

(9) Plaintiff was denied his constitutional right of due
process for a hearing.

(10) Defendant abused his discretion by terminating
plaintiff.

(11) Malice was involved in plaintiff's termination by
defendant.

(12) "At the pleasure" of the defendant implies conduct
that is not capricious.

(13) Municipalities can be sued for punitive damages.

DATED this 14th day of October 1977
NICK J. MANGIERI, Plaintiff
Pro Per

Shortly thereafter, accompanied by my 14-year-old son, and
my two daughters, ages 12 and 7, we boarded the Alaska Air
flight to Washington, D.C. I had just taken a leave of absence
from my federal job at Fort Richardson rather than resign outright, although I had a feeling that it would be permanent. With
my federal status, I thought that perhaps I could affect a transfer
to another agency in the Washington area, and that the best way
to accomplish such a transfer was to knock on doors rather that
submit the applications through the mail. It was to prove a good
decision, in the long run, but that *run* was to be much longer than

Frozen Shield

I expected.

All we were able to take with us were eight footlockers of clothing and personal possessions, which were two small trunks each. All other items, meager as they were, either were sold, given away or just left. After four years in Alaska, that was all I had to show for my efforts — in addition to a mountain of indebtedness. Of course, I had my three kids, and for that, I was very thankful.

Our arrival on the East Coast and reunion with family was good all the way around. Although we were forced to stay with my sister and my brother-in-law for a few weeks, it was pleasurable, though a little crowded. In a short time, however, I was able to locate a nice townhouse nearby, enroll the three children in local schools and attempt to settle in.

Although I was thousands of miles away, my legal work on two cases — the reinstatement case and the federal case — still needed a great deal of immediate attention.

Just before I left Anchorage, I filed my MOTION TO APPEAL AT PUBLIC EXPENSE. City Attorney Biss, in the interim, naturally filed an OPPOSITION and mailed it to me on October 24. I had left a forwarding address with him before I left Alaska, but he sent it to my Anchorage address anyway. Consequently, I received it almost two weeks later — too late to draft a response and mail it back to the court in a timely fashion.

I wasn't expecting such obvious subterfuge but wasn't so surprised by it that I didn't know what to do. I immediately fired off an explanatory telegram to the Clerk of the Superior Court at the Alaska Court System:

> "RE: _CASE NO. 75-8520,_ Defendants deliberately mailed OPPOSITION TO MOTION TO APPEAL AT PUBLIC EXPENSE to former address although possessed knowledge of current address. Said OPPOSITION mailed on Oct. 24th, but not received until Nov. 5th. Plaintiff's REPLY TO OPPOSITION to be mailed out on Nov. 10th."

The Clerk of the Court subsequently responded and granted me the extension.

Nick Mangieri

Accordingly, I filed the following abrasive cogent REPLY to Biss' OPPOSITION:

Case No. 75-8520
REPLY TO DEFENDANTS' OPPOSITION
TO MOTION TO APPEAL
AT PUBLIC EXPENSE

Defendants do themselves a disservice by utilizing the services of defense counsel. Defense counsel, in turn, "tries the patience of the court" by continually misinforming the court. His unethical actions border on contempt of court and have repeatedly been called to the court's attention. It is no small wonder that defense counsel finds himself a defendant, also, in plaintiff's federal case (No.A55-77 Civ.) for Civil Rights violation and conspiracy. Although the file is replete with plaintiff's allegations, for recent prime examples of plaintiff's specific allegations see:

■ OPPOSITION TO MOTION FOR JUDGMENT ON THE PLEADINGS, dated March 7, 1977.
■ AFFIDAVIT that accompanied OPPOSITION TO DEFENDANTS' MOTION FOR AWARD OF ATTORNEY'S FEES, dated March 26, 1977.

In reviewing defendants' present OPPOSITION, plaintiff notes that defense counsel again misadvises the court by stating that plaintiff's STATEMENT OF POINTS ON THE APPEAL, dated April 15, 1977, "differ materially" from the MEMORANDUM IN SUPPORT OF POINTS ON APPEAL, dated October 14, 1977. However, if the court will examine both Points on Appeal, it will note that they are virtually identical, the latter being copied from the former with the exception of a few words.

Plaintiff further notes that defense counsel has continued to perpetuate his personal attack against plaintiff in what would appear to be an unnatural vendetta against another party. Defense counsel's statements are deliberately taken out of context and for the specific purpose of misleading the court. (See companion Case No. 76-1271

354

E for Libel and the extensive MEMORANDUM OF PLAINTIFF IN SUPPORT OF ADDITIONAL ANSWERS TO INTERROGATORIES citing numerous examples of defense counsel's unethical tactics).

It is believed that plaintiff has ably demonstrated his indigence in his AFFIDAVIT in spite of his federal employment.

Defense counsel, again, inappropriately cites cases to bolster his weak position. The facts in *Johnson v. Johnson*, Alaska 1976, 544 P2d 1028, were totally unlike plaintiff's position. Mr. Johnson, Appellant in the above case:

(1) had some assets

(2) was receiving financial assistance from a "father's rights organization."

(3) refused to explain some expenses.

None of the above applied to plaintiff. Further, the holding of the court is likewise inconsistent with defense counsel's reporting of *United States v. Kras*, 409 U.S. 434 (1973) is even more inappropriate.

Defense counsel again misinforms the court when he asserts that plaintiff alleged the trial judge was biased "only *after* having received an adverse decision." (Emphasis supplied) Defense counsel is well aware that plaintiff initiated three MOTIONS before his adverse decision from the trial judge:

■ OPPOSITION TO ORAL REQUEST FOR CONTIN-
  UANCE OF TRIAL.

■ NOTICE OF CHANGE OF JUDGE. dated March 2,
  1977.

■ MOTION FOR DISQUALIFICATION OF JUDI-
  CIAL OFFICER FOR CAUSE, with AFFIDAVIT,
  dated March 4, 1977.

It should be noted by the court that not only was the MOTION FOR JUDGMENT ON THE PLEADINGS submitted to the court subsequent to the date in which any motions were to be allowed but the MOTION itself was suggested to defense counsel by the trial judge, himself, Judge Buckalew, in the in-chambers conference.

These actions themselves are supportive of plaintiff's contention of a biased judge. Further, Judge Buckalew's prejudicial remark in court, just prior to his dismissal of plaintiff's case, to the effect that "he had known defense counsel for twenty five (25) years and was an honorable man" are further evidence of bias against plaintiff.

Plaintiff's MOTION FOR RECONSIDERATION OF MOTION TO AMEND COMPLAINT, dated February 7, 1977, and PLAINTIFF'S OPPOSITION PURSUANT TO RULE 60 FOR RELIEF FROM ORDER, dated February 22, 1977, were improperly denied because plaintiff cited precise appropriate exceptions to the holding of a Municipality to punitive damages and accordingly plaintiff's MOTION should have been affirmed.

Defense counsel continues to confound the court by additional misinformation. He states that if plaintiff were merely an employee of the City that plaintiff could have been terminated "without cause at any time by the City Manager." Defense counsel in his misadvice to defendants and in their misreliance on it have failed to read the City's Personnel Regulations (which states that Appeal procedures are available to all employees and so specifies the mechanics of that procedure.)

It is believed that the attached Exhibit "A", entitled REPLY TO MEMORANDUM OPPOSING MOTION FOR ISSUANCE OF WRIT OF MANDAMUS, dated November 1, 1977, will satisfactorily cover in detail the other elements that defense counsel raised in his OPPO-SITION. In addition, MEMORANDUM OF PLAIN-TIFF IN SUPPORT OF PLAINTIFF'S OPPOSITION TO DEFENDANTS' MOTION FOR SUMMARY JUDGEMENT, dated September 27, 1976 should be reread by the court for additional due process citations.

Accordingly, it is hereby requested that PLAIN-TIFF'S MOTION TO APPEAL AT PUBLIC EXPENSE be granted.

Meanwhile, the federal case was heating up and needed to be

looked after.

Before I left Anchorage, I had filed a WRIT OF MAN-
DAMUS in the federal action hoping to obtain a preliminary
injunction from the federal court.

Defendants' attorney, Waggoner, then filed an OPPOSI-
TION with that forum in a renewed effort to obtain a dismissal.
With typical inconsistencies within Biss' office, the federal
case was mailed directly to my East Coast address, by his associate, Waggoner. Whereas, the reinstatement case, pending
before the Superior Court for consideration of appealing at
public expense before the Supreme Court. was mailed to my
Anchorage address, by Biss. Both were mailed the same day,
on October 24. Undoubtedly, because the importance of the
Supreme Court was a more threatening action, and consequently, had greater priority in a delaying tactic, the divergent
mailings to me — on the same day — were apparently done
with calculation, *not* inadvertence.

Fortunately, my receipt of the OPPOSITION, in the federal
case, was not received beyond the deadline to respond, but it
meant that I had to work through the night at a local law library
to have it mailed out on the day it should have been received by
the federal court.

Again, I was forced to send out another telegram to
Anchorage to explain my delay in not responding timely to
defendants' OPPOSITION to my WRIT OF MANDAMUS.

The latest telegram, however, was forwarded to the Clerk of
the U.S. Court before I mailed out my own REPLY:

"RE: case no. A-55-77 civ., 'Reply to memorandum
opposing motion for issuance of writ of mandamus'
mailed out on Nov. 1st. Defendants' opposition', dated
Oct. 24th, but not received until Oct. 29th."

I threw everything into that very minutely researched, and
very persuasive, REPLY. My initial goal was for a reinstatement,
and barring that, at least being able to forestall another attempt by
the City of Palmer for a Summary Judgment.

Although I did not have McShea around to ask any pertinent questions concerning format, I thought that I could handle

357

it fairly well myself, because I had done it so many times in the past:

Case No. A77-55 Civ.

REPLY TO MEMORANDUM OPPOSING MOTION
FOR ISSUANCE OF WRIT OF MANDAMUS

Defendants in their headlong pursuit to obtain summary judgment continue to misread and misinterpret the doctrine of res judicata to suit their own needs in spite of the law. The citation of *State v. Baker*, 393 P.2d 893, 897 (AK. 1964), in their opposition, was taken out of context and used for the purpose of misleading the court by attaching misplaced emphasis upon it because it was an Alaska case. In the *Baker* case the decision had been appealed to the Washington Supreme Court, which was also recognized as an impediment to the doctrine of res judicata — as it is in plaintiff's case.

In 1B *Moore's Federal Practice* 0.405 (1) at p. 624 citing *Com'r v. Sunnen* (1948) 333 US 591, 597, 68 S. Ct. 715, 92 L Ed 898, it states:

"The judgment puts an end to the cause of action, which cannot again be *brought* into litigation between the parties upon any ground whatever, absent *fraud* or *other* factor *invalidating the judgment*. (Emphasis supplied)

The court will note, and the record will reflect, that plaintiff raised the issue of prejudice by a biased judge before and after his State case was dismissed, thereby placing a new impediment to the application of res judicata.

It would further appear that defendants are bent upon a course of action to confound the court by additional loose wording dealing with Federal Rule of Procedure 81 (b). Although Rule 81 (b) abolished the writ of mandamus, "the rule is quite specific that the relief heretofore available by mandamus from a district court may now be obtained by appropriate action or motion and such relief can be granted in cases of which the district court has jurisdiction." Contrary to defendants' allegations that there is now "confusion in the law concerning the availability of alternate remedies that end up with the same result," perusal of Rule 81 (b) in its entirety does not impart that negative belief.

Defendants' reliance upon *Stern v. South Chester Tube Company*, 309 U.S. 606 (1968) is unclear but the holding that "neither the All Writs Act nor any other principle of federal law bars the granting of the mandatory equitable relief sought in this case," is consistent with plaintiff's statement above.

Defendants' statement that *Strait v. Laird*, 445 F.2d 843 (9th Cir. 1971) "reversed on other grounds" is equally confusing since it would be assumed because of its appearance in defendants' OPPOSITION that it had some bearing on the issue at hand regarding a writ of mandamus. However, the reversal in the *Strait* case was a jurisdictional question and had no relation at all to the present case. Further, defendants brief mention of "11 *Wright & Miller, Federal Practice & Procedure*, Section 2944" with no cases cited or holdings put forth, adds no support at all to their OPPOSITION.

Under this Section which deals with the Adequacy of the Legal remedy, plaintiff has repeatedly stated that he is without adequate legal remedy to accomplish his immediate reinstatement as Chief of Police. *Rogers v. U.S.*, D.C. Cal. 1958, 58 F Supp. 670, 679 holds that:

"For the exercise of equity jurisdiction, it must appear that there is no plain, speedy and adequate remedy at law..."

In addition, "Special circumstances" may excuse a plaintiff's "failure" to show an adequate legal remedy. Note 28 of Section 2944 offers the holding of *Teamsters Public Employees Union Local No. 594 v. City of West Point, Nebraska*, D.C. Neb. 1972, 338 F. Supp. 927: "In view of the time and cost already expended in connection with an action by former city employees who fought a preliminary injunction restraining the city from discriminating against them because of their union membership and ordering the city to restore them to their former employment with the city, it would be manifestly unjust to apply the exhaustion of remedies doctrine, and the court would proceed to consider the propriety of issuing a preliminary injunction."

Plaintiff believes that his long delay in his reinstatement and the burgeoning cost involved expended in this litigation plus the likelihood of a protracted delay in his State appeal places him directly within the holding of *Teamster v. West Point.*

Further analysis of *Section 2944* reveals that, "The legal remedy is inadequate if any one of a number of factors is present." Of these factors is that of "demonstrating that damages would not adequately compensate him." *Hoellen v. Annunzio*, C.A. 7th, 1972, 468 F.2d 522.

It would appear that the monetary damages of lost wages at some future date would not adequately compensate for the stigma of being terminated as Chief of Police and the many ramifications that have followed since that date as related by plaintiff in the instant case and in plaintiff's state action.

In addition to the insufficiency of remedy of monetary damages as discussed above, plaintiff has already offered what he believes is irreparable harm in his not being immediately reinstated. The tentacles of harm continue and follow plaintiff wherever he goes. As a former Chief of Police, who has been terminated, seeking similar employment on the East Coast (where plaintiff has been forced to go because of the "domino-effect" that defendants have initiated in plaintiff's marital life and produced irreversible damages), the odds are against being reemployed in a like position. However, if plaintiff were reinstated, the stigma would no longer attach and plaintiff would be "acceptable" in the eyes of his peers. As plaintiff has previously reiterated, every day that dawns produces new and greater harm and damage that can never ever fully be resolved. In *Studebaker Corp. v. Gittlin*, C.A. 2d, 1966, 360 F.2d 692, Judge Friendly cogently states that:

"A plaintiff asking an injunction because of the defendant's violation of a statute is not required to show that otherwise rigor mortis will set in forthwith; all that "irreparable injury" means in this context is that unless an injunction is granted, the plaintiff will suffer harm which cannot be repaired."

In defendants' OPPOSITION they advance the concept, "And courts are especially reluctant to grant affirmative injunctions," taken from 11 *Wright & Miller, Federal Practice & Procedure*, Section 2942. Again, defendants extract for the court only that which they would like considered. "In *Clune v. Publishers Assn. of New York City*, D.C. N.Y. 1963, 214 F. Supp. 520 (per Levet J.) affirmed per curiam C.A. 2d. 1963, 314 F. 2d 343, what was held was that, "courts are more reluctant to grant a mandatory injunction than a prohibitory one..." However, as McClintock, equity, 2d ed. 1948 Section J states:

"Nevertheless, injunctions compelling the doing of some act, as opposed to forbidding the continuation of a course of conduct, are an ancient and familiar tool of equity courts and will be used whenever the circumstances warrant."

Defendants also advance the proposition that they would be under hardship if required to allow plaintiff to resume his position as Chief of Police. If the Court will note, plaintiff offered to embark on a ten week annual leave (that being the approximation to which he would be entitled because of the time span from his initial hire). If such were the case, plaintiff would undoubtedly retain the present Chief as his second-in-command to be the Acting Chief in his absence. At the end of that period, plaintiff might very well retain the present Chief as his Deputy — having no quarrel with the Chief who now occupies his position. Court should further note that plaintiff at the inception of his legal suits with defendants, advised the present Chief that he was on tenuous ground. The present Chief agreed and advised plaintiff that he accepted the position with full knowledge of the results and the possibility that he might be out of a job as Chief of Police at any time. Plaintiff believes that

Nick Mangieri

with almost two (2) years in office, he cannot be found to complain too strenuously.

Defendants further state that the relationship between themselves and plaintiff has become severely strained and that there is no likelihood of harmonious working relationships and that the City of Palmer will be deprived of a functioning police force. These two concepts are without merit. First, defendants cannot be allowed to profit because of their wrongdoing. If plaintiff is reinstated, it is also incumbent upon defendants to work with plaintiff. If they cannot, they can submit their resignations — which are honorable ways to depart. If, on the other hand, they cannot and will not work with plaintiff for the best interests of the City, the electors can show their dissatisfaction and place in office those who place the City above their own petty behaviors. Plaintiff can see no hardship for defendants that they cannot resolve themselves. The keys to their predicament lie within their own pockets. Plaintiff's hardships continue to mount as discussed herein and in the files therein. In referring to the flexibility of an injunction decree, the court in *Hecht Co. v. Bowles*, 1944, 64 S. Ct. 587, 592, 321 U.S. 321, 329, 88 L. Ed. 754 found that:

"The essence of equity jurisdiction has been the poser of the Chancellor to do equity and to mold each decree to the necessities of the particular case. Flexibility rather than rigidity has distinguished it."

Plaintiff is cognizant of the contents of Section 2948, *Wright & Miller, Federal Practice & Procedure* and is grateful to the defendants for their reliance upon it. However, before plaintiff delves into the aspects of that Section that are beneficial to him he wishes to advise the Court that, again, defendants' choice of a citation in *Bishop v. Wood*, 96 S. Ct. 2074 (1976) is inappropriate because it is not "on point." At p. 2075 it states that:

"Discharge of public employee whose position is terminable at the will of the employer does not deprive such employee of liberty when there is no public disclosure of the reasons for the discharge."

Defendants are well aware that there was a "public disclosure" at a slanderous forty five (45) minute tirade by City Manager at a City Council meeting in which plaintiff was only allowed ten (10) minutes to respond and in which plaintiff's attorney and witnesses were forbidden to speak. Therefore, plaintiff's "good name, reputation, honesty or integrity" was impugned and his interest in "liberty" under the 14th Amendment should be protected as a constitutional right.

Although defendants are reluctant to have the court look through plaintiff's state case and the judgments therein, plaintiff welcomes that possibility. The court will note that plaintiff has raised many allegations, all provable, about the impropriety of plaintiff's termination. Of prime interest to the court should be the apparent mental instability of the defendant City Manager — a fact that defense counsel wished to suppress. Accordingly, defendant City Manager "abused his discretion" and unreasonably exercised his power to terminate plaintiff. See *Cara v. Delaware Liquro Comm. Del. Super*, 90 A2d 492, 494, *S. Terry 268 and County School Trustees of Callahan County v. District Trustees of Dist. No. 15 (Hart) Common School District of Callahan County, Texas* Civ. App., 192 S.W. 2d 891, 898.

Also, malice as grounds of attack on, or relief from, acts or regulations of public officers in exercise of discretionary powers, see *Speyer v. School District No. 1 City and County of Denver*, et al, 82 Colo. 534, 261 Pac. 859.

In *Moore v. Porter Field* (1925) 113 Okla. 234. 241 Pac. 346 (later appeal L (1927) 125 Okla 217, 257 Pac. 307) it was held that although as a general rule the discretionary powers of a public official will not be controlled by an injunction, yet an injunction may be issued in case of a gross abuse of such discretion, or where it appears that such action is founded on fraud, corruption, improper motive, plain disregard of duty, gross abuse of power or violation of the law.

In addition to defendant City Manager's apparent

mental instability, which was responsible not only for
plaintiff's ouster as Chief of Police, his erratic behavior
was also responsible for other terminations in the past.

Further, he and others in the City condoned and promoted what can only be described as "municipal corruption" and evidence indicates a participation in land fraud
in the surrounding area (*Exhibit A*).

It also has been brought out by defendants that because
plaintiff served "at the pleasure" of the City Manager, it was
not permanent employment. However, section 1017,
Williston on Contracts at pp. 132, 133 state that:

"If the employee has rendered additional consideration, other than merely quitting his current employment
and accepting his new duties, the contract of permanent
or life employment is valid..."

Plaintiff resigned a higher paying permanent State
position to accept, on good faith, from a prior City
Manager what purported to be a permanent position "to
straighten out the police department." Therefore, there
was "valuable consideration additional to the services
which he has contracted to render, a discharge without
good cause may constitute a breach of contract." (See
*Chesapeake and Potomac Tel. Co. of Baltimore City v.
Murray*, 198 Md. 526, 84 A2d 870).

Further, to enhance the "prima facie case" mentioned in Section 2948, the court should note that
Plaintiff has already alleged improprieties in the Superior
Court judge's dismissal of his state case — both in the in-
chambers conference and in a statement on the record in
court. These factors and others would give plaintiff a reasonable probability of success. There are numerous cases
at Note 55 bearing out this concept and the need for the
granting of an injunction.

Other factors to be considered by the court in their
granting of the injunction is that, "injury to reputation or
goodwill is not easily measurable in monetary terms, and
so often is viewed as irreparable." (See *Culter-Hammer,
Inc. v. Universal Relay Corp.*, D.C. N.Y. 1968, 285 F.
Supp. 636, 639.)

Even more important for the court to consider in its affirmative granting of an injunction is that, "when an alleged deprivation of a constitutional right is involved, most courts hold that no further showing of irreparable injury is necessary." (See *A Quaker Action Group v. Hickel*, CA 1969, 421 F.2d 1111, 1116, 137 U.S. App. D.C. 176, *Keefe v. Geanakos*, CA 1st 1969, 418 F.2d 359 and other cases cited in Note 39 of Section 2948. Further, a granting of this preliminary injunction would not give plaintiff all or most of the relief to which he would be entitled if he were successful at trial. (See list of cases at Note 48 of this Section).

A final factor in this area to be considered by the court in their discretion to grant an injunction is the public interest. If all, or a majority of plaintiff's allegations have merit that appear in Exhibit A concerning corruption in City Hall by the defendants, then the public interest would certainly best be served if plaintiff is reinstated immediately.

The question of the doctrine of abstention has been raised to cause the Federal Court to stay their proceedings. In *Weiner v. Shearson, Hammill and Co., Inc.*, 521 F.2d 817 (9th Cir. 1975) it held that:

"Abstention is required only in those relatively few instances where exercise of jurisdiction would create unwarranted friction between federal and state sovereigns."

It also stated that:

"Existence of prior pending state court action involving collateral dispute between same parties is not alone sufficient reason to invoke abstention."

Examination of Weiner reveals that, unlike plaintiff's case, the issues presented before the two courts in Weiner were identical. So much so, the federal complaint was virtually a carbon copy of the second amended state complaint. *Moore's Federal Practice*, Section 0.203 (4) at pp.2137, 2138 reveals several interesting cases in this area.

Crawford v. Seaboard Coast Line RR Co. (SD Ga 1968) 268 F Supp. 556 states, "that the federal court required the plaintiff to choose either the state or federal forums."

Clintila v. Diamond Reo Trucks Inc., (ED Pa 1975) 393 F Supp. 1392 states, "that the federal district court stayed a diversity action and the theory that since additional defendants had already been joined in the later filed state case, the state court suit would be tried earlier than the federal case."

Finally, in *Thompson v. Boyle* (CA 5th 1969) 417 F 2d 1041, the 5th Circuit affirmed the District Court stay of consolidated diversity actions because they reasoned; "that a stay of the federal action was appropriate because a number of defendants who had been joined in the state case were not before the federal court and therefore, the state case could better resolve all the rights of the parties."

It is not beyond the realm of supposition to believe that if in both the *Clintila* case and the *Thompson* case, where additional defendants were added, that if it occurred in the federal court and not the state court that the federal forum would prevail. In *Thompson* it was reasoned that the court with the greater number of defendants could better resolve the rights of the parties. Therefore, it would seem that because there are more defendants in plaintiff's federal case, that court can better resolve his case and should not invoke the doctrine of abstention. Further, the cause of action is different arising under Title 42 of the U.S. Code and the remedies more extensive.

In conclusion, it is earnestly requested that a preliminary injunction be granted allowing plaintiff to be reinstated as Chief of Police, Palmer, Alaska, to be effective immediately. Plaintiff is to be paid full back pay, at the rate he would have earned had he remained in office continuously, to November 4, 1975. Further, plaintiff is to be paid his full compensatory time accrued before his termination and still further, plaintiff is to be granted immediate annual leave for a period of approximately ten (10) weeks that being the leave he had earned."

Upon receipt and consideration of both our MOTIONS, U.S. District Judge von der Heydt issued a MEMORANDUM AND ORDER on November 15, 1977.

In it, he held in part:

"Accordingly IT IS ORDERED:

1. THAT plaintiff's motion for a writ of mandamus (preliminary injunction) is denied at this time without prejudice.
2. THAT this court will abstain from proceeding with this case pending final resolution of the related State court matters.
3. THAT the parties advise the court of the status of those proceedings every 6 months and upon their termination either party may move to reinstate this case to the active calendar or bring other appropriate motions."

Although I was disappointed in my primary objective of failing to have the federal judge rule in my favor, I did accomplish a secondary objective. I prevented the defendants from prevailing in the federal court in their OPPOSITION, and was able to keep them at bay even longer.

The judge, in his ruling, whether intentionally or unwittingly, was of assistance to me. In the body of his MEMORANDUM AND ORDER, he also wrote a cautionary — if not an instructional — comment to me, as the plaintiff:

"The court's only hesitation on the question of abstention arises from the fact that a ruling against plaintiff on appeal may well preclude this claim based upon *res judicata*. This difficulty, however, is caused by plaintiff's own error and demonstrates the manner in which subtle procedural traps may await pro se litigants. Had plaintiff filed both suits simultaneously and reserved the federal issues in the State court he would fall within the protection of *England v. Bd. of Medical Examiners*, 375 U.S. 411 (1964), which *sub silentio* precluded *res judicata* in such situations. Having failed to follow this pro-

Nick Mangieri

cedure plaintiff is now in serious difficulty in this litigation but abstention seems warranted nonetheless.

Should plaintiff prevail in the appeal in the State court he would be well advised to attempt to follow the *England* procedure or bring his federal claims in that forum. The court, of course, makes no determination of whether such a belated attempt will preclude the application of *res judicata*."

The advisory information obtained from the judge was appreciated, and duly noted, and would have certainly been applied if the opportunity arose. However, it did not, and I was therefore unable to avail myself of that future procedure.

In the interim, my concern for the children's welfare continued for the balance of 1977. Although I was 5,000 miles from Alaska, letters and telephone calls from my ex-wife constantly incited them. I began to realize that I couldn't leave them — even if it was temporarily.

It was a hard decision to make not to return to Anchorage to pursue my libel case against the Palmer figures after all that I had been through. Nonetheless, it was one that I knew that I not only had to make, but *would make* because of the children. They needed me, and the decision not to leave them to pursue my own interests 5,000 miles away — important as they were — was based on their need. Also, it would have been unfair to leave my three kids, who themselves had been through a lot, with my sister and her husband. They were in business for themselves and couldn't have devoted the time and effort required to look after my family while I was away for an unknown extended period.

... Chapter 24 ...

In mid January 1978 I wrote McShea to tell him I would not be returning to Anchorage to pursue my libel case and "to take whatever steps are necessary" to finalize that decision.

I never knew whether or not he understood my reasons. I never heard from him again, and I did not pursue any continued correspondence with him.

Meanwhile my disappointment in not being able to return to Alaska was sidetracked with fully occupied days. From 9 a.m. to 5 p.m., Mondays through Fridays, my activities were constantly devoted to going from one agency to another as I tried to find a job in Washington, D.C., At night, I tried to fill the father/mother duties in caring for the kids.

My long awaited break in finding a federal position finally came, but it didn't happen for many months.

Although I was unable to continue my libel case because of family responsibilities, I did not cease my efforts in the other legal areas. And while my appeal to the Alaska Supreme Court was still of foremost concern to me, it too, soon fell by the wayside. That high court ruled that I didn't meet the necessary criteria to enable me to file under public expense. The fact that I had relentlessly pursued my reinstatement case, at my own expense, and as my own attorney for two years, evidently didn't enter into the equation of *need*. For that matter, neither did my financial inability to file a transcript fee, nor post an appeal bond enter into their consideration. What apparently was considered was City Attorney Biss' statements that I was, and had been, living beyond my means, and that therefore I should not be permitted to avail myself of the *public expense* route. Undoubtedly, filing a divorce action in order to obtain custody — and then obtaining such — was unquestionably "living beyond my means." Obviously, anybody in his right mind wouldn't voluntarily engage in that type of legal action, especially if it was a man who sought the custody. Biss also was able to convince that august body that inasmuch as I was a federal employee with the U.S. Army that I couldn't possibly be indigent enough to qualify for court aid. My annual starting salary at Fort Richardson was $18,423, which was almost $200 less per month than my Police Chief's salary. My ending salary, a year later was $20,694, only $24 *more* per month than my Chief's salary. Of course, I also had lost my $800 additional monthly income as a part-time college instructor because of interference by Palmer officials.

The decision by the Alaska Supreme Court not to grant my public expense appeal, as disappointing as it was, came as no shock to me. It was just another frustration in a long string of defeats that would continue for an even longer period. My final lawsuit — the federal Civil Rights case against the Palmer defendants — was still open, however, and holding its own so I turned my attention to another area related to that complaint.

I decided I would personally follow up my Civil Rights complaints with the U.S. Department of Justice in our nation's capital. I had initially contacted the FBI office in Anchorage back in November 1975, and requested in writing — as per the Agent-in-Charge's suggestion — a "formal ruling from (the) Washington office to determine whether my Civil Rights and those of the citizens of Palmer (had) been violated."

I had received no response.

Ten months later, in September 1976, I grew tired of waiting for some word or action out of Washington and filed several Civil Rights complaints with the U.S. Attorney in Anchorage. Named in the complaints were all of the Palmer officials. A "prompt response" also was requested.

Again I heard nothing from the Department of Justice.

In April 1978, after relocating to the Washington area, I visited their Civil Rights Division in downtown D.C. and spoke briefly to a Richard Johnson, an attorney in their Criminal Section.

"I'd like status on my complaints," I asked him.

"We'll have someone look that up for you," he responded.

When he returned, he told me that my first complaint, the one that I had filed with the FBI in November 1975, was filed away with the notation that "no action would be taken."

"What about my second complaint, the one that I filed with the U.S. Attorney's Office in September 1976?" I wanted to know.

He looked through the file. "I'm sorry we have no record of it ever being received."

I was dumbfounded at his reply.

"Are you sure?" I asked in disbelief.

"I'm sorry," he said. "It's not here."

I shook my head, still trying to figure out what the hell had happened.

"I've got another copy at home," I told him confidently; "I'll be back."

A few days later I returned with a copy and gave it to him. He briefly looked over it and quickly advised me, "I'm sorry but the Civil Rights Division has more important cases that need attention."

I was somewhat amazed at his response, and when I asked him what they were, he mentioned "prisoner complaints."

When I looked at him questioningly, he added that they were "not adequately staffed to handle complaints by police officers." He continued, "even if your allegations of a conspiracy are true, as a police officer, you do not fall into the class of individuals protected by the section dealing with *Conspiracy Against The Rights Of Persons*."

I was astounded by his answer and wanted to know whether police officers were second class citizens?

His only reply was that it was "policy."

Unable to get any further satisfaction from an office that I thought should have jurisdiction over my type of complaint, I left. I still couldn't believe what I had heard and wondered what my next course of action should be. I still hadn't given up.

371

I had always heard that a Senator or Congressman was supposed to help their constituents. At that point I knew I didn't have a thing to lose. I looked up the name of one of my Senators in Maryland, a Charles Mathias Jr., and visited his office at the Russell Senate Office Building in Washington. I met with a Gordon Hawk of his staff and *again* reiterated my whole story of Alaska. I then followed up with my discussions with personnel in the Civil Rights Division at the Department of Justice. He was interested in the story and sympathetic to my plight — or at least seemed so — and suggested that I write the Senator what I had told him and forward whatever documentation I possessed.

On April 21, I wrote a six-page letter to the Senator that detailed what I had told his staff member and enclosed not only the two letter-complaints that I had filed in Alaska but some representative newspaper clippings as well. In the body of that letter, after I had reiterated my conversation with Johnson of the Civil Rights Division concerning their inability to handle complaints by police officers, I also added the pertinent comment:

> "It is no small wonder that corruption at all levels is able to flourish. If Police Chiefs or any other Police Officers are shackled to the political process and are immediately expendable at the whim of those who wish their corruption concealed, our nation is indeed in trouble."

The words were lofty and philosophical but nonetheless very sincere. I soon learned that apparently no one was on the same wavelength as me. That fact not only saddened me but also reinforced my belief that, as a nation, we were indeed "in trouble."

In closing my letter to the Senator I also mentioned:

> "In addition to my specific complaint concerning the inaction and lack of interest by the Civil Rights Division, it has also been my unwavering contention that massive land fraud has been perpetrated upon the U.S. Government and the State of Alaska by many within the State, including State officials. The State of Alaska will not investigate and the Federal Government will not

delve into the matter without hard facts or proof. As a former Police Chief, I was unable to obtain the proof that the federal authorities seek. Subpoena powers alone will produce that information."

I was satisfied with the letter, but regrettably, not as convinced as I would have been at one time that any real good would come of it. I was sustained, however, by the thought that I had left no stone unturned and was still doing my best.

On May 11, I received a welcomed reply from the Senator, which apparently indicated his interest in the matter:

"Dear Mr. Mangieri:
Thank you for writing to me, and for speaking with Gordon Hawk of my staff, regarding the events surrounding your termination as Chief of Police in Palmer, Alaska. I can appreciate your concern in this matter.

I have contacted the appropriate officials at the Department of Justice on your behalf and expect a reply in the near future. You may be assured that I will keep you informed of any developments.

With best wishes,
Sincerely,
Charles McC. Mathias, Jr.
United States Senator"

While waiting for the Senator's response, I called the office of the Assistant Attorney General of the Civil Rights Division to obtain confirmation of that stated "policy" of *hands-off* as it concerned police officer Civil Rights complaints. I still found it hard to believe that "prisoner complaints" would take precedence over police officer complaints, and that as such, police officers were then accorded second class citizen status. I was referred to a Donald Walker within the Division who also confirmed what Johnson had previously told me.

I was now past the non-belief stage because yet another attorney within the same division was telling me the same thing. It was still hard to swallow.

"Would you mind putting it in writing?" I asked.

Walker advised that he would relay the message to Johnson and that it would be done.

On May 17, the supposed *letter of confirmation* that I requested was mailed to me:

"Dear Mr. Mangieri:

Mr. Donald Walker of this Division has informed me that you desired a written reply to your allegations that a federal criminal Civil Rights violation occurred in connection with your dismissal as Chief of the Palmer City, Alaska, Police Department. This is in response to that request.

As you know, I have reviewed the written material which you submitted to the Department and have discussed the details of your allegations with you on two occasions. As I indicated to you in our last conversation, no criminal Civil Rights violation was disclosed in the information you provided. Consequently, the Department contemplates taking no further action with respect to this matter."

The letter was signed by Richard Johnson, under the name of the Assistant Attorney General for the Civil Rights Division, Drew S. Days III.

That was *not*, however, the letter that I requested or the one that was promised to me. It contained no reference to any policy concerning their inability to handle police officer Civil Rights complaints. After reading that innocuous reply, my knee-jerk reaction was spontaneous and I made a quick trip to the Civil Rights Office on May 18 and again saw Johnson. I wanted to rectify a distinct lack of communication among all parties. When I questioned him about the inconsistency between our prior conversation and his letter of May 17, he emphatically denied ever making such a statement to me. I knew then that such a *policy* was not about to be committed to paper.

At this point I realized that I was fighting a losing battle. Still I could not accept the fact that the entire system was disinterested not only in my allegations — which I *knew* to be valid — but in any other allegations that a police officer would raise.

I extracted the name of Drew S. Days III as the Assistant Attorney General, and wrote him a detailed six-page letter with the same attachments and cited my personal experiences with his office staff.

In the letter I wrote:

"Your immediate attention and resolution of this issue is requested as it would appear that such apathy and inaction is inappropriate not only to myself as a former Police Chief but to all other Police Officers nationwide who faithfully perform their duties and are not accorded the same safeguards and protection accorded all citizens — or even prisoners."

In closing out my letter to him, I used the same words, more or less, that I had used with Dan Hickey, the Alaska Deputy Attorney General, because I felt that they were just as appropriate:

"It is not my intention to become embroiled in any controversy with your office as I have always been of the belief that police and prosecutors should cooperate with each other fully. However, I have been through too much the past two-and-a-half years to ignore what I have seen and experienced in Alaska in widespread corruption, cover-ups and apathy. It is still my duty to expose that wrongdoing."

I waited for a reply from Days; there was none. I can't say I was surprised, because nothing surprised me anymore. I really didn't expect any affirmative action or favorable response from him but I did expect *something*. When nothing materialized after two weeks, I continued with my Congressional inquiries.

In early June I made an appointment to see Congressman Newton Steers, my local Congressman at the Cannon House Office Building in Washington. The contact produced the following letter:

CONGRESS OF THE UNITED STATES
HOUSE OF REPRESENTATIVES
June 8, 1978
Mr. Drew A. Days, III
Assistant Attorney General
Civil Rights Division
U.S. Department of Justice
Washington, D.C. 20530
Dear Mr. Days:

Enclosed you will find a letter from my constituent, Mr. Nicholas Mangieri, requesting your immediate attention to the issues raised therein.

My staff and I have spent considerable time reviewing Mr. Mangieri's particular case and the circumstances surrounding it. I believe it would be wise of the Department of Justice to do likewise.

I would appreciate being kept informed of your actions in this matter and look forward to hearing from you in the near future.

Yours sincerely,
Newton I. Steers, Jr.

As noteworthy as that letter was, and as forceful as the Congressman's advice to Days seemed to be that "it would be wise of the Department of Justice" to review my particular case — it still went unheeded.

Six weeks later, a reply to Congressman Steers from the Assistant Attorney General finally arrived. This time, however, it was signed by Maceo W. Hubbard, a Supervisory Trial Attorney in the Criminal Section. It again stated in part, that there was "nothing in the information he furnished that disclosed the existence of a criminal Civil Rights violation." The letter then advised the Congressman that, "Consequently, this office contemplates taking no further action with respect to his complaint."

That same type of letter, also signed by Maceo W. Hubbard, for Asst. A.G. Drew S. Days III, was dispatched to Senator Charles Mathias several weeks earlier. The only difference then was an added notation at the bottom of the letter that stated:

"Inasmuch as Mr. Mangieri feels that his Civil Rights have been violated, he may wish to consult with private counsel to determine what civil remedies may be available to him."

As Wayne Higgins would have said, "What a cop-out, Chief."

I had the same feeling several weeks earlier when I visited the administrative offices of the International Chiefs of Police in Gaithersburg, Maryland. I had gone there to ask what had happened to complaint I had registered with the association over two years earlier. The response that I received was that "the IACP did not get involved in local politics."

Although I was at the end of my rope trying to get justice done, events in my personal life surfaced again to completely overshadow my ongoing concerns about the Palmer situation.

One afternoon in mid June when the three kids were in their last day of school, the unthinkable happened.

My ex-wife kidnapped them from the school grounds. By the time I realized that she had taken them, it was too late. She and her new husband, a young airman who had recently been discharged in Alaska, drove to the school to pick up the children. They in turn drove to my house while I was still in downtown D.C., retrieved the kids' clothes and were gone by the time I got home.

Attempts to file child abduction charges against her were unsuccessful because there was no law on the books at the time.

Within the year such a law was enacted, but for me it was too late. For months afterward I didn't know where they were and how they were faring.

Just about that same time, however, fate did step in to rapidly change things in my favor.

Weeks before their disappearance, I had noticed an interesting article in the *Washington Post*. It stated that the U.S. Department of Labor was conducting a recruitment drive for Special Investigators to delve into CETA fraud that was rampant throughout the country. CETA was the Comprehensive Employment and Training Act program operated by the Labor

Department. Its aim was to take federal dollars and pay to train people in the workforce so they could be removed from public assistance rolls. Unfortunately, monies expended went into the pockets of those that were responsible for overseeing its distribution rather that to those for whom it was intended.

At the time I applied for the position I knew it entailed travel, but because I had been unemployed for many months, I didn't have much choice in the matter. If I were lucky enough to be selected, I knew that I could work the logistics out concerning the kids. The salary was good, and I needed the income.

I subsequently learned that they received 200 applications for the seven slots.

Within two weeks of the children being taken, I was called in for an interview, screened by a panel and hired. By the 4th of July, I, and six others, reported for duty to a newly formed Office of Special Investigations. It changed my life completely.

... Chapter 25 ...

My first assignment was to South Florida, where I worked out of the Organized Crime Bureau located at the Dade County Airport in Miami. In area, my cases ranged from West Palm Beach, about 65 miles north of Miami, to the Florida Keys. The work was hectic but rewarding. Periodically, I flew back to headquarters in Washington, made my reports, was briefed and then flew back to Florida to continue my investigations.

Although I continually kept busy, I never stopped worrying about my kids — nor could I forget my final *unfinished* Alaska case.

My first notification that the Palmer defendants also had not forgotten came in the form of a RENEWED MOTION FOR SUMMARY JUDGMENT in my federal case. Since I was not made aware of it until one of my sporadic trips back North, I sought additional time to respond to their MOTION.

On November 13, 1978, I sent a telegram to the Clerk of the U.S. District Court:

"RE: A77-55 CIVIL. DEFENDANTS REQUEST FOR RENEWED MOTION FOR SUMMARY JUDGEMENT JUST RECEIVED. AM FEDERAL AGENT ASSIGNED TO EXTENSIVE FLORIDA FIELD INVESTIGATION. REQUEST EXTENSION TO REPLY. PLEASE ADVISE DATE DUE." NICHOLAS

J. MANGIERI.

On November 14, the Honorable James A. von der Heydt issued a MINUTE ORDER FROM CHAMBERS, which stated, "Plaintiff shall have until Friday, December 8, 1978 to file an opposition to defendants' motion for summary judgment."

Again, because I was into heavy investigative efforts in Key West, I was forced to request a further extension of time.

On December 14, Judge von der Heydt issued still another MINUTE ORDER FROM CHAMBERS:

"The plaintiff is granted a final extension of time to file an opposition to defendants' motion for summary judgment by January 8, 1979."

At about this time, I also received further good news. I learned that my children were in Mississippi. I wasted no time in seeing that they were returned to me.

Because my assignment was still in the South Florida area, however, I hired a live-in housekeeper to cook and look after them.

It was not the most ideal arrangement since I was away for sustained periods, but I usually made a return flight on the week-ends to see them and then flew out again late Sunday nights.

On one of my return trips, because I had virtually no time to pursue my federal remedies, I engaged the services of a local attorney. He researched the law and regrettably informed me, in part, that:

"...the Defendants in the U.S. Court will prevail on res judicata grounds in their motion for summary judgment if the judge decides:

1) that the federal claim is based on the same asserted wrong as was the subject of the state action (namely, whether your dismissal as Police Chief was improper); and

2) that the addition of the City Attorney and City Council as parties does not sufficiently distinguish the federal and state actions."

Although his letter to me of January 9, 1979, was pessimistic, he closed it out with a slight glimmer of optimism:

"Therefore, your only reasonable hope is that you can overturn the State Court decision; hopefully the Rule 60 (b) motion will do so."

Having previously discussed a Rule 60 MOTION with him, as a sort of catch-all motion, to overturn Judge Buckalew's judgment against me in my reinstatement case, on January 4, I mailed the following MOTION to the Superior Court in Alaska:

No. 75-8520

MOTION FOR RELIEF FROM FINAL JUDGMENT

Plaintiff, pro se, respectfully moves this Honorable Court to relieve him from the final judgment in this case by vacating said judgment and for his reasons states:

1. Rule 60 (b) (6) of the Alaska Superior Court Civil Rules permits a court to relieve a party from a final judgment for "any...reason justifying relief from the operation of the judgment."
2. On March 4, 1977, I filed a MOTION FOR DISQUALIFICATION OF JUDICIAL OFFICER FOR CAUSE pursuant to Alaska Statues 22.20.020 in an attempt to have a Judge other than the Honorable Seaborn J. Buckalew hear my case.
3. In said MOTION, I noted that during a pretrial conference held March 1, 1977, involving myself, Burton C. Biss, attorney for the defendants, and Judge Buckalew, Mr. Biss stated that "contractual issues only are to be considered here."
4. Said MOTION was denied.
5. Subsequent to the hearing, Plaintiff ascertained or has reason to believe that Burton C. Biss and the Honorable Seaborn J. Buckalew are personal friends

and that said friendship may have caused the Judge to rule as he did.

6. In consideration of said friendship, Judge Buckalew should have disqualified himself from considering Plaintiff's case because of his bias for the Defendants.

7. In addition, it is impossible to know which issues were decided by the Court when Judge Buckalew entered JUDGMENT ON THE PLEADINGS on March 7, 1977, since the pretrial conference and the DEFENDANTS' MOTION FOR JUDGMENT ON THE PLEADINGS focused only upon the contractual issues raised in my complaint and ignored the Constitutional issues.

8. At present, there is pending in the United States District Court of the District of Alaska another action based upon some of the facts set forth in my complaint before this Court. The federal action may be disposed of adversely to Plaintiff by summary judgment on the grounds of res judicata unless the judgment in my case in the Superior Court (*No. 75-8520*) is vacated or modified to reflect that only the contractual issues were decided.

WHEREFORE, Plaintiff prays that:

A. The final judgment entered in *No. 75-8520* by the Honorable Seaborn J. Buckalew be vacated.

B. Alternatively, the final judgment be modified to reflect that only Plaintiff's contractual claims against the City of Palmer were decided adversely to Plaintiff.

NICHOLAS J. MANGIERI
Plaintiff, Pro se

My new use of the term *"Pro se,"* in my state case, when referring to myself as the Plaintiff, was a designation that I picked up from the judge in my federal case. Apparently, both *"Pro per"* and *"Pro se"* were synonymous when used to mean that a party represented himself.

The OPPOSITION to my MOTION was filed by City Attorney Biss on January 15. In typical twisted statements he mockingly stated in the body of his response:

> "Plaintiff further suggests that the judgment should be modified to show that only 'contractual issues' were decided, whatever Plaintiff means by that expression."

My reference to the "contractual issues," in my MOTION, were the very words that Biss had used in our in-chambers meeting with Judge Buckalew prior to Biss' JUDGMENT ON THE PLEADINGS, which Buckalew then granted. Apparently Biss had selective lapses of memory — especially where he was concerned.

Even Biss himself acknowledged the possible applicability of Rule 60, when he stated in his own OPPOSITION:

> "The most demanding standard for relief has been established for motions under Rule 60 (b)(6) with the courts requiring exceptional or extraordinary circumstances and a very special showing by the moving party."

If the announced *bias* by a particular judge in an in-chambers session wasn't considered "exceptional or extra-ordinary" — Judge Buckalew in this case — then I don't know what would have been an appropriate circumstance?

My reliance on a *Rule 60* in my MOTION FOR RELIEF FROM FINAL JUDGMENT, even if not deemed timely, was still a chance that I had to take. My Maryland attorney and I still considered it worthwhile raising, even if it appeared doomed from the onset. Undoubtedly, out there somewhere in that *great judicial field* would have been an understanding judge who would have been interested in fairness and justice in that State action.

Unfortunately, such was not to be in my own reinstatement case.

The Honorable Seaborn J. Buckalew, having first decided against me in March 1977 to have my lawsuit dismissed, had still a second chance. It was he who considered my MOTION FOR RELIEF FROM FINAL JUDGMENT, and it was he who considered Biss' OPPOSITION to that MOTION.

As was expected — and predicted — he denied my MOTION in a heavy bold script on March 28, 1979.

That dismissal of Case #75-8520, my long-pending reinstatement action, was the second case to die a slow death. My libel action, Case #76-1271E had also bitten the dust, 14 months earlier when I was unable to return to Alaska to have my day in court.

My final case, the federal Civil Rights action, No. A77-55 CIV, was all that remained.

Waggoner, attorney of record in that case for the defendants, including the Palmer City Attorney, pounced on the opportunity to finish me off.

On April 13, he followed up with a SUPPLEMENTAL MEMORANDUM REGARDING DEFENDANT'S MOTION FOR SUMMARY JUDGMENT and referred to Buckalew's "DENIAL":

> "Attached hereto as Exhibit A is the ORDER of the Superior Court refusing to set aside the Final Judgment entered therein. All the principals applicable to race judicada have been met, and this case should be dismissed."

In Waggoner's anxiety, and undoubtedly Biss' as well, to file the paper with the federal court, they both neglected to proofread their own legal copy. The word "principals" should have read "principles", and "race judicada" should obviously been "res judicata." However, there was little joy in dissecting, or calling attention to their errors in English usage to anyone, because I saw the handwriting on the wall.

I knew that it was just a matter of time before it would all be over. Because I had received his MEMORANDUM — again not in a timely fashion — I sent another telegram to the Clerk of the U.S. District Court on April 30, advising of the delay in my receipt of that MEMORANDUM, and requested a 15-day extension for a REPLY.

It was acknowledged and granted.

Although I knew that I had exhausted all my legal remedies, and that there was little hope of success, I still had to go down swinging.

I filed two final MOTIONS on May 14, and on May 16, I sent the U.S. Clerk of the Court an additional telegram informing her that my OPPOSITION was mailed.

The first MOTION, my OPPOSITION, sought reinstatement based on "aspects of fraud," and referred to my accompanying longer MEMORANDUM.

My OPPOSITION TO SUPPLEMENTAL MEMORAN-DUM REGARDING DEFENDANTS' MOTION FOR SUM-MARY JUDGMENT, stated that:

> "Plaintiff moves for partial summary judgment, i.e. immediate reinstatement with full back pay, including leave and compensatory time dating back to November 4, 1975, for defendants' actions in improperly dismissing Plaintiff as Chief of Police. Defendants admittedly have denied Plaintiff his constitutional right to a "hearing" and have thereby violated the "due process" clause of the Constitution.
>
> Plaintiff does not seek full summary judgment as he desires the merits of the case to be heard in open court and defendants' malignancy be exposed to the public.
>
> The court has the power to decide the case and move the forum from the State Court to Federal Court because of the fraud involved in both State actions and because of the actions of a biased State Judge, who admittedly knew and was a friend of defense counsel, who is also a defendant in this case.
>
> Aspects of fraud mitigate the doctrine of res judicata in the State case because the same biased trial judge, who refused to set aside the final judgment in Plaintiff's State action, was initially enjoined in the instant case.
>
> This Motion is supported by Plaintiff's MEMO-RANDUM filed herewith."

My harder-hitting MEMORANDUM contained all the elements that I had previously covered in numerous legal documents and in various correspondences with law enforcement sources, and I wanted it all to be "on the record."

Nick Mangieri

The following MEMORANDUM IN SUPPORT OF PLAIN-
TIFF'S OPPOSITION TO SUPPLEMENTAL MEMORAN-
DUM REGARDING DEFENDANTS' MOTION FOR SUM-
MARY JUDGMENT, contains that comprehensive effort:

"Plaintiff, for almost four years, has attempted not
only to fight the corruption he uncovered in City Hall in
Palmer, Alaska and in the Matanuska-Susitna Borough
but has fought his way through two cases in the State
Courts and one in the Federal Court in an attempt to find
justice in our legal system. Inspection of these cases by
the court would substantiate Plaintiff's continuing allegation that an ongoing conspiracy by all Defendants,
including defense counsel, forced Plaintiff from his position as Chief of Police and saw to it that he did not regain
it. Plaintiff has continually alleged that all Defendants
have lied — including defense counsel — and that several have perjured themselves during depositions conducted by the Plaintiff. Defendant Maze, the City Mayor,
a convicted embezzler still plies his trade. Defendant
Curtis, a proven psychotic, is involved in fraudulent land
transactions as is the majority of the City Council members. The others are involved in various forms of corruption, kickbacks and conflicts of interest.

Both Motions Judges in Plaintiff's State case have
acknowledged that Plaintiff had merit in his allegations
of fact and law and that the cases should have gone to
court. The Honorable Seaborn J. Buckalew, a hastily
installed trial judge not familiar with Plaintiff's case conceded to his friend's motion that the case not go to court
(Defense Counsel Biss). Buckalew further admitted a
friendship of long duration in open court with Biss.
Plaintiff objected, but to no avail. The case was dismissed but the Alaska Supreme Court granted Certiorari.
However, because Plaintiff could not post bond, the
appeal process was dropped. Plaintiff again reopened the
Supreme Court process and attempted to file at public
expense because he was a pauper. The Superior Court of
Alaska, however, declined to find Plaintiff destitute — a

Frozen Shield

ruling that was clearly inappropriate and unjust especially in light of the exhibited fact that Plaintiff had been unemployed for many months and had assets that were virtually nil.

In addition to Plaintiff's battle with Defendants' overt lies in an attempt to cover up a conspiracy and with Plaintiff's battle of litigation in courts manned by those friendly to Defense Counsel, Plaintiff has been subjected to other more personal battles. Two "contracts" had allegedly been put out on Plaintiff's life. His dogs shot and killed. His horses shot at. His phones tapped. His home foreclosed upon. His furniture and personal possessions taken from him — and eventually his family broken up.

Plaintiff's "battle" is not unique for Alaska, however. Many have come out second best to the controlling interest, better known as the Alaska Rural Rehabilitation Corporation — a supposedly non-profit corporation that is deeply entrenched in gigantic land manipulation in Alaska. Some who have challenged or become a threat to the system have been "accidentally" eliminated. Witness the untimely demise of an outspoken Chief Justice to the Alaska Supreme Court a few years ago and also the "accidental" death of a newspaper editor in the Matanuska Valley. Both departures from this life were by drownings under bizarre circumstances that had amateurish inquests and subsequent cover-ups. Both deaths were in Plaintiff's area before he assumed office. Both deaths have been investigated by Plaintiff and there is reasonable cause to believe that they were homicides.

Plaintiff has been extremely vocal in an attempt to call attention to his cries of corruption in his town and in the surrounding valley and in the encompassing borough. Unfortunately, the small handful of supporters and those knowledgeable of the pervasiveness of land fraud and other corrupt practices are powerless and disinclined to buck "the system." The public is apathetic and those charged with protecting the public interest are either corrupt themselves or unschooled in the fine art of uncover-

387

ing fraud.

Plaintiff is presently employed as a federal agent and is not unfamiliar with various aspects of fraudulent practices and all its ramifications, especially dealing with corruption prevalent in city halls. Plaintiff has conducted recent investigations into the Southern-most reaches of our country in the South Florida and the Florida Keys area, and is currently probing fraud in our Nation's Capital. Therefore, Plaintiff is able to speak with some air of authority when he states that Defendants — and others — are engaged in corrupt and fraudulent practices in Palmer, Alaska and in the Matanuska-Susitna Borough.

Plaintiff, therefore urgently prays that the court intercede and find that a partial summary judgment is proper to assure that justice finally be done."

My final attempt at intervention by a federal court jurisdiction also failed. It also came as no surprise, although in retrospect it seemed as though U.S. District Court Judge von der Heydt did his best to accommodate me and prolong the battle. He was one of the few judges with whom I was impressed. However, in response to Waggoner's MOTION TO STRIKE my last two pleadings, the judge finally acceded and dismissed my federal case on May 31, 1979.

When I received the final JUDGMENT in the mail, there was no great sense of loss, nor even anger, it was just *another* setback, nothing more and nothing less.

My sister and brother-in-law, who had been aware of all the ups and downs since the inception of the Palmer episode, made an appropriate sympathetic comment about a universally widely known fact.

"You can't fight City Hall."

I thought about it a moment, nodded my head in affirmation, and then added slowly, "Yeah, but there's always next time."

... Index ...

Nick Mangieri

Order Form

Postal Orders:
Veracity Press, Inc.
Nick Mangieri
P.O. Box 369, Lightfoot, VA 93090
Fax Orders:
(757) 565-0827
Payment:
by check or money order

Amount:
Frozen Shield $19.50
Broken Badge $19.50

Shipping:
$3.50 for the first book and . . . . _____
$1.00 for each additional book . . . . _____
Priority Mail: $4.50 per book. . . . . _____

Sales tax:
Add 4.5% for books shiped to Virginia addresses _____

TOTAL _____